11th edition

Chapter 13 Bankruptcy

Keep Your Property & Repay Debts Over Time

Attorney Stephen Elias & Kathleen Michon, J.D.

NOLO
LAW for ALL

ELEVENTH EDITION   MAY 2012

Editor   KATHLEEN MICHON

Book Design   TERRI HEARSH

Proofreading   SUSAN CARLSON GREENE

Index   JULIE SHAWVAN

Printing   BANG PRINTING

Elias, Stephen.
    Chapter 13 bankruptcy : keep your property & repay debts over time / Stephen Elias & Kathleen Michon. -- 11th ed.
        p. cm.
    Includes index.
    ISBN 978-1-4133-1712-1 (pbk.) -- ISBN 978-1-4133-1725-1 (epub e-book)
1. Bankruptcy--United States--Popular works. 2. United States. Bankruptcy. Chapter 13, Adjustment of debts of an individual with regular income--Popular works. I. Michon, Kathleen, 1966-. II. Title. III. Title: Keep your property and repay debts over time.
    KF1524.85.E39 2012
    346.7307'8--dc23

                            2011048778

Please note

We believe accurate, plain-English legal information should help you solve many of your own legal problems. But this text is not a substitute for personalized advice from a knowledgeable lawyer. If you want the help of a trained professional—and we'll always point out situations in which we think that's a good idea—consult an attorney licensed to practice in your state.

In Memoriam

Stephen Elias, 1941-2011

Stephen R. Elias, an important and beloved part of the Nolo family for more than 30 years, died in late 2011. His passing is a great loss to Nolo and to the communities and movements to which Steve gave so much.

Steve, a part of Nolo almost since its beginning, was passionate about access to law and tireless in his pursuit of anything that would get information and advice to people who needed it. To that end, he authored many Nolo books and software, including this book, *How to File for Chapter 7 Bankruptcy, The Foreclosure Survival Guide,* and more.

Authoring books and software were only part of his efforts. Steve and his wife, Catherine, helped create the profession of legal document preparer (independent paralegal, in his original term), founding an organization for California document preparers. Steve also personally provided low-cost, high-quality legal help to thousands of clients over the years. His strategy, unsurprisingly, was unique; for $100, Steve provided a phone consultation and written report designed to prepare clients to represent themselves.

Although Nolo will miss Steve deeply, we will also continue his legacy of bringing bankruptcy law to all. With our expert editors and stable of experienced and knowledgeable authors, Nolo will continue to publish up-to-date, accurate, and easy-to-understand bankruptcy books for many years to come.

About the Authors

Stephen R. Elias (1941-2011) was the author of many Nolo books, including *The Foreclosure Survival Guide: Keep Your House or Walk Away With Money in Your Pocket* and *The New Bankruptcy: Will It Work for You?* and coauthor of *How to File for Chapter 7 Bankruptcy*. Steve was a practicing attorney in California, New York, and Vermont before joining Nolo in 1980. Over his long career, he was featured in such major media as *The New York Times*, *The Wall Street Journal*, *Newsweek*, "Good Morning America," "20/20," *Money* magazine, and more. Steve died unexpectedly in December 2011, after completing the changes for the new edition of this book.

Kathleen Michon is an author, editor, and online legal content editor/manager at Nolo.com. She edits Nolo's bankruptcy and consumer books and writes, edits, and manages the bankruptcy information for Nolo.com and other Nolo-affiliated bankruptcy websites. Prior to joining Nolo, Kathleen was the directing attorney of Public Counsel's Consumer Rights Project. She received her undergraduate degree from Yale University and her law degree from Northwestern University School of Law. She authors Nolo's Bankruptcy, Foreclosure & Debt Blog (at blog.nolo.com/bankruptcy).

Table of Contents

Part 1: Is Chapter 13 Right for You?

Part II: Filing for Chapter 13 Bankruptcy

Part III: Making Your Plan Work

Part IV: Help Beyond the Book

Appendixes

Is Chapter 13 Right for You?

How Chapter 13 Works

Chances are good that you've picked up this book because your debts have become overwhelming. Maybe you are facing foreclosure on your home, repossession of your car, or constant letters and phone calls from debt collectors. Or perhaps, you've realized that your debts have grown far beyond your ability to repay them, and you're wondering if there's anything you can do to get back in control of your finances.

Chapter 13 bankruptcy could be the best way to resolve your debt problems. When you file for Chapter 13, you agree to repay all or a portion of your debts over time, under the supervision of the bankruptcy court. Chapter 13 allows you to keep your property while using your anticipated income to repay some or all of your debts.

This book opens up the world of Chapter 13 to anyone who wants to get a good idea of how Chapter 13 works and what it can do for you. The book stops short of giving you all the forms and instructions you would need to do your own Chapter 13 bankruptcy. That's because we believe that very few people would be able to successfully carry out this task without attorney representation. (See "Do You Need a Lawyer?" below.)

This chapter gets you started with an overview of Chapter 13 bankruptcy. It also explains other types of bankruptcy relief (including Chapter 7 bankruptcy) and options for dealing with your debts outside of bankruptcy.

Get Updates and More Online

When there are important changes to the information in this book, we'll post updates online, on a page dedicated to this book: **www.nolo.com/back-of-book/CHB11.html.** You'll find other useful information there, too, including author blogs, podcasts, and videos. You can even sign up to receive email notifications of updates—all for free.

An Overview of Chapter 13 Bankruptcy

Chapter 13 can be a good solution for people who need time to pay off certain debts and who have enough income to meet the Chapter 13 requirements.

In Chapter 13, you get to keep all of your property, regardless of its value. However, you will have to pay your unsecured creditors (those to whom you owe credit card debts, medical debts, and most court judgments, for example) at least as much as they would have received had you filed for Chapter 7 bankruptcy.

Chapter 13 has many benefits (discussed below in "Reasons to Choose Chapter 13"), but some of the most powerful involve your home. Chapter 13 bankruptcy allows you to catch up on mortgage arrears through your plan, so you can avoid foreclosure. (See Ch. 8) And if you have second mortgages that are no longer secured by the equity in your property, you can strip them off. (See "Lien Stripping: Getting Rid of Home Loans Other Than Your First Mortgage," below.)

Costs

Like everyone who files for Chapter 13 bankruptcy, you have to pay the filing fee of $281, due either when you file your initial bankruptcy paperwork or in four equal installments (with the court's permission). You'll also have to pay a fee—typically about $100 total—to the credit counseling agency where you receive your mandatory prefiling credit counseling and postfiling budget counseling. If you decide to hire a lawyer to help you with your case, you can expect to pay an additional $3,000 or more in legal fees. You won't have to come up with the entire fee all at once, but you will probably have to make a sizable initial payment and pay the rest over the course of your plan.

Do You Need a Lawyer?

For the vast majority of Chapter 13 filers, the answer is "yes." It's not that people can't understand the ins and outs of Chapter 13 bankruptcy law (although at times the law can be quite complicated) or fill out the petition and accompanying schedules and forms (although again, some of those can get tricky); instead, the rub lies with the Chapter 13 repayment plan. Calculating plan payments has become quite difficult without the assistance of computer software, which is extremely expensive. In addition, it is not uncommon for the trustee or creditors to challenge or object to various aspects of your plan. You may have to argue against objections, negotiate with creditors, or modify your plan. In fact, most Chapter 13 plans need at least one modification along the way, even when prepared by an attorney. Experienced Chapter 13 bankruptcy lawyers have software to prepare your Chapter 13 plan and the expertise to handle objections to your plan and to modify it as your case proceeds.

We believe that most Chapter 13 filers benefit from legal representation, assuming the lawyer is honest and competent. Having said that, it's still important to understand the Chapter 13 process, including options for dealing with debts and property, the possibility of reducing loan amounts (called cramdowns), and what you can expect to pay in your Chapter 13 plan. This book also helps you identify various tricky issues that might arise in your bankruptcy case.

It's also helpful to run some preliminary numbers yourself to determine if Chapter 7 is an option for you or if funding a Chapter 13 plan is even possible given your income and expenses. Chs. 4 and 5 take you through the means test (to see if you qualify for Chapter 7 bankruptcy) and provide step-by-step instructions on figuring out if you can fund a Chapter 13 plan.

To learn more about hiring and working with a bankruptcy lawyer, see Ch. 15.

Filing Your Papers

To begin a Chapter 13 bankruptcy, you fill out a packet of forms in which you disclose your property, debts, and economic transactions during the several years before you file. The official forms for Chapter 13 bankruptcy are the same as those for Chapter 7, with a few exceptions and additions.

In addition to the Chapter 7 forms, you must prepare or produce:

- a form (Form 22C: *Chapter 13 Statement of Current Monthly Income and Calculation of Commitment Period and Disposable Income*) that determines whether your income is more or less than the median income in your state. This calculation determines how long your repayment plan must last. If your income is more than the median, your plan must last five years; if your income is less, you can propose a three-year plan. If your income is more than the median, you must also use this form to calculate how much

disposable income you will have available to pay your unsecured creditors over the five-year period.
- your Chapter 13 repayment plan, showing how you propose to pay certain mandatory debts (child support, tax arrearages, and so on) and, if you have sufficient income, at least a portion of your other unsecured debts over the three- to five-year period. (See Ch. 8.)
- a certificate showing you have participated in a credit counseling program during the 180-day period before filing for bankruptcy (this requirement is explained in Ch. 9). If the credit counseling agency comes up with a proposed repayment plan that would allow you to pay your debts outside of bankruptcy, you must submit this as well.
- a certificate regarding child support obligations and your residence.
- pay stubs from the 60-day period before you file, along with a cover sheet.
- proof that you've filed your federal and state income tax returns for the previous four years.
- a copy of your most recent IRS income tax return (or a transcript of that return).

Chs. 7 through 9 discuss in detail the bankruptcy forms, repayment plan, and filing process.

The Repayment Plan

The repayment plan you submit with your other bankruptcy papers (or shortly after your initial filing) shows the judge how you will devote your disposable income to pay off all or some of your debt over the life of your plan.

Which Debts Must Be Repaid

Chapter 13 requires you to pay some of your debts in full within the life of the plan. You also must pay as much of your remaining debts as you can from the income you have available. Generally, you will have to be able to show, at the beginning of your case, that you are likely to have enough income to remain current on debts that secure collateral you want to keep (for example, a mortgage or car note) while fully paying off your back taxes, back child support owed to a child or an ex-spouse, and any mortgage and secured debt arrearages you owe. And, as explained in Ch. 3, your plan also has to allow for total payments to your unsecured creditors that are at least as much as they would have received had you filed for Chapter 7 bankruptcy. In other words, these payments must be at least equal to the value of your nonexempt property, less the costs, commissions, and fees that would have to be paid in order to sell that property.

Length of the Repayment Period

You must propose a repayment plan that lasts for either three or five years, depending on your income. As you'll learn in Ch. 4, the bankruptcy law now imposes a number of requirements on filers whose average gross monthly income over the six months before they file for bankruptcy is more than the median income in their state. Among other things, these filers must propose a five-year repayment plan unless the plan proposes to pay 100% of the filer's unsecured debt..

Filers whose average gross monthly income for the six-month period is less than the median usually have the choice of filing for either Chapter 7 or Chapter 13 bankruptcy. If they use Chapter 13, these filers may propose a three-year repayment plan and may use their actual expenses to calculate how much income they will have to devote to that plan.

Filers whose income is more than the median must use certain standard expense amounts set by the IRS—rather than their actual expenses—to calculate their plan payments. As a result, higher-income filers may have to devote more of their money, for a longer period of time, to repaying their debts.

To learn more about how to calculate your income, find out whether your income is above or below your state's median, and figure out which expenses to use in calculating your plan payments, see Ch. 4.

Coming Up With a Plan the Judge Will Approve

You can't proceed with a Chapter 13 bankruptcy unless a bankruptcy judge approves (confirms) your plan. As mentioned, some creditors are entitled to receive 100% of what you owe them, while others may receive a much smaller percentage or even nothing at all if you have insufficient disposable income left over after the mandatory debts are paid. For example, a Chapter 13 plan must propose that any child support you owe

to a spouse or child (as opposed to a government agency) will be paid in full over the life of your plan; otherwise, the judge will not confirm it. On the other hand, the judge can confirm a plan that doesn't repay any portion of your credit card debts if you won't have any disposable income left after paying your child support obligations.

TIP

You may have more—or less—disposable income than you think. Chapter 13 requires you to commit your "projected disposable income" to repaying your debts over the life of your plan. Some courts calculate your projected disposable income by subtracting your allowable expenses from your average income during the six months before you filed for bankruptcy, which may not give an accurate picture of your current income and expenses. Other courts look at your current income and expenses at the time you file, if those figures more accurately reflect your finances going forward. For more information on calculating your disposable income, see Ch. 5.

The Automatic Stay

When you file for Chapter 13 bankruptcy, the automatic stay goes into effect right away. The stay prevents most creditors from taking action to collect a debt against you or your property. So, for example, if a foreclosure sale of your home or a vehicle repossession is in the works, the stay stops the sale or repossession dead in its tracks. (However, the automatic stay doesn't apply if you've had two previous bankruptcy cases dismissed in the past year.) The automatic stay is discussed in more detail in Ch. 2.

The Meeting of Creditors

Once you file your bankruptcy papers, the court will schedule a meeting of creditors within 20 to 40 days after your filing date—and send notice of this meeting to you and the creditors listed in your bankruptcy papers. You (and your spouse if you have filed jointly) are required to attend. You'll each need to bring two forms of identification—a picture ID and proof of your Social Security number.

The creditors' meeting is conducted by the Chapter 13 bankruptcy trustee for your court. No judge is present, and the meeting is held outside of court, usually in the nearest federal building. Although the bankruptcy trustee is not a judge, you still have a duty to cooperate with the trustee as a condition of receiving a discharge.

A typical creditors' meeting lasts less than 15 minutes. The trustee will briefly go over any questions raised by the information you entered in the forms. The trustee is likely to be most interested in the fairness and legality of your proposed repayment plan and your ability to make the payments you have proposed. (See Ch. 8 for more on Chapter 13 plans.) The trustee has a vested interest in helping you successfully navigate the Chapter 13 process because the trustee gets paid a percentage of all payments doled out under your plan.

The trustee will also require proof that you have filed your tax returns for the previous four years. If you can't show that you filed returns, the trustee will continue the meeting to give you a chance to file these returns. Ultimately, you will not be allowed to proceed with a Chapter 13 bankruptcy unless and until you bring your tax filings up to date.

RESOURCE

Help if you are behind in tax payments. If you owe taxes, you may benefit from professional help in the form of a tax attorney, an enrolled agent (licensed by the IRS), or a tax preparer. For more information on getting current on taxes and getting professional help, read *Stand Up to the IRS*, by Frederick Daily (Nolo).

When the trustee is finished asking questions, any creditors who show up will have a chance to question you. Secured creditors often attend, especially if they have any objections to the plan you have proposed as part of your Chapter 13 filing. They may claim, for example, that your plan isn't feasible, that you're giving yourself too much time to pay your arrears on your car note or mortgage (if any), or that your plan proposes to pay less on a secured debt than the replacement value of the collateral.

An unsecured creditor who is scheduled to receive very little under your plan might show up, too, if that creditor thinks you should cut your living expenses and thereby increase your disposable income (the amount from which unsecured creditors are paid). This is more likely to happen if you are using your actual expenses to compute your disposable income (as filers whose income is less than the state median are allowed to do) instead of standard expense figures set by the IRS.

Come to the meeting prepared to negotiate with disgruntled creditors. If you agree to make changes to accommodate their objections, you must submit a modified plan. Keep in mind, though, that any decisions or agreements you make with creditors are not final at this point. The trustee or creditors will raise their objections (assuming they still have any after your negotiations) and then the bankruptcy judge (who is not at the meeting) will make a decision. As a general rule, the judge will go along with the trustee unless your lawyer can make a good case that the trustee (or creditor) is wrong.

The Confirmation Hearing

Chapter 13 bankruptcy requires at least one appearance by you or your attorney before a bankruptcy judge. (In some districts, the judge comes into the courtroom only if the trustee or a creditor objects to your plan, and you want the judge to rule on the objection.) At this "confirmation hearing," which is usually held a few weeks after the creditors' meeting, the judge either confirms (approves of) your proposed plan or sends you back to the drawing board for various reasons—usually because your plan doesn't meet Chapter 13 requirements. (For example, a judge might reject your plan because you don't have enough income to pay off your priority creditors in full while staying current on your secured debts, such as a car note or mortgage.)

You are entitled to amend your proposed plan until you get it right or the judge decides that it's hopeless. Each amendment requires a new confirmation hearing and appropriate written notice to your creditors. (For more information on the confirmation hearing, see Ch. 10.) Once your plan is confirmed, it will govern your payments for the three- to five-year repayment period.

Possible Additional Court Appearances

If your plan is drafted correctly from the beginning, your confirmation hearing will probably be the only time the bankruptcy judge deals with your case. However, additional appearances in court by you or your attorney may be necessary to:

- confirm your repayment plan if you later amend it
- value an asset, if your plan proposes to pay less for a car or other property than the creditor thinks it's worth (this might happen if you try to cram down the debt to the item's current value)
- respond to requests by a creditor or the trustee to dismiss your case or amend your plan
- respond to a creditor who opposes your right to discharge a particular debt (perhaps claiming that you incurred the debt through fraud)
- discharge a type of debt that can be discharged only if the judge decides that it should be (for example, to discharge a student loan because of undue hardship)
- eliminate a lien on your property that will survive your Chapter 13 bankruptcy unless the judge removes it, or
- reaffirm a debt owed on a car or other secured property or that would otherwise not survive your bankruptcy.

Many of these procedures are explained in Ch. 11.

Making Your Payments Under the Plan

You are required to make your first payment under your proposed repayment plan within 30 days after you file for bankruptcy. If the bankruptcy court ultimately confirms your plan, your payment will be distributed to your creditors in accordance with the plan's terms. If your Chapter 13 bankruptcy never gets off the ground, the trustee will return the money to you, less administrative expenses.

Once your plan is confirmed, you will make payments, usually monthly, to the bankruptcy trustee, an official appointed by the bankruptcy court to oversee your case. The trustee will usually require you to agree to an order that takes the payments directly out of your bank account or paycheck. The trustee uses your monthly payments to pay the creditors in accordance with the payment order contained in your plan. The trustee also collects a statutory fee (roughly 8% to 10% of the amount you will pay under your plan).

If you can show that you have a history of regular income spread out in uneven payments over the year— for example, quarterly royalty payments or predictable seasonal income fluctuations (for instance, if you do construction work in a location that has severe winters)—your plan may provide for payments when you typically earn income, rather than every month.

If Something Goes Wrong

Three to five years is a long time. What happens if you can't make a payment or it becomes apparent— perhaps because of a change in your income or life circumstances—that you won't be able to complete your plan? If you miss only a payment or two, you can usually arrange with the trustee to make up the difference. If you lose your income stream, however, and you definitely won't be able to complete the plan, you can convert your bankruptcy to Chapter 7 (if that makes sense), obtain a "hardship" discharge from the court, or modify the plan. In many cases, Chapter 13 bankruptcies that don't work out are dismissed entirely.

If your case is dismissed, you'll owe your creditors the balances on your debts from before you filed your Chapter 13 case, less the payments you made, plus the interest that accrued while your case was open. See Chs. 12 and 13 for more on what happens if you are unable to complete your plan.

Personal Financial Management Counseling

Before you make your last plan payment, you'll have to complete a personal financial management counseling course (called budget counseling)—and file an official form certifying that you did so—in order to get your discharge. This counseling covers basic budgeting, managing your money, and using credit responsibly. See Ch. 10 for more on this requirement.

After You Complete Your Plan

Once you complete your plan, certify that you've remained current on your child support or alimony obligations, and file proof that you've completed your personal financial management counseling, your remaining debts will be discharged, if they are the type of debts that can be discharged in Chapter 13. (See "Which Debts Are Discharged in Chapter 13 Bankruptcy," below, for more information.) For instance, if you have $40,000 in credit card debt, and you pay off $10,000 through your repayment plan, the remaining $30,000 will be discharged once you complete the plan. However, you will still owe whatever is left of the debts that you can't, by law, discharge in Chapter 13. Debts that you can't discharge include child support, alimony, and student loans (unless you can show that repaying the loan would cause undue hardship); most types of debts—including credit card debts—are discharged.

> **EXAMPLE:** Karen owes $60,000 in credit card debts, $60,000 in student loans, and $2,000 in alimony. Karen pays off the alimony in full (as required by law) and 10% of her credit card debts and student loans. The remainder of the credit card debts will be discharged, but she will still owe the rest of her student loan debt ($54,000) unless she can convince the judge to order it discharged because of undue hardship (typically, a very hard and expensive sell).

Which Debts Are Discharged in Chapter 13 Bankruptcy

Not all debts are discharged in Chapter 13 bankruptcy. Of course, if you will repay all of your unsecured debts in full over the life of your plan, no discharge is necessary. But if your plan provides for less than full repayment of your unsecured debts, whatever you still owe may or may not be discharged.

Debts That Are Discharged

As a general rule, whatever you still owe on most credit card debts, medical bills, and lawyer bills is discharged, as are most court judgments and loans. Also, under bankruptcy law, debts you owe to an ex-spouse arising from a divorce or separation agreement that are not for support are discharged in Chapter 13 (but not in Chapter 7), as are debts incurred for the purpose of paying taxes.

Debts That Are Not Discharged

Debts that survive a Chapter 13 bankruptcy (unless you pay them in full during the life of your plan) include:
- debts that you don't list in your bankruptcy forms
- court-imposed fines and restitution
- back child support and alimony

- student loans (with rare exceptions)
- recent back taxes
- taxes for years in which you did not file a return, and
- debts you owe because of a civil judgment arising out of your willful or malicious acts, or for personal injuries or death caused by your drunk driving.

Discharging Student Loans in Chapter 13 Bankruptcy: The *Brunner* Test

For the most part, student loans cannot be discharged in Chapter 13 bankruptcy. However, in rare circumstances, courts will discharge some or all of your student loans at the end of your Chapter 13 repayment period if paying them would cause undue hardship.

Many courts use a three-factor test to determine if repaying your student loans would cause undue hardship, called the *Brunner* test (after a court case of the same case). Not all courts use this test, however.

Under the *Brunner* test, a bankruptcy court looks at the following three factors to determine if repayment of your student loans would cause an undue hardship:
- Based upon your current income and expenses, you cannot maintain a minimal standard of living for yourself and your dependents if you are forced to repay your loans.
- Your current financial situation is likely to continue for a big part of the repayment period.
- You have made a good-faith effort to repay your student loans.

Debts That Are Not Discharged If the Creditor Successfully Objects

Some types of debts will survive your bankruptcy only if the creditor files a motion in court to prove that the debt shouldn't be discharged. For example, if a creditor successfully objects to a debt arising from your fraudulent actions or recent credit card charges for luxuries, those debts will be waiting for you after your bankruptcy, unless you managed to pay them all off during your repayment plan.

Special Chapter 13 Features: Cramdowns and Lien Stripping

In Chapter 13 bankruptcy, you may be able to reduce the amount of a secured loan (for example, your car loan) to the actual value of the property; this is called a cramdown. And you might be able to get rid of second or third mortgages, home equity lines of credit, or home equity loans if they are no longer secured by the equity in your home. This is called lien stripping.

Although these provisions are powerful, they don't apply to the first mortgage of your residential real property. Some people believe they can "modify" the first mortgage on their home through bankruptcy. For the most part, this is a myth, although there are a few exceptions, such as for vacation and rental properties.

TIP
You may be able to modify your mortgage through nonbankruptcy avenues. Although you can't modify a first mortgage on a residential home through bankruptcy, you may be able to negotiate with your lender directly to reduce your interest rate, payments, or more. Or, you might be able to take advantage of government programs designed to help homeowners modify their mortgages. For more information, check out Nolo's Foreclosure section at www. nolo.com or get *Your Foreclosure Survival Guide*, by Stephen Elias (Nolo).

Cramdowns: Reducing Secured Loans to the Value of the Property

If the amount you owe on personal property is more than the current value of that property, you may be able to take advantage of Chapter 13's cramdown provisions. When you cram down the loan, you reduce it to the value of the property.

How Cramdowns Work

When you cram down a secured loan, the court reduces the loan amount to the replacement value of the property. You pay this reduced amount over the life of your repayment plan. Most courts have held that you still owe the unsecured part of a loan, but it gets lumped in with your other unsecured debt. (See, for example, *In re Rodriguez*, 375 B.R. 535 (9th Cir. B.A.P. 2007).) But because of the way unsecured debt is treated in Chapter 13 bankruptcy, this usually means you pay pennies on the dollar.

Here's an example. Say you owe $20,000 on a car you bought three years ago. The car is only worth $15,000 (which means only $15,000 of the loan is secured by the property). You can cram down the loan to $15,000 and pay this amount through your Chapter 13 plan. The remaining amount—$5,000—will be added to your unsecured debt and treated like all of your other unsecured debt.

What Is Replacement Value?

When you cram down a secured claim, you use the property's replacement value—what a retail merchant would get for the property given its age and condition—as the value of the property. For example, you can use the *Kelley Blue Book* middle value for a car or prices from secondhand stores or eBay for other types of property. However, the creditor may disagree with the property value that you come up with. You can negotiate with the creditor to come up with a mutually agreeable value, or have the judge decide the issue.

Property That Is Eligible for Cramdown

You may cram down only certain types of secured debt. Significantly, you cannot cram down mortgages on your primary residence. However, you may be able to cram down mortgages on real estate that is not your primary residence, such as investment or commercial property, or on a mobile home that is considered to be personal property.

Car loans. Cramdowns are often used for car loans. There are a few restrictions to keep in mind, however. For cars, in order to cram down the loan, one of the following must apply:

- You incurred the debt at least 910 days before you filed for bankruptcy.
- The loan is not a purchase money loan (that is, you secured the debt with a car you already owned, not a car you bought with the loan.
- The car secured by the loan is not a personal vehicle (that is, you bought it for your business).

Cramming Down Negative Equity in the 9th Circuit

If you bought a car within 910 days of your bankruptcy filing (which means your loan is ineligible for cramdown), you might be able to cram down part of the loan if you traded in a car to buy the new car. You can only do this in the 9th Circuit (all other Circuits have rejected this interpretation of the law). Here's how it works:

If, when you purchase a car, you trade in a car that is underwater (you owe more on the car than the car is currently worth), the lender often adds the difference between the trade-in value of your car and the remaining balance on the loan to your new car loan. For example, say your old car is worth $5,000 but you still owe $8,000 on the car loan. The lender for your current car purchase takes your old car as a trade-in, and adds $3,000 ($8,000 balance on loan minus the $5,000 value of car) to your new car loan. This amount is called negative equity.

In the 9th Circuit, if you file for bankruptcy, you can treat the $3,000 as unsecured debt, even if you bought the second car within 910 days of your bankruptcy filing. (*In re Penrod*, 611 F.3d 1158 (9th Cir. 2010).)

Other personal property loans. You may cram down debts for all property (other than cars) only if you incurred them at least a year before you filed for bankruptcy or if the loan is not a purchase money loan (that is, you secured the debt with property you already owned).

For all other loans on personal property, you can only cram down the loan if you bought the property more than one year before filing.

Real estate loans. You can cram down (some people use the term "modify") your mortgage to the actual value of the real estate if any of the following is true:

- Your loan was for the purchase of a multiunit building (even if you live in the building).
- Your loan was for the purchase of a vacation or rental home.
- Your loan was for other buildings or an adjacent lot that is not likely to be considered part of your residence, such as farmland.

- Your loan was for a mobile home you live in that is considered personal property.
- The mortgage loan is not secured solely by your residence.

If you do modify your mortgage, you will have to pay it off completely in your plan. For instance, if the contract value of your mortgage is $150,000 and you modify it to $110,000 (the value of the real estate), you'll have to pay the entire $110,000 off as part of your plan. In order to do this, most people must propose a balloon payment at the end of the repayment period, and then demonstrate they have the ability to actually make the payment (for example, by selling other property). This alone prevents most mortgages from being crammed down, even if they meet one of the criteria above.

Lien Stripping: Getting Rid of Home Loans Other Than Your First Mortgage

Although you can't cram down mortgages on your primary residence, you may still be able to reduce your overall home payments through lien stripping. If your home is worth no more than you owe on your first mortgage, that means your second mortgage (and your third, if you have one) are no longer secured by your home. In this situation, you may be able to "strip off" the second mortgage and treat it as unsecured debt in your Chapter 13 plan. This procedure allows you to greatly reduce the amount you have to pay each month to keep your home.

For example, assume you pay $1,500 on your first mortgage, $750 on your second mortgage, and $400 on a third mortgage (such as a home equity loan). If your home is worth $200,000 and you still owe that much on your first mortgage, you can strip off the second and third mortgages. This would reduce your monthly payment from $2,650 to $1,500.

Not every bankruptcy circuit allows lien stripping, however. If yours doesn't, you won't be able to do this. To find out if lien stripping is an option in your area (and you haven't yet hired an attorney), you can pay for a consult with a local bankruptcy attorney, or do some legal research. (See Ch. 16 to learn how to do legal research.)

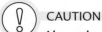 **CAUTION**

Lien stripping is not the same as lien avoidance. In Chapter 13 bankruptcy, you may also be able to "avoid" liens, or get rid of them, if the property is exempt. Although the end result may be the same, or similar, lien avoidance is different from lien stripping because it hinges on property exemptions. To learn more about lien avoidance, see Ch. 11.

Is Chapter 13 Right for You?

For most people, the two choices for bankruptcy relief are Chapter 7 and Chapter 13. In Chapter 7 bankruptcy, you immediately wipe out many debts, but in exchange you must give up any property you own that isn't protected by state or federal exemption laws.

Some of you won't have a choice between Chapter 7 and Chapter 13 bankruptcy; if you want to file for bankruptcy, you will have to use Chapter 13 and repay some of your debt. (See Ch. 4 to find out whether you'll be limited to Chapter 13.) Likewise, if you don't have a steady income, your only bankruptcy choice is Chapter 7. Many people who have a choice decide to file under Chapter 7, but there are some situations when Chapter 13 will be the better option.

Upper-Income Filers Must Use Chapter 13

If your average monthly income during the six months before you file for bankruptcy is higher than the median income for your state, you may not be able to use Chapter 7. If your average income is more than the median, you cannot file for Chapter 7 bankruptcy if your disposable income would allow you to pay your unsecured creditors at least $11,725 over a five-year period (about $195 a month). (See Ch. 4 for more on this "means" test.)

Reasons to Choose Chapter 7

Most people who have a choice traditionally have opted to file for Chapter 7 bankruptcy because it is relatively fast, effective, easy to file, and doesn't require payments over time. It also doesn't require you to be current on your income tax filings. In the typical situation, a case is opened and closed within three to four months, and the filer emerges debt free except for a mortgage, car payments, and certain types of debts that survive bankruptcy (such as student loans, recent taxes, and back child support).

If you have any secured debts, such as a mortgage or car note, Chapter 7 allows you to keep the collateral as long as you are current on your payments. However, if your equity in the collateral substantially exceeds the exemption available to you for that type of property, the trustee can sell the property, pay off the loan, pay you your exemption (if any), and pay the rest to your unsecured creditor. If you are behind on your payments, the creditor can come into the bankruptcy court and ask the judge for permission to repossess the car (or other personal property) or foreclose on your mortgage. As a general rule, however, most Chapter 7 filers are able to keep all their property, either because they don't own much to begin with or because any equity they own is protected by an exemption.

Changes in the bankruptcy law in 2005 put a few obstacles in the way of Chapter 7 filers. Nevertheless, assuming you qualify, you likely will find it easier—and more effective—to file for Chapter 7 than to keep up with a long-term payment plan under Chapter 13. And if you do file for Chapter 13 and don't keep up with your repayment plan, you will likely get no benefit from having engaged in the Chapter 13 process if you later convert to a Chapter 7 (unless the court lets you off the hook early for hardship reasons).

> **EXAMPLE:** Frank files for Chapter 13 bankruptcy. His five-year plan includes current payments on his mortgage, repayment of part of his $50,000 credit card debt, and payment in full of a $2,000 back child support debt. Frank remains current on his plan for three years and then loses his job. In that three-year period, Frank, through the Chapter 13 trustee, paid $12,000 on credit card debt as well as the child support debt.
>
> If Frank converts his case to Chapter 7, he can discharge all of the remaining credit card debt. But had Frank filed Chapter 7 from the beginning, he could also have discharged the $12,000 that he already paid to the credit card companies under his Chapter 13 plan. If Frank decides to skip Chapter 7 and negotiate a repayment schedule for the remaining $38,000, he will at least have made a $12,000 dent in the original $50,000 debt by filing for Chapter 13.

The moral of the story is that you should file for Chapter 7 in the first place if:

- You are eligible to use Chapter 7.
- You have significant doubts about your ability to complete a Chapter 13 repayment plan.
- None of the pressing reasons to use Chapter 13 are present in your case (see below).

For many people, the overriding reason to choose Chapter 7 is that they can do it themselves for little or no money (other than the filing fee), and they don't feel that they can handle their own Chapter 13 case nor afford to pay $3,000 or more in attorney fees.

Reasons to Choose Chapter 13

Although Chapter 7 is easier and doesn't require repayment, there are many good reasons why people who qualify for both types of bankruptcy choose Chapter 13 instead. Generally, Chapter 13 bankruptcy might make sense if you will have adequate, steady income to fund your plan for the appropriate period of time, and are in any of the following situations:

- You are facing foreclosure on your home or your car is being repossessed, and you want to keep your property. Using Chapter 13, you can make up the missed payments over time and reinstate the original agreement. You generally cannot do this in Chapter 7 bankruptcy—instead, you'll ultimately lose the property.
- You owe more on real estate that you own as a vacation or an investment property than that property is worth, and you can have your mortgage reduced to the value of the property. (This is possible only if you are not using the real estate as your primary residence.) (See "Special Chapter 13 Features: Cramdowns and Lien Stripping," above.)
- You have more than one mortgage and are facing foreclosure because you can't make all the payments. If your home's value is less than or equal to what you owe on your first mortgage, you can use Chapter 13 to change the additional mortgages into unsecured debts—which don't have to be repaid in full—and lower the amount of your monthly payments. (See "Special Chapter 13 Features: Cramdowns and Lien Stripping," above.)

- Your car is reliable and you want to keep it, but it's worth far less than you owe. You can take advantage of Chapter 13 bankruptcy's cramdown option (for cars purchased more than 2½ years before filing for bankruptcy) to keep the car by repaying its replacement value in equal payments over the life of your plan, rather than the full amount you owe on the contract. (See "Special Chapter 13 Features: Cramdowns and Lien Stripping," above.).
- You have a codebtor who will be protected under your Chapter 13 plan but who would not be protected if you used Chapter 7 (see Ch. 2).
- You have a tax obligation, student loan, or another debt that cannot be discharged in bankruptcy, but can be paid off over time in a Chapter 13 plan.
- You owe debts that can be discharged in a Chapter 13 bankruptcy but not in a Chapter 7 bankruptcy. For instance, debts incurred to pay taxes can't be discharged in Chapter 7 but can be discharged in Chapter 13.
- You want to use the Chapter 13 forum to sue one or more harassing creditors for violating state and federal antiharassment laws. For more information on these laws, see *Solve Your Money Troubles*, by Robin Leonard and Margaret Reiter (Nolo).
- You have a retail business that you would have to close down in a Chapter 7 bankruptcy but can continue to operate in Chapter 13.
- You have valuable personal property that you would lose in a Chapter 7 case, but could keep if you file for Chapter 13.
- You have a sincere desire to repay your debts, but you need the protection of the bankruptcy court to do so.

Alternatives to Bankruptcy

By now, you should have a pretty good idea of what filing a Chapter 13 bankruptcy will involve—and what you can hope to get out of it. Before you decide whether a Chapter 13—or Chapter 7—bankruptcy is the right solution for your debt problems, however, you should consider some basic options outside of the bankruptcy system. Although bankruptcy is the only sensible remedy for some people with debt problems, an alternative course of action makes better sense for others. This section explores some of your other options.

Do Nothing

Surprisingly, the best approach for some people who are deeply in debt is to take no action at all. You can't be thrown in jail for not paying your debts (with the exception of child support), and your creditors can't collect money from you that you just don't have.

Creditors Must Sue to Collect

Except for taxing agencies and student loan creditors, creditors must sue you in court and get a money judgment before they can go after your income and property. The big exception to this general rule is that a creditor can take collateral—foreclose on a house or repossess a car or furniture, for example—when you default on a debt that's secured by that collateral.

Under the typical security agreement (a contract involving collateral), the creditor can repossess the property without first going to court. But the creditor will not be able to go after your other property and income for any "deficiency" (the difference between what you owe and what the repossessed property fetches at auction) without first going to court for a money judgment.

To secure a money judgment, a creditor must have you personally served with a summons and complaint. In most states, you will have 30 days to file a response in the court where you are being sued. If you don't respond, the creditor can obtain a default judgment and seek to collect it from your income and property. If you do respond—and you are entitled to do so even if you think you owe the debt—the process will typically be set back several months until the court can schedule a trial where you can be heard. In most courts, you respond by filing a single document in which you deny everything in the creditor's complaint (or, in some courts, admit or deny each of the allegations in the complaint).

Much of Your Property Is Protected

Even if creditors get money judgments against you, they can't take away such essentials as:

- basic clothing
- ordinary household furnishings
- personal effects
- food
- Social Security or SSI payments necessary for your support
- unemployment benefits
- public assistance
- bank accounts with direct deposits from government benefit programs, and
- 75% of your wages (but more can be taken to pay child support judgments).

The general state exemptions described in Ch. 4 (and listed in Appendix A) apply whether or not you file for bankruptcy. Even creditors who get a money judgment against you can't take these protected items. (However, neither the federal bankruptcy exemptions nor the state bankruptcy-only exemptions available in California and a few other states apply if a creditor sues you in state civil court.)

When You Are Judgment Proof

A judgment is good only if the person who has it—the judgment creditor—can seize income or property from the debtor. If there is nothing to collect, the debtor is said to be "judgment proof." For example, if your only income is from Social Security (which can be seized only by the IRS) and all your property is exempt under your state's exemption laws, your judgment creditor can't take your income. Your life will continue as before, although one or more of your creditors may get pushy from time to time. While money judgments last a long time and can be renewed, this won't make any difference unless your fortunes change for the better. If that happens, you might reconsider bankruptcy at that time.

If your creditors know that their chances of collecting judgments from you any time soon are slim, they probably won't sue you in the first place. Instead, they'll simply write off your debts and treat them as deductible business losses for income tax purposes. After some years have passed (usually between four and ten), the debt will become legally uncollectible, under state laws known as statutes of limitation.

These statutes of limitation won't help you if the creditor sues or renews its judgment within the time limit, but most won't. Lawsuits typically cost thousands of dollars in legal fees. If a creditor decides, on the basis of your economic profile, not to go to court at the present time, it is unlikely to seek a judgment down the line to extend its claims. In short, because creditors are reluctant to throw good money after bad, your poor economic circumstances might shield you from trouble.

> **CAUTION**
> **Don't restart the clock.** The statute of limitations can be renewed if you revive an old debt by, for example, admitting that you owe it or making a payment. As soon as you acknowledge a debt, the clock starts all over again. Savvy creditors are aware of this loophole and may try to trick you into admitting the debt so they can sue to collect it. Sometimes, it might be a good idea to try to repay a debt, particularly one to a local merchant with whom you wish to continue doing business. But unless you are planning to make good on the debt or try to negotiate a new payment schedule, you should avoid any admissions.

Stopping Bill Collector Harassment

Many people file for bankruptcy to stop their creditors from making harassing telephone calls and writing threatening letters. As explained above and in Ch. 2, the automatic stay stops most collection efforts as soon as you file for bankruptcy. However, you don't have to start a bankruptcy case to get annoying creditors off your back. Federal law forbids collection agencies from threatening you, lying about what they can do to you, or invading your privacy. And some state laws prevent original creditors from taking similar actions.

Under federal law, you can legally force collection agencies to stop phoning or writing you by simply demanding that they stop, even if you owe them a bundle and can't pay a cent. (This law is the federal Fair Debt Collections Practices Act, 15 U.S.C. §§ 1692 and following.) For more information, see *Solve Your Money Troubles*, by Robin Leonard and Margaret Reiter (Nolo). Here's a sample letter asking a creditor to stop contacting the debtor.

Sample Letter Telling Collection Agency to Stop Contacting You

Sasnak Collection Service
49 Pirate Place
Topeka, Kansas 69000

November 11, 2011

Attn: Marc Mist

Re: Lee Anne Ito
     Account No. 88-90-92

Dear Mr. Mist:

For the past three months, I have received several phone calls and letters from you concerning an overdue Rich's Department Store account.

This is my formal notice to you under 15 U.S.C. § 1692c(c) to cease all further communications with me except for the reasons specifically set forth in the federal law.

This letter is not meant in any way to be an acknowledgment that I owe this money.

Very truly yours,

Lee Anne Ito

Lee Anne Ito

> 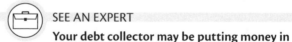 **SEE AN EXPERT**
> **Your debt collector may be putting money in your pocket.** The Fair Debt Collection Practices Act places a number of restrictions on debt collector activity. The remedies provided by the act include damages and attorneys' fees. More and more attorneys are interested in using these remedies, because they can earn some money without taking it out of a client's recovery. If you are suffering debt collection abuses, consider consulting with a bankruptcy or consumer rights attorney to find out if this type of lawsuit might be worth your while. For more information on the act and its remedies, see *Solve Your Money Troubles*, by Robin Leonard and Margaret Reiter (Nolo).

Negotiate With Your Creditors

If you have some income, or you have assets you're willing to sell, you may be a lot better off negotiating with your creditors than filing for bankruptcy. Negotiation may buy you some time to get back on your feet, or you and your creditors may agree to settle your debts for less than what you owe.

Creditors hate it when debtors don't pay their debts. They don't like the hassle of instituting collection proceedings, or the fact that these proceedings tend to turn debt-owing customers into former customers. To avoid the collection process and keep customers, creditors sometimes will reduce the debtor's expected payments, extend the time to pay, drop their demands for late fees, and make similar adjustments. They're most likely to be lenient if they believe you are making an honest effort to deal with your debt problems.

 TIP

More lenders are offering foreclosure "workouts." As the number of foreclosures has skyrocketed, lenders are increasingly willing to help homeowners keep their homes. These processes, called foreclosure workouts or modifications, might include:

- renegotiating the terms of the mortgage so that the arrearage is paid at the end of the mortgage term, either over additional time or as a balloon payment
- renegotiating the interest rate to lower the payments or keep them at the same level (if the interest rate is adjustable and will soon go up), or
- using a deed in lieu of foreclosure, where the debtor gives back the house in return for the lender's agreement not to foreclose and not to go after any additional money the debtor owes on the mortgage.

You might be wondering whether you should tell your creditors that you are thinking about filing for bankruptcy. After all, shouldn't they be willing to negotiate for a lesser amount—that you can pay—if you can get rid of the debt entirely? Unfortunately, experience shows that this tactic often backfires. Some creditors will call you every day demanding to know who your attorney is. When you tell them you don't have an attorney, they may well take the opportunity to berate you for not paying your debts and warn you to call them when you do get an attorney. In short, mentioning the "B" word is more likely to cause you grief than it is to produce a good result.

The Automatic Stay

One of the most powerful features of bankruptcy is the automatic stay: a court order that goes into effect as soon as you file, protecting you from certain actions by your creditors. The automatic stay stops most debt collectors dead in their tracks and keeps them at bay for the rest of your case. Once you file, all collection activity (with some exceptions, explained below) must go through the bankruptcy court—and most creditors cannot take any further collection actions against you while the bankruptcy is pending.

This chapter explains how the automatic stay applies to typical debt collection efforts, including a couple of situations in which you might not get the protection of the automatic stay. It also explains how the automatic stay protects your codebtors from collection activities. And, it covers how the automatic stay works in eviction proceedings—vital information for any renter who files for bankruptcy.

> **TIP**
>
> **You don't need bankruptcy to stop your creditors from harassing you.** Many people begin thinking about bankruptcy when their creditors start phoning them at home and on the job. Federal law prohibits debt collectors from doing this once you tell the creditors, in writing, that you don't want to be called. And if you orally tell debt collectors that you refuse to pay, it is illegal for them to contact you except to send one last letter making a final demand for payment before filing a lawsuit. While just telling a creditor to stop usually works, you may have to send a written follow-up letter. (You can find a sample letter in Ch. 1.)

How Long the Stay Lasts

The automatic stay is "automatic" because you don't have to ask the court to issue it, and the court doesn't have to take any special action to make it effective: Once you file, the stay is in place, automatically, by operation of law. The stay prohibits creditors and collection agencies from taking any action to collect most kinds of debts unless the law or the bankruptcy court says they can. In some circumstances, the creditor can file an action in court to have the stay lifted (called a "Motion to Lift Stay"). In a few others, the creditor can simply begin collection proceedings without seeking advance permission from the court.

Unless it is lifted by the bankruptcy court, the stay will remain in effect until one of the following:

- The court confirms your Chapter 13 plan (see Ch. 10).
- Your case is dismissed.

The stay ends when the court confirms your Chapter 13 plan because it is no longer necessary. Once the plan is confirmed, it governs all creditor and debtor behavior as to the debts included in the plan. The confirmation is a federal court order (just like the automatic stay), and any attempt by a creditor to collect a debt covered by the plan is a violation of that order.

How the Stay Affects Common Collection Actions

Most common types of creditor collection actions are stopped dead by the stay—including harassing calls by debt collectors, reporting debts to credit reporting bureaus, threatening letters by attorneys, and lawsuits to collect payment for credit card and health care bills.

Home Foreclosures

Many people file for Chapter 13 bankruptcy to prevent their homes from being taken in foreclosure. While the automatic stay will temporarily prevent a foreclosure no matter which type of bankruptcy is filed, in a Chapter 7 bankruptcy, the creditor may be able to have the stay lifted and proceed with the foreclosure. However, the forfeiture can be permanently stopped in a Chapter 13 bankruptcy.

> **EXAMPLE:** Angel owns his home. He has been faithfully making his monthly mortgage payment of $900 for eight years and has incurred $50,000 worth of credit card debt. In May 2012, Angel's job at a local telecommunications company is outsourced as part of a monster layoff. He obtains another job at a much lower salary and slowly but surely falls two months behind on his mortgage payments. His lender sends him a three-month notice of intent to foreclose on the mortgage.

Angel visits a bankruptcy lawyer, who explains that he can file for Chapter 7 bankruptcy to wipe out the credit card debt, but unless he can get current on his mortgage, the lender may be able to get permission from the bankruptcy court to proceed with the foreclosure. On the other hand, if Angel files for Chapter 13 bankruptcy, he can stop the foreclosure from proceeding and also buy some time to pay off the arrearage through his Chapter 13 plan.

As is true of just about everything related to bankruptcy, there is an exception to this wonderful remedy. The automatic stay won't stop a foreclosure in a Chapter 13 bankruptcy if you filed another bankruptcy case within the previous two years and the court, in that proceeding, lifted the stay and allowed the lender to proceed with the foreclosure. In other words, the law won't allow you to prevent a foreclosure by filing serial bankruptcies.

EXAMPLE: Julie falls three months behind on her mortgage and receives a notice of intent to foreclose from her lender. Julie stops making any further payments and tries to sell her home to recover her remaining equity, but the market has slowed, and she can't find a buyer. Julie files for Chapter 7 bankruptcy to prevent her home from being sold at auction (the procedure used in about half the states). The auction is postponed because of the automatic stay, but the creditor moves to have the stay lifted. The judge grants the motion two months after Julie filed for bankruptcy. The lender sets a new date for the auction.

Julie now files for Chapter 13 bankruptcy, intending to keep her home by paying the arrearage over the life of the plan. Because Julie filed her Chapter 7 bankruptcy within the previous two years, and the stay was lifted in that case, however, the stay will not apply in her Chapter 13 case. The lender will be allowed to proceed with the rescheduled auction.

Even if you are in Julie's position, you may still be able to keep your home. As mentioned, the automatic stay in Chapter 13 cases lasts only until the court confirms the plan filed by the debtor. Once the plan is confirmed, it governs the behavior of debtor and creditor alike. For example, if Julie continues with her Chapter 13 case, and the court confirms a plan that provides for repayment of the arrearage, the lender will have to abide by the plan and allow her to catch up on her payments.

If your lender is able to proceed with the foreclosure because of the two-year rule or because it obtained an order lifting the stay, and it sells your home before your plan is confirmed, you may have trouble getting the home back. The law favors purchasers who qualify as "bona fide purchasers for value" (BFPs)—third-party buyers who have no idea there might be a problem with the foreclosure or mortgage. If a BFP buys your house at auction, that might be the end of the story. Although not always. (See e.g. *In re Thaedine A. Brown,* ___ B.R. ___ (Bankr. S.D. Texas 2011).) If you are in this situation, talk to a bankruptcy attorney right away.

However, if the lender doesn't get a good offer at the auction and ends up with the house, it may not be able to claim BFP status. In this situation, you may be able to get your house back if you have grounds to challenge the legality of the foreclosure. This is a rapidly changing area of the law. To get up-to-date information for your state or region, talk to a local bankruptcy attorney or do some research. (See Ch. 16 to learn how to do legal research.)

Challenging Foreclosures in Automatic Stay Motion Hearings

Until the housing bubble burst, bankruptcy judges routinely granted a lender's motion to lift the stay and proceed with a foreclosure. However, more recently, bankruptcy courts have taken a closer look at these motions and discovered that the institutions filing them aren't necessarily entitled to ask the court to lift the stay. Only the holder of a promissory note is a "party in interest" with the right to request that the stay be lifted. Because of the way mortgages have been divided, bought, and sold lately, the institution asking to lift the stay often cannot produce a valid copy of the promissory note or otherwise prove that it is the legal holder of the note. Judges are increasingly likely to deny motions to lift the stay unless this type of proof is presented.

Vehicle Repossessions

Vehicle repossessions work in much the same way as foreclosures except that there is typically no advance repossession notice. If you fall behind on your car note and really don't want your car repossessed, you can file for Chapter 13 bankruptcy and schedule to repay your arrearage as part of your plan. If you file your bankruptcy petition before the repossession, the automatic stay will protect your car up until the time the judge confirms a plan that proposes to pay the arrearage. You'll have to include "adequate protection" payments in your proposed plan to cover the depreciation that occurs between the date you file for bankruptcy and the date your plan is finally confirmed. Typically, this means paying the same amount that you would otherwise pay monthly on your car loan.

Even if your car is repossessed before you file, if the judge confirms a repayment plan that provides for payment of the arrearage and the amount you owe monthly on the note, you will be able to get your car back, unless the vehicle has already been auctioned off to a bona fide purchaser for value, in which case, it is gone forever.

Often, a car is worth much less than the debtor owes on it. If you're in this situation, it may not be a bad idea to let the repossession go forward, especially if you bought the car fairly recently.

However, if you bought the car at least 2½ years ago, Chapter 13 gives you an alternative: You can reduce the amount you owe to the replacement value of the car (taking its age and condition into account), plus interest at a relatively low rate. This is called a cramdown. Even if you can't make your payments under your current car note, your monthly bill might be much more affordable once the loan has been crammed down. (Ch. 1 discusses cramdowns in more detail.)

Credit Card Debts, Medical Debts, and Attorneys' Fees

Anyone trying to collect credit card debts, medical debts, attorneys' fees, debts arising from breach of contract, or legal judgments against you (other than child support and alimony) must cease all collection activities after you file your bankruptcy case. They cannot:

- file a lawsuit or proceed with a pending lawsuit against you
- record liens against your property
- report the debt to a credit reporting bureau, or
- seize your property or income, such as money in a bank account or your paycheck.

Public Benefits

Government entities that are seeking to collect overpayments of public benefits, such as SSI, Medicaid, or Temporary Assistance to Needy Families (welfare), cannot reduce or terminate your benefits to get that money back while your bankruptcy is pending. If, however, you become ineligible for benefits, including Medicare benefits, bankruptcy doesn't prevent the agency from denying or terminating your benefits on that ground.

Criminal Proceedings

If a case against you can be broken down into criminal and debt components, only the criminal component will be allowed to continue; the debt component will be put on hold while your bankruptcy is pending. For example, if you were convicted of writing a bad check and have been sentenced to community service and ordered to pay a fine, your obligation to do community service will not be stopped by the automatic stay (but your obligation to pay the fine will).

IRS Liens and Levies

As explained in "When the Stay Doesn't Apply," below, certain tax proceedings are not affected by the automatic stay. The automatic stay does, however, stop the IRS from issuing a lien or seizing (levying against) any of your property or income.

Utilities

Companies providing you with utilities (such as gas, heating oil, electricity, telephone service, and water) may not discontinue service because you file for bankruptcy. However, they can shut off your service 20 days after you file if you don't provide them with a deposit or another means to assure future payment.

How the Stay Affects Actions Against Codebtors

Many people file for Chapter 13 bankruptcy to protect their codebtors from liability. For example, if your parent cosigns a loan and you file for bankruptcy, you certainly don't want the creditor to enforce the debt against your parent. With rare exceptions, the automatic stay also protects your codebtors unless the court lifts the stay. The court will lift the stay only in the following cases:

- Your codebtor received the item or services for which the debt was taken (for instance, the car obtained by the loan in question).
- Your repayment plan will not pay the debt.
- The creditor's interest would be irreparably harmed if the stay were allowed to continue.
- The debt is a tax debt.

If your Chapter 13 case is closed, dismissed, or converted to Chapter 7 or 11, your codebtor loses the protection of the automatic stay. Also, the stay does not protect a codebtor whose liability for the debt arose in the ordinary course of the codebtor's business.

When the Stay Doesn't Apply

The stay doesn't put a stop to every type of collection action, nor does it apply in every situation. Congress has determined that certain debts or proceedings are sufficiently important to "trump" the automatic stay. In these situations, collection actions can continue just as if you had never filed for bankruptcy. And even in circumstances when the stay would otherwise apply, you can lose the protection of the stay through your own actions.

Actions Not Stopped by the Stay

The automatic stay does not prohibit the following types of actions from proceeding.

Divorce and Child Support

Almost all proceedings related to divorce or parenting continue as before: They are not affected by the automatic stay. These include actions to:

- set and collect current child support and alimony

- collect back child support and alimony from property that is not in the bankruptcy estate (for instance, postfiling income that isn't included in your plan)
- determine child custody and visitation
- establish paternity in a lawsuit
- modify child support and alimony
- protect a spouse or child from domestic violence
- withhold income to collect child support
- report overdue support to credit bureaus
- intercept tax refunds to pay back child support, and
- withhold, suspend, or restrict drivers' and professional licenses as leverage to collect child support.

Tax Proceedings

The IRS can continue certain actions, such as conducting a tax audit, issuing a tax deficiency notice, demanding a tax return, issuing a tax assessment, demanding payment of an assessment, or pursuing a codebtor for taxes owed.

Pension Loans

The stay doesn't prevent withholding from a debtor's income to repay a loan from an ERISA-qualified pension (this includes most job-related pensions and individual retirement plans).

How You Can Lose the Protection of the Stay

Even if the stay would otherwise apply, you can lose its protection through your own actions. The stay may not protect you from collection efforts if you had one or more bankruptcy cases pending but dismissed within a year of your current bankruptcy filing.

The automatic stay will last only 30 days if you had one prior bankruptcy case pending but dismissed within the year before you file. You can ask the court to extend the stay, but you have to file a motion. And if you had two cases pending but dismissed within the last year, the automatic stay won't kick in at all (unless the court orders it). There are two lessons here for debtors:

- Don't let your case be dismissed (a dismissed case counts as a pending case).

- If your case is dismissed and you want to file again within the year, you should definitely talk to an attorney before you decide to file.

If the automatic stay terminates because of one or more prior pending cases, the property of the bankruptcy estate—in your current bankruptcy filing—is still protected. (Your bankruptcy estate includes most types of property that you own or are entitled to receive when you file your bankruptcy papers, but does not include money earned or most property received after filing.) For example, a creditor would not be entitled to seize money that was in your bank account on the date you filed, but it could levy on income you earned after filing, which is not part of the bankruptcy estate.

One Dismissal in the Past Year

With a couple of exceptions, if you had a bankruptcy case dismissed during the previous year for any reason, voluntarily or involuntarily, the court will presume that your new filing is in bad faith, and the stay will terminate 30 days after your new case is filed. You, the trustee, the U.S. Trustee, or the creditor can ask the court to continue the stay beyond the 30-day period, but the court will do this only if you (or whoever else makes the request) can show that your current case was not filed in bad faith.

The motion to extend the stay must be scheduled for hearing within the 30-day period after you file for bankruptcy and must give creditors adequate notice under local motion rules of why the stay should be extended. As a practical matter, this means the motion must:

- be filed within several days after you file for bankruptcy (unless you obtain an "Order Shortening Time" from the judge, a simple procedure)
- be served on all creditors to whom you want the stay to apply, and
- provide specific reasons why your filing was not in bad faith and the stay should be extended.

When deciding whether to extend the stay beyond 30 days, the court will look at a number of factors to decide whether your current filing is in good faith. Here are some of the factors that will work against you:

- More than one prior bankruptcy case was filed by (or against) you in the past year.
- Your prior case was dismissed because you failed to file required documents on time (for instance,

you didn't give the trustee your most recent tax return at least seven days before the first meeting of creditors) or amend the petition on a timely basis when required to do so. If you failed to file these documents inadvertently or because of a careless error, that won't help you with the judge—unless you used an attorney in the prior case. Judges are more willing to give debtors the benefit of the doubt if their attorneys were responsible for the mistakes.

- The prior case was dismissed while a creditor's request for relief from the stay was pending.
- Your circumstances haven't changed since your previous case was dismissed.

Two Dismissals in the Past Year

If you had more than two cases dismissed during the previous year, no stay will apply in your current case unless you convince the court, within 30 days of your filing, that your current case was not filed in bad faith and that a stay should therefore be granted. The court will look at the factors outlined above to decide whether you have overcome the presumption of bad faith.

Evictions

A landlord may evict a tenant, despite the automatic stay, if:

- The landlord obtained a judgment for possession before the tenant filed for bankruptcy. (If the judgment was for failing to pay rent, there is a possible exception to this rule—see below.)
- The landlord is evicting the tenant for endangering the property or the illegal use of controlled substances on the property.

If the landlord does not already have a judgment when you file, and he or she wants to evict you for reasons other than endangering the property or using controlled substances (for example, the eviction is based on your failure to pay rent or violation of another lease provision), the automatic stay prevents the landlord from beginning or continuing with eviction proceedings. However, the landlord can always ask the judge to lift the stay—and courts tend to grant these requests.

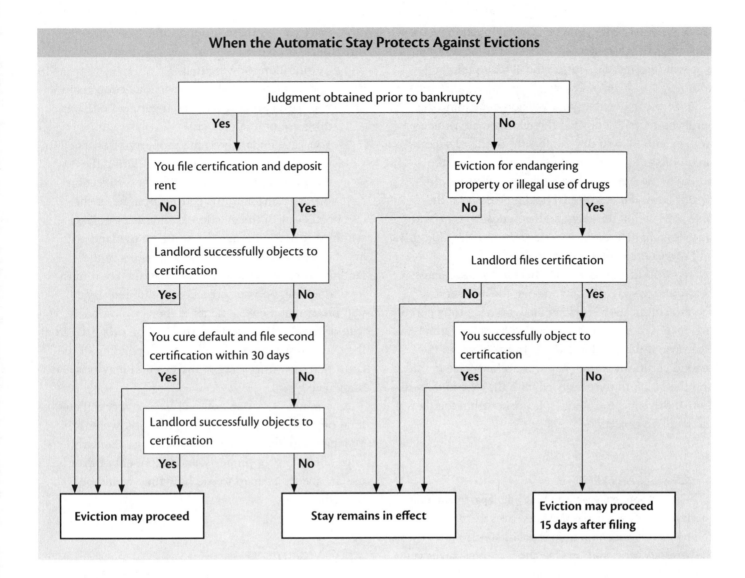

When the Automatic Stay Protects Against Evictions

Judgment obtained prior to bankruptcy

TIP

Different rules apply to evictions of an owner following foreclosure. The law that allows evictions to proceed despite the automatic stay doesn't apply to evictions of the former owner of the home following a foreclosure sale. If a court has ordered you to leave your home following foreclosure and the sheriff is trying to evict you, filing for bankruptcy will legally postpone the eviction until you receive a bankruptcy discharge or until the judge lifts the automatic stay, whichever happens first.

If the Landlord Already Has a Judgment

If your landlord already has a judgment of possession against you when you file for bankruptcy, the automatic stay won't help you (with the possible exception described just below). The landlord may proceed with the eviction just as if you never filed for bankruptcy.

If the eviction order is based on your failure to pay rent, you may be able to have the automatic stay reinstated. However, this exception applies only if your state's law allows you to remain in your rental unit and "cure" (pay back) the rent delinquency after the landlord has a judgment for possession. Here's what you'll have to do to take advantage of this exception:

Step 1: As part of your bankruptcy petition, you must file a certification (a statement under oath) that your state's laws allow you to cure the rent delinquency after the judgment is obtained and to continue living in your rental unit. Very few states allow this. To find out whether yours is one of them, ask the sheriff or someone at legal aid (if you have legal aid in your area). When you file your bankruptcy petition, you must deposit with the court clerk the amount of rent that will become due during the 30-day period after you file.

Once you have filed your petition containing the certification and deposited the rent, you are protected from eviction for 30 days unless the landlord successfully objects to your initial certification before the 30-day period ends. If the landlord objects to your certification, the court must hold a hearing on the objection within ten days, so theoretically you could have less than 30 days of protection if the landlord files and serves the objection immediately.

Step 2: To keep the stay in effect longer, you must, before the 30-day period runs out, file and serve a second certification showing that you have fully cured the default in the manner provided by your state's law. However, if the landlord successfully objects to this second certification, the stay will no longer be in effect and the landlord may proceed with the eviction. As in Step 1, the court must hold a hearing within ten days if the landlord objects.

SEE AN EXPERT

If you really want to keep your apartment, talk to a lawyer. As you can see, these new rules are somewhat complicated. If you don't interpret your state's law properly, file the necessary paperwork on time, and successfully argue your side if the landlord objects, you could find yourself put out of your home. A good lawyer can tell you whether it's worth fighting an eviction—and, if so, what tactics to use.

Endangering the Property or Using Controlled Substances

Under the new bankruptcy law, an eviction action will not be stayed by your bankruptcy filing if your landlord wants you out because you endangered the property or engaged in the "illegal use of controlled substances" on the property. And your landlord doesn't have to have a judgment in hand when you file for bankruptcy: The landlord may start an eviction action against you or continue with a pending eviction action even after your filing date if the eviction is based on property endangerment or drug use.

To evict you on these grounds after you have filed for bankruptcy, your landlord must file and serve on you a certification showing that:

- The landlord has filed an eviction action against you based on property endangerment or illegal drug use on the property.
- You have endangered the property or engaged in illegal drug use on the property during the 30-day period prior to the landlord's certification.

If your landlord files this certification, he or she can proceed with the eviction 15 days later unless, within that time, you file and serve on the landlord an objection to the truth of the statements in the landlord's certification. If you do that, the court must hold a hearing on your objection within ten days. If you prove that the statements in the certification aren't true or have been remedied, you will be protected from the eviction while your bankruptcy is pending. If the court denies your objection, the eviction may proceed immediately.

As a practical matter, you will have a very difficult time proving a negative—that is, that you weren't endangering the property or using drugs. Similarly, once allegations of property endangerment or drug use are made, it's hard to see how they would be "remedied."

CAUTION

Landlords can always ask the court to lift the automatic stay to begin or continue an eviction on any grounds. Although the automatic stay will kick in unless one of these exceptions applies, the judge can lift the stay upon the landlord's request. You can certainly argue that you need to keep your tenancy in order to make the payments required by your Chapter 13 plan. As a general rule, however, bankruptcy judges are more likely to lift the stay and allow landlords to exercise their property rights, figuring you will find another place to live.

RESOURCE

Need help with your landlord? For more information on dealing with landlords—including landlords who are trying to evict you—see *Every Tenant's Legal Guide*, by Janet Portman and Marcia Stewart (Nolo).

Are You Eligible to Use Chapter 13?

Before you can decide whether you should file for Chapter 13, you need to figure out whether you are legally eligible to do so. Not everyone can use Chapter 13: To qualify, you must meet certain eligibility requirements, and you must be able to propose a legally confirmable repayment plan. This chapter explains these requirements.

Prior Bankruptcy Discharges May Preclude a Chapter 13 Discharge

You can't get a Chapter 13 discharge if you received a discharge in a previous Chapter 13 case in the last two years or a discharge in a Chapter 7 case filed within the last four years. You aren't barred from filing for Chapter 13 bankruptcy in these circumstances, but you can't get a discharge. For instance, you can file for Chapter 13 bankruptcy the moment you receive a Chapter 7 discharge (to handle liens that survived your Chapter 7 case or debts that weren't discharged in that case), but you won't be able to discharge any debts that remain even if you complete your Chapter 13 repayment plan. (Filing for Chapter 13 immediately after filing for Chapter 7 is known colloquially as a "Chapter 20 bankruptcy.")

Business Entities Can't File for Chapter 13 Bankruptcy

To file a Chapter 13 bankruptcy case, you must be an individual (or a husband and wife filing jointly). If you own your own business as a sole proprietor or partner, you can include all business debts on which you have personal liability. You have to file the case in your own name, however, not in the name of the business, because a business entity cannot file for Chapter 13 bankruptcy. On your bankruptcy papers, you will need to list all fictitious business names or dba ("doing business as") names that you've used as a sole proprietor or partnership.

If you operate your business as a sole proprietorship or as a partnership with your spouse or someone else, you, or you and your partner, are personally liable for the debts of the business. For bankruptcy purposes, you and your business (or your share of a partnership)

are one and the same. You can include all of the business debts in your Chapter 13 bankruptcy case. There is one exception: Stockbrokers and commodity brokers cannot file a Chapter 13 bankruptcy case, even for personal (nonbusiness) debts.

Your Debts May Not Exceed Certain Limits

You do not qualify for Chapter 13 bankruptcy if your secured debts exceed $1,081,400 or your unsecured debts are more than $360,475. A secured debt is a debt secured by collateral (like your home or car). If you fail to pay, the creditor can take the collateral. Unsecured debts have no collateral guaranteeing payment.

For example, if you owe $2 million on your home, you can't file for Chapter 13 bankruptcy. The same would be true if you owed $100,000 on a student loan (unsecured), $100,000 on credit card debt (unsecured), and $200,000 on a court judgment due to injuries resulting from your negligent driving (unsecured). If you need help figuring out which of your debts are secured and which are unsecured, see "Classifying Your Debts" in Ch. 4.

When computing your debt load, include only debts that are both liquidated and uncontingent. A debt is liquidated if you know the exact dollar amount you owe; a debt is uncontingent if you owe it regardless of what happens in the future. For example, you don't have to include a debt that someone says you owe because you caused them property damage or personal injury, unless you have already settled the claim (or lost a lawsuit) for a set amount of money. Until that happens, you don't know how much you owe—and, if the person decides not to sue you, you might not owe anything at all.

You Must Be (and Stay) Current on Your Income Tax Filings

Within several months after you file for bankruptcy, you must prove that you have filed federal and state income tax returns for the four prior tax years. You can do this by submitting the returns themselves or transcripts of the returns obtained from the IRS. You are supposed to give the returns or transcripts to the trustee (the court official handling your case on behalf of the court) no later than the date set for your first meeting of creditors (about a month after you file). The trustee can keep the creditors' meeting "open" for an additional 120 days to give you time to file the returns and, if necessary, the court can give you an additional 30 days. Ultimately, if you don't produce your returns or transcripts of the returns for those four preceding years, the trustee will ask the court to dismiss your Chapter 13 case.

To obtain a transcript of your tax records, call 800-829-1040 or submit IRS Form 4506T, *Request for Transcript of Tax Return* (you can find a copy at www.irs.gov).

During the entire course of your plan, you must remain current on your tax filings and must provide the trustee—and any creditor who requests it—with copies of your returns. Failure to do so can result in your bankruptcy case being dismissed.

TIP

If you can't get current on taxes, file for Chapter 7. There is no requirement that you be current on your taxes in a Chapter 7 bankruptcy. If you need immediate bankruptcy relief and you know you won't be able to get current on your taxes within a relatively short period of time, Chapter 7 bankruptcy is your only practical option.

You Must Keep Making Your Child Support and Alimony Payments

Even if you owe back child support or alimony, you must meet your current support obligations during the course of your plan. If you don't keep up with your payments, your bankruptcy can be dismissed.

You Must File Annual Income and Expense Reports

You are required to file annual income and expense reports in order to keep your Chapter 13 case alive. Failure to file these reports can result in your case being dismissed.

Your Proposed Repayment Plan Must Pay All Required Debts

Certain debts must be paid in full in a Chapter 13 plan. If your expected monthly income, less reasonable living expenses, won't allow you to pay off those debts within the required plan period, the court will not confirm your plan. Ch. 5 explains the process you must use to determine whether you can propose a confirmable Chapter 13 plan over the appropriate time period.

In addition to paying your mandatory debts in full, your plan must show that you'll be able to pay a commission to the trustee equal to about 10% of your total monthly plan payment. For example, if you owe $50,000 in back taxes that would have to be paid in your Chapter 13 plan, your expected income must be sufficient to pay at least $10,000 a year for five years, plus interest, toward that debt. You would also have to come up with another $1,000 each year for the trustee. And, you would have to be able to show that you could pay your living expenses while making these required payments. If the judge doesn't think you'll have enough income to cover all of your obligations, your plan won't be approved.

Debts That Must Be Paid in Chapter 13

Here are the types of debts that must be paid in full over the course of your Chapter 13 plan.

Priority Debts

Priority debts are unsecured debts (that is, debts for which you haven't pledged collateral and for which the creditor has not filed or recorded a lien) that are considered sufficiently important to jump to the head of the bankruptcy repayment line. The general rule is that priority debts must be paid in full over the course of a Chapter 13 case. The most common priority debts that knock people out of Chapter 13 are back taxes and child support arrearages. (However, child support arrearages don't have to be paid in full during your repayment period if you owe the debt to a government agency rather than to your child or former spouse.) See "Classifying Your Debts" in Ch. 4 for a full list of priority debts.

Secured Debts That Will Outlive Your Plan

Your plan must provide that you will keep current on secured debts that are contractually scheduled to last longer than your repayment plan (such as mortgages). You must also pay off any arrearages you owe during the life of the plan, unless you are willing to surrender the collateral. If you do surrender the collateral, the arrearage becomes unsecured debt and is treated as such.

Other Secured Debts

All other secured debts must be paid in full under the plan, including tax liens on your property, promissory notes securing personal property collateral, and judgment liens that can't be removed for one reason or another.

Rough Calculation: Can You Repay Required Debts in Chapter 13?

To determine whether you could pay these mandatory debts during your repayment period, you must find out whether you will have enough income left over each month after paying your reasonable living expenses. (Remember, even though your income may be low enough to make you eligible for a three-year plan (see Ch. 1), you may propose a five-year plan if it will take you that long to pay off your mandatory debts.) Here's a quick way to figure out whether you can make these required payments:

Step 1: Compute your household's gross income over the past six months, divide it by six, and then multiply it by the number of months in your repayment period (60 for a five-year plan). (For help calculating your average monthly income, see Ch. 4.)

Step 2: Compute your actual monthly living expenses, including monthly installment payments on your car and other property necessary for your family's welfare, and multiply by the number of months in your repayment plan.

Step 3: Deduct your expenses computed in Step 2 from your income computed in Step 1.

Step 4: Add up all of your priority debts, secured debt arrearages for property you plan to keep, and

secured debts, as described in "Debts That Must Be Paid in Chapter 13," above.

Step 5: Subtract your total mandatory debts, as calculated in Step 4, from the total amount of income you will have left over after paying expenses, as calculated in Step 3.

If this amount is a positive number, it means you may have enough income to pay your mandatory debts. If the amount is negative, you may have to make some adjustments, such as giving up property on which you are making payments or lowering your expenses, to propose a confirmable Chapter 13 plan. Remember, however, that your expenses must appear to be reasonable to the court. If your expenses look too low, the court may reject your plan as unreasonable.

RELATED TOPIC

See Ch. 5 for detailed instructions on calculating income, expenses, and repayment obligations. This quick test is intended to give you a rough idea of which debts have to be paid in full and whether you might be able to pay them, but the actual math is much more complicated (especially if your income exceeds the median income in your state for a household of your size). Ch. 5 takes you step by step through the required income and expense computations and helps you figure out whether you can propose a confirmable Chapter 13 plan.

Your Unsecured Creditors Must Get at Least as Much as They Would Have Received in a Chapter 7 Bankruptcy

In a Chapter 7 bankruptcy, the trustee liquidates your nonexempt property and distributes the proceeds to your unsecured creditors. In a Chapter 13 bankruptcy, you can keep your property, whether or not it is exempt. Given this difference in the two types of bankruptcy, many people choose Chapter 13 rather than Chapter 7 because they want to hang on to some or all of their nonexempt property—that is, property they would have to surrender to the trustee in Chapter 7. For example, you may want to use Chapter 13 because you have a vacation home or valuable family heirlooms that you would lose if you filed for Chapter 7.

Although using Chapter 13 allows you to keep your property, it does not allow you to deprive unsecured creditors of the money they would have received if you had used Chapter 7. Your plan must propose payments to your nonpriority, unsecured creditors (those to whom you owe credit card debts, medical bills, lawsuit judgments, and so on) that are at least equal to what they would have received in a Chapter 7 case. In other words, your plan must show that they will be paid at least the value of your nonexempt property, less what it would cost to take that property and sell it (and less the trustee's fee for doing so). Ch. 5 provides detailed information on how to run these numbers and come up with the minimum amount you must pay to these creditors through your Chapter 13 repayment plan.

You Must Participate in an Approved Personal Financial Management Course

You must complete a personal financial management course before the court will discharge your debts. The agencies providing this service must be approved by the Office of the U.S. Trustee, which imposes specific curriculum requirements that are intended to require about two hours of your time. Typically, the agency where you get your prefiling credit counseling will also offer this personal financial management course. For more information about the requirements for these agencies and how to find one, visit the Office of the U.S. Trustee's website at www.justice.gov/ust (select "Consumer Information," then "Credit Counseling & Debtor Education" from the home page).

Do You Have to Use Chapter 13?

In October 2005, a massive change took place in the bankruptcy field. Believing that too many people were taking advantage of Chapter 7 bankruptcy to wipe out their debts, Congress passed the Bankruptcy Abuse Prevention and Consumer Protection Act of 2005 (BAPCPA). The stated purpose of this law is to force people who can afford to repay some of their debt to file for bankruptcy under Chapter 13 instead of under Chapter 7. To further this purpose, the BAPCPA makes it harder and more expensive to file under Chapter 7.

Because of the changes wrought by the BAPCPA, some debtors no longer have the option to use Chapter 7: If they want to file for bankruptcy, they have to use Chapter 13. However, most people will still have a choice. This chapter will help you figure out whether you have to use Chapter 13 or whether Chapter 7 is still an option for you.

CAUTION

Don't skip this chapter, even if you know you will use Chapter 13. Even if you have already decided to file for Chapter 13, make sure to read the instructions for Parts I, II, and III under "The Means Test," below. This information will help you compute your current monthly income and compare that figure to your state's median income. You will need these numbers to figure out the requirements of your repayment plan in Ch. 5.

Can You Pass the Means Test?

There are two income tests that determine whether you are eligible for Chapter 7 bankruptcy:

- **The means test.** Debtors whose average household income over the previous six months exceeds the median income in their state for a family of the same size must take this test. These debtors must answer a series of questions about their income and expenses to determine whether they have enough extra income to fund a Chapter 13 plan. If they do, their Chapter 7 filing will be labeled a presumed "abuse" and they will be forced out of Chapter 7.
- **The "abuse under all the circumstances" test.** This test compares your actual income to your actual

expenses to determine whether you have enough money coming in to repay some of your debts. Even if you pass the means test, you can be forced out of Chapter 7 if, under this test, you appear to be able to fund a Chapter 13 repayment plan.

If you fail the means test, you are presumed to be abusing the bankruptcy laws and will be forced into a Chapter 13 bankruptcy unless you can prove that the law shouldn't apply to you for some reason. If you fail the "abuse under all the circumstances" test, the Office of the U.S. Trustee—the government agency responsible for policing the bankruptcy system—has the burden of proving your ineligibility for Chapter 7. The only way to know for certain whether your income is too high under either of these tests is to complete a form that all Chapter 7 debtors must complete as part of their bankruptcy, Form 22A: *Chapter 7 Statement of Current Monthly Income and Means-Test Calculation.*

In the first part of the form, you determine whether your gross income (for the previous six months) is more or less than the median income for your state for your household size.

If your income is less than your state's median income. If your income (not including Social Security) is less than your state's median, you pass the means test and won't be presumed ineligible to use Chapter 7. But, as mentioned above, you might face another hurdle if you file under Chapter 7. If the U.S. Trustee believes that your actual income less your actual expenses leaves you with enough money to repay a reasonable portion of your debt over five years, it will ask the court to find that allowing you to use Chapter 7 would be an abuse. If the court agrees, you'll have to use Chapter 13.

Whether you choose or are required to use Chapter 13, you will have two advantages if your income is less than the state median: You may propose a three-year (rather than a five-year) repayment plan, and you may use your actual expenses—not amounts approved by the IRS—to calculate how much disposable income you will have left to devote to your plan.

If your income is more than your state's median income. If your income is more than the state median, you must take the rest of the means test—by completing the rest of Form 22A—to find out whether you'll have the option of using Chapter 7 or will have to use

Chapter 13. The purpose of this part of the form is to find out whether you would have enough income left over, after subtracting certain expenses and deductions, to pay a portion of your unsecured debts (credit card debts, medical bills, and the like) over a five-year period.

What Is Abuse Under All the Circumstances?

A number of bankruptcy judges have had to decide whether the facts of a particular case add up to abuse under all the circumstances. Generally, there are two situations in which the court is most likely to find an abuse: if it looks like your income will be higher, or your expenses should be lower, than the figures you used in the means test.

For example, the court might find an abuse under all the circumstances if it looks like you will have significant extra income in the future that didn't show up in the means test. (The means test looks only at your income in the six months before you file for bankruptcy.) If your spouse just landed a high-paying job in the last month, for instance, the court might push you into Chapter 13 if you now appear to have enough extra income to pay a significant portion of your unsecured, nonpriority debt over the next five years.

The court might also find an abuse if your expenses look extravagant or it appears that you could spend less for the same necessities. For example, if you are making large payments on a home or a luxury car, the court might decide that some of that money should be going toward debt repayment.

TIP

Debtors with primarily business debts can skip the means test. If your debts are primarily due to your business, you may choose between a Chapter 7 and Chapter 13 bankruptcy, regardless of the outcome of the means test. You are considered a business debtor if more than half of the total value of your debts comes from your business.

The Means Test

SKIP AHEAD

Those who initially filed for Chapter 7 bankruptcy can skip ahead. If you are using Chapter 13 because you initially filed under Chapter 7 and have already taken and flunked the means test, or if the Court has converted your case to Chapter 13, skip to "Forced Conversion to Chapter 13," below.

Getting the Official Bankruptcy Forms

Getting your hands on the most up-to-date forms required by the bankruptcy courts is easy. All the forms are on the website of the United States Courts (at www.uscourts.gov). You can complete the forms online, save, edit, and print at your convenience. Or, print out blank forms so you can review them as they are discussed in this book. The direct link to the forms is www.uscourts.gov/FormsAndFees/Forms/BankruptcyForms.aspx.

Pull up Official Form 22A from www.uscourts.gov so that you can fill it out as we go along. Or use the blank tear-out form in Appendix B and fill in the numbers by hand.

RESOURCE

Prefer to let your computer crunch the numbers? Rather than completing the means test form by hand, you can use an online calculator to run the numbers for you. You'll find an excellent online calculator at www.legalconsumer.com/bankruptcy/nolo. The calculator automatically enters IRS expense figures so you don't have to look them up. Just enter your zip code and away you go.

Part I.   Military and Non-Consumer Debtors

Line 1A. If all of the facts in the "Declaration of Disabled Veteran" are true of your situation, you can choose between Chapter 7 and Chapter 13 bankruptcy. If you know that you want to file for Chapter 13, however, you still have to calculate your "current monthly income" and compare it to your state's median income. This comparison will determine how long your Chapter 13 plan must last and how much income you will have to commit to your plan.

To qualify for the veterans' exclusion, you must have a disability rating of at least 30%, and more than half of your debt must have been incurred while you were either on active duty or performing homeland defense activity.

Line 1B. If the majority of your debts comes from running a business, check the box. Those who have primarily nonconsumer (business) debts don't have to take the means test and are free to choose between Chapter 7 and Chapter 13 bankruptcy. If the majority of your debts are personal, you must continue the means test to see whether you will have a choice of bankruptcy chapters. Back taxes (even unpaid personal income taxes) are considered to be business debts, even if you don't own a business. On the other hand, mortgage debt is considered to be consumer debt. Often, a debtor's mortgage debt tips the scale, making the case a consumer filing, even if the vast majority of the debtor's unsecured debt is business debt.

Line 1C. The law provides a temporary exclusion from taking the means test for reservists or National Guard members who were called to active duty or were performing homeland defense activities after September 11, 2001, for at least 90 days. The exclusion period lasts for 540 days after the 90-day period of active duty. If you fit this category, you may be eligible for a temporary exclusion from the means test requirement.

Part II. Calculation of Monthly Income for § 707(b)(7) Exclusion

Line 2a. If you are unmarried, check this box and follow the instructions (complete only Lines 3 through 11 in column A).

Line 2b. If you are married but filing separately because you have separate households, check this box and complete only Lines 3 through 11 in Column A. If you check this box, you are declaring, under penalty of perjury, that you are legally separated under the laws of your state or that you are living separately for reasons other than just to qualify for Chapter 7 bankruptcy.

Line 2c. If you are married but filing separately for reasons other than those stated on Line 2b, check

this box and complete Lines 3 through 11 in Columns A and B. Later, on Line 17, you will be allowed to deduct a nonfiling spouse's income that is not actually contributed to the filer's household.

Line 2d. If you are married and filing jointly, check this box and complete Lines 3 through 11 in Columns A and B.

> **CAUTION**
> **Use monthly figures.** All figures you enter in Lines 3 through 11 must be monthly averages of your actual income during the six months before you file for bankruptcy. The six-month period ends on the last day of the month before the month in which you file your bankruptcy. For instance, if you file on September 9, the six-month period ends on August 31. If your income is the same for each of those six months (for example, because you've held the same job and worked the same hours during that period), then use your monthly income. If your earnings vary, add them up for the six-month period, then divide the total by six to get a monthly average. You should include all income you actually received during the six-month period, even if you earned it or became entitled to receive it before the six-month period began. (*In re Burrell*, 399 B.R. 620 (Bkrtcy. C.D. Ill. 2008).)

Line 3. Enter your average monthly earnings over the last six months for gross wages, salary, tips, bonuses, overtime, and commissions. ("Gross" means before any taxes, Social Security, or other amounts are withheld.)

Line 4. If you operate a business, profession, or farm, you'll need to compute your necessary and ordinary business expenses for the six-month period and subtract them from your business receipts for that period. The lowest figure you can enter is zero—in other words, you can't enter a loss.

> **CAUTION**
> **Courts disagree on how to calculate business income.** In the context of reviewing Form 22C (in which this same item appears; see Ch. 5), a few courts have found that the form should not allow you to deduct business expenses here. These courts have held that only your gross receipts should go here, while your business expenses should be subtracted later, as part of the means test. (See, for example, *In re Wiegand*, 386

B.R. 238 (9th Cir. BAP 2008).) This interpretation means your average monthly income is likely to be higher, and you are more likely to have to take the means test. Whether courts will apply this interpretation to Form 22A (and which courts will follow along) remains to be seen. For more information on this issue, go to www.legalconsumer.com/bankruptcy/CH13, scroll down to the information for Ch. 4 of this book, and look for the appropriate link.

Line 5. Enter your average monthly rental income for the six-month period (if you have any), and deduct ordinary and necessary operating expenses for that same period. (Don't deduct mortgage payments.)

Line 6. Enter your average monthly income from interest, dividends, and royalties over the last six months.

Line 7. Here's where you include your average monthly pension and retirement income. Don't include Social Security retirement benefits.

Line 8. Enter the monthly average of any amounts another person contributes regularly to your household expenses. If you are filing separately but your spouse's income is included in Column B, don't include any contributions that your spouse makes to your household—his or her income is already being taken into account.

Line 9. Your average monthly unemployment compensation goes here.

Line 10. Insert the average monthly amount you receive from any other source. Do not include money or benefits received under the SSI, SSA, or TANF programs. These benefits are excluded from your current monthly income computation.

Line 11. Compute the subtotals for Columns A and B (if used). Remember, these subtotals should reflect an average monthly figure for all of the items you entered in Lines 3 through 10.

Line 12. Add the subtotals for Lines A and B together. This is what the 2005 bankruptcy law calls your "current monthly income." Because it's a six-month average, it might not match your actual monthly income at the time you file, especially if you've had a job loss or become unable to work in the last six months.

Courts have interpreted a number of other grey areas regarding income, such as:

- Should you count income you have earned but did not receive within the six-month period?
- Do loans from a retirement plan count as income?
- What other items that aren't included on the form might count as income?

Citations to court opinions on these income issues can be found at www.legalconsumer.com/bankruptcy/CH13; scroll down to the information for Ch. 4 of this book and look for the appropriate link.

Part III. Application of § 707(b)(7) Exclusion

This is where the rubber meets the road: In this part, you must compare the current monthly income figure you calculated in Part II with the median family income for your state. If your income is more than the median, you'll have to continue filling in the form to figure out whether you are barred from using Chapter 7. If your income is equal to or less than the median, you can skip the rest of the form and file for Chapter 7, if you wish.

Line 13. Convert your monthly figure on Line 12 to an annual figure by multiplying it by 12. This is your current annual income.

Line 14. Enter the median income for your state and household size. Note that your household might be larger than your actual family. For instance, you may have a relative or friend who is living with you as part of your household; if so, include the friend as a household member. The basic test for a household member is whether his or her income and expenses are intermingled with yours; he or she does not have to be your dependent for tax or other government purposes. (See *In re Ellinger*, 370 B.R. 905 (D. Minn. 2007).) (Citations to court opinions on who counts as a household member can be found at www.legalconsumer.com/bankruptcy/CH13; scroll down to the information for Ch. 4 of this book and look for the appropriate link.) The most recent state median income figures as of the date this book is published are in Appendix B. You can find the most current figures on the U.S. Trustee's website, www.justice.gov/ust (click "Bankruptcy Reform," then "Means Testing Information" and scroll down to the link to the state median income figures). You only need to check the website if your current monthly income is close to the median income figure in Appendix B (within $200 or so).

Line 15. Do the math. If your "current monthly income" exceeds the state median, check the bottom box on Line 15 and continue to Part IV to find out whether you can choose between Chapter 7 and Chapter 13.

If your income is equal to or less than the median, check the top box on Line 15. This means that you aren't banned from using Chapter 7. You don't need to proceed with the form any further. If you decide to proceed under Chapter 13, having an income that doesn't exceed the state median income offers you two big advantages: You can propose a three-year (rather than a five-year) plan, and you can calculate the income you must commit to the plan using your actual expenses rather than expense figures set by the IRS, which are often lower.

> ### TIP
> **Consider postponing your filing if you want to qualify for Chapter 7.** If you conclude, on the basis of your "current monthly income," that you'll have to complete the rest of Form 22A, think about whether your income will decrease in the next few months. If you recently lost a high-paying job or had a sudden decrease in commissions or royalties, for example, your average income over the past six months might look pretty substantial. But in a few months, when you average in your lower earnings, it will come down quite a bit—perhaps to even to less than the state median. If so, and if Chapter 7 would provide you a better remedy than Chapter 13, you might want to delay your bankruptcy filing.

Part IV. Calculation of Current Monthly Income for § 707(b)(2)

This is the beginning of the means test With a couple of exceptions, the values you will be entering in the form are fairly straightforward. The purpose of the means test is to find out whether you have enough income to pay some of your unsecured, nonpriority debts over a five-year period. (See "Classifying Your Debts," below, for help figuring out which debts fall into this category.)

Line 16. Enter the total from Line 12.

Line 17. If you checked the box on Line 2c (married, not filing jointly, and not making the declaration in Line 2b), you can subtract the amount of your spouse's income (as listed in Line 11, Column B) that was not

regularly contributed to your household expenses or those of your dependents. For example, if Line 11, Column B shows that your nonfiling spouse has a monthly income of $2,000, but your spouse contributes only $400 a month to your household, you can enter $1,600 here. Other examples of a nonfiling spouse's income that might not be contributed to the filing spouse's household are mortgage payments on a separately owned house, payments on a separately owned car, life insurance payments, payments into a retirement plan, and payments on credit cards or other revolving debt owned solely by the nonfiling spouse.

Line 18. Subtract the amount on Line 17 from the amount on Line 16. Enter the total here.

> ### SKIP AHEAD
> **If you know you will use Chapter 13.** If you have already decided to file for Chapter 13 bankruptcy, you can skip the rest of this chapter and continue on to Ch. 5. If you still want to know whether you have a choice between a Chapter 7 and Chapter 13 bankruptcy, continue completing this form.

Part V. Calculation of Deductions From Income

In this part, you will figure out which expenses you can deduct from your current monthly income. After you subtract all allowed expenses, you will be left with your monthly disposable income—the amount you would have left over, in theory, to pay into a Chapter 13 plan for the benefit of your nonpriority, unsecured creditors.

> ### CAUTION
> **National and local expense standards change every few years, or more often.** Many of the IRS expense standards are adjusted every three years. The next adjustment will occur on April 1, 2013. Other standards (such as local standards for housing) change more frequently. Be sure to check the most recent version of Form 22A (some of the expense figures are listed on the form itself) and the expense standards on the U.S. Trustee's website at www.justice.gov/ust (click on "Bankruptcy Reform" and "Means Testing") for the most recent figures.

Subpart A: Deductions under Standards of the Internal Revenue Service (IRS)

If you have to complete this part of the form—that is, if your current monthly income exceeds the state median income—you are not allowed to subtract all of your actual expenses. Instead, you must calculate some of your expenses according to standards set by the IRS. (The IRS uses these standards to decide how much a delinquent taxpayer should have to give the agency each month to repay back taxes on an installment plan.)

If you eventually decide to file under Chapter 13, you will have to use these same expenses to determine the amount of disposable income you must devote to your plan. (See Ch. 5 for more information.)

Line 19A. Enter the total IRS National Standards for Food, Clothing and Other Items for your family size and income level. This is the amount the IRS believes you should get to spend for food, clothing, household supplies, personal care, and miscellaneous other items. You can get these figures from www.justice.gov/ust. Click "Means Testing Information," then scroll down to find the right link. You also can get these figures from your court clerk.

Line 19B. Enter the amount you are allowed to claim for health expenses from the IRS National Standards for Out-of-Pocket Health Care. You can find these figures at www.justice.gov/ust. Click "Bankruptcy Reform," then "Means Testing Information," then scroll down to the appropriate link. As you'll see, you can claim more for household members who are at least 65 years old, which is reflected on the form. You'll also see that the total amount you can claim is quite small; if you spend more than you're allowed to claim here, you can claim it on Line 31.

Line 20A. Enter the amount of the IRS Housing and Utilities Standards, nonmortgage expenses for your county and family size. Get these figures from www. justice.gov/ust. Click "Bankruptcy Reform," then "Means Testing Information," then scroll down to the local Housing and Utilities Expense Standards section and enter your state in the drop-down menu. Find the figures for your county and family size, then enter the figure that appears under the heading "Non-Mortgage."

Line 20B. On Line a, enter the amount of the IRS Housing and Utilities Standards, Mortgage/Rent expenses for your county and family size. These figures appear on the U.S. Trustee's website, on the same chart as nonmortgage expenses; follow the instructions for Line 20A, above.

On Line b, enter the average monthly payment for any debts secured by your home, including a mortgage, home equity loan, taxes, and insurance. The average monthly payment is the total of all amounts contractually due to each secured creditor in the five years after you file for bankruptcy, divided by 60.

On Line c, subtract Line b from Line a. This may turn out to be a negative figure—if so, enter a zero in the right-hand column. Later in the means test, you'll be able to deduct your average monthly mortgage payment. Most courts allow you to take the IRS expense even if your actual expenses are less; for more information on this issue, go to www.legalconsumer. com/bankruptcy/CH13, scroll down to the information for Ch. 4, and look for the appropriate link.

Line 21. If your actual rental or mortgage expense is higher than that allowed by the IRS for shelter, you can claim an adjustment here. For instance, if the IRS mortgage/rental expense for a family of two is $550, you pay an actual rent of $900, and that amount is average for the area in which you live, enter the additional $350 here and explain why you should be able to subtract it (that you couldn't possibly find housing in your area for less, for example).

Line 22A. You are entitled to claim an expense here whether or not you actually have a car. First, indicate the number of cars for which you pay operating expenses or for which somebody else contributes the operating expenses as part of the amount entered on Line 8. If you don't have a car, enter the amount listed under "Public Transportation" from the IRS Local Standards: Transportation. You can find these at www.justice.gov/ust; click "Bankruptcy Reform," then "Means Testing Information," then scroll down to the appropriate link and choose your region. If you indicated that you have one or two cars, enter the amount listed for your region (and sometimes, your city) under "Operating Costs" in the same chart.

Line 22B. If you have a car and also use public transportation, you may claim a public transportation expense here. You can find the correct amount by following the instructions for Line 22A, above.

Line 23. These are your expenses for owning or leasing a car.

On Line 23a, enter the IRS Local Standards: Transportation for ownership of a first car. This amount is actually a national figure; currently, it is $496. To make sure you are using the most up-to-date numbers, check the website of the U.S. Trustee, www.justice.gov/ust. Click "Bankruptcy Reform," then "Means Testing Information," then scroll down to the Local Transportation Expense Standards drop-down menu and choose your region. The ownership figure is near the bottom of the page. If you aren't making loan or lease payments on a car, you can't claim this expense.

On Line 23b, enter your average monthly payment (over the next five years) for all debts secured by your first car. For example, assume you have three years left to pay on the car and the monthly payment is $350. The total amount you will owe in the next five years is $12,600 (36 months times $350). If you spread that amount over the next five years—by dividing the total by 60, the number of months in five years—you'll see that your average monthly payment is $210.

On Line 23c, subtract Line b from Line a and enter the result in the column on the right. Later on, if necessary, you will be able to deduct your car payments to figure out whether you have enough disposable income to fund a Chapter 13 plan.

Line 24. Complete this only if you are making payments on or leasing a second car (and you checked the "2 or more" box in Line 23). Follow the instructions for Line 23 to enter the required figures for your second car.

Line 25. Enter the total average monthly expense that you actually incur for all taxes *other than property or sales taxes*. Examples of taxes that you should enter here are income taxes, self-employment taxes, Social Security taxes, and Medicare taxes. In some cases, these taxes will show up on your wage stub. You'll need to convert the period covered by your wage stub to a monthly figure. Once you have figured out how much you pay each month for each type of tax, add them all together and enter them in the column on the right.

Converting Taxes to a Monthly Figure

If you are paid weekly, biweekly, or twice a month, you will have to convert the tax amounts on your pay stubs to a monthly amount. And, if you pay quarterly taxes (estimated income taxes, for example), you'll need to convert that figure as well. Here's how to do it:

- Weekly taxes: Multiply by 4.3 to get a monthly amount.
- Biweekly taxes: Divide by 2 to get a weekly amount, then multiply by 4.3.
- Bimonthly taxes: Divide by 2.
- Quarterly taxes: Divide by 3.

Line 26. Enter all of your mandatory payroll deductions here, other than those entered in Line 25. Use the conversion rules set out above to arrive at average monthly deductions. Make sure you deduct only mandatory deductions (such as required retirement contributions, union dues, and uniform costs). Contributions to a 401(k) should not be included, for example, because they are voluntary.

Line 27. Enter any monthly payments you make for term life insurance. Do not enter payments for any other type of insurance, such as credit insurance, car insurance, renters' insurance, insurance on the lives of your dependents, or whole life insurance on your own life. (Whole life insurance is the type that allows you to borrow against the policy.)

Line 28. Enter the amount of any payments you make pursuant to a court order. Child support and alimony are the most common examples, but you may also have to pay to satisfy a court money judgment or a criminal fine. Do not include court-ordered payments toward a child support or an alimony arrearage; only the payments you need to make to stay current should be entered here.

Line 29. Enter the total monthly amount that you pay for education required by your employer to keep your job and the total monthly amount you pay for the education of a physically or mentally challenged dependent child for whom no public education providing similar services is available. Included in this amount would be the actual costs of after-school enrichment educational services for a physically or mentally challenged child and the actual educational expenses you are paying in support of an individual educational plan (IEP).

Line 30. Enter the average monthly cost of child care. If your employment (and therefore, your need for child care) is seasonal, add up your child care costs for the year and divide the total by 12. Do not equate education with child care. For instance, child care for a child who is of public education school age should cover only the hours before and after school.

Line 31. Enter the average monthly amount you pay for out-of-pocket health care expenses, but only to the extent it exceeds the amount you were allowed to claim on Line 19B. Do not include health care expenses that are reimbursed by insurance or provided by an HMO or by Medicaid. Also, don't include premiums you pay for health insurance; you claim these on Line 34.

Line 32. Enter the average monthly expenses you pay for any communication devices that are necessary for the health and welfare of you or your dependents. Examples provided by the form are cell phones, pagers, call waiting, caller identification, and special long distance or Internet services. Virtually all of these devices arguably are necessary for the health and welfare of your family. However, some expenses might not be allowed (for example, a smartphone, cell phone you use for your business, or broadband Internet service). When in doubt, list the expense.

Line 33. Add the expenses you entered in Lines 19 through 32 and put the total in the column at the right.

Note: If your average monthly income, as calculated on Line 18, less the expenses totaled on Line 33, is less than $110, you can file for Chapter 7 if you desire. Remember, however, that you can still be forced out of Chapter 7 if the U.S. Trustee successfully argues that your actual income, less your actual expenses, would produce enough disposable income to pay off a significant portion of your unsecured debts over a five-year period. Just what percentage of your unsecured debts would have to be paid off to warrant pushing you into Chapter 13 varies from court to court, but 20% is a pretty good working minimum.

Subpart B: Additional Living Expense Deductions

The expenses in this subpart are allowed by the Bankruptcy Code, in addition to the IRS expenses. However, you can't list an expense twice; if you already claimed it in Subpart A or on Lines 4 or 5 in Section II (business expenses), don't list it again here.

Line 34. Here, list your reasonably necessary monthly expenses for health insurance, disability insurance, and health savings accounts (HSAs) on the lines provided. The form was revised in 2008 to clarify that you can list a "reasonable" expense here whether you actually pay that amount each month or not. If, however, you pay less than the reasonable amount you list, you must indicate how much you actually spend each month on the additional line provided. If the U.S. Trustee or one of your creditors later wants to challenge your expense claims—for example, to argue that you really have more disposable income than the form indicates—they can use this information.

Line 35. Anything you spend to care for a member of your household or immediate family because of his or her age, illness, or disability can be deducted here. If your contributions are episodic—a wheelchair here, a vacation with a companion there—estimate your average monthly expense and enter it here.

> **CAUTION**
>
> **Your response here could affect eligibility for government benefits.** Expenses you list here could render the person you are assisting ineligible for Social Security or other government benefits. For example, if you state that you are spending $500 a month for the care of a relative, and that relative is receiving SSI, your relative might receive a lower benefit amount each month, to reflect your contribution. On the other hand, if you are making such expenditures, you are required to disclose them here. If you find yourself in this predicament, talk to a lawyer.

Line 36. The average monthly expense of security systems and any other method of protecting your family should be entered here.

Line 37. If your actual home energy costs exceed the figure you entered on Line 20A, enter the extra money you spend here. As the form indicates, you may need to prove this extra expense to the trustee. Whether you need to prove this extra expense will depend on the results of the means test. If the amount you enter here is the deciding factor in determining that you don't have enough disposable income to fund a Chapter 13 plan, proof will definitely be required.

Line 38. This item is for money you spend on your children's education. If your average monthly expense is $147.92 or more, put $147.92 in this blank; that's the maximum you can deduct. Remember not to list an amount twice; if you already listed an expense on Line 29 or 30, for example, don't repeat it here. Education expenses for children with special needs may be deductible later as a "special circumstance," as (perhaps) can expenses required by individual education plans (IEPs). (Special circumstance claims are explained in Ch. 5.)

Line 39. Here, you can list the amount by which your actual expenses for food and clothing exceed the IRS allowance for these items as entered in Line 19. However, you cannot list more than 5% over the IRS allowance.

Line 40. If you have been making charitable contributions to an organization before your bankruptcy filing date, you can enter them here as long as the group is organized and operated exclusively for religious, charitable, scientific, literary, or educational purposes; to foster national or international amateur sports competition (but only if no part of its activities involve the provision of athletic facilities or equipment); or for the prevention of cruelty to children or animals. You can't take this deduction if the organization has been disqualified from tax exemption status because of its political activities.

Line 41. Enter the total of Lines 34 through 40 in the column on the right.

Note: If you subtract the amounts on Line 41 and 33 from the amount on Line 18 and the total is less than $110, you won't be prohibited from using Chapter 7 on the basis of the means test. Remember, however, that the U.S. Trustee can still challenge your Chapter 7 filing if your actual income less your actual expenses would give you enough disposable income to fund a Chapter 13 plan.

Subpart C: Deductions for Debt Payment

Here, you deduct average monthly payments you will have to make over the next five years. Once you've completed this section, you can put all the numbers together to figure out whether you pass the means test.

Line 42. List the average monthly payment you will have to make over the next five years to creditors that hold a secured interest in your property (for example, the mortgage holder on your house or the creditor that holds your car note). As explained in the instructions for Line 23, you can calculate this amount by figuring out the total amount you will owe over the next five years, then dividing that total by 60. Courts are divided as to whether you can include this deduction if you aren't making the payments and plan to surrender the property to the creditor. Some courts have found that allowing debtors to deduct payments they aren't making is contrary to the purpose of the means test; other courts have ruled that these "phantom" payments should be deducted because the purpose of the means test is to provide a snapshot of your financial situation. For a listing of the cases that have ruled on this issue, go to www.legalconsumer.com/bankruptcy/CH13, scroll down to the information for Ch. 4, and look for the appropriate link.

Line 43. Here, list the average monthly payment you would have to make to pay off any past amounts due to creditors on property that you must keep for your support or support of your dependents. That would typically include a car, your home, and any property you need for your employment. (Come up with the monthly figure by dividing the total amount you would have to pay by 60.)

Line 44. List the average monthly amount you will have to pay for priority claims over the next five years. (See "Classifying Your Debts," below, for a list of priority claims.) Typical priority claims include back taxes and back child and spousal support. Divide the total of all priority claims by 60 to arrive at the monthly average. Don't include payments you've already listed on the form, such as current child support obligations. This line is only for debts you owe at the time of filing.

Line 45. Here, you must calculate the fee that the trustee would charge if you ended up in Chapter 13 bankruptcy. The fee depends on how much you would be paying, through the trustee, to your secured and unsecured creditors. It's impossible to come up with a figure at this point in the form, so leave it blank for now. If you don't pass the means test with this line left blank, come back here when you've completed Part VI and follow these instructions to come up with a figure:

- Add Lines 42, 43, and 44.
- Divide the total on Line 54 by 60 (to calculate the average monthly payment you would have to make to pay down 25% of your unsecured debt over five years).

- Add this number to the total of Lines 42, 43, and 44, and put the result on Line 45a. This is the average amount you would have to pay into a Chapter 13 plan to cover your secured debts, arrearages on those debts, priority debts, and 25% of your unsecured debts.
- On Line 45b, enter the multiplier percentage from the U.S. Trustee's website for your state and district. Go to www.justice.gov/ust, click "Bankruptcy Reform" and then "Means Testing Information," scroll down to the section called "Administrative Expenses Multipliers" and click "Schedules," then select your state and district to get the percentage.
- Multiply Line 45a by Line 45b and enter the result in the column on the right.

Line 46. Add Lines 42 through 45, and enter the total in the column on the right.

Subpart D: Total Deductions from Income

Line 47. Enter the total of Lines 33, 41, and 46 in the column at the right. This is the total amount you can subtract from your current monthly expenses to arrive at your disposable income.

Part VI. Determination of § 707(b)(2) Presumption

This is where you find out whether you received a passing grade on the means test.

Line 48. Enter the amount from Line 18 in the column on the right.

Line 49. Enter the amount from Line 47 in the column on the right.

Line 50. Subtract Line 49 from Line 48 and enter the result in the column on the right.

Line 51. Multiply the total from Line 50 by 60 (to find out how much disposable income you will have over the next five years, according to these figures). Enter the result in the column at the right.

Line 52. Here you must check one of three boxes. If the amount on Line 51 is less than $7,025, check the top box. This means that you don't have enough money left over to make a Chapter 13 plan feasible, so you have the choice of filing for Chapter 7. If the total on Line 51 is more than $11,725, you have enough income to make a Chapter 13 plan feasible, and you probably won't be allowed to use Chapter 7. If your total is at least $7,025 but no more than $11,725, you will have to do a few more calculations to figure out where you fall. Proceed to Line 53.

Line 53. Enter the total of your nonpriority, unsecured debts. See "Classifying Your Debts," below, for help figuring out which of your debts qualify.

Line 54. Multiply the amount on Line 53 by 0.25 and enter the result in the box on the right. This amount represents 25% of your total nonpriority, unsecured debt.

Line 55. Here, you determine whether the income you have left over (listed on Line 51) is sufficient to pay 25% of your unsecured, nonpriority debt (listed on Line 54). If Line 51 is less than Line 54, you have passed the means test and may choose to file for Chapter 7 bankruptcy. (Remember, however, that you might still face a challenge if your actual income less your actual expenses would leave you with enough money to fund a Chapter 13 repayment plan.)

If Line 51 is greater than Line 54, you have failed the means test. If you fail the means test, you can complete Part VII, in which you list additional expenses that were somehow not included in the earlier parts of the form. Those expenses would be taken into account by the U.S. Trustee if you file a Chapter 7 case, as long as they don't duplicate expenses you already listed and are reasonably necessary for the support of you and your family.

 TIP

Make sure not to understate your expenses. If you want to use Chapter 7 but have failed the means test, go back over the form and carefully examine the expenses you listed for categories that aren't mandated by the IRS. People often underestimate their actual expenses. If you underestimated one or more expenses or left an expense out that is provided for in the form, make the adjustments and see whether you can get a passing grade. Because this form is so complex, we recommend that you go through it at least twice before arriving at your final figures.

Classifying Your Debts

To complete the means test, you need to know how to categorize each of your debts. As explained above, you have to calculate what you owe on your priority debts and your secured debts for the next five years, and you have to add up all of your nonpriority, unsecured debts to figure out what portion of them you could repay in a Chapter 13 plan. This section will help you determine which debts are which. The classifications you make here will also help you draft your repayment plan and complete your bankruptcy forms.

Secured Debts

A debt is "secured" if you stand to lose a particular piece of property when you don't make your payments to the creditor. Most secured debts are created when you sign loan papers giving a creditor a security interest in your property—such as a home loan or car loan. But a debt might also be secured if a creditor has filed a lien (a legal claim against your property that must be paid before the property can be sold). Here is a list of common secured debts and liens:

- **Mortgages.** Called deeds of trust in some states, these are loans to buy or refinance houses or other real estate. If you fail to pay, the lender can foreclose on your house.
- **Home equity loans (second mortgages).** If you fail to pay, the lender (typically a bank or finance company) can foreclose on your house.
- **Loans for cars, boats, tractors, motorcycles, or RVs.** If you fail to pay, the lender can repossess the vehicle.
- **Store charges with a security agreement.** Almost all store purchases on credit cards are unsecured. Some stores, notably Sears and J.C. Penney, however, claim to retain a security interest in all hard goods (durable goods) purchased, or they make customers sign security agreements when they use their store charge card.
- **Personal loans from banks, credit unions, or finance companies.** Often, you must pledge valuable personal property, such as a paid-off motor vehicle, as collateral for these loans. The property can be repossessed if you don't make the payments.
- **Judicial liens.** A judicial lien can be imposed on your property only after somebody sues you and wins a money judgment against you. In most states, the judgment creditor then must record (file) the judgment with the county or state. The recorded judgment creates a lien on your

real estate and, in some states, on some of your personal property as well.
- **Statutory liens.** Some liens are automatic, by law. For example, in most states, when you hire someone to work on your house, the worker and the supplier of materials automatically gets a mechanics' lien (sometimes called a materialmen's or contractor's lien) on the house if you don't pay.
- **Tax liens.** If you owe money to the IRS or another taxing authority, the debt is secured if the agency has recorded a lien against your property. (See "Tax Debts," below, for more information.)

Priority Debts

Priority debts are unsecured debts that are considered sufficiently important to jump to the head of the bankruptcy repayment line. Priority debts that may come up in consumer bankruptcies include:

- wages, salaries, and commissions owed by an employer
- contributions to employee benefit plans
- money owed to certain farmers and fishermen
- up to $2,600 in deposits made for the purchase, lease, or rental of property or services for personal, family, or household use that were not delivered or provided
- alimony, maintenance, or support
- claim for death or personal injury the debtor caused while intoxicated
- nondischargeable taxes (see "Tax Debts," below), and
- customs, duties, and penalties you owe to the federal, state, or local government.

Nonpriority, Unsecured Debts

Not surprisingly, nonpriority, unsecured debts are all debts that are neither secured nor priority. Debts in this category include:

- credit and charge card purchases and cash advances
- department store credit card purchases, unless the store retains a security interest in the items you buy or requires you to sign a security agreement
- gasoline company credit card purchases
- back rent
- medical bills

- certain tax debts (see "Tax Debts," below)
- student loans
- utility bills
- loans from friends or relatives, unless you signed a promissory note secured by some property you own
- money judgments for breach of contract or negligence
- health club dues
- lawyers' bills (unless there's a lien on your property to secure payment)

- church or synagogue dues, and
- union dues.

Tax Debts

A tax debt can be secured, priority, or unsecured. If a taxing agency has placed a lien on your property, the debt is secured. If the tax debt is not dischargeable in bankruptcy, the debt is priority. And if the tax debt can be discharged, it is unsecured. The chart below will help you figure out what category particular tax debts fall into.

Classifying Your Tax Debt	
If ...	**Your tax debt is ...**
All of the following are true: • The taxes first became due at least three years before you file for bankruptcy (taxes first become due for a particular year on April 15 of the following year, or on October 15 of the following year if you request an extension). • You timely filed your tax return at least two years prior to your bankruptcy filing date (tax returns filed after the due date and returns filed by the IRS for you do not qualify as filed returns). • The IRS has not assessed the taxes due within 240 days prior to your bankruptcy date. • The IRS is not arguing that you willfully intended to avoid paying the tax.	**dischargeable,** meaning you can completely eliminate your income tax debt, and the interest and penalties associated with it
The IRS has recorded a Notice of Federal Tax Lien.	**secured,** meaning you may be able to discharge your personal liability in bankruptcy, but the lien remains. If you don't pay off the entire debt during your case, the IRS can seize property you owned before filing to cover the rest. Practically speaking, the IRS looks to collect from real estate and retirement plans.
Your tax debt is not dischargeable or secured.	**priority,** which means that it must be paid in full in your Chapter 13 plan
Both of the following are true: • Your tax debt is not dischargeable or secured. • The IRS has recorded a Notice of Federal Tax Lien, but your property won't cover what you owe the IRS.	**undersecured** (if you have no seizable assets) or partially undersecured (if you have some). The undersecured portion is dischargeable if the first three conditions listed above for dischargeable taxes are met.

Forced Conversion to Chapter 13

If you already filed for Chapter 7 and flunked the means test, the U.S. Trustee, the trustee, or a creditor will have filed a motion under 11 U.S.C. § 707(b)(2) to have the court declare your filing "abusive." If the court agrees, it will give you the choice of having your case dismissed or converted to Chapter 13. If you consent to the conversion, the court will order it.

To remain in Chapter 13, you will have to file a confirmable plan within 15 days of the conversion, start making payments on the plan within 15 days after that, and otherwise comply with the eligibility requirements unique to Chapter 13 (see Ch. 3 for more on these requirements).

> **CAUTION**
>
> **You may not be eligible for either type of bankruptcy.** It's entirely possible to be kicked out of Chapter 7 because your income is too high, then be unable to come up with a Chapter 13 repayment plan that's acceptable to the judge. In other words, there may be no bankruptcy remedy for you. For instance, you may get tossed out of Chapter 7 because your current monthly income was too high when you filed. If, however, you don't have a steady income by the time you convert to Chapter 13, your plan won't be confirmed. If you find yourself in this situation, talk to a lawyer right away.

Can You Propose a Plan the Judge Will Approve?

Before you are allowed to proceed with your Chapter 13 bankruptcy, the judge must approve your repayment plan. As explained briefly in Ch. 3, your plan will be approved only if it shows that you will have enough steady income to:

- pay certain types of debts in full over the life of your plan, and
- pay your nonpriority, unsecured creditors at least what they would have received if you had filed under Chapter 7.

The plan must also show that all of your "projected disposable income" (as defined by the bankruptcy laws) will go toward paying your remaining debts for the duration of your plan.

How long your plan must last and how much money you must devote to it depends on whether your current monthly income, which you calculated in Ch. 4, is more or less than your state's median income. If your current monthly income is less than the median income for your state, you can propose a three-year plan, and you may use your actual expenses to calculate your disposable income.

If your current monthly income is more than the median income for your state, your plan must last five years, and you must use expense amounts set by the IRS (which might differ from your actual expenses) to calculate your disposable income. In essence, this means that you will probably have to devote more money to your plan for a longer period of time.

RELATED TOPIC

If you haven't calculated your current monthly income, go back to Ch. 4. Ch. 4 explains how to come up with this figure and compare it to your state's median. You'll need to know your current monthly income—and whether it is more or less than your state's median—to figure out whether you can come up with a confirmable repayment plan.

This chapter will give you a fairly accurate idea as to whether you can propose a repayment plan that meets the legal requirements. If you decide to go ahead with a Chapter 13 bankruptcy, your attorney (or your attorney's software) will do the fine-tuning to come up with your repayment plan.

SEE AN EXPERT

Talk to a lawyer if you can't make the numbers work. This chapter will help you determine whether you can come up with a plan the judge will approve if you decide to file for Chapter 13. If the numbers don't work out, you may want to talk to a lawyer before you give up. An attorney may be able to provide a different slant on the numbers you provide in the form and the choices you make when completing this chapter.

Repayment Plan Calculations: An Overview

Upon first glance, this chapter might look intimidating. It asks you to fill in a long form and requires you to come up with numerous income and expense figures. Our advice: Don't sweat the details yet. The purpose of the chapter is to get a rough idea as to whether you have enough income, given your expenses and debts, to propose a plan that will work within the law. The forms are pretty self-explanatory (and we provide instructions). You'll eventually need to provide your attorney with this information, so it doesn't hurt to run through them. If you don't have an exact figure for something, enter your best estimate.

Below, we've provided an overview of how these calculations work—so you can see the forest through the trees as you go through these forms. Or, you can use the overview below to rough out some numbers before you visit an attorney, and skip the details altogether.

Start with your current monthly income as you computed it in Ch. 4.

Subtract living expenses. This is where your income as it compares to your state median income comes into play. If your income is below the state median income (as determined in Ch. 4), you get to subtract your *actual* living expenses (as long as they are reasonable). If your income is above the state median income, you must use set dollar amounts dictated by national and local IRS standards. You are allowed to include certain additional living expenses that are not covered by the IRS expense standards.

Subtract installment payments on secured debts. These are your monthly payments on debts secured by property you plan to keep, like your mortgage or car note. If you have 60 or more monthly payments left, list the monthly payment. If you have less than 60 monthly payments left, divide the amount still owed by 60 and list that amount.

Subtract priority debts. Your priority debts (listed in Ch. 3) must be paid off in full through your plan. Total up the remaining balance on all priority debts and divide by the length of your plan (36 months if your income is less than the state median, 60 months if your income is more than the state median).

Subtract secured debt arrearages. Your plan must propose to pay 100% of arrearages on secured debts if you want to keep the property. For example, you must pay off mortgage arrears through the plan. Total up your arrearages and divide by 60 to get the monthly deduction.

Subtract debts secured by liens. You have to pay off some liens by the end of the plan. To learn which ones, see Step 6 below. Total up these liens and divide by the length of your plan.

Subtract payments to unsecured creditors. You must pay your unsecured, nonpriority creditors at least what they would have received had you filed for Chapter 7 bankruptcy. To get a rough estimate of what this figure will be, start with the value of your nonexempt property, subtract the trustee's commission and costs of sale, and divide the total by your plan length.

Subtract the trustee's commission. You must pay the trustee a percentage of your plan payment, usually 10%. To get a rough estimate, subtract all of the above items in this list from your monthly income and multiply this number by 0.1 (10%).

TOTAL. The resulting number is a rough estimate of what your monthly plan payment will be if you file for Chapter 13 bankruptcy. If you get zero or a negative number, you may not be able to fund a plan.

If Your Current Monthly Income Is Less Than Your State's Median Income

If your current monthly income is less than your state's median income, you can propose a plan that lasts for three years or less. However, the court can authorize a plan lasting up to five years, if necessary. Because certain debts must be paid off in full in a Chapter 13 plan, debtors often need a longer plan period so they can afford the monthly payments. For example, if you

owe a $20,000 arrearage on your mortgage, a three-year plan would require monthly payments of at least $555. If you stretched out those payments over five years, you would owe only $333 each month.

 SKIP AHEAD

This section is only for those whose current monthly income is less than their state's median income. If your income—as calculated in Ch. 4—is equal to or more than the state median, skip ahead to "If Your Current Monthly Income Is More Than Your State's Median Income," below.

Step 1: Calculate Your Base Income

Your base income is the amount you will use to determine whether you have sufficient income to fund a Chapter 13 plan. Your base income is simply your current monthly income (your average gross income over the six-month period before you filed for bankruptcy, as calculated in Ch. 4) less any child support payments, foster care payments, or disability payments you receive for a dependent child, as long as those amounts are necessary for the child's care.

Current Monthly Income (from Ch. 4): _____

Child Support, Foster Care, or
   Disability Payments: − _____

Base Income: = _____

If Your Actual Income Is Different From Your "Current Monthly Income": *Hamilton v. Lanning*

The income figure you use in this section, although labeled "current monthly income," actually describes your average monthly income over the last six months. (The same is true if you calculate your income under the next section, "If Your Current Monthly Income Is More Than Your State's Median Income.") And yet, bankruptcy law says you must put all of your "projected disposable income" towards your repayment plan (unless you plan to pay your unsecured creditors 100%). So what happens if your "currently monthly income" doesn't match your actual or projected income? For example, what if you recently lost your job or your hours were greatly reduced? Or what if you received a one-time bonus or payout in the previous six months that you won't receive again (which would inflate your "current monthly income")?

Until recently, courts have been divided in how they treat debtors whose "current monthly income" does not reflect what their actual income is at the time of the bankruptcy filing or what their income will be during the repayment period.

Some courts followed the "mechanical approach," and required a debtor to use the income figure from Forms 22A or 22C, even if it didn't match the debtor's true income. This meant that some debtors whose income had decreased in recent months were unable to fund a Chapter 13 plan—the plan payment as calculated by the formula was more than they could afford given their current income. Other courts followed the "forward-looking approach." These courts took into consideration a debtor's actual or future income when calculating disposable income.

In 2010, the U.S. Supreme Court ruled on this issue in *Hamilton v. Lanning* (130 S.Ct. 2464 (2010)) and endorsed the "forward-looking approach." It held that when calculating a debtor's projected disposable income, the court may account for changes in the debtor's income or expenses that are "known or virtually certain at the time of [plan] confirmation."

If your income has changed substantially from your "current monthly income" calculation, the court can consider this in approving your plan payments. If you anticipate an income change, you'll have to convince the court that the change is "virtually certain." What constitutes "virtually certain" is likely to be the source of further litigation in the bankruptcy courts.

The Court in *Hamilton* also noted that changes in projected expenses may be considered by the court in approving plan payments. This too, is likely to foster further litigation.

Is Social Security Income Included as "Disposable Income"?

Although Social Security income is not included when calculating current monthly income on Form 22C, some trustees believe that the decision in *Lanning v. Hamilton* (which allows courts to consider a debtor's actual income, rather than the debtor's income on Form 22C, when figuring out how much income is available for plan payments) means that Social Security

income should be factored into plan payments. Some courts agree and consider Social Security income when determining plan payments, other courts have ruled that Social Security income should not be factored into plan payments.

Step 2: Subtract Your Expenses

When determining your disposable income, you can subtract only those expenses that are reasonably necessary for you and your dependents and any child support or alimony obligation that first arose after you filed your bankruptcy petition.

The best way to calculate these expenses is to use one of the official bankruptcy forms—Schedule J: *Current Expenditures of Individual Debtor(s)*—as a starting point, then add certain other expenses allowed by the bankruptcy code.

Use Schedule J to Determine Reasonably Necessary Expenses

Tear out the blank version of Schedule J from Appendix B. If you and your spouse have separated but are filing jointly, you can each complete a separate Schedule J and combine your expenses at the end of this procedure.

For each listed item, fill in your monthly expenses for you and any dependents. Remember to include payments you make for your dependents' expenses in your figures only if those expenses are reasonable and necessary for the dependents' support.

If you make some payments biweekly, quarterly, semiannually, or annually, prorate them to show your monthly payment.

1. Rent or home mortgage payment. If your rent or mortgage payment is unusually high for your area, the court might suggest that you move in order to bring this expense down, if alternate housing is easily available. If you are facing foreclosure and will be surrendering your home in your Chapter 13 bankruptcy, what amount should you list for your rent or home mortgage payment? You can either hunt around the neighborhood where you plan to live and use an average rental amount or you can use the IRS figure for average rentals in your area. (You can find them at www.justice.gov/ust; click "Bankruptcy Reform," and

"Means Testing Information," then scroll down to "Local Housing and Utilities Expense Standards" and choose your state.)

2. Utilities. List your monthly utility expenses. Be sure to take a monthly average of gas, heating fuel, and electricity if your bills vary month to month. Also under the utility category, put expenses for satellite TV, cellular telephone, pager, caller identification, and special long distance and Internet subscriptions necessary for the welfare of you or your dependents. Some courts might refuse high phone bills (for example, if you call a parent or child in a distant city every day). A court might also question the expense of full-service cable or satellite TV, so you may have to adjust your plan to keep the basic service but drop the premium channels.

3. Home maintenance. If your estimates of maintenance and upkeep are high, you may have to provide the court with documentation for past years' expenses. Obviously, the court will want you to maintain your home's condition, but in a reasonably inexpensive manner.

4. Food. To determine whether or not your figure is reasonable, the court will most likely compare it to the federal cost of living figure for your area. (See "What's a Reasonable Expense?" below.) If your expenses are higher than average, be ready to explain them—for example, because a family member needs a special diet. If the expenses are high because you eat out a lot, be prepared to explain why.

5. Clothing. You are not expected to wear only second-hand clothing, especially if your employment requires a high-end dress standard. But extravagant or frequent purchases may not be allowed. A court might also suggest that you buy used clothing for your still-growing children. To get an idea of how much you spend now, total up the clothing purchases for which you have receipts, credit card statements, or an entry in your checkbook, and arrive at a monthly average.

6. Laundry and dry cleaning. Enter your expenses here. Especially if you have to dress up for work, the court will allow you to spend some money on dry cleaning every month.

7. Medical and dental expenses. The court will want you to maintain your medical insurance coverage, so it will allow medical insurance for you and your dependents as an expense. Don't list payments you're making on bills from medical providers and hospitals for services that you've already received. The court will probably want you to pay those through your Chapter 13 plan. The court might let you include 100% of the bill as part of your monthly expenses if you need ongoing medical care and the provider won't continue to provide it unless you pay your bill in full. If you are in this situation, include the expense on this worksheet. The court may also reject expenses for mental health therapy and instead suggest that you visit a free or low-cost county mental health facility, if you qualify.

What's a Reasonable Expense?

When it comes to expenses, what is considered reasonable varies from debtor to debtor, court to court, and even region to region. In general, expenses for luxury items or services (such as a gardener) will not be allowed. If an expense seems particularly high, the court will look to see whether you can achieve the same goal by spending less; the court will let you live adequately, but not high on the hog. For example, if you are making payments of $550 per month on a Cadillac, the court may allow only $300 per month toward a less expensive car, freeing up another $250 per month of disposable income. Courts also tend not to allow any voluntary payments to retirement plans, unless the debtor is approaching retirement age or is financially challenged. (See *In re Behlke*, 358 F.3d 429 (6th Cir. Ohio 2004).)

Your best approach when completing Schedule J is to enter your actual expenses. If you want to know whether your expenses will later be considered reasonable, compare them with the cost of living schedules published by the federal government and collected for your convenience by the U.S. Trustee's Office at www.justice.gov/ust. These are the same expenses you used in Ch. 4 if you completed the means test there. If you didn't, click "Bankruptcy Reform," and "Means Testing" on the U.S. Trustee's website and check out the following categories:

- National Standards: Food, Clothing & Other Items
- Local Housing and Utilities Expense Standards, and
- Local Transportation Expense Standards.

You can also find out the applicable IRS standards for your area by taking the free, online means test at www.legalconsumer.com.

8. Transportation. The court will let you pay a reasonable amount to get to and from work and provide necessary transportation for your children. The court will allow expenses for vehicle insurance, maintenance, and registration. The IRS figures for a reasonable operating and public transportation expense vary from $200 to $400, depending on where you live and whether you have one or two cars. As mentioned on the form, you shouldn't put your car payments on this line: They come later.

9. Recreation, clubs and entertainment, newspapers, magazines, etc. Many debtors are tempted to leave this line blank because they think it will look bad for them to incur expenses for recreation. For now, don't worry what it will look like. Just list your actual expenses. Later on, if you lack adequate disposable income, you might need to tighten your belt, and recreation may be one category where you can cut back.

10. Charitable contributions. You can include donations to charity, in an amount up to 15% of your income for the year in which you make them. You can subtract charitable contributions even if you are paying your nonpriority, unsecured creditors only 1% of what you owe them. (*In re Tony and Martha Petty*, Case No. 4:05-BK-26362 (E.D. Ark. 2006).)

11. Insurance. The court generally will let you maintain your disability or life insurance, especially if your health is compromised and you may need to use the disability insurance, or if you have young children or other dependents who would need the life insurance money if you died. If you have a whole life insurance policy, you may be told to convert it to a term policy, which has much lower premiums.

12. Taxes. List the monthly average of all taxes that are deducted from your wages or that you pay as a self-employed person or an independent contractor.

13. Installment payments. Don't list your installment payments here—you will include them elsewhere in your repayment plan.

14. Alimony, maintenance, and support paid to others. List your current support obligations only. Don't list any back support you owe.

15. Payments for support of additional dependents not living at your home. Your expenses listed so far have included expenses for your dependents living at home. You also are permitted to claim expenses for the support of other dependents not living at home,

including your children. These expenses include child care, clothes, books, an occasional movie, and the like.

16. Regular expenses from operation of business, profession, or farm. If you run a business, enter all ordinary and necessary expenses paid for the continuation, preservation, and operation of the business. This would include monthly payments on business assets as well as any expenses you would include on your IRS Schedule C. You can include expenses only if you own the business as a sole proprietor or as a partner with your spouse.

17. Other. List any additional expenses here, except payments you are making on back income taxes and on unsecured installment debts, such as student loans, credit card accounts, and personal loans: These debts must be paid out of your disposable income through your Chapter 13 plan. Be ready to explain why the expenses you list here are reasonable. Other expenses not already listed might include:

- **Educational expenses for your children.** Courts are reluctant to let you send your children to private school if it means your creditors won't be paid. You may be able to convince the court of the need for private school, however, if the public schools in your area are quite bad or dangerous, you want your children to receive religious education, or your child has special educational needs. If your child is in college, a court may not let you deduct tuition at an expensive private university, but may let you count the payments for a state college.

- **Your or your spouse's educational expenses.** If either you or your spouse is currently in school, list your expenses here. The court may reject a portion of these expenses if you or your spouse could be working and increasing the family's income.

- **Miscellaneous personal expenses.** Often, these are the expenses that your creditors, the trustee, and the court scrutinize the most. Some courts do not think you should be allowed to spend anything for entertainment, to participate in any hobbies that cost money, or to buy gifts for friends or relatives. As with all expenses, the key to getting these expenses approved is their reasonableness. You can't include in your budget money to see Broadway shows, go sailing once a week, keep a subscription to an expensive journal, or renew your country club membership. You can probably budget to rent movies, go bowling, get a daily newspaper, keep your membership at the local Y, and take care of your pet.

Once you have completed the form, add up all of the expenses you have listed. Subtract these expenses from your base income, as calculated above.

Base Income (from Step 1): _____

Schedule J Expenses: – _____

Total: = _____

If you still have a positive number—that is, if it looks like you will have some money left over after paying the expenses listed on Schedule J—you may be able to propose a confirmable Chapter 13 plan. If the number is negative, you won't have anything left to put toward a repayment plan. If you find yourself in this situation, revisit your expenses. Some of them may not be reasonable.

Step 3: Subtract Your Installment Payments

Here is where you figure out the monthly average of any installment payments you are making on property that is collateral for a secured debt. These are typically mortgage, car, and home furniture payments, but you may also be making payments on other valuable items, such as jewelry and electronic equipment.

Add up all of the installment payments you are contractually obligated to make each month, then subtract that amount from what you had left at the end of Step 2.

Base Income Less Expenses
(from Step 2):   _____

Installment Payments: – _____

Total: = _____

If you still have money left over after subtracting your expenses and your installment payments from your base income, you may be able to propose a confirmable Chapter 13 plan. If your total is zero (or less), revisit your installment payments. If you are paying $600 a month for a Corvette and you could get by with a more economical car or with no car at all, make the adjustment here so that you will have some

income left over. (Incidentally, the IRS national standard for a reasonable monthly car payment is $496.)

 TIP

Reduce installment payments with cramdowns. You might be able to reduce the amount of a secured loan to the replacement value of the property. (See "Special Chapter 13 Features: Cramdowns and Lien Stripping" in Ch.1 for details.) Doing so could significantly reduce the amount of your installment payments on that loan.

Step 4: Subtract Your Priority Debts

As mentioned in Ch. 3, you must pay certain debts in full over the life of your plan—three years, unless the court authorizes a longer time. Among the debts that have to be paid in full are priority debts. (You can find a list of priority debts in Ch. 4, "Classifying Your Debts.")

If you owe any priority debts, divide the total amount you owe by 36 to determine how much you would have to pay each month in order to pay off these debts in three years. Subtract this amount from what's left of your base income after subtracting expenses and installment payments, in Step 3, above.

Remaining Income
(from Step 3, above):   _____

Monthly Priority Debt
Payments: – _____

Total: = _____

If you have a positive number, move on to the next section. If the number is negative, you still might propose a confirmable plan under the following conditions:

- If one of the priority debts was child support or alimony that was assigned to a government agency (rather than money you owe directly to your child or ex-spouse), you don't have to pay the full amount in your plan. However, you do have to include the debt in your plan and commit all of your disposable income to a plan for five years rather than three years, unless it won't take you that long to pay the child support debt in full. If some of the debt still remains when your repayment period is over, it won't be discharged. You'll still have to pay the remainder.

- As mentioned, if you could pay off all of your priority debts over a five-year period rather than a three-year period, you can ask the court to allow a five-year plan as part of your confirmation hearing.

Step 5: Subtract Secured Debt Arrearages

One of the main reasons people file Chapter 13 is to deal with arrearages—amounts past due—on their home or car note, to prevent a foreclosure or repossession. Chapter 13 allows you to keep your home or car while paying off the arrearages under your plan. If you owe an arrearage and your plan shows that you are keeping the collateral (your home, car, or the like), you'll have to pay 100% of the arrearage and stay current on the main debt.

Add up all arrearages on debts securing collateral you want to keep. Divide the total by 60 to arrive at a monthly amount. Subtract this total monthly payment from your remaining income, from Step 4, above.

Remaining Income (from Step 4, above):	_____
Monthly Secured Debt Arrearage Payments:	− _____
Total:	= _____

If the number is positive, proceed to Step 5 below. If the number is negative, even over a five-year repayment period, you won't be able to present a confirmable plan.

> **TIP**
> **Giving up the property might help.** If you surrender the collateral to the lender (and therefore, don't have to pay the full past due amount), you might have some income left over. This means you may be able to come up with a confirmable plan.

Step 6: Subtract Debts Secured by Liens

In most cases, if you have a lien on your property other than a purchase money lien, you'll have to pay the lien off in full in your plan. For example, if the IRS has recorded a lien against your property for back taxes, or a contractor has placed a mechanics' lien on your property for work that you didn't pay for, your plan will not be confirmed unless it provides for payment of these liens in full.

> **TIP**
> **What is a purchase money lien?** Your property is encumbered by a purchase money lien if you took out the loan to buy the property that secures the loan. Typical examples include a car loan or a mortgage.

> **TIP**
> **Different rules apply to judgment liens.** If there is a lien on your property because you lost a lawsuit and owe someone money as a result, you might be able to remove the lien in a separate proceeding called "lien avoidance." If you use lien avoidance to remove a lien, you won't have to pay it under your plan. See Ch. 11 for information on lien avoidance.

Add up all liens on your property (other than judgment liens and liens created when you obtained loans to purchase the property). Divide the total by 36 for a three-year plan (or by 60 if you are proposing a five-year plan) to obtain the monthly amount you will have to pay. Then, subtract this total from your remaining income from Step 5, above.

Remaining Income (from Step 5):	_____
Monthly Lien Payment:	− _____
Total Disposable Income:	= _____

If you still have money left over, you can move on to Step 7. If your total disposable income is zero or less, your plan won't be confirmed.

Step 7: Compare Your Disposable Income to What Your Creditors Would Get If You Used Chapter 7

As explained briefly in Ch. 3, if you own nonexempt property, you will have to pay your nonpriority, unsecured creditors at least what they would have received if you had filed for Chapter 7: the value of your nonexempt property, less what it would cost for the trustee to take and sell that property, less the trustee's commission. To find out whether you have nonexempt property, skip to "Understanding Property Exemptions," below, for information on which exemptions you can use and how to apply them to your possessions.

If you find that all of your property is exempt, you don't have to worry about this step. As long as you came up with a positive number in Step 6, you should be able to propose a confirmable plan. If you do have nonexempt property, however, you will have to perform what's called a "liquidation analysis" to determine how much your unsecured creditors would actually receive if you used Chapter 7 (and therefore, how much they are entitled to receive under your Chapter 13 plan).

Start with the value of your equity in the property (see "Value Your Property," below, for tips on coming up with an estimated value). If a portion of the property is exempt, subtract the exempt amount. For example, many states exempt up to a certain amount of equity in a car. If you own a car outright that's worth $10,000, and the exemptions you are using allow you to exempt $4,000 of equity in a car, your total nonexempt amount is $6,000.

Next, subtract the trustee's commission. This amount represents what the trustee would get to keep if your property were taken and sold in a Chapter 7 case. Because this amount would not be distributed to your creditors, you can subtract it from the amount you have to pay them in a Chapter 13 case.

For each item of property sold, the trustee gets 25% of the first $5,000, 10% of the next $50,000, and 5% of the rest up to one million dollars. So, if you have a nonexempt bank account containing $25,000, the trustee gets to keep $1,250 (25% of $5,000) plus $2,000 (10% of the remaining $20,000) for a total of $3,250. Put another way, your creditors would receive $21,750 instead of $25,000.

In addition to the trustee's commission, you can also subtract the costs of taking the property and selling it. For certain types of property, there are few (if any) costs of sale. Cash on hand, bank accounts, and investments that can easily be converted to cash fit within this category of property. However, other types of property—such as a home, a car, or furniture—have significant resale costs. Because your unsecured creditors wouldn't get any of this money in a Chapter 7 case, they also aren't entitled to it in your Chapter 13 case. And, because personal property (a piano or furnishings, for example) often sells at auction for significantly less than its replacement value, you might be able to argue for an even lower total.

EXAMPLE 1: Jane has a savings account containing $50,000, and none of it is exempt. She can subtract the trustee's commission: 25% of $5,000 ($1,250) plus 10% of the remaining $45,000 ($4,500) for a total of $5,750. If Jane were to file for Chapter 13, her unsecured creditors would be entitled to at least $44,250.

EXAMPLE 2: John owns his home, appraised at $100,000, free and clear. The exemption system he is using allows him to exempt $50,000 worth of equity, so his nonexempt equity is worth $50,000. From this amount, he can subtract the commission the trustee in a Chapter 7 case would earn from selling the property: 25% of $5,000 ($1,250) plus 10% of the remaining $45,000 of his equity ($4,500), or a total of $5,750. He can also subtract the costs of selling his house. Typically, sales costs come to about 8% of the sales price. If John's home sold for $100,000, he could subtract $8,000 in sales costs. So if John were to file for Chapter 13, his unsecured creditors would be entitled to at least $36,250: his nonexempt equity of $50,000, minus the trustee's commission of $5,750, minus $8,000 in sales costs.

EXAMPLE 3: Juan owns a car worth $10,000 free and clear. He can exempt $3,000 of his equity, so the value of his nonexempt amount is $7,000. From this amount, he can subtract the trustee's commission of $1,450 (25% of $5,000 plus 10% of $2,000), for a nonexempt total of $5,550. Then he can subtract the costs of sale, including the cost of picking up the car, storing it, and holding an auction at which the car will likely sell for well less than its replacement value. If Juan wants to play it safe, he could use the out-of-pocket expense rate typically agreed to by trustees, which is 5% of the car's value, or $500. This means his unsecured creditors in a Chapter 13 case would be entitled to $5,050. If Juan is willing to argue with the trustee, he could advocate for a higher expense rate, to account for the lower price the car is likely to fetch at auction.

Once you come up with the total amount your unsecured creditors would actually receive if you filed for Chapter 7, convert it to a monthly figure. For example, if you find that your unsecured creditors are entitled to $7,200 and you are proposing a three-year repayment plan, divide $7,200 by 36 months to come up with the monthly amount you would have to pay: $200. Subtract this monthly total from the disposable income you calculated in Step 6.

Disposable Income
  (from Step 6):   _____
Monthly Amount for
  Unsecured Creditors: – _____
Total: = _____

Step 8: Subtract the Trustee's Fee

Your Chapter 13 trustee is entitled to roughly 10% of all payments you make under the plan, as a fee. It's hard to compute what that figure will be at this point; the total trustee's cut may depend on whether your mortgage (if you have one) and other secured debts will be paid under the plan or directly to the creditor. For example, assume your mortgage payment is $2,000 a month, and you want to use Chapter 13 to cure an arrearage of $5,000. If you make your mortgage payment directly to the creditor, you will owe the trustee only $500 (10% of the arrearage). However, if you also make your mortgage payment to the trustee as part of the plan, the trustee will be entitled to another $7,200 over the life of a three-year plan. Although some courts permit debtors to make mortgage payments directly to a creditor (see *In re Lopez*, 372 B.R. 40 (9th Cir. B.A.P. 2007)), others require debtors to make these payments through the plan, so the trustee gets paid more (see *In re Breeding,* 366 B.R. 21 (E.D. Ark. 2007)).

To get a rough figure, multiply the amount you came up with in Step 6 by 0.1 (10%), then subtract that amount from your total disposable income.

Remaining Income
  (from Step 7):   _____
Monthly Trustee's Fee
  (remaining income x 0.1): – _____
Total Disposable Income: = _____

As long as your total is a positive number, you may be able to propose a confirmable plan. If your total is zero, this means you will have exactly enough money to meet your plan obligations, not a penny more or less.

If all of your property is exempt, and the disposable income you calculated in Step 6 was zero, your unsecured creditors won't get paid a cent. This is called a "zero-percent" plan. Before the bankruptcy law changed in 2005, many courts wouldn't confirm a plan that paid unsecured creditors less than a particular percentage (anywhere from 20% to 80%, depending on the court). Under the revised law, however, there is no legal reason why a zero-percent plan should not be confirmed, as long as your expenses are reasonable (that is, the court can find any money you are paying for expenses that should go to your creditors instead).

If Your Current Monthly Income Is More Than Your State's Median Income

If your current monthly income is more than your state's median income, you are required to use Form 22C, *Chapter 13 Statement of Current Monthly Income and Calculation of Commitment Period and Disposable Income*, to compute your disposable income. You'll find instructions for completing that form below and a blank, tear-out form in Appendix B.

These calculations are essentially the same as the calculations you would perform if your income was below the state median income, with two exceptions:

- Instead of using your actual living expenses, you must set amounts found in national and local IRS expense standards.
- For most people, your plan length will be 60 months instead of 36 months.

Step 1: Use Form 22C to Calculate Your Disposable Income

In Ch. 4, you may have completed Form 22A to find out whether you are required to use Chapter 13 or whether you have a choice between Chapter 13 and Chapter 7. If you completed that form, be aware that Lines 19 though 47 of Form 22A are the same as Lines 24 though 52 of Form 22C. If you completed Form 22A, you can start Form 22C by transferring the amount you entered in Line 47 of Form 22A to Line 52 of Form 22C, then starting with our instructions below for Line 53.

Otherwise, start computing your disposable income with Line 24.

RESOURCE

Finding national and regional expense standards. To fill out Form 22C you must find IRS National Standards and Local Standards for various expenses (for example, housing, transportation, health care, and the like). You can find all of these figures on the U.S. Trustee's website at www.justice.gov/ust. Click on "Bankruptcy Reform" and then "Means Testing Information." From the drop-down menu, select the time period that covers when you will file for bankruptcy. Scroll down to find the applicable link. At times you'll have to select your state or region from the drop-down menu to get the figures for your location.

"Current Monthly Income" or Actual Projected Income: *Hamilton v. Lanning*

What if your "current monthly income" as calculated on Form 22C (which is your average income over the past six months) does not match your actual income or the income you will receive during your repayment period? The U.S. Supreme Court recently held that bankruptcy courts may account for changes in the debtor's income or expenses that are "known or virtually certain at the time of [plan] confirmation" when calculating projected disposable income for purposes of the plan payments. (*Hamilton v. Lanning,* 130 S.Ct. 2464 (2010).) For details, see "If Your Actual Income Is Different From Your 'Current Monthly Income': *Hamilton v. Lanning*".

Line 24A. Enter the total IRS National Standards: Food, Clothing, and Other Items for your family size and income level. This is the amount the IRS believes you should get to spend for food, clothes, household supplies, personal care, and miscellaneous other items.

Line 24B. Enter the amount you are allowed to claim for health expenses from the IRS National Standards: Out-of-Pocket Health Care Expenses. As you'll see, you can claim more for household members who are at least 65 years old, which is reflected on the form. You'll also see that the total amount you can claim is quite small; if you spend more than you're allowed to claim here, you can claim it on Line 36.

Line 25A. Enter the amount of the IRS Local Housing and Utilities Expense Standards, nonmortgage expenses for your county and family size.

Line 25B. On Line a, enter the amount of the IRS Housing and Utility Expense Standards, Mortgage/Rent expenses for your county and family size.

On Line b, enter the average monthly payment for any debts secured by your home, including a mortgage, home equity loan, taxes, and insurance. The average monthly payment is the total of all amounts contractually due to each secured creditor in the five years after you file for bankruptcy, divided by 60. Even if you are planning to move or have stopped making your payments, you should still enter your contractual mortgage payment here. If your mortgage payment is higher than the IRS allowance for housing in the area where you live, the court might calculate your disposable income using the IRS allowance. (See *In re Meek,* 370 B.R. 294 (D. Idaho 2007).)

On Line c, subtract Line b from Line a. This may turn out to be a negative figure; if so, enter a zero in the right-hand column. Later, as you'll be able to claim your average monthly payment as a deduction.

Line 26. If your actual rental or mortgage expense is higher than that allowed by the IRS, you can claim an adjustment here. For instance if the IRS mortgage/rental expense for a family of two is $550, you pay an actual rent of $900, and that amount is average for the area in which you live, enter the additional $350 here and explain why you should be able to subtract it (that you couldn't possibly find housing in your area for less, for example).

Line 27A. You are entitled to claim an expense here whether or not you actually have a car. First, indicate the number of cars for which you pay operating expenses or for which somebody else contributes the operating expenses as part of the amount entered on Line 7. If you don't have a car, enter the amount listed under "Public Transportation" from the IRS Local Transportation Expense Standards. If you indicated that you have one or two cars, enter the amount listed for your region (and sometimes, your city) under "Operating Costs" in the same chart.

Line 27B. If you have a car and also use public transportation, you may claim a public transportation expense here. You can find the correct amount by following the instructions for Line 27A, above.

Line 28. These are your expenses for owning or leasing a car.

 CAUTION

You can only claim this deduction if you own or lease a car. Until recently, courts were divided as to whether a debtor who did not own or lease a car could deduct the standard ownership expense. In January of 2011, the U.S. Supreme Court ruled that for purposes of calculating disposable income, only debtors who own or lease a car may claim the ownership deduction. (*Ransom v. FIA Card Services*, 131 S.Ct. 716 (2011).) The court left up in the air what happens if you own or lease a car, but your actual ownership expenses are less than those set forth in the ownership expense standards. So far, two courts have ruled that debtors in this situation may deduct the full amount in the standards, rather than the (lower) amount of their actual expense.

On Line 28a, enter the IRS Local Transportation Standards for ownership of a first car. This amount is actually a national figure; currently, it is $496. The most up-to-date number is in the Local Transportation Expense Standards. The ownership figure is near the bottom of the page.

On Line 28b, enter your average monthly payment (over the next five years) for all debts secured by your first car. For example, assume you have three years left to pay on the car and the monthly payment is $350. The total amount you will owe in the next five years is $12,600 (36 months times $350). If you spread that amount over the next five years—by dividing the total by 60, the number of months in five years—you'll see that your average monthly payment is $210.

On Line 28c, subtract Line b from Line a and enter the result in the column on the right. Later on, if necessary, you will be able to deduct your car payments to

figure out whether you have enough disposable income to fund a Chapter 13 plan.

Line 29. Complete this only if you have a second car (and you checked the "2 or more" box in Line 28). Follow the instructions for Line 28 to enter the required figures for your second car.

Line 30. Enter the total average monthly expense that you actually incur for all taxes *other than property or sales taxes*. Examples of taxes that you should enter here are income taxes, self-employment taxes, Social Security taxes, and Medicare taxes. In some cases, these taxes will show up on your wage stub. You'll need to convert the period covered by your wage stub to a monthly figure. Once you have figured out how much you pay each month for each type of tax, add them all together and enter them in the column on the right.

Converting Taxes to a Monthly Figure

If you are paid weekly, biweekly, or twice a month, you will have to convert the tax amounts on your pay stubs to a monthly amount. And, if you pay quarterly taxes (estimated income taxes, for example), you'll need to convert that figure as well. Here's how to do it:

- Weekly taxes: Multiply by 4.3 to get a monthly amount.
- Biweekly taxes: Divide by 2 to get a weekly amount, then multiply by 4.3.
- Bimonthly taxes: Divide by 2.
- Quarterly taxes: Divide by 3.

Line 31. Enter all of your mandatory payroll deductions here, other than those entered in Line 30. Use the conversion rules set out above to arrive at average monthly deductions. Make sure you deduct only mandatory deductions (such as required retirement contributions, union dues, and uniform costs). Contributions to a 401(k) should not be included here, for example, because they are voluntary. (You may deduct contributions to a retirement plan, including loan repayment, on Line 55.)

Line 32. Enter any monthly payments you make for term life insurance. Do not enter payments for any other type of insurance, such as credit insurance, car insurance, renters' insurance, insurance on the lives of your dependents, or whole life insurance on your own life. (Whole life insurance is the type that allows you to borrow against the policy.)

Line 33. Enter the amount of any payments you make pursuant to a court order. Child support and alimony are the most common examples, but you may also have to pay to satisfy a court money judgment or a criminal fine. Do not include court-ordered payments toward a child support or alimony arrearage; only the payments you need to make to stay current should be entered here.

Line 34. Enter the total monthly amount that you pay for education required by your employer to keep your job and the total monthly amount you pay for the education of a physically or mentally challenged dependent child for whom no public education providing similar services is available. Included in this amount would be the actual costs of after-school enrichment educational services for a physically or mentally challenged child, and the actual educational expenses you are paying in support of an individual educational plan.

Line 35. Enter the average monthly cost of child care. If your employment (and therefore, your need for child care) is seasonal, add up your child care costs for the year and divide the total by 12. Do not equate education with child care. For instance, child care for a child who is of public education school age should cover only the hours before and after school.

Line 36. Enter the average monthly amount you pay for out-of-pocket health care expenses, but only to the extent it exceeds the amount you were allowed to claim on Line 24B. Do not include health care expenses that are reimbursed by insurance or provided by an HMO or Medicaid. Also, don't include premiums you pay for health insurance; you can claim these on Line 39.

Line 37. Enter the average monthly expenses you pay for any communication devices that are necessary for the health and welfare of you or your dependents. Examples provided by the form are cell phones, pagers, call waiting, caller identification, and special long distance or Internet services. Virtually all of these devices arguably are necessary for the health and welfare of your family. However, some expenses might not be allowed (for example, a smartphone, cell phone you use for your business, or broadband Internet service). When in doubt, list the expense.

Line 38. Add the expenses you entered in Lines 24 through 37 and put the total in the column at the right.

Subpart B: Additional Living Expense Deductions

The expenses in this subpart are allowed by the Bankruptcy Code, in addition to the IRS expenses. However, you can't list an expense twice; if you already claimed it in Subpart A, don't list it again here.

Line 39. Here, list your reasonably necessary monthly expenses for health insurance, disability insurance, and health savings accounts (HSAs) on the lines provided. The form was revised in 2008 to clarify that you can list a "reasonable" expense here whether you actually pay that amount each month or not. If, however, you pay less than the reasonable amount you list, you must indicate how much you actually spend each month on the additional line provided. If the U.S. Trustee or one of your creditors later wants to challenge your expense claims—for example, to argue that you really have more disposable income than the form indicates—they can use this information.

Line 40. Anything you spend to care for a member of your household or immediate family because of his or her age, illness, or disability can be deducted here. If your contributions are episodic—a wheelchair here, a vacation with a companion there—estimate your average monthly expense and enter it here.

> **CAUTION**
> **Your response here could affect eligibility for government benefits.** Expenses you list here could render the person you are assisting ineligible for Social Security or other government benefits. For example, if you state that you are spending $500 a month for the care of a relative, and that relative is receiving SSI, your relative might receive a lower benefit amount each month, to reflect your contribution. On the other hand, if you are making such expenditures, you are required to disclose them here. If you find yourself in this predicament be sure to alert your lawyer.

Line 41. The average monthly expense of security systems and any other method of protecting your family should be entered here.

Line 42. If your actual home energy costs exceed the figure you entered on Line 25A, enter the extra money you spend here. As the form indicates, you may need to prove this extra expense to the trustee.

Line 43. This item is for money you spend on your children's education. If your average monthly expense is $147.92 or more, put $147.92 in this blank; that's the maximum you can deduct. Remember not to list an amount twice; if you already listed an expense on Line 34 or 35, for example, don't repeat it here.

Line 44. Here, you can list the amount by which your actual expenses for food and clothing exceed the IRS allowance for these items as entered in Line 24. However, you cannot list more than 5% over the IRS allowance.

Line 45. You can claim the charitable contributions you ordinarily take, but you can't suddenly decide to make them and then deduct them here. See the discussion of Line 40 on Form 22A in Ch. 4 for information on what types of organizations qualify for charitable deductions.

Line 46. Enter the total of Lines 39 through 45 in the column on the right.

Subpart C: Deductions for Debt Payment

Here, you deduct average contractually due monthly payments you will have to make over the next five years.

Line 47. List the average monthly payment you will have to make over the next five years to creditors that hold a secured interest in your property (for example, the mortgage holder on your house or the creditor that holds your car note). Calculate this amount by figuring out the total amount you will owe over the next five years, then dividing that total by 60. You can list the full amount of your contractual payment even if you are planning to cram it down as part of your plan. (For details on cramdowns, see Ch. 1.) If you have stopped making your mortgage payments or are planning to move, some courts will allow you to take this deduction anyway; other courts will not. Check with your lawyer. If your mortgage payment is higher than the IRS allowance for housing in the area where you live, the court might calculate your disposable income using the IRS allowance. (See *In re Meek,* 370 B.R. 294 (D. Idaho 2007).)

Line 48. Here, list the average monthly payment you would have to make to pay off any back amounts due to creditors on property that you must keep for your support or support of your dependents. That would typically include a car, your home, and any property you need for your employment. (Come up with the monthly figure by dividing the total amount you would have to pay by 60.)

Line 49. List the average monthly amount you will have to pay for priority claims over the next five years. (See "Classifying Your Debts," in Ch. 4, for a list of priority claims.) Typical priority claims include back taxes and back child and spousal support. Divide the total by 60 to arrive at the monthly average. Don't include payments you've already listed on the form, such as current child support obligations. This line is only for debts you owe at the time of filing.

Line 50. Calculate the fee the trustee will charge if you file Chapter 13 bankruptcy. That fee will depend on how much you would be paying, through the trustee, to your secured and unsecured creditors. It's impossible to come up with a figure at this point in the form, so leave it blank for now. (Ch. 8 explains how to come up with a rough figure.)

Line 51. Add Lines 47 through 50, and enter the total.

Subpart D: Total Deductions from Income

Line 52: Enter the total of items 38, 46, and 51 in the column at the right. This is the total amount you can subtract from your current monthly income to arrive at your disposable income.

Part V: Determination of Disposable Income Under § 1325(b)(2)

Here is where you subtract your expenses from your income to arrive at your total disposable income.

Line 53. Enter your current monthly income, as calculated in Ch. 4.

Line 54. Enter the monthly average of any child support payments, foster care payments, or disability payments for a dependent child, that:

- are necessary to spend on the child, and
- you included in Line 8 when computing your current monthly income, in Ch. 4.

Line 55. Enter the monthly average of:

- all contributions or wage deductions made to qualified retirement plans, as specified in Section 541(b)(7) (these include virtually all defined-benefit pension plans arising from employment), and
- all repayments of loans from retirements plans, as specified in Section 362(b)(19) (employment pension plans and 401(k)s).

Line 56. Bring down the total expenses from Line 52.

Line 57. Special circumstances are situations that give rise to unexpected expenses that don't qualify as "additional expense claims" on Line 60. The law lists a serious medical condition (such as cancer, Alzheimer's disease, or Parkinson's disease) or a call to active duty in the armed forces as examples of special circumstances. It's not enough just to show that special circumstances exist: You must also show that they justify additional expenses or adjustments to your current monthly income "for which there is no reasonable alternative." And, you must be able to document the expenses. If you believe that something in your life—that is not already provided for in this form—will eat up part of your disposable income, list the expense here and line up your documentation.

Cases on Special Circumstances

Here are some cases in which the court has allowed a particular special circumstance claim, but remember that courts in your area may see the issue differently:

- unusually high transportation expenses (*In re Batzkiel*, 349 B.R. 581 (Bkrtcy N.D. Iowa 2006); *In re Turner*, 376 B.R. 370 (Bkrtcy D. N.H. 2007))
- mandatory repayment of 401(k) loan (*In re Lenton*, 358 B.R. 651 (Bkrtcy E.D. Pa. 2006))
- reduction in income (*In re Martin*, 371 B.R. 347 (Bkrtcy C.D. Ill. 2007) (diminished future availability of overtime hours); *In re Tamez*, No. 07-60047 (Bkrtcy W.D. Tex. 2007) (reduction in income due to voluntary job changes))
- wife's pregnancy in a joint case (*In re Martin*, 371 B.R. 347 (Bkrtcy C.D. Ill. 2007))
- joint debtors who have two separate households (*In re Graham*, 363 B.R. 844 (Bkrtcy S.D. Ohio 2007); *In re Armstrong*, No. 06-31414 (Bkrtcy N.D. Ohio 2007))
- unusually high rent expenses (*In re Scarafiotti*, 375 B.R. 618 (Bkrtcy D. Colorado 2007)), and
- court-ordered child support payments (*In re Littman*, 370 B.R. 820 (Bkrtcy D. Idaho 2007)).

Line 58. Add Lines 54, 55, 56, and 57, and enter the total.

Line 59. Subtract Line 57 from Line 53 and enter the result. This is your first calculation of disposable income, but you're not through yet. Now return to Line 50 and enter the amount on Line 58 on Line 50a. On Line 50b, multiply the amount on Line 50a by the correct multiplier, which can be found on the U.S. Trustee's website (www.justice.gov/ust). Enter the result on Line 50c. Then, subtract Line 50c from Line 58.

Line 60. If you have additional expenses that you couldn't include anywhere else on the form, you can enter them here, provided they really are necessary for the health and welfare of you and your family. The court will look at these expenses with special scrutiny. If you include additional expenses here, subtract them from the total on Line 58, less the amount on Line 50c, for a final disposable income figure.

To find out whether you have enough disposable income to get a Chapter 13 plan confirmed, divide the total of any secured debts that weren't included in Line 47 by 60, to figure out how much you'd have to pay each month to pay off these liens in five years. Subtract the result from your disposable income. If this results in a negative figure, then you can't propose a confirmable plan, given your current expenses and property holdings. If your disposable income is zero or more, then you can propose a confirmable plan, as long as the total is at least equal to the value of your nonexempt property (see Step 2, below).

Plan Length If You Have No Disposable Income

If your income is above the state median, you normally must propose a 60-month plan. However, if you don't have any disposable income left after deducting living expense and repayment of secured and priority debts, some courts will let you propose a 36-month plan. Other courts won't.

Step 2: Determine What Your Creditors Would Get If You Used Chapter 7

As explained in Step 7, above (for those whose incomes are less than the state median), your plan must pay your unsecured creditors at least what they would have received if you had filed under Chapter 7: the value of your nonexempt property, less what it would cost to take and sell it, less the trustee's commission for doing so. See Step 7, above, for information on how to make this calculation.

Once you come up with the total amount your unsecured creditors would actually receive if you filed for Chapter 7, convert it to a monthly figure. For example, if you find that your unsecured creditors are entitled to $7,200 and you are proposing a five-year repayment plan, divide $7,200 by 60 months to come up with the monthly amount you would have to pay: $120. Subtract this monthly total from the disposable income you calculated in Step 1.

> Disposable Income
> (from Step 1):   _____
>
> Monthly Amount for
> Unsecured Creditors: – _____
>
> Total: = _____

As long as your total is a positive number, you may be able to propose a confirmable plan. If your total is zero, this means you will have exactly enough money to meet your plan obligations, not a penny more or less.

If all of your property is exempt, and the disposable income you calculated in Step 1 was zero, your unsecured creditors won't get paid a cent. This is called a "zero-percent" plan. Before the bankruptcy law changed in 2005, many courts wouldn't confirm a plan that paid unsecured creditors less than a particular percentage (anywhere from 20% to 80%, depending on the court). Under the revised law, however, there is no legal reason why a zero-percent plan should not be confirmed, as long as your expenses are reasonable (that is, the court can find any money you are paying for expenses that should go to your creditors instead).

Understanding Property Exemptions

This section covers exemptions—the rules that determine how much, if any, your Chapter 13 plan will have to pay to your nonpriority, unsecured creditors.

Your Bankruptcy Estate

Your bankruptcy estate refers to all of your property that is part of your bankruptcy case. Not all property is in your bankruptcy estate; for example, most property you acquire after you file for bankruptcy is not part of the estate, and you need not account to the trustee about what you do with it. If property falls outside of your bankruptcy estate, you don't need to worry about whether or not it's exempt, because the court can't touch it or ask you to pay its value to your creditors.

Several broad categories of property make up your bankruptcy estate:

- **Property you own and possess.** Everything in your possession that you own, whether or not you owe money on it—for example, a car, real estate, clothing, books, television, stereo system, furniture, tools, boat, artworks, or stock certificates—is included in your bankruptcy estate. Property that you have in your possession but that belongs to someone else (such as the car your friend stores in your garage or the television you borrowed from your sister) is not part of your bankruptcy estate, because you don't have the right to sell it or give it away.

- **Property you own but don't possess.** You can own something even if you don't have physical possession of it. For instance, you may own a car that someone else is using. Other examples include a deposit held by a stockbroker, a security deposit held by your landlord or a utility company, or a business in which you've invested money.

- **Property you are entitled to receive.** Property that you have a legal right to receive but haven't gotten yet when you file for bankruptcy is included in your bankruptcy estate. Common examples include:
  - wages, royalties, or commissions you have earned but have not yet been paid
  - a tax refund legally due you
  - vacation or termination pay you've earned
  - property you've inherited but not yet received from someone who has died
  - proceeds of an insurance policy, if the death, injury, or other event that gives rise to payment has already occurred, and
  - money owed you for goods or services you've provided (often called "accounts receivable").

- **Community property.** If you live in a community property state, all property and income either spouse acquires during the marriage is ordinarily considered "community property," owned jointly by both spouses. (The community property states are Arizona, California, Idaho, Louisiana, Nevada, New Mexico, Texas, Washington, and Wisconsin, and—if you have a written community property agreement or trust—Alaska.) Gifts and inheritances to only one spouse are the most common exceptions; these are the separate property of the spouse who receives them. If you're married and file jointly for bankruptcy, all the community property you and your spouse own, as well as all of both of your separate property, is considered part of your bankruptcy estate. If your spouse doesn't file, then your bankruptcy estate consists of all of the community property and all of your separate property—your spouse's separate property isn't included.

- **Marital property in a common law property state.** If you are married and filing jointly, your bankruptcy estate includes all the property you and your spouse own, together and separately. If you are filing alone for bankruptcy in a common law property state (all states other than the community property states listed above), your bankruptcy estate includes:
  - your separate property (property that has only your name on a title certificate or that was purchased, received as a gift, or inherited by you alone), and
  - half of the property that is jointly owned by you and your spouse, unless you own the property as tenants by the entirety. If you own property as tenants by the entirety, and both spouses file for bankruptcy, then the property is part of your bankruptcy estate. If only one spouse files, however, it's likely that none of the property is part of the bankruptcy estate. The rules that determine whether you own property as tenants by the entirety differ from state to state. Also, some states allow only real estate to be owned as tenants by the entirety, while other states also allow personal property to be owned this way.
- **Certain property you receive within 180 days after filing for bankruptcy.** Most property you acquire or become entitled to after you file for bankruptcy

isn't included in your bankruptcy estate. But there are a few exceptions. If you acquire or become entitled to the following items within 180 days after you file, you must notify the trustee:
  - an inheritance (but not money "inherited" through a living trust or beneficiary designation form; see *In re Szwyd*, 370 B.R. 882 (1st Cir. B.A.P. 2007) and *In re Kester*, 493 F.3d 1208 (10th Cir. 2007))
  - property you receive or have a right to receive from a marital settlement agreement or divorce decree, and
  - death benefits or life insurance policy proceeds.
- **Property (revenue) generated by estate property.** This type of property typically consists of the proceeds of contracts—such as those providing for rent, royalties, and commissions—that were in effect at the time of the bankruptcy filing, but which produced earnings after that date. For example, if you are a composer or an author and receive royalties each year for a composition or a book that was written before you filed for bankruptcy, the trustee may collect those royalties as property of your estate. Proceeds from work you do after your filing date belong to you.
- **Property transferred within the previous two years.** If you transferred personal or real property to anyone within the last two years for less than it's worth, the trustee may decide to treat the property as part of you bankruptcy estate and initiate legal action to recover the property for the benefit of your creditors.

Property That's Not Part of Your Bankruptcy Estate

Property that is not in your bankruptcy estate is not subject to the bankruptcy court's jurisdiction, which means that you don't have to worry about whether or not it's exempt.

The most common examples of property that doesn't fall within your bankruptcy estate are:
- property you buy or receive after your filing date (with the few exceptions described above)
- pensions subject to the federal law known as ERISA (commonly, defined benefit pensions, 401(k)s, and Keogh plans)

- property owned as tenants by the entirety when only one spouse files
- property pledged as collateral for a loan where a licensed lender (pawnbroker) retains possession of the collateral
- property in your possession that belongs to someone else (for instance, property you are storing for someone)
- wages that are withheld and employer contributions that are made for employee benefit and health insurance plans, and
- funds in a qualified tuition plan or Coverdell education savings account if you deposit the funds into the account at least one year before filing, and the beneficiary is your child, stepchild, grandchild, step-grandchild, or in some cases, foster child. There are monetary limits depending on how long the funds have been in the account.

Value Your Property

As you'll see below, many exemptions apply only up to a certain dollar value. This means that you need to know what your property is worth in order to figure out whether it's exempt. You must use the property's replacement value: what it would cost to buy that specific property from a retail merchant, considering its age and condition.

It's easy to enter a dollar amount for cash and most investments.

If you own a car, start with the middle *Kelley Blue Book* price. If the car needs repair, reduce the value by what it would cost you to fix the car. You can find the *Kelley Blue Book* at a public library or online at www.kbb.com. Or, use the NADA guide at www.nada.org.

Online, visit eBay (www.ebay.com) to get a fix on the going price for just about anything. Or briefly describe the item in Google (or your search engine of choice) and see what turns up. As long as your valuations are based on the going retail price for the item in question, you should generally use the lowest value you can find. That means it is more likely to be exempt and not require payments to your nonpriority, unsecured creditors. On the other hand, low-ball valuations might provoke arguments with the trustee or your creditors about what the property is really worth.

As long as the exemptions available to you cover the value you use, pricing your property more reasonably can help you avoid unnecessary hassles.

If you are filing separately and own something jointly with someone (other than a spouse with whom you would file for bankruptcy), reduce the value of the item to reflect only the portion you own. For example, you and your brother jointly bought a music synthesizer worth $10,000. If your ownership share is 40% and your brother's is 60%, the value of your portion is $4,000.

If you are married and filing separately in a community property state, include the total value of all the community property as well as the value of your separate property.

If you are married, you own the property with your spouse as tenants by the entirety, and you are filing separately, your ownership interest may not be 50% for purposes of computing your exemption. (Talk to your lawyer to find out what percentage of your tenancy by the entirety property you can claim as exempt.)

Applying Exemptions

Bankruptcy is intended to give debtors a fresh start—not to leave them utterly destitute. Exempt property can literally range from "the shirt on your back" to a million-dollar estate, depending on which state's exemptions you use.

State and Federal Exemption Systems

Every state has its own fairly lengthy list of exempt property. (You can find these lists in Appendix A.) In addition, some states offer bankruptcy filers an alternative choice of exemptions—a list of exempt property found in the federal Bankruptcy Code. States that offer this choice are: Arkansas, Connecticut, Hawaii, Massachusetts, Michigan, Minnesota, New Hampshire, New Jersey, New Mexico, New York, Pennsylvania, Rhode Island, Texas, Vermont, Washington, and Wisconsin. In these states, you must choose between the state exemption system and the federal exemption system; you can't mix and match.

California Note: Although California doesn't make the federal Bankruptcy Code exemptions available, it has two separate exemption systems—both created by state law. Debtors who use the California exemptions must choose between System 1 (the regular exemptions available to debtors in and out of bankruptcy) and System 2 (available only in bankruptcy and very similar to the federal exemptions).

How Exemptions Work

Under both the federal and state exemption systems, some types of property are exempt regardless of value. For example, in some states, home furnishings, wedding rings, or clothing are exempt without regard to value. In Florida and Texas, homes are exempt regardless of their value or the value of the bankruptcy filer's ownership (equity) in the home.

Other kinds of property are exempt up to a limited value. For instance, cars are often exempt up to a certain amount—typically $2,500 to $3,000. The home equity exemption ranges from thousands of dollars to hundreds of thousands, depending on the state. When there is a dollar limit on an exemption, any equity above the limit is considered nonexempt. (Your equity is the amount you would get to keep if you sold the property.)

Many states offer a "wildcard" exemption—a dollar amount that you can apply to any property, in order to make it (or more of it) exempt. This type of exemption typically runs from a few hundred to several thousand dollars (but more than $22,000 in California's System 2 exemptions).

> **EXAMPLE:** Fred and Susan are married and live in Virginia. They rent rather than own their home. Under the Virginia exemptions, equity in an automobile is limited to $2,000 ($4,000 for couples). Fred and Susan own $12,000 of equity in their cars. Fortunately for Fred and Susan, Virginia allows debtors to use the Virginia homestead exemption as a wildcard for their personal property, if they don't use it for a home. Because Fred and Susan rent, they can use this wildcard for their cars. The homestead exemption is $10,000 for couples. So, by adding $8,000 of the wildcard to their $4,000 car exemption, Fred and Susan can exempt all of their equity in their cars. They can apply the other $2,000 of the wildcard exemption to property that isn't otherwise protected by the Virginia exemptions.

Property Typically Not Exempt

The kinds of property listed below are typically not exempt unless you use a wildcard exemption:

- interests in real estate other than your home
- substantial equity in a newer-model motor vehicle
- expensive musical instruments unrelated to your job or business
- stamp, coin, and other collections
- cash, deposit accounts, stocks, bonds, and other investments
- business assets (except property that qualifies as tools of your trade, which you can typically exempt up to several thousand dollars)
- valuable artwork
- expensive clothing and jewelry, or
- antiques.

Domicile Requirements for Exemption Claims

In 2005, Congress passed domicile requirements that filers have to meet before claiming a state's exemptions. Your domicile is where you are living and plan to continue living for the indefinite future. For most people, their domicile is where they are living, period. But for some people, such as those in the armed forces, their domicile may be in one state and their residence in another (such as when they live on an army base in North Carolina but maintain a home in Tennessee). Here are the domicile rules:

- If you have been living (been domiciled) in your current state for at least two years, you must use that state's exemptions (or the federal exemptions, if they are available).
- If you have been living (been domiciled) in your current state for less than two years, you must use the exemptions of the state where you were domiciled for the better part of the 180-day period immediately prior to the two-year period preceding your filing—unless that state allows only current residents to use its exemptions. In that case, you can use the federal exemptions.
- If you have been domiciled in your current state for fewer than 91 days, you'll need to wait until you have lived there for 91 days to file in that state (and then use whatever exemptions are available to you according to the rules set out above).

- If the state you are filing in makes the federal exemptions available, you can use that exemption list regardless of how long you've been living in the state.
- If these rules deprive you of the right to use any state's exemptions, you can use the federal exemptions (even if your state doesn't make them available). For example, if you were living in another country during the 180-day period prior to the two years before you filed for bankruptcy, you can use the federal exemptions.

A longer domicile requirement applies to homestead exemptions: If you acquired a home in your current state less than 40 months before your filing date, your homestead exemption may be subject to a $146,450 cap regardless of which state's exemption system you use. People convicted of felonies and certain securities violations are also subject to this cap.

Using the Exemptions Appendix

You can find the exemptions for all 50 states in Appendix A. If you are considering filing for bankruptcy in one of the states listed below, you'll also want to look at the federal exemptions, which are listed in that appendix right after Wyoming.

Use Appendix A to find the applicable exemptions for your property, using the domicile rules set out above. Compare the type and value of your property, and the amount of equity you have in the property, with the exemptions.

Remember, if you are filing in a state that offers the federal bankruptcy exemptions, you should also check the federal exemption chart. Items that aren't exempt under the state exemptions available to you may be exempt under the federal system, and vice versa. However, you must pick one system or the other; you can't mix and match.

If you are married and filing jointly, you can double your exemptions unless the chart says that you can't. This will be indicated either at the top of the chart or next to a particular exemption.

If you have been domiciled in California for more than two years when you file, you may choose System 1 (the regular state exemptions) or System 2, a state list that is derived from the federal exemptions but differs in important particulars. If you file in California but haven't been domiciled there for two years, you can't use either California system—you'll have to use the domicile rules set out above to figure out which exemptions you can use.

States That Offer the Federal Exemptions

Arkansas	New Hampshire	Rhode Island
Connecticut	New Jersey	Texas
Hawaii	New Mexico	Vermont
Massachusetts	New York	Washington
Michigan	Pennsylvania	Wisconsin
Minnesota		

Federal Nonbankruptcy Exemptions

If you are using the exemptions of a particular state rather than the federal exemptions, you may also exempt property listed in Appendix A under Federal Nonbankruptcy Exemptions. Don't confuse those with the federal bankruptcy exemptions, which may be used only if a state allows it and only as an alternative to the state exemptions.

Making the Decision

Now you have all of the information you need to decide whether you can—and should—file for Chapter 13 bankruptcy. To help you sort through this information, weigh the pros and cons, and reach a decision, this chapter provides a transcript of a consultation between a debtor and a lawyer.

As you'll see, the debtor, Georgia Cox, is trying to figure out whether to file for bankruptcy under Chapter 7 or Chapter 13. She has decided to consult with a bankruptcy lawyer to help her with her decision. The questions the lawyer asks will help remind you of factors you should consider as you evaluate your own situation.

Lawyer: Good morning. What's your name?

Debtor: Georgia Cox.

Lawyer: Hi, Georgia. How can I help you today?

Debtor: Well, I've run up quite a bit of debt, and I've decided to file for bankruptcy. I know there are different types of bankruptcy, but I think I need to learn more about them. I need some help figuring out what my options are.

Lawyer: Okay, I can help you with that. The two basic types of bankruptcy for individuals are Chapter 7 bankruptcy and Chapter 13 bankruptcy. There are a couple of major differences between them. In a Chapter 13 bankruptcy, you pay down some or all of your debts over a three- to five-year period and discharge (cancel) whatever is left at the completion of your plan. In a Chapter 7 bankruptcy, you don't pay down any of your debt, and the entire process takes between three and four months. But you may have to give up property you own so it can be sold and the proceeds distributed to your creditors.

In either type of bankruptcy, some types of debts will survive your bankruptcy, such as criminal fines and penalties. Some types of debts will survive a Chapter 7 bankruptcy but will be discharged at the end of a Chapter 13 bankruptcy, such as an obligation to an ex-spouse under a marital settlement agreement.

But we'll get to that later. Are you with me so far?

Debtor: Yes. I kind of already knew most of what you just told me by reading some articles on the Nolo website. Right now, I'm leaning toward Chapter 7 since it's over a lot sooner and seems like it's a lot simpler. But I wouldn't want to choose Chapter 7 if Chapter 13 would clearly be the better choice for me.

Lawyer: Okay. Well, let's start by figuring out whether you even have a choice. Some people aren't eligible to file for Chapter 7 bankruptcy. If both options are available to you, then we can talk about which one makes more sense.

Debtor: Okay.

Lawyer: What state do you live in?

Debtor: New Hampshire.

Lawyer: Who lives with you as part of your household? That includes not only relatives and dependents, but anyone else whose income and expenses are combined with yours to maintain your home.

Debtor: Just me and my two children. One is eight and the other just turned 12.

Lawyer: Okay. And do you operate a business?

Debtor: Actually, I do. What difference does that make?

Lawyer: Well, in some cases, your eligibility for Chapter 7 may turn on whether your debts are classified as business or consumer debts.

Debtor: Okay. I run my own business, repairing used electronic equipment.

Lawyer: Have you incorporated your business or is it a partnership?

Debtor: No, just me, a sole proprietor.

Lawyer: And do you have other work? In other words, do you have a regular job and operate your business on the side?

Debtor: No, just the business.

Lawyer: Is your income pretty steady?

Debtor: It was until recently. Near the end of 2010, my business tanked and I'll be lucky to bring in half of what I was earning not too long ago. Also, I receive alimony and child support, which helps stabilize my income, but my ex told me just last week that he's been laid off and can't find another job, so I expect that source of income to dry up as well.

Lawyer: So, to dig in a little deeper about the nature of your debt, I see from the worksheet you completed when you first contacted me that you have about $100,000 in mortgage debt and that you currently don't owe any back taxes. Is that right?

Debtor: Yep.

Lawyer: I gather from the worksheet that your overall debt, other than your mortgage, is far short of $100,000, is that right?

Debtor: Right again.

Lawyer: Well, since mortgages count as personal debts, that means that your personal debts are higher than your business debts. If your business debts comprised more than 50% of your debts you would qualify for Chapter 7 without having to deal with what's known as the means test, which we'll get to in a moment. But since that's not the case, we'll have to see if your income is low enough to qualify you for Chapter 7. First, let's look at your income over the previous six months. More specifically, what was your gross income from all sources, taxable or not, minus the expenses that were reasonable and necessary for operating the business?

Debtor: About $3,000 a month after expenses.

Lawyer: You mentioned you've been receiving child support and alimony. How much during that six-month period?

Debtor: About $1,000 a month in alimony and $800 a month for child support.

Lawyer: Any other income?

Debtor: No, that's it.

Lawyer: So, it looks like your average monthly earnings over the past six months are $3,000 from your business, $1,000 in alimony, and $800 for child support, for a total of $4,800. Does that sound right?

Debtor: Yes.

Lawyer: Under the bankruptcy law, if your income is less than the median annual income for a family of your size in your state, you are presumed to be eligible to file for Chapter 7 bankruptcy. You don't have to fill out a lengthy form comparing your income to your expenses and deductions for contractual obligations, such as a car note and mortgage. Does any of this sound familiar to you?

Debtor: Yes, I remember reading a few years ago that higher-income people won't be able to file for Chapter 7 anymore. Is that what you are talking about?

Lawyer: Yes, that's it. Also, if your income is less than the median for your state and you decide to file a Chapter 13 bankruptcy anyway, your repayment plan need only last for three years. If, on the other hand, your income is more than the median, your plan would have to last for five years.

Debtor: I didn't know that.

Lawyer: So, let's see how these numbers work out. Your annual income based on your gross income for the last six months is $57,600. The New Hampshire median income for a household of three people is $79,349. So, you're under the median income and don't have to take the means test to prove your eligibility for Chapter 7 bankruptcy. And if you decide to use Chapter 13, you can repay your debts over three years, instead of five.

Debtor: I guess that's good news, but when it comes right down to it, I wish I earned more, even if that meant I had to take the means test and have a Chapter 13 case last longer. Of course, if I had more money, I guess I wouldn't be talking to you about filing for bankruptcy in the first place.

Lawyer: Even though you will be presumed to qualify for Chapter 7 bankruptcy on the basis of your average income over the past six months, you may still be forced into a Chapter 13 bankruptcy (or optionally have your case dismissed) if it appears that your actual monthly net income going forward will be substantially more than your actual monthly expenses—which would make it feasible for you to pay off some of your debts under a repayment plan.

Debtor: Oh dear, I wish I did have some extra income, but I always fall short at the end of the month.

Lawyer: Well, as long as your basic living expenses are reasonable and more or less equal to your net income, and because your income is below the state median income, you have the option of filing for Chapter 7 bankruptcy.

Let's turn now to your residence. How long have you lived in New Hampshire?

Debtor: About three years.

Lawyer: Have you lived there continuously for the last three years, or did you live or maintain a residence somewhere else?

Debtor: I've lived here the whole time. I moved here from Vermont because of a job, but I didn't keep a home in Vermont. I vote and get my mail here.

Lawyer: Great. Because you've been living in New Hampshire for more than two years, we'll be able to use our state's property exemptions. These will determine what property you can keep if you file a Chapter 7, and the minimum amount you'll have to pay your unsecured creditors if you file a Chapter 13 bankruptcy.

Debtor: Why do the exemptions matter in a Chapter 13 bankruptcy? I thought I could keep all of my property if I use Chapter 13.

Lawyer: Yes, you're right about that. But the law doesn't want your creditors to be worse off if you use Chapter 13 rather than Chapter 7. A Chapter 13 repayment plan has to give your unsecured, nonpriority creditors at least what they would have received if you had filed for Chapter 7 bankruptcy. So, if you have some nonexempt property, your plan will need to pay your unsecured, nonpriority creditors at least the value of that property, less the trustee's commission and the costs of taking and selling the property.

Lawyer: Now, let's see if you have any nonexempt property. You own your own home, right?

Debtor: Yeah, although as you know, I owe $100,000 on my mortgage, which kind of means that the bank owns the home.

Lawyer: I know how you feel, but for bankruptcy purposes, if you are the owner on the title deed, you are considered the owner. Are you on the title deed?

Debtor: When I last looked.

Lawyer: Okay. How large are your mortgage payments?

Debtor: $1,200.

Lawyer: Are you current on your payments?

Debtor: Yes.

Lawyer: What's your home worth?

Debtor: $150,000. It used to be worth $200,000 just last year.

Lawyer: Okay. Under the New Hampshire homestead exemption, you are entitled to protect up to $100,000 of equity in your home. You have $50,000 of equity, so all of your equity is protected.

Debtor: What's a homestead exemption?

Lawyer: That's an exemption for equity you have in your home. You are entitled to keep that much equity in your home, even if you file for Chapter 7 bankruptcy. If your equity exceeded the exemption, you might lose the extra equity if you filed for Chapter 7. The trustee could sell your home, pay off the mortgage, pay you your exemption, and still have money left over to distribute among your creditors. But because your equity is protected by the exemption, there wouldn't be anything left for your creditors after you got your exemption amount and the mortgage was paid. That's how exemptions work.

We already discussed how exemptions work in Chapter 13. If you have equity in personal property or real estate that isn't protected by an exemption, your repayment plan has to pay out at least what your unsecured creditors would have gotten from the sale of that property if you had used Chapter 7.

Debtor: I remember reading that a new bankruptcy law made it harder for people to keep their homes. Will that affect me?

Lawyer: Nope. The law puts a cap of roughly $150,000 on the exemption amount for people who bought their home within the 40 months before they filed for bankruptcy. So it affects only people who bought a home more recently, and then only if their state would otherwise allow them to take a higher exemption. For example, even if you bought your home in New Hampshire within the previous 40 months, the New Hampshire homestead is only $100,000, so the cap wouldn't make any difference.

Debtor: So, I don't have to worry about that.

Lawyer: Right. Oh, your homestead exemption might be affected if you used nonexempt property in the last ten years to buy your home in order to cheat your creditors. I guess I should ask how you got the money to pay for your home.

Debtor: I borrowed money from my parents.

Lawyer: Great. Your home equity is covered by your state's homestead exemption and you can keep it if you file for Chapter 7 bankruptcy.

Debtor: What happens to my home if I file for Chapter 13 bankruptcy?

Lawyer: As long as you keep making your mortgage payments and the other payments required by your Chapter 13 plan, there won't be a problem. However, if you fall behind on your payments, your lender can request permission from the court to proceed with a foreclosure, just as if you hadn't filed for bankruptcy.

Debtor: So I have to keep my mortgage payments current, no matter which type of bankruptcy I file?

Lawyer: That's right.

Debtor: While we're talking about mortgages, would you mind if I asked you about something my sister's going through?

Lawyer: Shoot.

Debtor: My sister owns a house that is now worth $100,000, but she owes $150,000 on her first mortgage and another $50,000 on her second mortgage. She's several months behind on her mortgage payments and her lender told her it's about to start foreclosure proceedings. She also lives in New Hampshire and she's been told that the lender can foreclose without having to go to court. Could bankruptcy help her keep her home?

Lawyer: The short answer is that Chapter 13 might help her keep her home. Chapter 7 would only delay the process for several months. Even in Chapter 13, she might have to give up her home but at least, unlike Chapter 7, she would have an opportunity for the bankruptcy judge to rule on the legality of the foreclosure and mortgage documents. And finally, she could get rid of the second mortgage lien on the property as part of her Chapter 13 plan, since the second mortgage lien is no longer secured by any equity in the home.

Debtor: That's really interesting

Lawyer: It is, isn't it? Anyway, moving on, what other debts do you owe?

Debtor: Mainly credit card debts, and one SBA bank loan for my business.

Lawyer: Is the SBA loan secured by any of your property?

Debtor: No, it's just a bank loan.

Lawyer: How much are you paying on that loan?

Debtor: About $300 a month.

Lawyer: And how much credit card debt do you owe?

Debtor: About $20,000.

Lawyer: What were the credit card debts for?

Debtor: About $14,000 for personal expenses and $6,000 for paying off back taxes.

Lawyer: Oh yeah? What period did you owe the taxes for?

Debtor: The last couple of years.

Lawyer: That's interesting. I'll come back to this later. Bankruptcy law allows you to discharge credit card charges used to pay off taxes in a Chapter 13 bankruptcy but not in a Chapter 7 bankruptcy. So, if there is no other reason to choose one type of bankruptcy over the other, you would be wise to choose Chapter 13.

So, having paid those taxes, are you now current on your taxes for the past four years?

Debtor: Yes.

Lawyer: That's good. You can't file for Chapter 13 unless you have filed your state and federal taxes for the previous four years. How much was the bank loan for?

Debtor: $40,000.

Lawyer: Did anybody cosign on that loan?

Debtor: As matter of fact, my mother did.

Lawyer: Hmm. Even if you could get rid of that debt in bankruptcy, your mother would still be on the hook to repay it if you filed under Chapter 7. Even though you wouldn't be responsible for the debt any more, she would be.

But if you file for Chapter 13 bankruptcy, your mother won't have to repay it while your plan is in place, as long as your plan provides for payment of some or all of that debt. So, assuming your plan lasts for three years, your mother won't be on the hook for that period. However, she will still be responsible for any amount you haven't paid when your plan ends. So, again, if there is no other reason to choose one type of bankruptcy instead of the other, it looks like Chapter 13 might be a good choice.

Do you have any other debts?

Debtor: Nothing significant, maybe a total of $2,000 in miscellaneous bills. And, oh, does child support count?

Lawyer: I thought you were receiving child support.

Debtor: I am, but I also owe child support, for a child from a previous marriage. I never paid because my ex never asked, but now he's seeking current support as well as $5,000 in back support.

Lawyer: How much will you owe?

Debtor: Under the court order, $300 a month.

Lawyer: Have you started paying the support?

Debtor: No. I have to start paying it next month.

Lawyer: If you decide to file for Chapter 13, you will have to remain current on your child support payments throughout the life of your plan. If you don't, your case will be dismissed or converted to a Chapter 7 bankruptcy.

Debtor: I understand.

Lawyer: Let's talk later about the back support you owe. When were you divorced?

Debtor: A couple of years ago.

Lawyer: Did you assume any of the debts in the course of your divorce?

Debtor: Yes, I assumed the credit card charges for personal expenses in exchange for my ex-husband's share of our home.

Lawyer: Okay. How much were these charges?

Debtor: About $3,000.

Lawyer: Hmmm, in a Chapter 7 bankruptcy, you can discharge this debt as regards to the creditor, but your ex can come after you for this debt if he is sued by the creditor. In Chapter 13 bankruptcy, the debt would be fully discharged, with respect to both the creditor and your ex.

Debtor: It sounds like I should probably file for Chapter 13.

Lawyer: Maybe, but we're not through yet. Let's talk about your other property. Other than your home, do you have any other property you would want to keep in your bankruptcy?

Debtor: Oh, yes. I have a concert piano and some copyright interests in several songs I wrote. Also, I have

a car I want to hold on to and the tools I use in my business.

Lawyer: How much are the tools worth?

Debtor: About $3,000.

Lawyer: Great. New Hampshire allows you to keep up to $5,000 worth of tools for your occupation, so those are exempt. How much is the car worth?

Debtor: About $4,000 according to *Kelley Blue Book.*

Lawyer: Are you making payments on it?

Debtor: Yes.

Lawyer: How much is left on your note?

Debtor: About $8,000.

Lawyer: When did you buy it?

Debtor: Three years ago.

Lawyer: If you file for Chapter 13, you can pay off the value of the car rather than what you still owe on the note. This is called a cramdown, and it's another great reason for you to file for Chapter 13. And it's a good thing you didn't buy your car more recently: You couldn't use this cramdown procedure if you had bought the car within 2½ years of your bankruptcy filing date.

Now let's take a look at the New Hampshire exemptions, to see whether your other property is covered. Remember, exemptions like the homestead exemption and the tools of your occupation exemption are laws that determine what property you can keep in your bankruptcy. As I read them, the car is covered because you owe more than it's worth, so your creditors wouldn't get anything if it were sold. Because you don't have any equity in the car, you don't need to protect it with an exemption. As for the piano and your copyright interests, there are no state exemptions that specifically cover those items.

Debtor: Does that mean I'll lose my piano?

Lawyer: Not necessarily. Remember, if you file for Chapter 13, you don't lose any property—you just have to make sure you pay your creditors at least what they would have received in a Chapter 7 case. This would be a lot less than the value of the piano, because of the trustee's commission and the costs of taking the piano, storing it, and selling it at auction. And even though New Hampshire doesn't specifically exempt pianos, it has a $3,500 exemption for all your furniture. So depending on your piano's value, it might be covered by the furniture exemption.

Debtor: I think my piano would sell for about $12,000 and I guess my copyrights are pretty much worthless.

Lawyer: Why do you say your copyright interests are worthless?

Debtor: Well, they belong to three songs I wrote, but I've never had the songs published, so there is no one to sell them to.

Lawyer: Okay, let's forget about the songs. We're only talking about the piano. Looking at the New Hampshire exemptions, in addition to the portion of the piano's value arguably covered by the furniture exemption—$3,500—there are also some "wildcard" exemptions. This type of exemption can be used to protect any property you choose. New Hampshire's wildcard exemptions will provide an additional $8,000 that you can put toward the piano: That takes into account a $1,000 straight wildcard, plus a $7,000 wildcard that you can use if you don't fully take advantage of certain other exemptions. If you use these wildcards for your piano, only about $500 of its value is not exempt. Because of the trustee's commission and the costs of selling the piano, your creditors probably wouldn't get any of the proceeds if you use Chapter 7. So the nonexempt portion of your piano's value will add little or nothing to the cost of your Chapter 13 plan.

Debtor: Okay.

Lawyer: Here is a copy of the New Hampshire exemptions. Other than the piano, do you have any property that exceeds the exemption limit or that isn't listed in the exemption list?

Debtor: No, the piano is the only problem. But if I use the furniture exemption for my piano, my furniture won't be exempt. It's old furniture I bought at the Goodwill. I have nothing that would be of any value.

Lawyer: Well, that's up to the trustee. If you choose to use the entire furniture exemption for your piano, you might have to place some value on your furniture equal to what it would cost you to replace it.

Debtor: That would probably be about $1,000.

Lawyer: Okay, so you would have about $1,500 worth of nonexempt property, total. That's under the New Hampshire state exemptions. Some state allow a person to choose to use a different set of exemptions set out in the federal Bankruptcy Code termed the "federal exemptions." As it turns out, New Hampshire does allow use of the federal exemptions as an alternative to the New Hampshire state exemptions. You can choose from the federal exemption list or from the New Hampshire state list, but you can't mix or match.

Let's take a look and see if the federal exemptions would do you any good. The federal exemptions protect only $21,625 in your home equity. You have $50,000 equity to protect, so you wouldn't want to choose the federal exemptions.

So, we know you can file for Chapter 7 bankruptcy if you wish. You could keep your home and probably your piano, even though it isn't completely exempt. The cost of collecting and storing the piano, then selling it at auction, would probably be more than $500—the nonexempt portion—which means there wouldn't be anything left after selling it to pay to your unsecured creditors. If you had to use part of the furniture exemption for other pieces of furniture, however, $1,500 of the value of your piano would be nonexempt. If that were the case, the trustee might decide to take it and sell it, giving you the exempt amount and paying the rest to your unsecured creditors. Or, you could keep the piano if the trustee was willing to sell it to you for a negotiated price. Because the trustee would probably have to pay about $1,000 to sell it, you might be able to keep it by paying the trustee $500. But that's all in a Chapter 7 bankruptcy.

Debtor: It's still sounding to me like Chapter 13 is a good idea. But you said I have to make sure I'm eligible. What are the requirements?

Lawyer: Before we get to that, I have a couple more questions.

Debtor: Okay.

Lawyer: During the previous year, have you made payments on any loans you owe to relatives?

Debtor: Nope.

Lawyer: Good. If you had, the trustee might require the relative to return the money so it could be added to the amount your creditors would get.

Debtor: I wouldn't want that to happen.

Lawyer: Have you given away or sold any property to anyone within the past two years?

Debtor: No.

Lawyer: That also simplifies things. If you had given away some property, or you had sold some property for less than what it was worth, the difference in value might be considered nonexempt property. You'd have to add that to the amount you have to pay under your Chapter 13 plan. But you didn't sell any property, so this rule doesn't affect you.

Debtor: Wow, there's a lot to consider here. Are we done—isn't it clear that Chapter 13 is the right route for me?

Lawyer: Bear with me, just a few more issues to consider. Chapter 13 has some limitations on how much debt you can owe in order to be eligible. Let's see, you owe a total of $70,000 of unsecured debt—a $40,000 bank loan, $23,000 in credit card debts, $5,000 in child support arrearage, and $2,000 other debts. You owe a total of $108,000 secured debt (your home and car). This means you fall within the eligibility guidelines, which are $1,081,400 for secured debts and $360,475 for unsecured debts.

Debtor: That's good.

Lawyer: Now, let's see what debts you would have to pay in your Chapter 13 bankruptcy. Some debts have to be paid in full while others can be paid in part, depending on your income. Let's start with administrative expenses, which consist of part of my attorneys' fees and the trustee's fee. My total fees for a Chapter 13 bankruptcy are $3,000. I will need $1,500 up front and you can pay me the additional $1,500 through your plan. You'll also have to pay the trustee a fee, which is roughly 10% of whatever is paid out over the course of your plan. So, before we can know how much the trustee's fee will be, we'll need to figure out how much your plan will pay out.

Debtor: What happens to my credit card debts and my SBA loan?

Lawyer: That will depend on how much income you have left over after deducting your living expenses. If you'll have no income left over, you won't be able to file a Chapter 13 bankruptcy. If you'll have enough extra income to pay the debts that must be paid off in a Chapter 13 bankruptcy, but you won't have enough income to pay off any of your credit card debts or SBA loan, then those debts will be discharged at the end

of your Chapter 13 without your paying a cent. This is what's known as a "zero percent" plan. Some judges refuse to confirm "zero percent" plans, so I can't tell you for sure what would happen in your particular case.

Debtor: So what are the mandatory debts that must be paid through the plan?

Lawyer: We start with the $5,000 child support arrears, which must be paid in full. Plus, you might have to pay a portion of the $1,500 nonexempt equity in your piano as well as my fee. Those items total $8,000. If that's all you'll have to pay under your plan, the trustee's fee would be $800, which means the total amount you'd have to pay through your plan would be $8,800. This amount might be a little less (depending on what you work out with the trustee about the piano) or perhaps a bit more if your bankruptcy judge makes you pay your car note through the plan because you are cramming it down. And, of course, if your disposable income is high enough to repay some of your unsecured debt in addition to the mandatory debts, then the total amount would be even higher.

Debtor: How can I tell whether I have enough income to meet the Chapter 13 requirements?

Lawyer: If you decide to file for Chapter 13 bankruptcy, you have to fill out some forms to determine your income and your expenses. These forms will basically show whether you can afford a Chapter 13 bankruptcy. If you don't have enough income to pay all necessary debts in three years, you can ask the judge to let you propose a five-year plan, so you can pay less each month.

Debtor: So, do you suggest that I file for Chapter 7? Or should I use Chapter 13?

Lawyer: As long as you have enough income left over in your budget to use Chapter 13, that would be an excellent choice for you because:

- It will protect your codebtor—your mother—for the life of the plan.
- It will allow you to keep your car and pay it off at market value rather than reaffirming the current note, which is twice what it's worth.
- Unlike Chapter 7, it fully discharges the credit card debts you assumed in your divorce.

- Unlike Chapter 7, it will allow you to discharge the credit card debts you incurred to pay off your taxes.
- It will allow you to pay off your child support arrearage—that is, the back child support you owe—over the life of your plan, without worrying about wage garnishments and bank levies.

So, assuming you have enough income to propose a confirmable Chapter 13 plan and pay my fees, I recommend Chapter 13. If you can't propose a confirmable Chapter 13 plan, even over a five-year period, you might consider filing a Chapter 7 bankruptcy. It won't discharge your child support debt, and you can't cram down your car note. And you'll still owe the debt you assumed in your divorce, but you will be able to discharge all of your credit card debt and the SBA loan, as well as any other miscellaneous unsecured debts that you owe, and you'll be able to keep your home and your car as long as you remain current on your payments. If you hired me to represent you, my fees would be $1,500 up front, but that's all, plus the court filing fee of $306 and about $100 for prefiling and postfiling mandatory counseling sessions. And, if you wanted, you could probably represent yourself (and save yourself my $1,500 fee). Nolo publishes a great book called *How to File for Chapter 7 Bankruptcy*, which provides step-by-step instructions for filling out the official forms, which you can get off the Internet.

Filing for Chapter 13 Bankruptcy

Complete Your Bankruptcy Forms

In this chapter, we review the Chapter 13 bankruptcy petition as well as the schedules and other forms you will have to file for your Chapter 13 case (except for your repayment plan, which is covered in Ch. 8).

We discuss the purpose of each form, the type of information required, and legal issues to consider when completing the forms. Your bankruptcy attorney will prepare the forms for you, but it's important to know what information must be disclosed in a Chapter 13 bankruptcy, and why. This knowledge will help you:

- prepare for your first visit with your lawyer
- make decisions with your lawyer about how to proceed, and
- ensure that your petition is accurate and complete.

Required Forms, Fees, and Where to File

Here's a quick rundown of the official bankruptcy forms, fees to file your case, special local requirements, and where to file your petition.

Filing in the Right Bankruptcy Court

Because bankruptcy is a creature of federal, not state, law, you must file for bankruptcy in a special federal court. There are federal bankruptcy courts all over the country.

The federal court system divides the country into judicial districts. Every state has at least one judicial district; most have more. You can file in either:

- the district where you have been living for the greater part of the 180-day period before you file, or
- the district where you are domiciled—that is, where you maintain your home, even if you have been living elsewhere temporarily (such as on a military base).

Bankruptcy Filing Fees

The total fee to file for Chapter 13 bankruptcy is $281. Fees change, however. Your local bankruptcy attorney will have the up-to-date figures, or check with the court. This fee is due upon filing, unless you qualify for a waiver of fees or obtain court permission to pay in installments. Chapter 13 filers seldom qualify for

either of these remedies, since the income level that is necessary to file a Chapter 13 is usually higher than the level of income required to qualify for a waiver or installment payments.

Required Bankruptcy Forms

Bankruptcy uses official forms prescribed by the federal office of the courts. These are the standard forms that must be filed in every Chapter 13 bankruptcy:

- ☐ Form 1—*Voluntary Petition*
- ☐ Form 6, which consists of:
  - ☐ Schedule A—*Real Property*
  - ☐ Schedule B—*Personal Property*
  - ☐ Schedule C—*Property Claimed as Exempt*
  - ☐ Schedule D—*Creditors Holding Secured Claims*
  - ☐ Schedule E—*Creditors Holding Unsecured Priority Claims*
  - ☐ Schedule F—*Creditors Holding Unsecured Nonpriority Claims*
  - ☐ Schedule G—*Executory Contracts and Unexpired Leases*
  - ☐ Schedule H—*Codebtors*
  - ☐ Schedule I—*Current Income of Individual Debtor(s)*
  - ☐ Schedule J—*Current Expenditures of Individual Debtor(s)*
  - ☐ *Summary of Schedules A through J*
  - ☐ *Declaration Concerning Debtor's Schedules*
- ☐ Form 7—*Statement of Financial Affairs*
- ☐ Form 21—*Statement of Social Security Number*
- ☐ Form 22C—*Chapter 13 Statement of Current Monthly Income and Calculation of Commitment Period and Disposable Income*
- ☐ Form 201A—*Notice to Individual Consumer Debtor Under §342 of the Bankruptcy Code*
- ☐ Attorney Fee Disclosure Under Rule 2016
- ☐ Mailing Matrix
- ☐ Chapter 13 repayment plan (covered in Ch. 8), and
- ☐ required local forms, if any.

With the exception of Form 22C, which requires you to some math, the forms addressed in this chapter are fairly straightforward.

All together, these forms usually are referred to as your "bankruptcy petition," although technically your petition is only Form 1. (In case you're wondering, Forms 2, 4, and 5 aren't used in voluntary Chapter 13 bankruptcy filings. Form 3 is an application to pay the filing fee in installments, which Chapter 13 filers generally won't file since they won't qualify.)

Where to Get the Official Forms

You can find copies of the official bankruptcy forms on the website of the United States Courts at www. uscourts.gov/FormsAndFees/Forms/BankruptcyForms. aspx. You may want to take a look at the forms as we describe each one in this chapter, or review them before you visit an attorney.

Your bankruptcy attorney will have software for completing all of the official forms.

Local Forms and Requirements

In addition to the official forms that every bankruptcy court uses, your local bankruptcy court may require you to file one or two additional forms that it has developed. Your local bankruptcy court may also have special requirements or rules for filing your petition. Your bankruptcy attorney should have the local court forms and be familiar with what your local court requires. You can also get these forms and requirements from the bankruptcy court clerk.

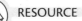 **RESOURCE**
Finding your local bankruptcy court's website. Go to www.justice.gov/courtlinks for a list of links to local courts. Or try http://www.uscourts.gov/court_locator.aspx.

Things to Think About When Reviewing the Forms

Here are some things to keep in mind as you provide your attorney with the necessary information to complete the forms or review the forms completed by your attorney.

Be ridiculously thorough. Always err on the side of giving too much information to your attorney and the court, rather than too little. If you leave information out, the bankruptcy trustee may become suspicious of your motives. If you leave creditors off the forms, the debts you owe these creditors won't be discharged—hardly the result you would want. If you intentionally or carelessly fail to list all your property and debts, or fail to accurately describe your recent property transactions, the court, upon a request by the trustee, may rule that you acted with fraudulent intent. It may deny your bankruptcy discharge altogether.

Don't worry about repetition. Sometimes different forms—or different questions on the same form—may ask for the same or overlapping information. Your attorney may provide the same information multiple times—too much information is never a sin in bankruptcy.

Be scrupulously honest. As part of your official bankruptcy paperwork, you must complete declarations, under penalty of perjury, swearing that you've been truthful. It's important to realize that you could be prosecuted for perjury if it's evident that you deliberately lied. Carefully review all forms completed by your attorney before you sign them.

For Married Filers

If you are married, you and your spouse will have to decide whether one of you should file alone or whether you should file jointly. To make this decision, you'll first have to make sure that you're married in the eyes of the federal law (a trickier issue than you might think), and then consider how filing together or separately will affect your debts and property.

Are You Married?

If you are married to a partner of the opposite sex, and you were married with a valid state license, you are married for purposes of filing a joint petition—and you can skip down to "Should You File Jointly?" below. However, if you were not married with a license and ceremony, or if you are married to a same-sex partner, read on.

Common Law Marriage

Some states allow heterosexual couples to establish "common law" marriages, which the states will recognize as valid marriages even though the couples do not have a state marriage license or certificate. Contrary to popular belief, a common law marriage is not created when two people simply live together for a certain number of years. In order to have a valid common law marriage, the couple must do all of the following:

- live together for a significant period of time (not defined in any state)
- hold themselves out as a married couple—typically this means using the same last name, referring to the other as "my husband" or "my wife," and filing a joint tax return, and
- intend to be married.

Alabama, Colorado, the District of Columbia, Georgia, Idaho, Iowa, Kansas, Montana, New Hampshire (but only for inheritance purposes), Ohio, Oklahoma, Pennsylvania, Rhode Island, South Carolina, Texas, and Utah recognize some form of common law marriage, but the rules for what constitutes a marriage differ from state to state. Several of these states will only recognize common law marriages that were created before a certain date.

If you live in one of these states and you meet your state's requirements for a common law marriage, you have the option to file jointly, if you wish.

Same-Sex Marriage

If you married your same-sex partner in a state, country, or province that recognizes same-sex marriage, you may be wondering if you can file for bankruptcy together with your spouse.

Until recently, same-sex married couples were not allowed to file a joint bankruptcy petition, primarily because of the federal Defense of Marriage Act or DOMA (1 U.S.C. § 7 and 28 U.S.C. § 1738C). DOMA states that the federal government does not recognize same-sex marriage and that states may disregard such marriages performed in other states.

However, recent events have signified big changes in this area of the law. In June 2011, a bankruptcy opinion, signed by 20 of the 24 bankruptcy judges in the Central District of California, allowed a same-sex couple who legally married in California in 2008 to file a joint petition for Chapter 13 bankruptcy. (*In re Balas and Morales*, 449 B.R. 567 (C.D.Cal. 2011).) In the written opinion, the court declared that DOMA was

unconstitutional. Shortly after the *Balas* decision, the U.S. Department of Justice announced that it would no longer oppose joint bankruptcies filed by same-sex couples legally married in their state.

Despite these recent events, however, it's still up in the air how different courts and districts will treat joint petitions filed by same-sex married couples. If you are considering filing a joint bankruptcy petition with your same-sex spouse, talk to an attorney who is familiar with these issues.

RESOURCE

Get the latest news on same-sex marriage and bankruptcy. The list of states that recognize same-sex marriage is changing every year, and legal issues involving same-sex couples (including in bankruptcy) are evolving rapidly. To get the latest news on same-sex couples in bankruptcy, check Nolo's Bankruptcy, Debt, and Foreclosure Blog. For other legal news affecting same-sex couples and LGBT folks, check Queer Justice: Nolo's LGBT Law Blog. Both blogs are found at www.nolo.com.

Should You File Jointly?

Unfortunately, there is no simple formula that will tell you whether it's better to file alone or with your spouse. In the end, it will depend on which option allows you to discharge more of your debts and keep more of your property. Here are some of the factors you and your attorney should consider:

- If you are living in a community property state and most of your debts were incurred, and your property acquired, during marriage, you should probably file jointly. Even if only one spouse files, all community property is considered part of the bankruptcy estate—and any of the property that is nonexempt will determine the amount that nonpriority unsecured creditors will be paid (see Ch. 5 for more information). The same is generally true for debts—that is, all community debts must be listed and most will be dealt with in the repayment plan even though only one spouse files.
- If you have recently married, you haven't acquired any valuable assets as a married couple, and one of you has all the debts, it may make sense

for that spouse to file for bankruptcy alone (especially if the nonfiling spouse has good credit to protect).

- You may want to file alone if you and your spouse own property as tenants by the entirety, most of the debts are in your own name, and you live in a state that excludes such property from the bankruptcy estate when one spouse files. This is a particularly important consideration if your home would be nonexempt property if both spouses filed—that could push the level of payment to your nonpriority unsecured creditors past the point that you could afford to pay in your repayment plan.
- If the exemption system you are using allows married spouses to double their exemptions, filing jointly may reduce the amount you would have to pay to your nonpriority unsecured creditors.
- If you are still married but separated, you may have to file alone if your spouse won't cooperate. Still, if your debts and property are joint rather than separate, a joint filing would probably be to your best advantage.

Form 1—*Voluntary Petition*

The voluntary petition (Official Form 1) provides the court with basic information about you, where you live, and your bankruptcy case. It also lets the court know if you have completed the required prebankruptcy credit counseling or if you qualify for an exception to the requirement.

Here are a few other tidbits you'll have to provide on the voluntary petition:

Nature of your debts. You must let the court know if your debts are primarily consumer or business debts. Keep in mind that mortgages on personal residences are considered consumer debts, so homeowners will have primarily consumer debts. On the other hand, tax debts are considered business debts, so if you owe a lot of back taxes and don't have a mortgage, your debts may be primarily business debts.

Prior bankruptcy cases. You are required to disclose all prior bankruptcy cases filed by you (or your spouse if you're filing jointly) within the last eight years. You must also disclose any pending cases filed by your

spouse. (Ch. 3 discusses when previous bankruptcy discharges bar a current discharge.)

Information about a pending eviction. As explained in Ch. 2, certain evictions are allowed to proceed after you file for bankruptcy, despite the automatic stay. The petition asks a series of questions to figure out whether your landlord has already gotten a judgment for possession (eviction order) and whether you might be able to postpone the eviction.

Exhibits to the Voluntary Petition

There are four additional forms, called exhibits, which make up the voluntary petition. The only one worthy of note is Exhibit D. This is where you tell the court that you've met the debt counseling requirement. (See Ch. 9 for more details on this requirement.)

Form 6—Schedules

"Form 6" refers to a series of schedules that provides the trustee and court with a picture of your current financial situation.

 CAUTION
Get the correct addresses for your creditors. On many of these schedules, you must provide your creditors' addresses. If the creditor has sent you something within the last 90 days, provide the address that the creditor listed as its "contact address" on at least two of those written communications. If the creditor hasn't written to you within the last 90 days, provide the address the creditor listed in its last two communications to you. If you no longer have the address of the original creditor, use the contact address of the most recent creditors on that debt—for instance, a collection agency or an attorney's office.

Schedule A—*Real Property*

Here your attorney will list all the real estate you own as of the date you'll file the petition.

The Definition of "Real Property"

Real property—land and things permanently attached to land—includes more than just a house.

It can also include unimproved land, vacation cabins, condominiums, duplexes, rental property, business property, mobile home park spaces, agricultural land, airplane hangars, and any other buildings permanently attached to land.

You may own real estate even if you can't walk on it, live on it, or get income from it. This might be true, for example, if:

- You own real estate solely because you are married to a spouse who owns real estate and you live in a community property state.
- Someone else lives on property that you are entitled to receive in the future under a trust agreement.

Your attorney will list leases and time-shares on a different schedule (Schedule G).

What Is Your Legal Interest in the Property?

Your attorney will also have to provide the legal definition for the interest you (or you and your spouse) have in each piece of real estate. The most common type of interest—outright ownership—is called "fee simple." Even if you still owe money on your mortgage, as long as you have the right to sell the house, leave it to your heirs, and make alterations, your ownership is fee simple. A fee simple interest may be owned by one person or by several people jointly. Normally, when people are listed on a deed as the owners—even if they own the property as joint tenants, tenants in common, or tenants by the entirety—the ownership interest is in fee simple. Other types of real property interests include:

- **Life estate.** This is the right to possess and use property only during your lifetime. You can't sell the property, give it away, or leave it to someone when you die. Instead, when you die, the property passes to whomever was named in the instrument (trust, deed, or will) that created your life estate. This type of ownership is usually created when the sole owner of a piece of real estate wants a surviving spouse to live on the property for the rest of his or her life, but then have the property pass to the owner's children. In this situation, the surviving spouse has a life estate. Surviving spouses who are beneficiaries of AB, spousal, or marital bypass trusts have life estates.

- **Future interest.** This is your right to own property sometime in the future. A common future interest is owned by a person who—under the terms of a deed or an irrevocable trust—will inherit the property when its current possessor dies. Simply being named in a will or revocable living trust doesn't create a future interest, because the person who signed the deed or trust can amend the document to cut you out.

- **Contingent interest.** This ownership interest doesn't come into existence unless one or more conditions are fulfilled. Wills sometimes leave property to people under certain conditions. If the conditions aren't met, the property passes to someone else. For instance, Emma's will leaves her house to John, provided that he takes care of her until her death. If John doesn't care for Emma, the house passes to Emma's daughter Jane. Both John and Jane have contingent interests in Emma's home.

- **Lienholder.** If you are the holder of a mortgage, deed of trust, judgment lien, or mechanics' lien on real estate, you have an ownership interest in the real estate.

- **Easement holder.** If you are the holder of a right to travel on or otherwise use property owned by someone else, you have an easement.

- **Power of appointment.** If you have a legal right, given to you in a will or transfer of property, to sell a specified piece of someone's property, that's called a power of appointment and should be listed.

- **Beneficial ownership under a real estate contract.** This is the right to own property by virtue of having signed a binding real estate contract. Even though the buyer doesn't yet own the property, the buyer does have a "beneficial interest"— that is, the right to own the property once the formalities are completed. For example, property buyers have a beneficial ownership interest in property while the escrow is pending.

Valuing Your Real Property

You'll have to provide the court with the actual value of your real estate ownership interest. Your attorney will help you do this. But if your ownership is the usual "fee simple," and you want to get a head start, or a good estimate, you can compare it to similar real estate parcels in your neighborhood that have recently sold (comparables). You can also get information about the value of your real estate from websites such as www.homevalues.com, www.zillow.com, www.domania.com, www.homeradar.com, and http://list.realestate.yahoo.com/re/homevalues.

If you own the property with someone else who is not joining you in your bankruptcy, your attorney will list only your ownership share. And if your ownership interest is one of the unusual types, like a life estate, the value of that interest will have to be set by a real estate appraiser.

Mobile Home Note

If you own a mobile home in a park, use the value of the mobile home in its current location. Many parks are located in desirable areas, and the park adds value to the mobile home even though you may not have any ownership interest in the park itself. A mobile home that may not be worth much on its own could be worth quite a bit if it's sitting in a fancy park.

Mortgages, Liens, and Other Debts Secured by the Property

Your attorney will also list all mortgages, deeds of trust, home equity loans, liens (judgment liens, mechanics' liens, materialman's liens, tax liens, or the like) that are claimed against the property.

If you don't know the balance on your mortgage, deed of trust, or home equity loan, call the lender. Your attorney can help you find out the existence and values of liens recorded against your property. Or your attorney may order a title search which will identify the existence of liens. If you are trying to get this information before visiting an attorney, you can visit the land records office in your county and look up the parcel in the records; the clerk can show you how.

 TIP

You might be able to get rid of liens. If you have liens on your property that are no longer secured by your equity in the property, you may be able to strip them off and reduce the amount of your current mortgage expense. For example, if your property is worth $250,000, and you owe $250,000 or more on your first mortgage, any other liens listed here can be "stripped off" in your Chapter 13 bankruptcy and reclassified as unsecured debt. If your total mortgage payment is $2,500, and $1,750 of that is attributable to your first mortgage, you can reduce your mortgage payment by the remaining $750, which will make a Chapter 13 plan more feasible. (For more on lien stripping, see Ch. 1.)

Schedule B—*Personal Property*

Here your attorney will list and value all of your personal property, including property that is security for a debt and property that is exempt. Schedule B also lists the address where each piece of property is located. A few things to keep in mind:

Be honest and thorough. Don't give in to the temptation to "forget" any of your assets. Bankruptcy law doesn't give you the right to decide that an asset isn't worth mentioning. Even if, for example, you've decided that your CD collection is worthless given the advent of the iPod, you still have to list it. You can explain on the form why you think it's worthless. If you omit something and get caught, your case can be dismissed—or your discharge revoked—leaving you with no bankruptcy relief for your current debts.

Use the property's replacement value. When estimating your property's worth, use the replacement value—what it would cost to purchase the property from a retail vendor, given its age and condition.

Type of Property That Will Be Listed on Schedule B

Your attorney will probably ask you to fill out a detailed questionnaire with lots of categories for property. In addition to the usual suspects (personal goods, real estate, cars, and the like), here are some other things that count as property:

- **Cash on hand, money in financial accounts.** Be sure to explain the source of any money—for example, from wages, Social Security payments, or child support. This helps in figuring out whether any of this money qualifies as exempt property.

- **Education IRAs and qualified state tuition plans.** They may not be part of the bankruptcy estate, but tell your attorney about them anyway.
- **ERISA-qualified pension plans, IRAs, and 401(k)s.** Although probably not part of your bankruptcy estate, tell your attorney about them anyway.
- **Stock options.**
- **Accounts receivable.** If you are a sole proprietor or an independent contractor, you likely will be owed money by one or more of your customers. These debts belong to your bankruptcy estate as of your filing date, and may be used by the trustee to compute payments to your nonpriority, unsecured creditors under your plan unless you are able to claim them as exempt.
- **Child support or alimony arrears**—that is, money that should have been paid to you but hasn't been.
- **Debts owed you from a property settlement incurred in a divorce or dissolution.**
- **Money owed to you and not yet paid,** including judgments you've obtained.
- **"Equitable or future interests."** This is property owned by someone else that sooner or later you will get. For instance, if your parents' irrevocable trust gives you their home when they die, you have an "equitable interest" in the home while they're alive.
- **Contingent interests in property.** For example, you are named the remainder beneficiary of an irrevocable trust (a trust that can't be undone by the person who created it). It's contingent because you may or may not get anything from the trust—it all depends on whether there's anything left by the time it gets to you. This includes wills or revocable living trusts that name you as a beneficiary. Even though you don't have an absolute right to inherit under these documents (they can be changed at any time prior to the person's death), the trustee wants to know this information. An inheritance becomes part of your bankruptcy estate if the person dies within the six-month period following your bankruptcy filing date—and can result in your plan being

modified to increase payments to your nonpriority unsecured creditors.

- **Claims that you have against others that might end up in a lawsuit.** For instance, if you were recently rear-ended in an automobile accident and are struggling with whiplash, you may have a cause of action against the other driver (and that driver's insurer). If you fail to list this type of claim, you might not be allowed to pursue it after bankruptcy.
- **Intellectual property,** such as patents, copyrights, and trademarks.
- **Licenses and franchises.**
- **Customer lists.**
- **Crops.**

Schedule C—*Property Claimed as Exempt*

On this form, your attorney will list all your property that is legally exempt. In most bankruptcies filed by individuals, all—or virtually all—of the debtor's property is exempt. If, however, you have any property that is not exempt, you will have to pay your nonpriority, unsecured creditors at least what they would have received from the sale of this property if you had used Chapter 7 (see Ch. 5 for more information).

On the form you will state which exemption system you wish to use. If you live in one of the states that allows you to use the federal exemptions (below), you and your attorney will decide which system is better for you—the state exemptions or the federal exemptions. See Ch. 5 for information on residency requirements for using a state's exemptions and tips on how to choose between the federal and state exemption systems. As explained in Ch. 5, if you are living in a state that offers the federal exemption system, but you haven't been there long enough to meet the two-year residency requirement for the state exemptions, you can choose the federal system.

Note that if you didn't acquire your home at least 40 months before filing, and you didn't purchase it from the proceeds of selling a home in the same state, your homestead exemption may be capped at $146,450 regardless of the exemption available in the state where your home is located. (See Ch. 5 for detailed information on the homestead exemption cap.)

Bankruptcy law allows married couples to double all exemptions unless the state expressly prohibits it. That means that each of you can claim the entire amount of each exemption, if you are both filing and your state permits it.

States That Offer the Federal Exemptions		
Arkansas	New Hampshire	Rhode Island
Connecticut	New Jersey	Texas
Hawaii	New Mexico	Vermont
Massachusetts	New York	Washington
Michigan	Pennsylvania	Wisconsin
Minnesota		

Schedule D—*Creditors Holding Secured Claims*

In this schedule, your attorney will list all creditors who hold claims secured by your property. These include:

- holders of a mortgage or deed of trust on your real estate
- creditors who have won lawsuits against you and recorded judgment liens against your property
- doctors or lawyers to whom you have granted a security interest in the outcome of a lawsuit, so that the collection of their fees would be postponed (the expected court judgment is the collateral)
- contractors who have filed mechanics' or materialmen's liens on your real estate
- taxing authorities, such as the IRS, that have obtained tax liens against your property
- creditors with either a purchase-money or nonpurchase-money security agreement (see "What is the Nature of the Lien" below), and
- all parties who are trying to collect a secured debt, such as collection agencies and attorneys.

If you originally had a secured debt but the collateral was repossessed or foreclosed prior to your bankruptcy filing, the remaining debt is no longer secured and you should list it on Schedule F (see below).

When Credit Card Debt Is Secured

Most credit card debts, including a card issued by a bank, gasoline company, or department store, are unsecured and will be listed on Schedule F. Some department stores, however, claim to retain a security interest in all durable goods, such as furniture, appliances, electronics equipment, and jewelry, bought using the stores credit cards. Also, if you were issued a bank or store credit card as part of a plan to restore your credit, you may have had to post property or cash as collateral for debts incurred on the card. If either of these exceptions applies to you, you'll list the credit card debt on Schedule D.

What Is the Nature of the Lien?

You will also have to list the type of lien held by the creditor. Your attorney will help you figure this out, but here are the possible answers:

- **First mortgage.** You took out a loan to buy your house. (This is a specific kind of purchase-money security interest.)
- **Purchase-money security interest.** You took out a loan to purchase the property that secures the loan—for example, a car note. The creditor must have perfected the security interest by filing or recording it with the appropriate agency within 20 days. (*Fidelity Financial Services, Inc. v. Fink*, 522 U.S. 211 (1998).) Otherwise, the creditor has no lien and your attorney will list the debt on Schedule F (unsecured debt) instead.
- **Nonpossessory, nonpurchase-money security interest.** You borrowed money for a purpose other than buying the collateral. This includes refinanced home loans, home equity loans, or loans from finance companies.
- **Possessory, nonpurchase-money security interest.** This is what a pawnshop owner has when you pawn your property.
- **Judgment lien.** This means someone sued you, won a court judgment, and recorded a lien against your property.
- **Tax lien.** This means a federal, state, or local government agency recorded a lien against your property for unpaid taxes.

- **Child support lien.** This means that another parent or a government agency has recorded a lien against your property for unpaid child support.
- **Mechanics' or materialmen's lien.** This means someone performed work on your real property or personal property (for example, a car) but didn't get paid, and recorded a lien on that property. Such liens can be an unpleasant surprise if you paid for the work, but your contractor didn't pay a subcontractor who got a lien against your property.

CAUTION

Only "perfected" liens count. Every state has a law specifying the procedures that must be followed to make a mortgage or another secured agreement or lien valid (called perfecting the lien). If a lien is not properly recorded, or the document creating the lien is defective (because of a faulty notarization on a deed of trust, for instance), it won't count as a lien in bankruptcy. And liens that have not been perfected won't reduce your equity in your home. So, if you are counting on a lien to bring your equity within the exemption amount for your state, make sure the lien has been perfected through recording and proper notarization.

Is the Claim Contingent, Unliquidated, or Disputed?

You also have to note whether a particular claim is contingent, unliquidated, or disputed. If you have any such claims, be sure to tell your attorney about them. Here's what each of these terms means.

- **Contingent.** The claim depends on some event that hasn't yet occurred and may never occur. For example, if you cosigned a secured loan, you won't be liable unless the principal debtor defaults. Your liability as cosigner is contingent upon the default.
- **Unliquidated.** This means that a debt may exist, but the exact amount hasn't been determined. For example, say you've sued someone for injuries you suffered in an auto accident, but the case isn't over. Your lawyer has taken the case under a contingency fee agreement—the lawyer will get a third of the recovery if you win, and nothing

if you lose—and has a security interest in the final recovery amount. The debt to the lawyer is unliquidated because you don't know how much, if anything, you'll win.

- **Disputed.** A claim is disputed if you and the creditor do not agree about the existence or amount of the debt. For instance, suppose the IRS says you owe $10,000 and has put a lien on your property, and you say you owe $500. List the full amount of the lien, not the amount you think you owe.

TIP

You're not admitting you owe the debt by listing it in your petition. You may think you don't really owe a contingent, unliquidated, or disputed debt, or you may not want to "admit" that you owe the debt. By listing a debt on this schedule, however, you aren't admitting anything. Instead, you are making sure that, if you owe the debt after all, it will be discharged in your bankruptcy (if it is dischargeable).

Schedule E—*Creditors Holding Unsecured Priority Claims*

Schedule E identifies certain creditors who—with the exception of child support claims assigned to a government agency—are entitled to be paid in full in your Chapter 13 case.

Here is a list of priority claims.

- **Domestic support obligations.**
- **Wages, salaries, and commissions owed by you (as an employer) to a** current or former employee that was earned within 180 days before you filed your petition or within 180 days of the date you ceased your business. In certain circumstances, this also includes money owed to an independent contractor who did work for you. Only the first $11,725 owed per employee or independent contractor is a priority debt.
- **Contributions to employee benefit plans if you are an employer.**
- **Money owed to a grain producer or U.S. fisherman for fish or fish products if you are a farmer or fisherman.** Only the first $5,775 owed per person is a priority debt.

- **Deposits by individuals.** If you took money from people who planned to purchase, lease, or rent goods or services from you that you never delivered, you may owe a priority debt. For the debt to qualify as a priority, the goods or services had to have been planned for personal, family, or household use. Only the first $2,600 owed (per person) is a priority debt.
- **Taxes and certain other debts owed to governmental units,** such as unsecured back taxes or fines imposed for driving under the influence of drugs or alcohol. Not all tax debts are unsecured priority claims. For example, if the IRS has recorded a lien against your real property, and the equity in your property fully covers the amount of your tax debt, your debt is a secured debt and will be listed on Schedule D.
- **Claims** against you for death or personal injury resulting from your operation of a motor vehicle or vessel while intoxicated from using alcohol, a drug, or another substance. This priority doesn't apply to property damage—only to personal injury or death.

As in Schedule D, you'll have to note whether someone else can be legally forced to pay your debt to a priority creditor (this would be a codebtor).

Schedule F—*Creditors Holding Unsecured Nonpriority Claims*

In this schedule, your attorney will list all creditors you haven't listed in Schedules D or E. This will include debts that are or may be nondischargeable, such as a student loan. Even if you believe that you don't owe the debt or you owe only a small amount and intend to pay it off, you must include it here. It's essential that you list every creditor to whom you owe, or possibly owe, money. The only way you can legitimately leave off a creditor is if your balance owed is $0.

Inadvertent errors or omissions on this schedule can come back to haunt you. If you don't list a debt you owe to a creditor, it won't be discharged in your Chapter 13 bankruptcy. Also, leaving a creditor off the schedule might raise suspicions that you deliberately concealed information, perhaps to give that creditor preferential treatment in violation of bankruptcy rules.

Creditors That Are Often Overlooked

One debt may involve several different creditors. Remember to tell your lawyer about:

- your ex-spouse, if you are still obligated under a divorce decree or settlement agreement to pay joint debts, turn any property over to your ex, or make payments as part of your property division
- anyone who has cosigned a promissory note or loan application with you
- any holder of a loan or promissory note that you cosigned for someone else
- the original creditor, anybody to whom the debt has been assigned or sold, and any other person (such as a bill collector or attorney) trying to collect the debt, and
- anyone who might sue you in the future because of a car accident, business dispute, or the like.

Schedule G—*Executory Contracts and Unexpired Leases*

In this form, you list every executory contract or unexpired lease to which you're a party. "Executory" means the contract is still in force—that is, both parties are still obligated to perform important acts under it. Similarly, "unexpired" means that the contract or lease period hasn't run out—that is, it is still in effect.

Common examples of executory contracts and unexpired leases are:

- car leases
- residential leases or rental agreements
- business leases or rental agreements
- service contracts
- business contracts
- time-share contracts or leases
- contracts of sale for real estate
- personal property leases, such as equipment used in a beauty salon
- copyright and patent license agreements
- leases of real estate (surface and underground) for the purpose of harvesting timber, minerals, or oil
- future homeowners' association fee requirements

- agreements for boat docking privileges, and
- insurance contracts.

CAUTION

If you're behind in your payments. If you are not current on payments that were due under a lease or an executory contract, the delinquency should also be listed as a debt on Schedule D, E, or F.

What Happens to Executory Contracts and Unexpired Leases in Chapter 13 Bankruptcy?

The trustee has until the confirmation hearing on your plan (see Ch. 10) to decide whether an executory contract or unexpired lease should be assumed (continued in force) as property of the estate or terminated (rejected). As a general matter, most leases and contracts are liabilities and are rejected by the trustee.

If the trustee rejects the contract or lease, you can assume or reject the contract or lease in your Chapter 13 plan. If your plan rejects the lease or contract, you and the other parties to the agreement are cut loose from any obligations, and any money you owe the creditor will be treated as an unsecured debt in your plan, even if the debt arose after your filing date. For example, say you are leasing a car when you file for bankruptcy. You want out of the lease. The car dealer cannot repossess the car until the trustee rejects the lease, or you reject the lease in your plan. During that period, technically you can use the car without paying for it (although you will have to make "adequate protection" payments equal to your monthly payments, unless you have sufficient equity in the car to cover the value it will lose in depreciation while you're using it; see *In re Singer*, 368 B.R. 435 (E.D. Pa. 2007)). The payments you don't make during this period will be treated as an unsecured debt just as if they were incurred prior to your bankruptcy.

Bankruptcy law has special rules for executory contracts related to intellectual property (copyrights, patents, trademarks, or trade secrets), real estate, and time-share leases. If you are involved in one of these situations, discuss it with your lawyer.

Schedule H—*Codebtors*

In Schedules D, E, and F, you will identify those debts for which you have codebtors. You will also list those codebtors here. In addition, you must list the name and address of any spouse or former spouse who lived with you in Puerto Rico or in a community property state during the eight-year period immediately preceding your bankruptcy filing.

The most common codebtors are:

- cosigners
- guarantors (people who guarantee payment of a loan)
- ex-spouses with whom you jointly incurred debts before divorcing
- joint owners of real estate or other property
- coparties in a lawsuit
- nonfiling spouses in a community property state (most debts incurred in a community property state by a nonfiling spouse during marriage are considered community debts, making that spouse equally liable with the filing spouse for the debts), and
- nonfiling spouses in states other than community property states, for debts incurred by the filing spouse for basic living necessities such as food, shelter, clothing, and utilities.

In Chapter 13 bankruptcy, your codebtors will be responsible for whatever portion of the debts that are left after you complete your plan. For instance if the debt they cosigned on is $2,000, and you pay 50% of the debt in your Chapter 13 bankruptcy, they will be responsible for the remaining $1,000.

Schedule I—*Current Income of Individual Debtor(s)*

In this schedule, you calculate your current income (not your average monthly income in the six months before you file, which you calculated in Form 22C in Ch. 4).

You'll have to provide information about how many dependents you have, your current employment, and your income, including:

- estimated monthly gross income
- estimated monthly overtime pay

- payroll deductions
- income from the operation of a business or farm
- income from real property (real estate rentals, leases, or licenses, such as mineral exploration, oil, and the like)
- interest you receive from bank or security deposits and other investments, such as stocks
- payments from alimony, maintenance, and child support
- amounts you receive from Social Security, SSI, public assistance, disability payments, veterans' benefits, unemployment compensation, workers' compensation, or any other government benefit (although you don't have to report Social Security benefits on Form 22C, you do have to include them here—and some courts may consider them in determining how much you have to pay into your Chapter 13 plan every month)
- the value of any food stamps you receive
- pension or retirement income, and
- any other monthly income you receive on a regular basis (such as royalty payments or payments from a trust).

You will also be required to describe any increase or decrease in income reasonably anticipated to occur within the year following the filing of this schedule.

Three Different Income Figures

In your bankruptcy papers, you will report three different income figures.

- Your "current monthly income" in Form 22C (this is your average gross income for the six months before you file).
- Your actual income in Schedule I (this is your net income going forward).
- Your annual income in your *Statement of Financial Affairs* (see below).

The figures on Form 22C and Schedule I may be different. For example, if you lost your job a couple of months ago and now earn much less in your new job, your income on Schedule I will be less than it is on Form 22C.

RELATED TOPIC

How your income figures help determine your plan payment. See "If Your Actual Income Is Different From Your 'Current Monthly' Income: *Hamilton v. Lanning*" in Ch. 5 to learn how these various income figures help determine your Chapter 13 plan payment.

Schedule J—*Current Expenditures of Individual Debtor(s)*

Schedule J is discussed in Ch. 5. On it, you list your average monthly expenses and then describe any increases or decreases you anticipate might occur within the year after you file for bankruptcy.

Summary of Schedules

This form helps the bankruptcy trustee and judge get a quick look at your bankruptcy filing. It summarizes the figures you entered onto your schedules and then lists your total assets and total liabilities.

Declaration Concerning Debtor's Schedules

In this form, you are required to swear that everything you have said on your schedules is true and correct. Deliberate lying is a major sin in bankruptcy and could cost you your bankruptcy discharge, a fine of up to $500,000, and up to five years in prison.

Form 7—*Statement of Financial Affairs*

This provides detailed information about financial transactions made within certain time periods prior to your bankruptcy filing. You'll have to include information about things such as your employment and business income, payments to creditors, repossessions, foreclosures, lawsuits, wage attachments, garnishments, gifts, losses (for example from fire, theft, or gambling), property transfers, closed financial accounts, safe deposit boxes, and property you are holding for someone else. If you want to know the details, take a look at the form. Some of the items merit extra discussion, which you'll find below.

This information is required because under certain circumstances, the trustee may be entitled to take back property that you transferred to others prior to filing for bankruptcy and sell it for the benefit of your unsecured creditors. This rarely happens in Chapter 13 cases, however, unless a plan proposes to pay nonpriority, unsecured creditors only a small percentage of what is owed them.

> ! **CAUTION**
>
> **Be honest and complete.** Don't give in to the temptation to leave out a transfer or two, assuming that the trustee won't find or go after the property. You must sign this form under penalty of perjury. And, if the trustee or a creditor discovers that you left information out, your bankruptcy may be dismissed and you may be prosecuted.

Payments to creditors. When you list payments to creditors, you must distinguish between regular creditors and insiders. An insider is essentially a relative or close business associate. All other creditors are regular creditors.

If your debts are primarily consumer debts, you'll have to list all payments made to a regular creditor that total more than $600 if those payments were made to repay a loan, an installment purchase, or another debt during the 90 days before you file your bankruptcy petition.

If your debts are primarily business debts, you'll have to list all payments or other transfers made to a creditor within 90 days your bankruptcy filing if the payments involve property that is worth $5,850 or more.

Everyone (whether your debts are primarily consumer or business) will have to list all payments or other transfers made to an insider creditor within one year before filing the bankruptcy petition. This includes alimony and child support payments.

The purpose of these questions is to find out whether you have preferred any creditor over others. If you have paid a regular creditor during the 90 days before you file, or an insider during the year before you file, the value of the payment will be part of your bankruptcy estate and will not be considered exempt. Rather, you will have to pay your unsecured creditors at least the value of the amount you paid to these creditors before you filed for bankruptcy. Exceptions to this rule are payments you made toward a domestic support obligation (child support or alimony) or payments you made under an alternative repayment schedule arranged by an approved nonprofit budget and credit counseling agency.

Losses. If the loss was for an exempt item, most states also exempt the insurance proceeds, up to the exemption limit for the item. If the item was not exempt, the trustee is entitled to the insurance proceeds, if any. In either case, list any insurance proceeds you've received or expect to receive. If you experience a loss after you file, you should promptly amend your papers, as this question applies to losses both before you file and afterwards.

Payments related to debt counseling or bankruptcy. If you paid an improperly high fee to an attorney, bankruptcy petition preparer, a debt consultant, or a debt consolidator, the trustee may try to get some of it back to distribute to your creditors.

Other transfers. You must list all real and personal property that you've sold or given to someone else during the two years before you file for bankruptcy. Examples include selling or abandoning (junking) a car, pledging your house as security (collateral) for a loan, granting an easement on real estate, or trading property. This doesn't include gifts or property you've parted with as a regular part of your business or financial affairs.

Transfers to irrevocable trusts. You must list all transfers of your own property you have made in the previous ten years to an irrevocable trust that lists you as a beneficiary. These types of trusts—referred to as self-settled trusts—are commonly used by wealthy people to shield their assets from creditors and by disabled people to preserve their right to receive government benefits. In bankruptcy, however, assets placed in a self-settled trust will be considered nonexempt, which means you will have to pay your unsecured creditors at least the value of those assets. There is an exception that applies to assets placed in certain special needs trusts. (*In re Schultz,* 368 B.R 832 (D. Minn. 2007).)

Setoffs. A setoff is when a creditor, often a bank, uses money in a customer's account to pay a debt owed to the creditor by that customer. You must include any setoffs your creditors have made during the last 90 days.

Form 21—*Statement of Social Security Number*

This schedule requires you to list your full Social Security number. It will be available to your creditors and the trustee but, to protect your privacy, will not be part of your regular bankruptcy case file.

Form 22C—*Chapter 13 Statement of Current Monthly Income and Calculation of Commitment Period and Disposable Income*

In this form, you'll calculate your "disposable income" which will determine whether you have enough income to propose a confirmable plan and help determine what your monthly plan payments will be. By comparing your income to your state's median income, the form also calculates whether your plan will last three or five years.

More details about this form are found in Ch. 5.

Form 201A—*Notice to Individual Consumer Debtor Under §342(b) of the Bankruptcy Code*

This form, required by the new bankruptcy law, gives you some information about credit counseling and the various types of bankruptcy available. It also warns you sternly of the consequences of lying on your bankruptcy papers, concealing assets, and failing to file the required forms on time.

Attorney Fee Disclosure

Rule 2016(b) of the Bankruptcy Code requires that your attorney file a form disclosing the fees he or she is charging in your case. You might want to check the form to make sure what you are paying matches the fees listed on the form.

Mailing Matrix

As part of your bankruptcy filing, your attorney will submit a list of all of your creditors so the court can give them official notice of your bankruptcy. This is called the mailing matrix.

Income Deduction Order

Your bankruptcy court might require you to draft and submit an income deduction order with the rest of your Chapter 13 bankruptcy papers. This is an order the bankruptcy court sends to your employer. It requires the employer to automatically deduct your monthly repayment plan amount from your wages and send it to the bankruptcy court.

The Chapter 13 Plan

Your Chapter 13 plan is the cornerstone of your bankruptcy case. The plan tells the court and your creditors how you intend to repay your debts, including the total amount you will pay each month, how much each creditor will receive under your plan, and how long your plan will last. As we've discussed in earlier chapters, you will pay some of your creditors in full and others only a portion of what you owe them. Some creditors are entitled to be paid before other creditors. All of these details will be in your plan, along with some automatic conditions required by law (commonly termed "boilerplate").

Your repayment plan will control your financial life while your bankruptcy is pending. With a few exceptions, once the court confirms your plan, both you and your creditors are bound by its terms.

As we discussed in the beginning of this book, putting together a plan has become quite complicated. It's possible, but very difficult, to come up with a plan without using computer software. Even with software, experienced Chapter 13 bankruptcy attorneys often find it necessary to amend an original plan several times in the course of a Chapter 13 bankruptcy. For this reason, we no longer recommend that Chapter 13 filers go it alone. To get the best possible outcome in your case, it's almost always best to hire an attorney.

This chapter explains the basics of a Chapter 13 plan, so you know what you will be getting into should you choose to file for Chapter 13 bankruptcy.

What You Must Pay

To propose a plan that the judge will confirm, you must show that you will have sufficient income, after deducting allowed expenses, to pay certain debts in full over the life of your plan. Some of these debts must be paid through your Chapter 13 plan—that is, you must pay the trustee, who will then pay the creditor (after collecting a fee). Others may be paid outside of your plan.

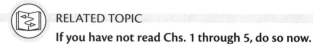 **RELATED TOPIC**

If you have not read Chs. 1 through 5, do so now. In order to understand what goes into your plan, you need to know the basic rules for calculating your income and expenses, how to classify your debts, which debts you have to repay in Chapter 13, and how to determine how long your plan will last. All of this information is explained in detail in Chs. 1 through 5.

How Long Your Plan Will Last

If your income is more than the median for your state and household size, your plan must last for five years (with a few exceptions). If your income is less than the median, your plan may last for only three years. If you are a lower-income filer and you don't have enough income to pay all mandatory debts within the three-year period, you can ask the court to extend your repayment time to five years. If you don't have enough income to pay your mandatory debts within five years, you can't propose a feasible Chapter 13 plan. (See Ch. 4 for more on calculating your base income and finding your state's median income.)

What You Must Pay Through Your Plan

At a minimum, you must pay all of the following debts through your Chapter 13 plan:

- all priority debts other than child support owed to a government agency
- all secured debts that are contractually due to end within the life of your plan, such as a home equity loan (if the debt is no longer secured when you file, you can strip off the lien and classify the debt as unsecured, then treat it just like your other unsecured debts)
- all other secured debts that aren't contractually due within the life of your plan (for example, a government tax lien on your property)
- any arrearage necessary to keep your home, car, or other secured property
- an amount equal to what your unsecured, non-priority creditors would have received if you had filed for Chapter 7 bankruptcy (you figured this out in Ch. 5 when you calculated the amount creditors would have received from the sale of your nonexempt property)
- all administrative expenses, including lawyer fees and trustee fees (trustee fees are usually about 10% of your plan payment), and
- all of your remaining income (called your "disposable" income).

The last category of debt—your disposable income—is often the most difficult figure to calculate. Essentially, you start with your income and subtract the following: living expenses, payments you'll make through the plan (listed above), and ongoing payments you'll make outside of the plan. There are lots of rules about what counts as income and what you can and cannot subtract for expenses. All of this is discussed in detail in Ch. 5.

What You Must Pay Either Through or Outside of Your Plan

As discussed above, there are certain payments that you must make through your plan. If a payment type is not listed above, you might be able to make it outside of the plan (that is, you pay the creditor directly rather than the trustee). Common examples include ongoing mortgage payments, ongoing car payments, and current expenses.

If you are required to make these payments through your Chapter 13 plan, you will have to pay significantly more over the life of your plan to cover the trustee's fee. The trustee gets 10% on all payments made through the plan, but gets nothing on payments made outside of the plan. If your current monthly mortgage payment is $2,000, the trustee would get 10% of your monthly payment, or $200 a month, if you paid through your plan. This amount is added to what you're already paying into the plan. Over the life of a five-year plan, paying your mortgage this way would require you to pay an extra $12,000. The lesson here is that it makes a huge difference whether you pay through or outside of the plan.

Obviously, you should try to pay outside of the plan if at all possible. Unfortunately, courts are split on whether mortgages must be paid through the plan. Ask your bankruptcy attorney about the policy in your local court. If you are paying an arrearage on a car note through the plan, you may also have to make the current payment through the plan. The same is true of other secured property for which you are using Chapter 13 to make up an arrearage. On the other hand, current payments for rent, utilities, Internet services, telephone, child support, taxes, and the like can—and should—be made outside of the plan.

Repayment of Unsecured Debts: Allowed Claims

Payments of unsecured debts under your Chapter 13 plan will be based on "allowed claims" filed by your creditors. After receiving notice of your bankruptcy, unsecured creditors that want a share of the payments you make under your plan must file a *Proof of Claim*. Once the creditor files a *Proof of Claim*, you or the trustee can object to the claim; you can argue that you don't really owe the claim or that you owe less than the creditor says, for example. (Objections to creditors' claims are covered briefly in Ch. 11.) The court will then decide which claims are allowed; creditors with allowed claims are entitled to share in the money you pay into your plan.

Which Creditors Must File a *Proof of Claim*

All unsecured creditors—whether you owe them priority or nonpriority debts—must file *Proofs of Claim* in order to be paid by the trustee. Only a secured creditor does not have to file a *Proof of Claim*

The deadline for filing a *Proof of Claim* is 90 days after the date set for the first meeting of creditors (Rule 3002). However, the confirmation hearing—at which the judge either confirms your repayment plan or sends you back to the drawing board to make changes—must be held between 20 and 45 days after the first meeting of creditors (or earlier, if the court approves). This means that a creditor could file a *Proof of Claim* after your plan is confirmed. Because of this scheduling oddity, you can't assume that your plan must include only those claims for which proofs have been filed.

Dealing With Unfiled Claims

If a creditor doesn't file a *Proof of Claim* within the deadline and you want that creditor to be paid in your plan, you'll have 30 days after the deadline to file a claim for the creditor. You might want to do this if, for example, the debt cannot be discharged in bankruptcy: By filing a *Proof of Claim,* you can make sure that at least part of the debt is paid off through your plan, so you won't owe as much when your bankruptcy case is over. (Ch. 11 covers filing *Proofs of Claim* on behalf of a creditor.)

Most likely your attorney will assume that all of your creditors will file *Proofs of Claim* in a timely manner when drafting your plan. This means your plan will include:

- payment in full to all secured creditors, except those with debts contractually lasting longer than your plan, such as a mortgage (these are the creditors listed in Schedule D, as explained in Ch. 7)
- payment in full to all priority creditors, except child support owed to a government agency (these are the creditors listed in Schedule E, as explained in Ch. 7), and
- payment in whole or in part to all unsecured, nonpriority creditors (these are the creditors listed in Schedule F, as explained in Ch. 7). Of course, the amounts these creditors receive depend on your disposable income; they each get a share of the amount of your payment that doesn't go to secured debt arrearages, priority debts, the trustee's fee, and so on.

Your plan will also state whether you intend to object to (that is, claim that you don't owe) any of the debts listed on Schedules D, E, or F. If one or more of those creditors don't file timely *Proofs of Claim,* you can either file *Proofs of Claim* on the creditors' behalf (see Ch. 11) or amend your plan to take those defaults into account.

Discharging Student Loans in Your Plan

Generally, student loans cannot be discharged in bankruptcy unless there is a separate hearing at which the debtor convinces the judge that repayment would constitute an undue hardship (typically, a difficult thing to prove). In the past, some bankruptcy courts have discharged student loans or the interest on student loans if they were included in a plan that proposed repayment in whole or in part, without a showing of undue hardship.

This practice was denounced in a recent U.S. Supreme Court decision, *United Student Aid Funds, Inc. v. Espinosa* (559 U.S. 130 S. Ct. 1367, 2010). In that case, the Court ruled that even if a student loan creditor does not object to the discharge of the student loan or fails to appear at the hearing on the issue, the bankruptcy court must still determine whether repayment would pose an undue hardship on the debtor.

The Parts of Your Plan

At the end of this chapter, you will find a sample plan. Many of the details for drafting a repayment plan (including the required format) are determined by individual bankruptcy districts and courts. However, the general rules for drafting a repayment plan are the same everywhere. Here we discuss the basic information that you'll find in all repayment plans.

Plan Payments

Your plan will indicate how much you will pay each month, what that money will be used for, and how long the repayment period will be.

Monthly payment amount. Usually the plan starts off with what you will pay to the trustee each month. All of the figures for coming up with this number will be included in various other sections of the plan.

> **TIP**
>
> **Your first plan payment.** You must make the first monthly plan payment to the trustee within 30 days after filing the petition. Failure to make this payment can result in dismissal of your Chapter 13 case.

Length of plan. Your plan will indicate how long the repayment period will be. (For more information, review Chs. 4 and 5.)

How much your unsecured, nonpriority creditors will get paid. Your plan will state how much you will pay to your nonpriority unsecured creditors. This is expressed as a percentage. For example, your plan might state that you will pay each nonpriority, unsecured creditor 18% of its total claim.

Other payments. Most plans contain boilerplate language stating that the trustee:

- can secure any amount of your future property or income to use in the event that claims are filed postpetition, and
- will get your tax refunds to add to the other payments you make under the plan. If your plan pays 100% of your unsecured creditors' claims then the trustee is not entitled to your tax refunds.

Adequate protection payments. Because a long time can elapse between your bankruptcy filing and your plan confirmation, secured creditors may demand a premium (called adequate protection payments) to protect their property interests before the plan is confirmed. The trustee typically pays these amounts out of your first plan payment. (See Ch. 10 for more information.)

Classification and Treatment of Claims

Your plan will list all of your debts according to category and calculate how much you will pay on each during your plan.

For example, your plan must classify and list:

Class 1—Priority claims. The plan will list the total amount due and the interest rate, if any. Usually you don't pay interest on priority debts. You might have to pay interest, however, if you signed a contract that requires interest.

Class 2—Secured claims. This class includes your mortgage. Usually, the plan indicates whether you will make payments directly to the creditor or to the trustee, who will then pay the creditor. The plan will also list any arrearages you owe on secured debts.

Class 3—Secured claims that must be paid in full under the plan. These are tax liens, mechanics' liens, judicial liens that can't be avoided, and secured claims that are to be paid in full under a contract that expires during the plan period. For example, if you owe $20,000 on a claim for a secured debt under a contract that will expire in three years, and you are drafting a five-year plan, the claim must be paid in full unless it qualifies for a cramdown (see Class 4, below).

You don't have to list secured claims that will outlive your plan—you can pay these on your own, to keep the trustee's fee down. If you owe an arrearage on any of these debts, your plan will list them as well.

Class 4—Secured debts on which you owe more than the value of the collateral. This is where you list loans you intend to cram down or liens you intend to strip. For example, you might owe $10,000 on a car that is worth only $6,000. In some cases, you can modify the claim so that the secured portion is reduced to the value of the property ($6,000 in this case). The rest of the claim ($4,000 in this example) is treated as an unsecured, nonpriority claim. As a general rule, you can't cram down your mortgage, but there are exceptions. Also, you might be able to strip off some second or third mortgages that are no longer secured by the property. (For details on how cramdowns and lien stripping work, see Ch. 1, "Special Chapter 13 Features: Cramdowns and Lien Stripping.")

Determining Interest Rates for Secured Debts in Chapter 13 Plans

In 2004, the U.S. Supreme Court announced a formula to be used in setting interest rates for secured claims other than mortgages in Chapter 13 cases. (*Till v. SCS Credit Corporation, 541 U.S 465 (2004).*) The Court said the rate should be the national prime rate, adjusted upward slightly for the additional risk of lending to a bankruptcy debtor. In that case, the risk was deemed to be 1.5% over prime. Lower courts have generally approved adjustments in the range of 1% to 3% over prime. The 2005 bankruptcy law did not address the *Till* case, so its holding still stands.

The bankruptcy court in your district may already have a rate stated on its standard Chapter 13 plan form. If your court has not set an interest rate, you and your creditor will have to negotiate a rate or ask the court to decide, using the formula announced by the Supreme Court.

TIP

You can surrender your car. If you don't qualify for a cramdown and you simply give your car back to the lender, a few courts may consider your debt to be cancelled. (See, for example, *In re Ezell, 338 B.R. 330 (E.D. Tenn. 2006).*) However, most courts have ruled that you will still owe any deficiency that results from the surrender (the difference between what the property is worth and what you owe on it), and that you must include this debt with your other unsecured, nonpriority debt in your plan. This will usually have no effect on your budget or plan payment. Since you are required to devote 100% of your disposable income to your plan payments, owing a deficiency on a formerly-secured debt will simply reduce the percentage that all of your unsecured creditors will be paid.

Class 5—Claims (other than residential mortgages) on which the last payment is due after the final plan payment. These debts are typically arrearages on leases or licenses, six- or seven-year car notes, and long-term secured and unsecured promissory notes that last beyond five years.

Class 6—Nonpriority, unsecured claims. This is where your plan will list the debts from Schedule F, plus the unsecured portion of any bifurcated secured claim (listed in Class 4, above).

Comparison With Chapter 7

Your plan will list the total amount your unsecured, nonpriority creditors would receive from the sale of your nonexempt property in a Chapter 7 case (see Ch. 4) and what percentage of your total allowed unsecured, nonpriority debt (the debts listed in Schedule F) that amount would pay off over the course of your plan.

Plan Analysis

This section summarizes your payments for each class of debts. After coming up with a subtotal, your attorney (or the software) will multiply this subtotal by 10% (or the multiplier in your district) to get the trustee's fee.

The total payment, divided by the number of months your plan will last, is the amount of your monthly payment to the trustee.

Order of Payment

This section of your plan tells the trustee how to prioritize the creditors to be paid under your plan. Usually, the order of payment is this:

- the trustee's fee
- domestic support orders
- administrative expenses (such as attorney fees) in an amount up to 10% of each plan payment until paid in full
- ongoing payments on secured debts that are made through your plan (as opposed to those you pay directly to the creditor), and
- all other claims.

The plan will not pay unsecured claims until all secured and priority claims are paid in full.

Sample Plan

Here is a sample Chapter 13 repayment plan. The debtor is Carrie Ann Edwards, divorced mother of two children who lives in Lakeport, California. Carrie was forced into Chapter 13 bankruptcy by the means test. She was faced with possible foreclosure on her mortgage because of an arrearage—which she can pay off over time through her Chapter 13 plan. She owns a car, which she bought four years ago, that is currently valued at $8,000. The balance on the car loan is $15,000. In Chapter 13, she can cram down the secured loan to $8,000. The remaining $7,000 becomes unsecured debt. Finally, she will surrender her second car, a 2009 Mitsubishi Galant, to the lender.

UNITED STATES BANKRUPTCY COURT

_____ Northern _____ DISTRICT OF _____ California _____

In re _____ Edwards, Carrie Anne _____)
    [*Set forth here all names including married,*)
    maiden, and trade names used by debtor)
    within last 8 years.])
                    Debtor)
)   Case No. _____

Address __ 3045 Berwick St. _____)

Lakeport, CA 95453 _____)   Chapter 13
)
Last four digits of Social Security or Individual)
Tax Payer Identification (ITIN) No(s). (if any): __ 6287 __)

Employer's Tax Identification (EIN) No(s). (if any):)
_____)

Chapter 13 Repayment Plan

Notice

This plan is proposed by the above debtor under penalty of perjury. Any creditor can object to this plan being confirmed by written notice filed with the court and served upon the debtor, the trustee, and other parties in interest not less than eight days before the date set for the meeting of creditors. Absent a timely objection, the court may confirm this plan as drafted. The plan, and payments under the plan, will be subject to all relevant Bankruptcy Code provisions.

With certain exceptions, a confirmed plan holds the debtor and creditors to the treatment provided in the plan—even if the plan modifies rights and duties held by the debtor and creditor. The exceptions are:

a. Each creditor will retain its lien until the earlier of payment of the underlying debt determined under nonbankruptcy law or discharge under Section 1328. If the case under this chapter is dismissed or converted without completion of the plan, the holder of such lien shall retain it to the extent recognized by applicable nonbankruptcy law.

b. Defaults will be cured using the interest rate set forth below in the plan. Any ongoing obligation will be paid according to the terms of the plan.

c. Holders of secured claims and Class 1 claimants will be paid according to the plan after confirmation unless the secured creditor or Class 1 claimant files a *Proof of Claim* in a different amount than that provided in the plan.

d. If a secured creditor files a *Proof of Claim*, that creditor will be paid according to that creditor's *Proof of Claim*, unless the court orders otherwise. Holders of all other claims must timely file *Proofs of Claim*, if the code so requires, or they will not be paid any amount. A debtor who confirms a Chapter 13 plan may be eligible thereafter to receive a discharge of debts to the extent specified in 11 U.S.C. Section 1328.

Plan Payments

The debtor proposes the following Chapter 13 plan and makes the following declarations:

Monthly Amounts Paid to Trustee Under the Plan

The debtor submits the following to the supervision and control of the trustee:

A. Payments by debtor of $___1,226___ per month for sixty (60) months. The monthly payment will begin within 30 days of the date the petition was filed.

B. The base plan amount is $___42,660 (disposable income x 60)___, which will pay ___27__% of the allowed claims of nonpriority unsecured creditors. If that percentage is less than 100%, the debtor will pay the plan payment stated in this plan for the full term of the plan.

C. Amounts necessary for the payment of postpetition claims allowed under 11 U.S.C. Section 1305.

D. If the plan provides for less than 100% payment of nonpriority unsecured claims, all postpetition tax refunds received by the debtor during the plan term.

E. Preconfirmation adequate protection payments for any creditor who holds an allowed claim secured by personal property: _____ .

F. Other property: _____ .

Classification and Treatment of Claims

Class 1: Allowed unsecured claims entitled to priority under 11 U.S.C. 507

The debtor will pay Class 1 allowed claims in full; except the debtor may provide for less than full payment of domestic support obligations assigned to a government agency.

Category	1. Amount of Priority Claim	2. Interest Rate If Any	3. Monthly Payment	4. Number of Months	5. Total Payment
Administrative					
1. Trustee's fee	$6,540		$109.00	60	$6,540
2. Attorneys' fees					
3. Ch. 7 trustee fees					
4. Other Admin.					
5. IRS	3,000	7%	59.50	60	3,570
6. State tax					
7. Support	4,500	7%	89.11	60	5,346
8. Other					
9. Support not to be paid in full					
Totals	$14,040		$257		$15,456

Class 2: Claims secured solely by real property that is the debtor's principal residence

☐ 1. The postconfirmation monthly mortgage payment will be made by the trustee from the plan payment to: _____

_____ .

☑ 1.2. The postconfirmation monthly mortgage payment will be made by the debtor directly to: ___LENDERS___ .

The debtor will cure all prepetition arrearages for the primary residence through the plan payment as set forth below. If the debtor pays the cure amount while timely making all required postpetition payments, the mortgage will be reinstated according to its original terms, extinguishing any right of the mortgagee to recover any amount alleged to have arisen prior to the filing of the petition.

1. Name of Creditor	2. Last Four Digits of Loan #	3. Amount of Arrearage	4. Interest Rate	5. Monthly Payment	6. Number of Months	7. Total Payment
Grand Junction Mortgage	1861	$5,200		$86.67	60	$5,200.00
Lending Tree	5555	$800		$13.33	60	$800.00

Class 3: Secured claims to be paid in full through the plan

1. Name of Creditor	2. Last Four Digits of Loan #	3. Amount of Claim	4. Interest Rate	5. Monthly Payment	6. Number of Months	7. Total Payment

The debtor will cure all prepetition arrearages on these claims through the plan payment as set forth below:

1. Name of Creditor	2. Last Four Digits of Loan #	3. Amount of Arrearage	4. Interest Rate	5. Monthly Payment	6. Number of Months	7. Total Payment

Class 4: Secured claims to be bifurcated under the plan

1. Name of Creditor	2. Last Four Digits of Loan #	3. Claim Total	4. Secured Claim	5. Unsecured Claim	6. Interest Rate	7. Equal Monthly Payments	8. Number of Months	9. Total Payment	10. Purchase for Debtor's Personal Use?	11. Date of Purchase	12. Purchase Money Loan?
GMAC	2753	$15,000	$8,000	$7,000	7%	$158.41	60	$9,504.60	Y ☑ N ☐	03/05/xx	Y ☑ N ☐

The debtor will cure all prepetition arrearages on these claims through the plan payment as set forth below:

1. Name of Creditor	2. Last Four Digits of Loan #	3. Amount of Arrearage	4. Interest Rate	5. Monthly Payment	6. Number of Months	7. Total Payment

Class 5: Secured or unsecured claims other than residential mortgages on which the last payment is due after date on which final payment under the plan is due

☐ 3. The postconfirmation monthly payment pursuant to the promissory note will be made by the trustee from the plan payment to: _____ .

☐ 3.4. The postconfirmation monthly payment pursuant to the promissory note will be made by the debtor directly to:

_____ .

The debtor will cure all prepetition arrearages on these claims through the plan payment as set forth below:

1. Name of Creditor	2. Last Four Digits of Loan #	3. Amount of Arrearage	4. Interest Rate	5. Monthly Payment	6. Number of Months	7. Total Payment

Class 6: Nonpriority unsecured claims

The debtor estimates that allowed nonpriority unsecured claims will be the sum of $ 155,915 .

Class 6 claims will be paid as follows (*check one box only*):

☑ Class 6 claims (including the unsecured claims in Class 4) are of one class and will be paid pro rata.

☐ Class 6 claims will be divided into subclasses as shown below and the creditors in each class will be paid pro rata.

Claim	Reason for Subclass	Amount

Comparison With Chapter 7

The value as of the effective date of the plan of property to be distributed under the plan on account of each allowed claim is not less than the amount that would be paid on such claim if the estate of the debtor were liquidated under Chapter 7 of the Bankruptcy Code on such date. The amount distributed to nonpriority unsecured creditors in Chapter 7 would be $ 9,246 , which is estimated to pay   6   % of the scheduled nonpriority debt. The plan proposes to pay   27   % of the debtor's nonpriority unsecured debt.

Plan Analysis

Total Payments Provided for Under the Plan	
Class 1 (Priority Claims)	$8,916
Class 2 (Residence, current and arrearage)	6,000 (arrearage only)
Class 3 (Secured claims paid in full)	
Class 4 (Secured claims bifurcated)	9,504
Class 5 (Claims due beyond final payment)	
Class 6 (Nonpriority unsecured)	42,660
Subtotal	67,080
Trustee's fee (10% unless otherwise)	6,540
Total Payment	$73,620

Order of Payment

Except as otherwise provided in the plan or by court order, the Chapter 13 trustee shall disburse all available funds for the payment of claims in the following order:

First: The Chapter 13 trustee's fee up to but not more than the amount accrued on payments made to date

Second: Any domestic support orders

Third: Administrative expenses (including, but not limited to, attorneys' fees) in an amount up to but not more than 10% of each plan payment until paid in full

Fourth: Ongoing payments on secured debts that are to be made by the trustee from the plan payment

Fifth: Pro rata to all other claims except as otherwise provided in the plan

Sixth: No payment shall be made on general unsecured claims until all secured and priority claims have been paid in full

Other Plan Provisions

A. The debtor rejects the following executory contracts and unexpired leases: _sales contract with Herman Jones_ _____ .

B. The debtor assumes the executory contracts or unexpired leases set forth in this section. The debtor has a leasehold interest in personal property and will make all postpetition payments directly to the lessor(s): _Beauty Products Leasing_ _____

C. In addition to the payments specified in Class _____ and Class _____, the debtor will make regular payments directly to the following: _____

D. The debtor hereby surrenders the following personal or real property (identify property and creditor to which it is surrendered):

Property	Creditor
2009 Mitsubishi Galant	ZYX Auto Financing

E. Preconfirmation adequate protection payments will be paid to the trustee for the following creditor(s) in the following amounts:

Creditor Name	Amount

Each adequate protection payment will commence on the 30th day from the date of filing of the case. The trustee shall deduct the foregoing adequate protection payment(s) from the debtor's plan payment and disburse the adequate protection payment to the secured creditor(s) at the next available disbursement or as soon as practicable after the payment is received and posted to the trustee's account. The trustee will take his or her statutory fee on all disbursements made for preconfirmation adequate protection payments.

F. The debtor shall incur no debt greater than $_____ unless the debt is incurred in the ordinary course of business pursuant to 11 U.S.C. Section 1304(b) or for medical emergencies.

G. The debtor will pay timely all postconfirmation tax liabilities directly to the appropriate taxing authorities as they come due.

H. The trustee is authorized to disburse funds after the date of confirmation in open court.

I. The debtor will pay all amounts required to be paid under a domestic support obligation that first became payable after the date of the filing of the petition.

Revestment of Property

Property of the estate shall not revest in the debtor until such time as a discharge is granted or the case is dismissed or closed without discharge. Revestment shall be subject to all liens and encumbrances in existence when the case was filed, except those liens avoided by court order extinguished by operation of law. In the event the case is converted to a case under Chapter 7, 11, or 12 of the Bankruptcy Code, the property of the estate shall vest in accordance with applicable law. After confirmation of the plan, the Chapter 13 trustee shall have no further authority or fiduciary duty regarding use, sale, or refinance of property of the estate except to respond to any motion for proposed use, sale, or refinance as required by the local bankruptcy rules. Prior to any discharge or dismissal, the debtor must seek approval of the court to purchase, sell, or refinance real property .

Filing the Bankruptcy Case

After preparing the necessary forms and drafting your repayment plan, your attorney will file your bankruptcy case. Here's a rundown of the documents you'll have to gather, whether you can pay the filing fee in installments, what's required to file an emergency bankruptcy petition, and what happens to your property immediately after you file.

File Documents in Addition to the Bankruptcy Forms

In addition to a sizable stack of official bankruptcy forms and your repayment plan, you must also submit a number of other papers. These are:

- your credit counseling certificate
- any repayment plan that was developed during your credit counseling session
- your most recent tax return or a transcript of the return
- proof that you've filed your tax returns for the last four years with the IRS, and
- your wage stubs for the last 60 days, if you were working.

Credit Counseling

As explained in Ch. 1, almost everyone who files a consumer bankruptcy must first attend credit counseling. This credit counseling must be provided by an agency approved by the United States Trustee's Office within the 180-day period before you file for bankruptcy. The counseling can be done by phone, on the Internet, or in person. You can obtain a list of approved counselors by visiting the website of the U. S. Trustee at www.justice.gov/ust (click on "Consumer Education" and then "Credit Counseling & Debtor Education"). The agencies are listed by state, but you can use any agency in any state or region that is on the list. Most likely your attorney will recommend a particular counseling agency that he or she has worked with before.

Repayment Plans

The purpose of this counseling is to get you to sign up for a debt repayment plan instead of filing for bankruptcy. Indeed, if the plan makes sense and you believe you can faithfully make the payments required to complete it, you might reasonably consider signing up for it. However, keep in mind that even if you make the required payments on the plan month after month, the creditors can pull out of the plan if you later fall behind—and they can go after you for the remaining debt. If you then decide to file for bankruptcy protection, you may well have paid back all that money for no good reason. This is why most bankruptcy professionals—including the authors of this book—discourage their clients from signing up for a debt repayment plan.

Counseling Fees

Most of these credit counseling agencies charge a modest sum ($30 to $50 is common) for the counseling, creating a repayment plan (if it gets that far), and the certificate of completion that you'll need to file with your other bankruptcy papers.

Agencies are legally required to offer their services without regard to your ability to pay. If an agency wants to charge more than you can afford (which is rare in the case of Chapter 13 filers), inform the agency of this legal requirement.

Exceptions to the Counseling Requirement

You don't have to get counseling if the U.S. Trustee certifies that there is no appropriate agency available to you in the district where you will be filing. However, counseling can be provided by telephone or online, so it is unlikely that approved debt counseling will ever be "unavailable."

You can also avoid the requirement if you move the court to grant an exception and prove to the court's satisfaction that "exigent circumstances" prevented you from meeting the counseling requirement. To prove exigent circumstances, you must show that:

- you had to file for bankruptcy immediately, and
- you were unable to obtain counseling within five days after requesting it.

Many of the agencies on the U.S. Trustee's list will counsel you the same day you ask for it, so it will be tough to show that you couldn't get counseling when you requested it. In other words, once you decide to file for Chapter 13 bankruptcy, you should immediately seek credit counseling and don't rely on the exigent circumstances exception.

CAUTION

A foreclosure may not be "exigent" enough. Some courts look with disfavor on debtors who wait until the last minute to get their credit counseling. For example, courts found that no exigent circumstances exist when a debtor files for bankruptcy on the day of a scheduled foreclosure sale.

If you can prove that you didn't receive counseling due to exigent circumstances, your attorney must file a certification with the court explaining your situation, then complete the counseling within 30 days after you file (you can ask the court to extend this deadline by 15 days).

You may also escape the credit counseling requirement if, after notice and hearing, the bankruptcy court determines that you couldn't participate because of:

- a physical disability that prevents you from attending counseling (this exception probably won't apply if the counseling is available on the Internet or over the phone)
- mental incapacity (you are unable to understand and benefit from the counseling), or
- your active duty in a military combat zone.

CAUTION

"Same-day" counseling might not count. Some courts have ruled that getting credit counseling on the same day you file for bankruptcy does not satisfy the requirement that the counseling take place "within 180 days prior to your filing date." Other courts have allowed same-day counseling. Your local bankruptcy attorney will know what your bankruptcy court requires. To be safe, get your counseling no later than the day before you file.

Your Tax Return or Transcript

You must give the trustee your most recent IRS tax return no later than seven days before the 341 hearing. (11 U.S.C. §521(e)(2).) You also have to provide the return to any creditor who asks for it. To protect your privacy, you can redact (black out) your date of birth and Social Security number. If you don't provide your tax return on time, your case will likely be dismissed.

If you can't find a copy of your most recent tax return, you can ask the IRS to give you a transcript of the basic information in your return—and you can use the transcript as a substitute for your return. Because it can take some time to receive the transcript (the IRS says two weeks), you should make your request as soon as you can.

CAUTION

Your taxes must be current for the last four years. Before you file for Chapter 13 bankruptcy, you must be able to show that you have filed tax returns for the previous four years. If you are behind on your tax filings, contact an accountant, enrolled tax agent, or a tax preparation service right away.

Wage Stubs

If you are employed, you receive stubs or "advisements" with your paycheck. You are required to produce these stubs for the 60-day period before you file. If you have already tossed your stubs, you have three options: Ask your employer for copies; wait 60 days (and keep your stubs) before filing; or go ahead and file, hand over the stubs you have, and explain why you don't have 60 days' worth.

If you do not have an employer—for instance you are self-employed or operate a business as a sole proprietor—you won't have to produce wage stubs. However, most courts have a local form requiring you to declare the reason you aren't submitting wage stubs.

Paying the Filing Fee in Installments

In theory, you can pay the $281 filing fee in up to four installments over 120 days. In practice, however, this is almost never done. One reason is that you must pay your filing fee before you pay your attorney. Most attorneys require you to pay at least some attorneys' fees before he or she begins preparing your paperwork and proposed repayment plan. If you want to try to pay in installments, discuss it with your attorney.

Electronic Filing

Virtually all bankruptcy courts require attorneys to file bankruptcy petitions electronically. The attorney is required to have what's called a "wet copy" in his or her files, meaning a print copy of your papers that you have actually signed with pen and ink. At any point in a bankruptcy case, the trustee can demand that your attorney produce the wet copy, although this is rarely done. The advantage of electronic filing is that papers can be filed around the clock, holidays and weekends included. So, if you are faced with an emergency and have to get your bankruptcy filed right away in order to stop a foreclosure or repossession, the calendar should not present a barrier to getting that done.

Emergency Filing

If you want to file for bankruptcy in a hurry—typically, to get the protection of the automatic stay (described in Ch. 2)—you can accomplish that (in most places) by filing your bankruptcy *Petition,* mailing matrix and cover sheet (if required by local rules), Form 21 (*Statement of Social Security Number*), and your credit counseling certificate. Some courts also require you to file a cover sheet and an order dismissing your Chapter 13 case, which will be processed if you don't file the rest of your required papers within 14 days.

If you don't follow up by filing the additional documents within 14 days, your bankruptcy case will be dismissed. You can file again, if necessary. However, if your case was dismissed when you opposed a creditor's request to lift the stay, you'll have to wait 180 days to refile. And even if you don't have to wait to file, you'll have to ask the court to keep the automatic stay in effect once 30 days have passed after you file. (See Ch. 2.)

After You File

Filing a bankruptcy petition has a dramatic effect on your creditors and your property.

The Automatic Stay

The instant you file for Chapter 13 bankruptcy, your creditors are subject to the automatic stay, as described in detail in Ch. 2.

Property Ownership

When you file your bankruptcy papers, the trustee becomes the owner of all the property in your bankruptcy estate as of that date. However, the trustee won't actually take physical control of the property and the property will revert to your legal possession after your plan is confirmed. Until your plan is confirmed, do not throw out, give away, sell, or otherwise dispose of property you owned as of your filing date, unless and until the bankruptcy trustee says otherwise.

If you are a sole proprietor with business inventory, the trustee takes legal control of your inventory, although you still keep physical control of it. Your attorney will find out if you can continue running your business. Usually you can, but you must be prepared to account for any inventory you sell before your Chapter 13 plan is confirmed.

In a Chapter 13 case, with a few exceptions, the trustee has no claim to property you acquire or income you earn after you file but before your plan is confirmed. You are free to spend it as you please. The exceptions are: property from an insurance settlement, a marital settlement agreement, or an inheritance that you become entitled to receive within 180 days after your filing date. (See "Understanding Property Exemptions," in Ch. 5, for more information.) To the extent that this property is not exempt, it could increase the amount you have to pay your nonpriority, unsecured creditors in your plan.

Handling Routine Matters
After You File

Once you have filed all of your Chapter 13 bankruptcy papers, including your repayment plan, the bankruptcy trustee and the court take over. They will examine your papers and schedule court hearings. Your creditors also get into the act; it's time for them to file their claims, so they can get paid by the trustee once you start making plan payments. They may also object to your plan if they think they are getting shortchanged.

This chapter tells you how to move your bankruptcy case along once you file. Your attorney will probably have to make two or three brief court appearances and do some negotiating with creditors.

CAUTION
Emergency filing reminder. If you have not filed all your bankruptcy papers, you must do so within 15 days of when you filed your petition. (Bankruptcy Rules 1007(c), 3015(b).) If you do not, the bankruptcy court will dismiss your case and might even fine you.

The Automatic Stay

When you file your bankruptcy papers, the automatic stay will go into effect. (See Ch. 2 for detailed information on how the automatic stay works.) Creditors won't know about your case until they receive notice of your bankruptcy filing from the court, however. It might take several days—or weeks—for this notice to reach your creditors. If you want quicker results (particularly if you are facing aggressive collection efforts), you can send out your own notice.

The court almost always lifts (removes) the stay at the end of the confirmation hearing, because your creditors are now bound by your plan. This means they cannot sue you or take other action to get paid. Their only means of being paid is through the terms of the confirmed plan.

Dealing With the Trustee

Within a few days after you file your bankruptcy petition, the bankruptcy court assigns a Chapter 13 trustee to oversee your case. You will receive a *Notice of Appointment of Trustee* from the court, giving the name, address, and phone number of the trustee. It may also include a list of any financial documents the trustee wants copies of, such as bank statements, canceled checks, and tax returns, and the date by which the trustee wants them.

Within a few days after the trustee is appointed, the court will send you and your creditors a *Notice of Chapter 13 Bankruptcy Case*. This notice usually contains:

- a summary of your Chapter 13 plan (if you filed it with your petition)
- an explanation of the automatic stay
- the date, time, and place of the meeting of creditors (see below)
- the date, time, and place of the confirmation hearing (see below), and
- the date by which creditors must file their claims (see below).

You and your attorney may also receive a letter of introduction from the trustee explaining how this trustee runs a Chapter 13 case. For example, the letter may inform you that the trustee only accepts payments by cashier's check or money order.

Many Chapter 13 trustees play a fairly active role in the cases they administer. This is especially true in small suburban or rural judicial districts or districts with a lot of Chapter 13 bankruptcy cases. For example, a trustee may:

- give you financial advice and assistance, such as helping you create a realistic budget (the trustee cannot, however, give you legal advice)
- actively participate in modifying your plan at the meeting of the creditors, and
- participate at any hearing on the value of an item of secured property, possibly even hiring an appraiser.

For more information on the role of the Chapter 13 trustee, see Ch. 1.

Hold on to Property You Owned Before Filing

Once you file your bankruptcy papers, the property you owned before filing is under the supervision of the bankruptcy court. Don't throw out, give away, sell, or otherwise dispose of any property unless and until the bankruptcy trustee says otherwise.

Report Certain Property You Receive After Filing

Despite the trustee's great interest in your finances, your financial relationship with the trustee is not as stifling as it may sound. In general, you still have complete control over money and property you acquire after filing—as long as you make the payments called for under your repayment plan and you make all regular payments on your secured debts. If you don't make those payments, your creditors may object at the confirmation hearing or even file a motion to dismiss your case.

You can use income you earn after filing that's not going toward your plan payments to purchase everyday items such as groceries, personal effects, and clothing. If you have any questions about using your postfiling income, ask your attorney.

If you receive certain kinds of property (or become entitled to receive it) within 180 days after filing for bankruptcy, you must report it to the bankruptcy trustee. Here's the list:

- property you inherit or become entitled to inherit
- property from a marital settlement agreement or divorce decree, or
- death benefits or life insurance policy proceeds.

If any of this property is nonexempt, you might have to modify your plan to make sure your unsecured creditors are still getting paid at least as much as they would have gotten if you had filed under Chapter 7. (Ch. 5 explains how to calculate how much your unsecured creditors are entitled to receive.)

Provide the Trustee With Proof of Insurance

If you are behind on payments on a secured debt, such as a car loan, and you plan to make up the payments and get back on track during your Chapter 13 case, you may have to give the trustee proof that you have adequate insurance on the collateral. This requirement is meant to protect the creditor if the collateral is destroyed or damaged.

Make Adequate Protection Payments

Within 30 days after you file for bankruptcy, you will have to start making payments (called adequate assurance payments or adequate protection payments) to secured creditors to cover the period between the date you file and the date your plan is confirmed. Usually, you will have to pay the same amount you were obligated to pay before you filed for bankruptcy. These payments are intended to protect the creditor's rights: The creditor cannot repossess the property or go after you for payment because of the automatic stay, so these payments protect the creditor's interest in the property before your repayment plan kicks in.

Make Your First Payment

Within 30 days after you file your petition, you must make the first payment proposed in your Chapter 13 repayment plan. This deadline usually comes up before the meeting of creditors, and always before your confirmation hearing. The reason you must make the payment so early is to show that you are filing in good faith and that you can, in fact, make the payments.

It's crucial to meet this first deadline. So that you don't forget, count out 30 days from the date you filed your petition and mark the deadline on a calendar. It might be better, though, to make the payment a little earlier—for example, the day after you get paid, so you'll be sure to have the funds. If your wages are currently subject to wage attachments, garnishments, or voluntary payroll deductions, your attorney will get those removed so that you have the money to make your Chapter 13 payments.

If you do not make your first payment on time, the bankruptcy court can convert your case to a Chapter 7 bankruptcy, dismiss your case, or deny confirmation of your plan. A few courts consider the failure to make the first payment evidence that the plan was not submitted in good faith and is an abuse of the Chapter 13 bankruptcy system. In that case, the court would lift the automatic stay and allow your creditors to continue their collection efforts. If the court felt you were egregiously abusing the system—for example, this is the fourth Chapter 13 bankruptcy case you've filed without making payments in any of them—the court would likely dismiss your case and possibly fine you and bar you from ever filing for Chapter 13 bankruptcy again.

How a Typical Chapter 13 Bankruptcy Proceeds	
Step	**When It Happens**
1. You file for Chapter 13 bankruptcy.	
2. The automatic stay takes effect. It bars your creditors, once they learn of your filing, from taking any actions to collect what you owe.	When you file the bankruptcy petition
3. The court appoints a trustee to oversee your case. You will receive a *Notice of Appointment of Trustee* from the court.	Within a few days after you file the bankruptcy petition
4. The court sends you and your creditors a *Notice of Chapter 13 Case*, which usually contains: • general information about Chapter 13 bankruptcy • a summary of your Chapter 13 plan • the date of the meeting of creditors • the date of the confirmation hearing, and • the deadline by which creditors must file their claims.	Within a few days after you file your Chapter 13 plan
5. Creditors file written objections to your plan, if they wish.	At least 25 days before the confirmation hearing
6. You provide your most recent tax return to the trustee. You may black out certain personal information, such as your Social Security number.	At least seven days before the scheduled date of the first meeting of creditors
7. You begin making payments under your repayment plan. (If your plan is never approved, the trustee will return your money, less administrative costs.)	Within 30 days after you file the bankruptcy petition
8. You attend the meeting of the creditors, where the trustee and any creditors who show up can ask you about information in your papers. A creditor may raise objections to your plan with the hope of getting you to modify it before the confirmation hearing. You must bring any documents the trustee requests and proof that you've filed tax returns for the last four years.	Within 40 days after you file the bankruptcy petition
9. You file a modified plan, if you wish.	Anytime before the confirmation hearing. You must send a copy of the modified plan to all creditors, who are entitled to 20 days' notice before the confirmation hearing. If you don't give 20 days' notice, you will have to schedule a new hearing date.
10. You or your attorney attend the confirmation hearing, where the court addresses any objections raised by creditors or the trustee and approves your repayment plan.	The hearing must be held between 20 and 45 days after the creditors' meeting, unless the court wants to hold it earlier and there is no objection to the earlier date.
11. Creditors file their *Proofs of Claim*, specifying how much they are owed. You may also have to file *Proofs of Claim* for creditors who don't file their own proofs.	Within 90 days after the creditor's meeting (180 days for creditors that are government agencies). If you have to file *Proofs of Claim* on behalf of creditors, you must do so within 30 days after the 90-day or 180-day limit.

How a Typical Chapter 13 Bankruptcy Proceeds (continued)	
Step	**When It Happens**
12. You or the trustee files written objections to creditors' claims, if you have a reason to object.	As soon as possible after the creditors file their claims. You must notify your creditors at least 30 days in advance of the hearing on your objections.
13. The trustee sends you periodic statements showing: • who has filed claims and for how much • how much money has been paid to each creditor, and • the balance due each creditor.	Commonly, twice a year
14. You give the trustee annual income and expense statements.	Every year while your Chapter 13 plan is in effect, if requested by the court, trustee, U.S. Trustee, or a creditor
15. You file a *Certificate* (Form 23) showing that you completed a course in personal financial management.	Before you make your last plan payment
16. The court grants your discharge. The court may schedule a brief final court appearance called a "discharge hearing." If there's no discharge hearing, you'll be mailed formal notice of your discharge.	36 to 60 months after you file if you complete your plan payments; sooner if you seek and obtain a hardship discharge

If You Operate a Business

If you operate a business, by all means keep running it after you file your Chapter 13 papers. If your business has employees, don't forget to make all required payroll tax and withholding deposits with the IRS and your state taxing authority.

The trustee can require the following from you:
• an inventory of your business property, and
• a report on the recent operation of the business, including a statement of receipts and disbursements, if you didn't include one in your bankruptcy papers (you may already have attached one to Schedule I—*Current Income of Individual Debtor(s)* or Form 7—*Statement of Financial Affairs*). (11 U.S.C. § 1304; Bankruptcy Rule 2015(c).)

As in a regular Chapter 13 case, you must file an income and expense statement every year through the life of your plan. If your net business income increases while the plan is in effect, the trustee may require you to amend the plan to reflect your higher income.

The trustee may also direct you to send notice of your bankruptcy case to all entities who hold money or property that belongs to you. This includes financial institutions where you have accounts, landlords and utility companies who hold security deposits, and insurance companies where you have business insurance with a cash surrender value. If the balance of the money or value of the property is significant and your plan provides little or no payment to your unsecured creditors, the trustee might try to take this money or property for them.

The Meeting of Creditors

Your first court appearance is a fairly informal one; the bankruptcy judge isn't even present. The purpose of the creditors' meeting is to allow the trustee and your creditors to ask you about the information in your bankruptcy papers, including your repayment plan. The trustee will want to be sure that you can make the payments you've proposed in your plan.

You (and your spouse, if you are filing jointly) must attend. If you don't, you may be fined $100 or so by the judge. Even worse, your case may be dismissed. If you know in advance that you can't attend the creditors' meeting, your attorney should try to reschedule it.

Prepare for the Meeting

Some courts require you to bring at least the following documents:

- file-stamped copies of all the papers you've filed with the bankruptcy court
- copies of all documents that describe your debts and property, such as bills, deeds, contracts, and licenses, and
- financial records, such as recent tax returns, checkbooks, and bank statements.

Bring proof of your state and federal tax filings for the previous four years to the creditors' meeting. Also be prepared for the trustee to ask you to hand over all of your major credit cards. (Not all trustees require this.) You should be able to hold on to your debit cards that have the Visa or MasterCard logo on them. This will give you a card to use for your online accounts and rental cars.

If you lack the necessary documents at the creditors' meeting, the trustee will postpone the meeting to a later date when you can produce them. Often, if you get the documents to the trustee before the rescheduled meeting, you won't have to appear again; the trustee will simply review your documents, then close the meeting.

If you are feeling anxious about the meeting of creditors, find out when and where the next scheduled meeting will occur. Then, attend the meeting. That way, you can observe the proceedings and get comfortable with the process before you have to attend your own meeting.

The night before the creditors' meeting, thoroughly review the papers you filed with the bankruptcy court. If you discover mistakes, make careful note of them. You may have to correct your papers after the meeting, an easy process that your attorney can handle.

If your papers are internally consistent and there are no problem areas, the trustee is likely to ask you very few questions, perhaps nothing more than whether you have provided complete and accurate information. But sometimes the trustee may delve into a particular subject in more detail. For instance, the trustee may be interested in how you put a value on property such as real estate or a business. Or, if you recently sold some property, the trustee may want to know the details of the transaction and what you did with the proceeds. Or, if one part of your bankruptcy papers shows that you owe a debt but that debt hasn't been identified on the appropriate schedule, the trustee will want to know why. And finally, the trustee may want a better understanding of how your plan proposes to pay your creditors.

Clearly, there are an infinite number of situations where the trustee may want to go deeper into the facts. So how can you prepare for this? The single best way is to do a complete and accurate job of providing your attorney with information in the first place. Then, as mentioned, carefully review your papers before the meeting to make sure you understand all the information they contain and how you arrived at particular estimates and appraisals. Even if your attorney prepared your papers, you and you alone are responsible for what goes in them.

Getting to the Meeting

Most creditors' meetings take place in a room in or near the bankruptcy courthouse or federal courthouse. The date and time of the meeting are commonly stated on the notice of filing sent out by the court; if they are not, ask your attorney. Give yourself at least an extra 30 minutes to find the right place, park, find the right building, go through security, and find the right room.

> **CAUTION**
>
> **You'll have to prove your identity.** To show that you are really who you say you are, you'll need to produce a picture ID and official proof of your Social Security number, such as a Social Security card, wage stubs, or a passport. Failure to produce such documents will result in your meeting being reset for a later date. Also, you'll need your picture ID to gain entrance to the federal building where the meeting is being held.

When you get to the right room, look for your attorney and then give your name so the trustee knows you are present. Then just sit down and wait your turn.

Tight Court Security

On your way to any court hearing, you will probably spend some time getting through security. Like airports, federal buildings have metal detectors, but set to an even higher sensitivity. If you set the detector off, you'll have to empty your pockets, take off any offending articles, such as a jacket or belt, and go through again. If you set it off again, the security guard may scan your body with a hand-held metal detector. In addition, items you're carrying—such as a purse, briefcase, or knapsack—must go through an X-ray scanner. The security guard may confiscate objects such as pocket knives; you can reclaim them after your hearing.

What Happens at the Meeting

Most bankruptcy trustees set aside one or two days a month to hold Chapter 13 bankruptcy creditors' meetings. This means that when you show up for your creditors' meeting, many other people who have filed for bankruptcy will be there, too. And commonly, everyone is told to come at the same time. That means that 25 to 30 cases may all be scheduled for 9:00 a.m.

To get a rough idea of when your name will be called, check the schedule that should be posted outside the door. If your name is near the top of the list, you may not have too long to wait. If you're toward the bottom, you may be sitting there for quite some time. This time doesn't have to be wasted. The opportunity to observe other people at their meetings can be to your advantage; you'll quickly find out what to expect, where to stand, and maybe even what to say. And if you're nervous, watching other cases will probably help you calm down.

Your creditors' meeting, if it's typical, will last less than 15 minutes. When your name is called, you'll be asked to sit at a table near the front of the room. Your attorney will sit next to you. The trustee will swear you in and ask your name, address, and other identifying information. The trustee will also ask to see your photo ID and proof of Social Security number.

Your Attorney's Role at the Creditors' Meeting

Even though you are represented by an attorney, it will be your job to answer directly any questions put to you by a creditor or the bankruptcy trustee. With rare exceptions, your attorney will sit quietly and not object to the questions or intervene with answers he or she thinks would be best. Only if a question is inappropriate or the attorney has reason to believe your answer might incriminate you will he or she pipe up. Of course if the question is about a legal matter that only the attorney would know about, you can refer the question to the attorney for an answer.

The Trustee's Questions

The trustee will briefly go over your forms with you, probably asking at least a few questions. Your answers should be both truthful and consistent with your bankruptcy papers. The trustee is likely to be most interested in the fairness of your plan (that is, that it treats all similarly situated creditors the same) and your ability to make the payments you have proposed.

If you have valued some of your property at or near the exemption limit, the trustee may question you more closely on how you came up with your valuation figures. For example, if you estimate that your home is worth $100,000, and your state's homestead exemption protects $100,000 worth of equity, the trustee may dig a little to see whether your property might be worth more. Depending on home price trends in your area when you file, the trustee might even initiate an independent appraisal in the hopes that the value of your property exceeds the homestead protection enough to add significantly to your nonexempt property—and, therefore, require an increase in plan payments to your unsecured creditors. The trustee will be motivated to take steps like these because of the commission fee structure: The more you pay into your plan, the more the trustee collects as a fee.

Questions From Your Creditors

When the trustee is finished, any creditors who showed up will have a chance to question you. Often, secured creditors come, especially if they have any objections to the plan—for example, that the interest rate you propose is too low, the schedule takes too long to pay your arrearage, or the value you assigned the collateral is wrong (if you are proposing a cramdown). An unsecured creditor who is receiving very little under your plan might show up too, if that creditor thinks you can cut your expenses and increase your disposable income. Creditors may also challenge your exemption claims or the value assigned to property.

At the end of the meeting, be ready to negotiate. If you agree to make changes to accommodate a creditor's objections, you must submit a modified plan.

Modifying Your Plan Before the Confirmation Hearing

You have an absolute right to file a modified plan with the bankruptcy court any time before the confirmation hearing, and most Chapter 13 debtors modify their plan at least once. Your attorney will file the new plan with the bankruptcy court clerk and send notice of the new plan to all of your creditors. The new plan replaces the old one.

Here are some common reasons to modify a plan:
- to correct errors—such as to add overlooked creditors or debts
- to reflect financial changes—such as a new job, a raise, an inheritance or insurance settlement, reduction in income, or destruction of property secured by a debt
- to reduce your proposed payments—for example, if you just lost your job or had your income reduced
- to respond to creditors' objections (for instance, that you undervalued property) or include terms you negotiated with a creditor at the end of the meeting of the creditors, or
- to add debts you incurred after filing. In general, you should not incur debts after you file, other than day-to-day expenses. (In fact, the trustee will probably make you hand over your credit cards.) You can modify your plan, however, to add any debts that are necessary for you to keep following your plan (such as a medical bill) or

unanticipated debts (such as a tax bill). (This is covered in Ch. 12.)

At a minimum, the notice of your plan amendment must:
- identify the debtor (you)
- identify each creditor whose claim is affected by your modification
- describe your proposed modification with particularity (for instance, if you're proposing to reduce your payment to a creditor, your notice has to make that clear), and
- if secured property is involved, state (or restate) whether you plan to keep making payments or surrender the collateral.

(See *In re Friday*, 304 B.R. 537 (N.D. Ga. 2003).)

The Confirmation Hearing

A judge must approve your Chapter 13 plan for it to be valid. This is done at a confirmation hearing, where the judge addresses any objections raised by creditors or the trustee. Typically, Chapter 13 debtors don't attend the confirmation hearing; it is handled by the attorney. In a few courts, a confirmation hearing is held only if a creditor has filed a formal motion objecting to the plan. If no hearing is scheduled, it means your plan is approved as filed.

The confirmation hearing must be held no sooner than 20 or later than 45 days after the creditors' meeting, unless the court wants to hold it earlier and no one objects. However, the deadline for filing *Proofs of Claims*—which creditors must file to get paid through your plan—is 90 days after the date set for the first creditors' meeting. Assuming that the creditors' meeting is actually held on the scheduled date (it usually is), creditors might not have to file their *Proofs of Claim* until 45 to 70 days after the confirmation hearing. This means that plans up for confirmation often have to estimate which debts will be paid, and in what amounts. If creditors file claims after the court approves your plan, you may need to pay more into the plan than you expected. Later, we explain how to handle claims that are filed late and when you should file a claim on a creditor's behalf.

Dealing With Disputed Debts

If you want to dispute whether you actually owe a particular debt, you'll need to file your objection with the court. The court will issue a ruling on whether you owe the debt. Similarly, you may need to ask the court to rule on whether a nondischargeable debt is dischargeable in your particular circumstances.

Ideally, you want the court to rule on your objection before your plan is confirmed. Otherwise you'll have to modify your plan if the court ultimately agrees with your objection. And until you get the court's ruling, you'll also have to start paying off the debt if these payments come due under your Chapter 13 plan. Unfortunately, many courts hold confirmation hearings early in the case—even as early as the creditors' meeting—so it may be difficult if not impossible to get a ruling prior to confirmation.

What Happens at the Confirmation Hearing

As mentioned, your attorney can represent you at the confirmation hearing. However, if you plan to attend, here's what to expect.

Unlike a creditors' meeting, the confirmation hearing usually is run by a bankruptcy judge. Judges like to get easy cases in and out of their courtrooms as quickly as possible. This means that all uncontested matters will be heard first. Next will be cases where the outcome is fairly obvious—often motions to dismiss in cases where the plans were approved but the debtors have missed several payments. If the trustee or a creditor has filed an objection in your case, your confirmation hearing will probably be toward the end. Bring a big book with you.

The judge is most interested in your ability to make the payments under your plan and will question your attorney about that or about plan provisions that are unclear.

After these questions, the judge will ask whether objections raised by the trustee or creditors have been resolved. If they haven't, the judge may ask the trustee or creditors to elaborate on their objections, ask your attorney for any response, and then make a ruling. If the trustee doesn't think your plan is feasible, the trustee will raise that issue now. If the judge still has a lot of cases to get through, the judge may reschedule the rest of the hearing to a less busy day.

If the judge agrees with an objection, you will probably be allowed to submit a modified plan. (See "Modifying Your Plan After the Confirmation Hearing," below.) But if it's obvious that Chapter 13 bankruptcy just isn't realistic for you—for example, you earn very little money to pay into a plan—the judge will order that your case be dismissed or converted to Chapter 7 bankruptcy.

TIP

If you were already forced out of Chapter 7. If you had to file for Chapter 13 because you couldn't pass the means test (see Ch. 4), you may also be unable to propose a confirmable Chapter 13 repayment plan. If your income has declined since the six-month period before you filed, however, you may now find yourself eligible to use Chapter 7. (Remember, the means test is based on your average monthly income in the six months before you file.)

If you convert to Chapter 7 from a Chapter 13 case, you may avoid the means test altogether. Some courts have ruled that the means test doesn't apply to Chapter 7 cases that have been converted from Chapter 13. (See, e.g., *In re Guarin*, 2009 WL 4500476 (Bankr. D. Mass. 2009); *In re Willis*, 408 B.R. 803 (Bankr. W.D. Missouri 2009); *In re Dudley*, 405 B.R. 790 (Bankr. W.D. Va. 2009).) Other courts have gone the opposite way, ruling that if you convert to Chapter 7 from Chapter 13, you must still pass the means test in order to be eligible for Chapter 7 relief. (See, e.g., *In re Chapman*, 447 B.R. 250 (B.A.P. 8th Cir. 2011); *In re Lassiter*, 2011 WL 2039363 (Bankr. E.D. Va. 2011); *In re Phillips*, 417 B.R. 30 (Bankr. S.D. Ohio 2009).)

Income Deduction Orders

If you have a regular job with regular income, the bankruptcy judge may order, at the confirmation hearing, that your monthly plan payments be automatically deducted from your wages and sent to the bankruptcy court. (11 U.S.C. § 1325(c).) This is called an income deduction order. Income deduction orders work if you are regularly paid a salary or wages. They are almost impossible to use, however, if you are:

- self-employed
- funding your plan with public benefits, such as Social Security (the Social Security Act prohibits the Social Security Administration from complying with an income deduction order), or
- funding your plan with pension benefits— many pension plans prohibit the administrator from paying proceeds to anyone other than the beneficiary (you), which means that the administrator will ignore the income deduction order.

In many districts, the bankruptcy court automatically issues an income deduction order at the confirmation hearing—and possibly even earlier. In some districts, the bankruptcy court leaves it up to the debtor whether or not to issue an order. And in a few districts, the court doesn't issue the order unless you miss a payment in your plan.

You may not like the idea of the order, but the court is likely to deny your plan for lack of feasibility if you refuse to comply with it. And you should realize that the order will probably make it easier for you to complete your plan. The success rate of Chapter 13 cases is higher for debtors with income deduction orders than for debtors who pay the trustee themselves.

Your Employer Can't Fire You for Filing for Bankruptcy

Don't be worried that your employer, who will learn of your bankruptcy when the income deduction order arrives, will fire you because you filed for bankruptcy. Employers rarely care. If your employer does punish you for having filed for bankruptcy, let someone in charge know that the Bankruptcy Act prohibits all private and public employers from terminating you or otherwise discriminating against you solely because you filed for bankruptcy. (See Ch. 14 for more on the laws against this kind of discrimination.)

One benefit of an income deduction order is that it usually forbids your employer from making other deductions from your paycheck. This means that all wage attachments, garnishments, and voluntary payroll deductions will end (if they haven't already) when the order takes effect.

If the court does issue an income deduction order, you might inform the payroll department at your job that you've filed for Chapter 13 bankruptcy and to expect an income deduction order from the bankruptcy court.

Once the income deduction order takes effect, your attorney will need to tell the trustee if you change jobs.

The Judge's Order Confirming Your Plan

A court order granting confirmation of your repayment plan is binding on your creditors; they must accept the payments the trustee will make to them under the terms of your plan. This includes creditors who do not file claims by the deadline and creditors who unsuccessfully objected to your plan. (11 U.S.C. § 1327(a).)

When the court approves your plan, your attorney will file an *Order Confirming Chapter 13 Plan* with the bankruptcy court clerk and send notice that your plan was confirmed to all your creditors.

Modifying Your Plan After the Confirmation Hearing

If your plan isn't confirmed at the hearing, the court will usually give you a certain amount of time in which to try again. If you don't submit a modified plan by the deadline (or if the court found that you acted in bad faith or that Chapter 13 is not a feasible option for you), the court will dismiss your case or convert it to a Chapter 7 bankruptcy case. In that situation, the trustee must return your payments to you, less administrative expenses.

In most cases, you'll need to do one or more of the following to get your modified plan confirmed:

- extend your plan (if it's for less than five years)
- arrange to pay off your secured debt arrears faster
- change an interest rate on secured debt arrears
- increase the secured portion of a debt that is partially secured and partially unsecured
- create or eliminate a class of unsecured creditors, or

- increase the amount a particular class of creditors receives.

When your attorney files the modified plan, he or she will also schedule a new confirmation hearing. The hearing must be at least 25 days after the modified plan is filed. This gives your creditors an opportunity to object.

Amending Your Bankruptcy Forms

You have a right to amend the bankruptcy forms you have filed at any time before your final discharge. (You can also modify your plan after it's confirmed if the judge consents.) This means that if you made a mistake on your schedules, you can correct it easily. Also, you must amend your papers if you receive certain property within 180 days after filing. (These are described in "Dealing With the Trustee," above.)

If your mistake means that notice of your bankruptcy filing must be sent to additional creditors (for instance, if you inadvertently left off a creditor who must be notified), you'll have to pay a fee to file the amendment. If your mistake doesn't require new notice (for example, you just add information about property you owned when you filed), you may not have to pay an additional filing fee. If you amend your schedules to add creditors before the meeting of creditors, you'll usually be required to provide the newly listed creditors with notice of the meeting as well as notice of your amendment.

If you become aware of debts or property that you should have included in your papers, amending your papers will help you avoid any suspicion that you're trying to conceal things from the trustee. If you fail to amend your papers in this situation and someone else discovers your error, the judge may dismiss your bankruptcy petition or rule that one or more of your debts is nondischargeable.

Filing a Change of Address

If you move while your bankruptcy case is still open, you must give the court, the trustee, and your creditors your new address.

Filing Tax Returns

The court, a creditor, the trustee, or the U.S. Trustee may request that you file copies of your federal tax returns (or transcripts) with the bankruptcy court when you file those returns with the IRS, while your case is pending. This rule applies to returns for current years and for the three years before you file your bankruptcy petition. Because this rule is new, it's too soon to know whether these requests will be common or rare. But this much is clear: If you don't comply with a request to file your returns, your case will be dismissed.

Before you provide your returns to the court or a creditor, you can redact (black out) information that identifies you personally. The following information may be redacted:

- **Social Security number.** You may redact all but the last four digits of any Social Security number that appears in the documents.
- **Names of minor children.** You may redact the names and use only initials.
- **Dates of birth.** You may redact the day and month of birth and use only the year.
- **Financial account numbers.** If any account numbers are included, you may redact all but the last four digits.

Filing Annual Income and Expense Statements

The court, a creditor, the trustee, or the U.S. Trustee may request that you file an annual income and expense statement. This statement must include your income and expenditures during the most recently concluded tax year, and it must show how you calculated your income (both monthly and annually) and your expenses.

You must file the first statement 90 days after the end of the last tax year or one year after the date you filed your case (whichever is later), if your plan has not yet been confirmed by the later date. Once your plan is confirmed, you must file an annual statement at least 45 days before the anniversary of the date your plan is confirmed. It's hard to imagine that anyone will be paying close attention to these dates, as long as you are proceeding in good faith. Still, you should mark these dates on your calendar, just in case someone makes the request.

The income and expense statement must identify the amount and sources of your income, any person who contributed money to your household, and the amount that person contributed. Unless the trustee tells you otherwise, the best way to prepare this statement is to use blank copies of Schedules I and J to compute your annual and monthly income and your expenses. You can find these forms at www.uscourts.gov. (For more information, see "Getting the Official Bankruptcy Forms," in Ch. 4.)

Personal Financial Management Counseling

Before your last plan payment is due, you must complete a two-hour course in financial management and file a certificate of completion with the court. If you don't complete the course and file the certificate, the court can close your case without granting you a discharge. Although it isn't terribly difficult to reopen your case and file the certificate, it's better to avoid that extra step. Along with the certificate, your attorney will also file Form 23.

You must use an agency that's been approved by the U.S. Trustee's office. You can find a list of approved providers at the U.S. Trustee's website, www.justice. gov/ust. If you were satisfied with the agency that provided you with credit counseling before you filed your case, you can probably use it again—typically, the same agencies are approved to provide both types of counseling.

You might think that requiring you to complete this course is overkill. After all, to complete your repayment plan, you have had to live on a pretty strict budget for three to five years. Nevertheless, the court will require proof that you've completed this counseling before it will grant your discharge.

Form 283—Domestic Support and Homestead Exemption

Before you get your discharge, your attorney must file a form certifying that you have paid any required domestic support obligations (child support and alimony). On the same form, you must provide information on your use of a homestead exemption, if applicable. This information is used to determine whether your homestead exemption should be limited because you were convicted of a felony or securities violation. Hopefully, this won't be an issue for most filers.

Making Your Plan Work

Common Legal Issues

Hopefully, your bankruptcy case will go smoothly, without any challenges or unexpected complications. In some situations, however, your attorney might have to make an extra court appearance or two. This might happen if you need to ask the court to rule in your favor on an issue—for example, to eliminate a lien from your property. You might also have to defend against a creditor's objections to your plan or object to a creditor's claim for repayment. This chapter explains these types of contingencies in more detail.

Filing Motions

While your bankruptcy case is pending, you may learn that you need the judge to rule on a particular point. For example, you may have to modify your repayment plan (see Ch. 10) or have your debts discharged on the basis of hardship because you can't complete your plan (see Ch. 13). Requests for the court to intervene in your case—to make a decision or take some action, for example—are called motions.

In this section, we briefly review the general requirements that apply to all motions brought in bankruptcy court.

There are two basic types of motions:

- ex parte motions, which are typically decided by the judge on the application of one party, without a hearing, and
- noticed motions, which give the other side enough time to come into court and oppose your request.

Ex Parte Motions

Ex parte motions are typically used when you are clearly entitled to the action you are asking the court to take. For example, let's say you want to file a noticed motion to modify your repayment plan, but you can only give the creditor 20 days' notice, rather than the 25 days generally required for a noticed motion. In this situation, your attorney could file an ex parte motion seeking an "order shortening time." With the motion, the attorney includes an order for the judge to sign and a declaration—a statement signed under penalty of perjury—that the attorney contacted or tried to contact the other side about the motion.

Ex parte motions can also be used to dismiss your Chapter 13 bankruptcy case, because you have an absolute right to do so.

Noticed Motions

Noticed motions are much more common. Your attorney will prepare the motion, which explains what you want the court to do and why, along with other required documents, such as declarations (signed statements of fact) and a memorandum of points and authorities (this part sets out the law and explains why the court should grant the motion). In addition to filing the motion and accompanying documents, your attorney must send notice to the affected parties.

There are two types of notice:

- Notice of the date and time of the hearing. In this situation, your attorney will schedule a hearing. The opposing side will have an opportunity to respond in writing.
- Notice that the other side must schedule a hearing if it wants to contest the motion. In this situation, if the opposing party doesn't respond within the 25-day notice period, your attorney can ask the court for a default (which means you automatically win the motion).

At the hearing on the motion, your attorney and the opposing side will have an opportunity to argue their points.

Then, the judge will either announce a decision or take the matter under submission (think about it for a while). The judge typically files a written memorandum explaining the decision. The judge will also ask the party that won the motion to prepare a formal order.

Dealing With Creditors' Motions

In most Chapter 13 cases, you'll be able to work out any minor glitches as they arise. On rare occasions, however, a creditor throws a monkey wrench into the works by filing a motion that, if successful, could mean a major disruption or even a dismissal of your case.

If you are faced with a creditor motion, take heart: Even when creditors file motions to challenge your right to file for Chapter 13 bankruptcy or discharge a particular debt, few Chapter 13 trustees want to deal with them. Most trustees handle thousands of cases a year. They do not want to get involved in drawn-out court battles unless the result is likely to have an impact on many other debtors in your district. In most cases, the trustee will encourage you and the creditor to work things out without a hearing. Some trustees even discourage creditors from filing a lot of motions (and a creditor needs to stay on the trustee's good side).

If you receive a motion from a creditor, your attorney will have a certain period of time to file a written response. If you don't respond, you will mostly likely lose the motion.

Here are a few common types of motions a creditor might file.

Objections to Your Eligibility to Use Chapter 13

A creditor might file a motion claiming that your debts exceed the Chapter 13 bankruptcy limits; as explained in Ch. 3, these limits are $360,475 for unsecured debts and $1,081,400 for secured debts. A creditor may raise this kind of objection if your liability for a debt is relatively certain (even though it hasn't yet been determined), and the creditor is afraid you'll wipe it out in bankruptcy.

> **EXAMPLE:** A few years ago, you and a partner started a business. It failed, you both lost a lot of money, and your former partner blames you for the whole mess, with some justification. He has been threatening to sue you for the money he claims you are responsible for causing him to lose. During your business's lean times, you missed several house payments, didn't pay your personal income taxes, and charged up your credit cards. You have filed for Chapter 13 bankruptcy, and your plan proposes to pay only 10% of your unsecured debts. Your ex-partner objects, claiming that you owe him at least $400,000, which puts you over the limit for unsecured debts.

Motion for Adequate Protection

Your secured creditors will probably insist that you agree to protect the property securing their debts against loss, damage, or general depreciation. This is called providing adequate protection. (See Ch. 10 for more information.) The protection you provide could take the form of money, additional liens, or proof of insurance. If you refuse to provide adequate protection, the creditor may file a motion asking the court to order you to do so. If this happens, you might as well comply: Because the creditor has a right to protect its interest in the property, you have no chance of winning this type of motion.

Motion for Relief From the Automatic Stay

When you file for bankruptcy, the automatic stay prohibits most creditors from taking any action to collect the debts you owe them, unless and until the court says otherwise. If you have had two or more dismissals entered in bankruptcy cases within the past year, you are not protected by the automatic stay and will need a court order to protect you against actions by a specific creditor. If you have one dismissal entered in the past year, the automatic stay only lasts for 30 days, absent a court order. (For more on the automatic stay, see Ch. 2.)

In a Chapter 13 bankruptcy, the automatic stay bars creditors from going after the property and wages you acquire after you file your petition and before your confirmation hearing. The court almost always removes (lifts) the stay after the confirmation hearing, because your creditors are bound by your plan at that point. If the confirmation hearing is delayed, however, your creditors may file a motion asking the judge to lift the stay early. The court is likely to grant such a motion if any of the following are true:

- You refuse to provide adequate protection to a secured creditor. (See "Motion for Adequate Protection," above.)
- Your filing is obviously in bad faith, or your plan is completely unfeasible.
- You have no equity in an item of secured property, and the creditor (who wants to repossess it) claims that you don't need the item to carry out your Chapter 13 plan. You may be able to get around a motion that makes this argument if:
  - Your plan includes payments on the secured item.
  - You can show that you need the property to generate income. For example, you could

argue that you need to keep a car because you have to drive to work and have no adequate alternative means of transportation.

- The property is your family home. Many courts rule that the family home is always necessary. Some courts rule otherwise, however, if the creditor can show that comparable housing is available to you for less money. You would have to emphasize your children's ties to their school and neighborhood, your proximity to work, and/or the cost of finding new housing and moving.

Motions to Lift the Stay and Proceed With Foreclosure

If your mortgage lender or servicer initiated foreclosure proceedings before you filed for bankruptcy, the lender will likely ask the court to lift the automatic stay so it can proceed with the foreclosure. To obtain this type of relief, the lender's motion must be accompanied with paperwork demonstrating that it has an ownership interest in the property. The foreclosing party can do this by way of a promissory note listing the lender (or other party bringing the foreclosure action) as the note's owner, or in some courts, by showing that the promissory note was properly assigned to the party by an earlier owner. Absent such evidence, the bankruptcy court may refuse to lift the stay on the ground that the foreclosing party did not have "standing" to bring the stay-relief action.

If the court finds that the foreclosing party has standing and lifts the automatic stay, you still might be able to challenge the legality of the foreclosure or the mortgage by opposing the lender's *Proof of Claim*. (See, "Objecting to a Creditor's Claim," below.)

Motions to Lift the Stay and Proceed With an Eviction

The same basic rules apply to evictions: The bankruptcy court is likely to lift the automatic stay and allow the landlord to proceed with an eviction. And, in some cases, that might not even be necessary. If the landlord already has a judgment of possession when you file for bankruptcy, or the landlord wants to evict you for endangering the property or illegally using controlled substances on the premises, the automatic stay generally won't apply to stop the eviction, except in the limited circumstances described in Ch. 2.

Motions to Dismiss by the Trustee and Others

Creditors and trustees can file a variety of motions to dismiss your case. Typically, these motions argue that the filer failed to comply with procedural bankruptcy rules. For example, you might face:

- a motion by the trustee to dismiss your case because you failed to provide your most recent tax return at least seven days before the creditors' meeting
- a motion by the trustee to dismiss or convert your case (to Chapter 7) if you fail to prove that you filed your tax returns for the previous four years
- a motion by the trustee, the U.S. Trustee, or a creditor to dismiss your case because you failed to provide them, on their request, with the income tax returns you filed while your case was pending
- a motion by the trustee to dismiss your case because you didn't stay current on your income tax filings, or
- a motion by an ex-spouse or the trustee to dismiss your case because you didn't stay current on your child support or alimony payments while your case was pending.

If the person bringing this type of motion is right—that is, you really didn't file your tax returns or stay current on your child support payments—your only defense is that the failure was beyond your control. If you can show, for example, that a natural disaster prevented you from filing your tax return on time, you might have a shot at success.

If an Unsecured Creditor Objects to Your Plan

It might seem odd to you that an unsecured creditor would object to your Chapter 13 plan. After all, in a Chapter 13 case, the creditor might get some money. By contrast, if you ignored the creditor or filed for Chapter 7 bankruptcy, the creditor probably wouldn't get anything.

A creditor who objects to your plan isn't trying to derail your bankruptcy, however: Instead, the creditor wants you to modify your plan to ensure that you will be able to make the payments it requires. Because so many Chapter 13 filers eventually dismiss their cases or convert to Chapter 7, your creditors have good reason to doubt that you'll be able to follow through. A creditor objects to a plan precisely because the creditor wants it to succeed.

A creditor who objects to your plan will probably attend the creditors' meeting and try to convince you to modify your plan before the confirmation hearing, which typically takes place from 20 to 40 days after the creditors' meeting.

> **CAUTION**
>
> **If a creditor requests a deposition.** It's rare, but a creditor who thinks you are hiding assets and could pay more into your plan might try to gather evidence about your finances through a formal legal process called "discovery." The discovery technique the creditor is most likely to use is a deposition (also called a "Rule 2004" examination in bankruptcy)—a proceeding in which you answer questions posed by the creditor's attorney orally, under oath, before a court reporter. If a creditor sends you a discovery request, the court will postpone the confirmation hearing to give the creditor time to gather evidence.

This section describes the four most common objections creditors raise to Chapter 13 plans.

The Plan Is Not Submitted in Good Faith

Probably the most common objection creditors raise is that a Chapter 13 plan was not proposed in good faith. The bankruptcy rules don't define good faith, but bankruptcy courts will take this type of objection seriously if you have proposed a plan that appears to be impossible for you to carry through. However, if you filed your papers with the honest intention of getting back on your feet and making all payments required in a Chapter 13 case by the bankruptcy code (11 U.S.C. §§ 1322 and 1325), you should be able to overcome this objection.

Occasionally, creditors make a good-faith objection as a negotiating ploy. They want you to change your plan to satisfy them rather than argue the issue to the judge. If you think this is going on, your lawyer will help you figure out whether you have anything to worry about—that is, whether there are any valid, good-faith objections to your plan.

When a creditor makes a good-faith objection, most bankruptcy courts look at these factors:

- **How often you have filed for bankruptcy.** Filing multiple bankruptcies in and of itself does not show bad faith. If, however, you've filed and dismissed two or more other bankruptcy cases within a year, the court may find that you lack good faith if your papers are inconsistent or you can't show that your circumstances have changed since the previous dismissal. Changed circumstances sufficient to support a refiling might include:
  - an increase in your income
  - a reduction of your debt
  - a new job that will permit use of an income deduction order
  - your spouse's decision to file jointly with you, or
  - the end of a condition that required your previous dismissal, such as illness or unemployment.

  The court might also find a lack of good faith if you file for Chapter 13 bankruptcy within four years after filing a case in which you received a Chapter 7 discharge, and you propose to pay your unsecured creditors substantially less than what you owe them. In this situation, the court may well find that you are using Chapter 13 to circumvent Chapter 7's prohibition on filing a second Chapter 7 case within eight years of receiving a prior discharge.

- **The accuracy of your bankruptcy papers and statements.** The court is likely to find a lack of good faith if you misrepresent your income, debts, expenses, or assets or you lie at the creditors' meeting or a deposition. Creditors will look for discrepancies by comparing your written and oral statements with credit applications and financial data you submitted to them—such as tax returns and bank statements. Even if your mistakes were purely accidental, the appearance of sloppiness (such as failing to mention property or minor debts, providing the wrong Social Security number, listing insufficient or incorrect information about creditors, or incorrectly valuing your property) will lead some courts to dismiss your case on the ground that you failed to meet your obligations as a debtor. If you discover any inaccuracy in your papers after you file them, be sure to point it out to the trustee at the creditors' meeting and promptly make the appropriate amendments.

- **Your motive for filing for Chapter 13 bankruptcy.** If you want to cure your mortgage default and get back on track with your house payments, pay off a tax debt, or get some breathing room to pay off your creditors, you have nothing to worry about. If the court finds that you have either of the following motives, however, it might also find a lack of good faith:
  - You filed for bankruptcy solely to reject a lease or contract, such as a time-share or car lease.
  - You filed for bankruptcy to handle only one debt, other than mortgage arrears or back taxes. The court is particularly likely to find lack of good faith if you file only to restructure payment on a nondischargeable debt, such as a student loan or criminal fine.
- **Your efforts to repay your debts.** If you will pay your nonpriority, unsecured creditors less than the full amount you owe, you will have to show the court that you are stretching your budget as much as you can. The court will want to see that the expenses you deduct from your income when calculating your disposable income are reasonably necessary to support yourself and your dependents. You'll have few problems if you can show that you've eliminated payments on luxury items, depleted your investments, canceled your country club membership, brought down your living expenses, and/or increased your hours at work.
- **The cause of your financial trouble.** Bankruptcy courts are reluctant to find bad faith if your financial problems are due to events beyond your control, such as exceptional medical expenses or an accident, job loss, or death in the family.

The Plan Is Not Feasible

The second most likely objection is that your plan is not feasible—that is, that you won't be able to make required payments or comply with the other terms of the plan.

There are two arguments a creditor might make:

- Your Form 22C (along with Schedules I and J) do not show that you have enough income to pay all required debts. For instance, if you owe $35,000 in priority taxes (which must be paid in full) but your current monthly income won't allow you to pay $583 a month ($34,980) for the next five years, you can't propose a feasible plan.
- Your income as shown in Schedule I (your actual current income) does not exceed your expenses as listed in Schedule J by enough to pay all required debts. If, on the other hand, your Schedule I income, when compared to your Schedule J expenses, is sufficient to pay all your mandatory debts, you may be able to propose a feasible plan even if you have nothing left over to pay your unsecured creditors. This will depend on whether or not your bankruptcy court lets you use your Schedules I and J to propose a feasible plan or whether you are forced to use the figures listed on Form 22C. (For more information, see "If Your Actual Is Different From Your "Current Monthly Income": *Hamilton v. Lanning*," in Ch. 5.)

Your creditors might also question your job stability, the likelihood that you'll incur extraordinary expenses, and whether you have any outside sources of money. The court will likely find that your plan is not feasible—and refuse to confirm it—if any of the following is true:

- Your business has been failing, but you have predicted a rebound (on a wing and a prayer) and intend to use the proceeds to make your plan payments.
- You propose making plan payments from the proceeds of the sale of certain property, but a sale isn't imminent. For example, if your house

has been on the market for a long time and you haven't received any offers, the court probably won't confirm a plan that depends on your house selling.

- Your plan includes a balloon payment, but you haven't identified a source of money you'll use to make the payment.
- You owe back child support or alimony and have been held in contempt of court for failing to pay.
- You've been convicted of a crime and face a likely jail sentence.

The Plan Is Not in the Best Interests of the Creditors

When you file for Chapter 13 bankruptcy, you must pay your unsecured creditors at least as much as they would have received if you had filed for Chapter 7 bankruptcy—in other words, you must pay them at least the value of your nonexempt property less the trustee's fee and costs of sale. (See Ch. 5 for more information on this requirement.) This is called the "best interests of the creditors" test.

If a creditor raises this objection, your attorney will prepare a written "liquidation analysis" that provides the value of the property (including how you came up with that value), the exemption you are claiming, the trustee's statutory commission, and the costs of sale, if any. The final result—the value of the property, less your exempt amount, the trustee's commission, and the costs of sale—is the proper value to use when determining whether your plan satisfies the best interests of the creditors. You may be called on to negotiate one or more numbers in your liquidation analysis, but the burden will be on the creditor to prove why your numbers are wrong.

If you lose on this point, you'll need to raise the amount of your monthly payments to your nonpriority, unsecured creditors or extend the life of your plan (if it doesn't already last for five years).

The Plan Unfairly Discriminates

In your plan, you must specify which unsecured creditors will be paid in full and which, if any, will get less. To do that, you can create classes of unsecured creditors, specifying how much (or what percentage of your payments) each class will receive, as long as you do not unfairly discriminate against any particular creditor. (Classes of creditors are explained in Ch. 8.)

Handling Creditor Claims

After you file for bankruptcy, the trustee sends a notice of your bankruptcy filing to all the creditors you listed in your papers. In general, creditors who want to be paid must file a claim within 90 days after the meeting of creditors is first scheduled to be held. If the meeting is rescheduled, the deadline is still 90 days from the originally scheduled date.

Sometimes, a creditor you want to pay through your Chapter 13 plan forgets to file a claim. If this happens, you may have to file a *Proof of Claim* on behalf of the creditor. For example, if you want the trustee to pay the creditor under your plan and the trustee won't make the payment without a *Proof of Claim*, you will have to file one for the creditor. The time limit for filing a *Proof of Claim* on a creditor's behalf is short—you have only 30 days after the deadline the creditor missed to file your papers. (Bankruptcy Rule 3004.)

Secured creditors. The bankruptcy code does not expressly require secured creditors to file claims in order to be paid, but few trustees will pay secured creditors unless there's a claim on file. (Even if a secured creditor doesn't file a claim, however, the creditor's lien stays on the property.)

> ! CAUTION
> **To pay arrearages on a secured debt, you must file a *Proof of Claim*.** If you want to make up missed payments on a secured debt in your Chapter 13 case and the secured creditor doesn't file a claim, you will have to file it on the creditor's behalf. For example, if you have missed three house payments, but the lender doesn't file a claim, the trustee won't pay your arrears through your plan unless you file the claim yourself. If you don't, the lender would probably ask the court for permission to proceed with a foreclosure.

New Rules and Forms: Mortgage Holders and Servicers Must Make Additional Disclosures in *Proofs of Claim*

Chapter 13 bankruptcy has become an increasingly important remedy for people who are at odds with their mortgage servicers. Mortgage-related issues in Chapter 13 usually center around the lender's *Proof of Claim*. In the past, many such *Proofs of Claim* have not adequately documented arrears and fees, and have contained statements that are misleading or untrue. Also, after the Chapter 13 discharge, many mortgage servicers have attempted to collect arrears and fees that supposedly accrued in the course of the bankruptcy without giving the debtor notice of these charges and fees.

Recently, new bankruptcy rules and forms were promulgated in an effort to address these issues. New Rule 3002.1, revised Official Form 10 (*Proof of Claim*), and a new required attachment to Form 10 (*Mortgage Proof of Claim Attachment*) require servicers to provide debtors with details regarding alleged prepetition mortgage arrears and fees, and to provide continuous notification to the debtor of postpetition arrears and fees that allegedly accrue during the bankruptcy. Finally, the new rule and forms require that the person signing the *Proof of Claim* have personal knowledge of the contents of the *Proof of Claim*. Hopefully this will eliminate or reduce robosigning—the practice where many lenders and servicers used a signing clerk who prepared and signed mortgage-related documents but who had no knowledge of the facts alleged in the documents.

Priority creditors. Priority creditors must file a claim to be paid. Most priority creditors must file the claim within 90 days after the date set for the first meeting of creditors. Government agencies must file a *Proof of Claim* within 180 days after the date you filed your case. The government can get an extension if it formally requests one before the 180 days expire. (Bankruptcy Rule 3002(c)(1).) The IRS is notoriously late in filing claims, but it is usually granted extensions.

Nonpriority, unsecured creditors. Nonpriority, unsecured creditors must file a claim to be paid. If a nonpriority, unsecured creditor does not, that creditor's debt will be discharged when you complete your plan, unless the debt is nondischargeable.

If you want to pay a nondischargeable unsecured debt through your Chapter 13 plan (to avoid having the debt remain after your case ends) and the creditor doesn't file a claim, you will have to file it on the creditor's behalf.

Objecting to a Creditor's Claim

Unless you file a written objection to a creditor's claim, the trustee will pay the claim. (In bankruptcy legalese, claims the trustee pays are called "allowed" claims.) You can file an objection at any time, but the sooner the better. You'll have to give notice and schedule a court hearing, at which the creditor must prove you owe the claim. This is where you get to contest the validity of a disputed debt, such as a mortgage or tax debt.

Possible reasons for objecting to a creditor's claim include:

- You owe less than the creditor claims you do.
- A secured creditor has overstated the value of the collateral.
- The creditor has characterized the debt as secured (meaning you'll have to pay it in full), and you think it's unsecured.
- The claim was filed late. Most courts disallow late claims. Some, however, allow late claims if the creditor shows "excusable neglect" or another good reason for the failure to file on time.
- The creditor hasn't provided a paper trail proving that it owns the lien—for example, the creditor can't come up with a copy of your original promissory note and security agreement or can't produce assignments linking itself to those original documents. (This ground for objecting to a claim is increasingly common in cases involving foreclosures.)

Asking the Court to Eliminate Liens

During your Chapter 13 case, you may be able to get the court to reduce or eliminate liens on your property. If you succeed, you'll still owe the debt, but it will be unsecured. The creditor then shares in what you are paying your other unsecured creditors and you keep the property. Even if you're paying your other

Objecting to a *Proof of Claim* for a Credit Card Debt

The court will presume that a *Proof of Claim* submitted on a credit card debt (most likely by your credit card company) is valid if it is accompanied by a statement that includes the following information"

- if the entity filing the *Proof of Claim* is not the original lender or card issuer (for example, if the claim holder is a collection agency or the original issuer sold your account to someone else), the name of the entity that the claim holder purchased the account from
- the name of the entity to whom the debt was owed when you made your last transaction on the account
- the date of your last transaction on the account
- the date of your last payment on the account, and
- if the account was charged off, the date on which this was done.

The claim holder must also state the amount of the debt prior to your bankruptcy filing and break down any additional charges, such as interest, late fees, and attorneys' fees.

If the *Proof of Claim* includes this information, then you have the burden of refuting the claim as part of your objection. If the *Proof of Claim* doesn't include this information, the creditor must prove the claim. Finally, if the holder of the claim is not the original creditor, the creditor must provide documentation that ownership of the claim has been transferred, in addition to providing the other information. (See *In re Armstrong*, 320 B.R. 97 (N.D. Tex. 2005).)

If you are proposing to pay a very small percentage of your nonpriority, unsecured debt, it may not be worth your time to object to a credit card claim. Even if you win, that just means you will have to pay your other nonpriority, unsecured creditors a little more. Remember, the amount you have to pay to these creditors is based on your disposable income. You shouldn't spend time worrying about which creditors get what. Or, as the old saying goes, "Don't sweat the small stuff."

unsecured creditors 100%, avoiding the lien is still worthwhile, because you get to keep your property with clear title. (See *In re Lane*, 280 F.3d 663 (6th Cir. 2002).)

Which Liens Can Be Avoided

Lien avoidance is a procedure by which you ask the bankruptcy court to allow you to "avoid" (eliminate or reduce) certain liens. If your Chapter 13 repayment plan proposes to pay nothing or very little on your unsecured debts, lien avoidance makes a lot of sense. As long as there's a lien, you have to pay it in full to keep your secured property.

Lien avoidance is available only in very limited circumstances, and only for certain types of liens.

Security Interest Liens

A security interest is a secured debt you take on voluntarily, by pledging property as collateral for the debt. The creditor's interest in the collateral is secured by a lien. Common security interests include mortgages, home equity loans, car loans, store charges that contain a security agreement, and bank loans for which you pledge collateral.

You can avoid a security interest lien only if it meets these criteria:

1. **You obtained the loan by pledging property you already own (not property you purchased with the loan).** This is called a nonpossessory, nonpurchase-money security interest. It sounds complicated, but it's easier to understand when you break it down:
   - Nonpossessory means the creditor does not physically keep the property you pledge as collateral—you do. (In contrast, if you leave you property at a pawn shop to get a loan, that would be a possessory security interest, for which lien avoidance is not available.)
   - Nonpurchase money means you didn't use the money from the loan to buy the collateral.
   - Security interest means the lien was created by agreement between you and the creditor.
2. **The property you pledged is exempt.** Exemptions are explained in Ch. 5.

3. The collateral you pledged fits into certain categories of property. These categories are:

- household furnishings, household goods, clothing, appliances, books, musical instruments, or jewelry that is primarily for your personal, family, or household use
- health aids professionally prescribed for you or a dependent
- animals or crops held primarily for your personal, family, or household use (but only the first $5,000 of the lien can be avoided), or
- implements, professional books, or tools used in a trade (yours or a dependent's), but only the first $5,000 of the lien can be avoided.

These rules prevent you from eliminating liens on real estate or on motor vehicles, unless the vehicle is a tool of your trade. Generally, a vehicle is not considered a tool of the trade unless it is an integral part of your business—for example, you are a door-to-door salesperson or make deliveries. If you just use your vehicle to get to and from work, it isn't considered a tool of the trade, even if you have no other way to commute.

 TIP

You can strip certain liens from your home. Although you cannot avoid liens like the first mortgage on your residence, you may be able to get rid of second mortgages and home loans through a process known as lien stripping. See Ch. 1 for details.

Nonconsensual Liens

A nonconsensual lien—a secured debt that you didn't agree to—can be avoided only if:

- It's a judicial lien.
- You can claim the property as exempt.
- The lien, if honored, would deprive you of your full exemption.

You can remove judicial liens from any exempt property, including real estate and cars.

Tax Liens

If your federal tax debt is secured, you may have a basis for challenging the lien. Quite often, the IRS makes mistakes when it records a Notice of Federal Tax Lien.

Here are some possible grounds for asking the court to remove a tax lien:

- The Notice of Federal Tax Lien was never recorded, though the IRS claims it was.
- The Notice of Federal Tax Lien was recorded after the automatic stay took effect.
- The Notice of Federal Tax Lien was recorded in the wrong county—it must be recorded where you own real estate for it to attach to the real estate in that county.
- The Notice of Federal Tax Lien was recorded against the wrong assets, such as your child's house, not yours.

Even if the Notice of Federal Tax Lien was recorded correctly, you still may have a basis to fight it if:

- The lien expired (liens last only ten years).
- The lien is based on an invalid tax assessment by the IRS.

Carrying Out Your Plan

Once the court has approved your repayment plan, you should be in for smooth sailing as long as you make your monthly payments. If an unforeseen problem arises, and you think you're going to have trouble making a payment, notify your attorney right away. Your attorney will notify the trustee and help you work something out.

The trustee is interested in your successful completion of your Chapter 13 plan. Remember, the trustee gets a cut of everything paid to creditors under your plan. If you have to convert to Chapter 7 or your case is dismissed, the trustee's income from your case will be cut off.

This chapter covers issues that might arise after your plan is confirmed as well as what happens once you complete your plan.

Your Income Increases

There are a couple of ways for the trustee to keep track of your income as your case proceeds. You may be asked to submit an annual income and expense statement to the trustee (and to any creditor who requests one). In addition, you must remain current on your tax returns throughout your case and provide a copy of your tax return to the trustee (and to any creditor who makes a request). (For more information on these requirements, see Ch. 10.) From these documents, the trustee can determine whether your income has increased.

If your financial condition improves sufficiently to allow you to pay more to your unsecured creditors (assuming your plan doesn't provide for them to be paid in full), the trustee or an unsecured creditor may file a motion with the bankruptcy court to amend your plan. The motion will request that the court order you to increase each payment, pay a lump sum amount (especially if you've inherited valuable property or won the lottery), or extend your plan (unless it already lasts for five years). The bankruptcy court will most likely grant the motion.

What If Your Income Increases Because You Pay Off a 401(k) Loan?

If, during the course of your Chapter 13 plan, you pay off a loan you took out from your 401(k) plan, your income will effectively increase (since you'll no longer be making those loan payments). Do you have to modify your plan to pay more into it?

One court has ruled that in this situation your plan payments can remain the same. The idea being that you can contribute the amount formerly dedicated to repaying the loan to your 401(k) plan. (*In re Egan*, 458 B.R. 836 (Bankr. E.D. Pa. 2011).)

However, other courts have ruled the opposite: That you must modify your plan so that unsecured creditors get paid more. (See, for example, *In re Noll* ___ B.R. ___ No. 10-35209 (Bankr. E.D. Wis. 2010) and *In re Brann* 457 B.R. 738 (Bankr. C.D. Ill. 2011).)

If You Get a Windfall

If you win the lottery, get a substantial raise, or receive an inheritance, or if your house goes way up in value, you may be able to dismiss your case and pay off your debts outside of bankruptcy. But keep in mind that the interest (and sometimes the penalties) on your debts that stopped accruing while you were in bankruptcy can be added back when you dismiss your case. And, don't assume you can use the equity in your home to apply for and obtain a loan. Don't dismiss your case and then apply for the loan. If you are rejected, you'll just have to refile for bankruptcy.

Selling Property

Certain property remains under the control of the bankruptcy court even after your plan is approved. (See Ch. 10 for more information.) If you want to sell any of this property, the court (or in some cases, the trustee) will have to approve the sale. And your unsecured creditors might object if you'd pocket any cash left over after paying off any liens on the property, rather than use it to pay their claims.

Modifying Your Plan When Problems Come Up

Chapter 13 bankruptcy isn't easy. You must live under a strict budget for three to five years. Problems are bound to arise. Fortunately, the Chapter 13 bankruptcy system has built-in procedures designed to handle the disruptions. Any time after your plan is confirmed, you, the trustee, or an unsecured creditor who filed a claim can file a motion with the court, asking permission to modify the plan. Keep in mind that your modified plan cannot last more than five years after the date your plan originally began.

This section discusses five common situations in which you might need to modify your plan.

You Miss a Payment

If the trustee doesn't receive a plan payment, expect a phone call. Sometimes, the problem will be easy to solve—the payment got lost in the mail, your employer forgot to send it (if there is an income deduction order), or you changed jobs and forgot to change the income deduction order.

If you missed the payment because you are struggling to make ends meet, resolving the problem may be more complicated. But don't lose heart. If the problem looks temporary, and you are several months or years into your plan, the trustee may suggest that you modify your plan to do any of the following:

- skip a few payments altogether, meaning your unsecured creditors would receive less than you originally proposed
- skip a few payments now and extend your plan to make them up, assuming your plan is not already scheduled to last five years
- make a lump sum payment to make up the payments you've missed, or
- increase several payments to cover the payments you missed.

If the problem looks likely to continue, or it happens very early in your Chapter 13 case, the trustee is less likely to support a modification of your plan. Instead, the trustee (or a creditor) is likely to file a motion to have your case dismissed or require you to convert to Chapter 7.

If you file a motion to modify your plan because you've missed some payments, a creditor may ask that the modified plan contain what is called a drop-dead clause. Such a clause provides that if you miss another payment, your case will automatically convert to Chapter 7 bankruptcy or be dismissed by the court. Many courts include drop-dead clauses in modified plans.

Your plan payment isn't the only payment you might miss. If the court approved your request to make direct payments to certain creditors (such as a mortgage lender) and you miss a payment, the creditor will run to the court. Most likely, the creditor will file a motion to have the automatic stay lifted, which would let the creditor go after any property you've acquired since filing for bankruptcy. Alternatively, the creditor may ask the court to dismiss your case or convert it to Chapter 7. If it's early in your plan and you haven't missed any other payments, ask the court for permission to modify your plan to pay the new arrears immediately.

Your Disposable Income Decreases

You wouldn't have filed for Chapter 13 bankruptcy if you hadn't had debt problems in your past—perhaps because of job losses or reduced work hours. Filing for bankruptcy doesn't make those kinds of problems go away.

If your income goes down, you or your spouse suffers a serious illness or goes on maternity leave, or you incur an extraordinary expense, call the trustee. The trustee is likely to suggest that you suspend payments for a month or two. You can make up the difference by modifying your plan to:

- make a lump sum payment when your income goes back up
- extend your plan, if it is scheduled to last less than five years, or
- decrease the amount or percentage that a certain class of creditor receives—for example, you might have originally proposed to pay your general unsecured creditors 75% of what you owe but will now file a modified plan that calls for them to get only 45%.

Creditors rarely object to a short suspension in payments, and bankruptcy courts routinely grant those modifications. If you propose a longer-term suspension, however, your secured creditors may object, especially if collateral is involved that is decreasing in value. You may have to continue your payments on secured debts and suspend only the unsecured portion for a while.

You Need to Replace Your Car

A lot can go wrong with a car during the three to five years you're paying into your Chapter 13 plan—especially if you bought a used car before you filed to minimize your expenses. Chapter 13 trustees often hear from debtors whose cars have died or are on their last legs. This situation raises several issues in a Chapter 13 bankruptcy case.

Taking out a new loan. Let's say your car dies, you need another one, and you want to take out a loan to pay for it. You file a motion to modify your plan to include payments for the new loan. Will the court confirm the new plan? The court is likely to say "yes" if you *must* have the car to complete your plan—for example, you're a salesperson. If, however, the car is just a convenience, the payments will significantly increase your monthly expenses, and you've had trouble making your plan payments, the court will probably turn you down.

For most people, the need for a car isn't all or nothing. In that case, the court will probably allow you to take out the loan if the effect is to lower your bills (for example, you were still making payments on your previous car and the loan will reduce your payments) or to increase your income (for instance, it would take two hours each way to get to work by public transit and only 30 minutes by car, so with a car you can get paid for three more hours' work a day).

Giving back a wrecked car. Now let's assume that after your plan is confirmed, your car is wrecked or won't run. You want to give the car back to the lender and modify your plan to treat the balance due (called a deficiency) as an unsecured claim. Several courts have allowed this. Other courts have ruled that a secured creditor cannot be reclassified as an unsecured creditor after a plan has been confirmed and that the debtor still must pay the full balance owed the lender.

A court might look at how you got into the situation. If your negligence or recklessness caused the problem, the court may be more inclined to deny modification of your plan.

What happens to insurance proceeds. If your car loan is paid off and your car is damaged in an accident, you may get some insurance money. The court will probably want you to use that money to get the new car you need. If your car wasn't paid off, the insurance money will go to pay off your lender. If the insurance proceeds exceed what you owe the lender under your plan, you get to keep the difference. Remember, once the court determines the amount a secured creditor is entitled to get under the plan, that's all the creditor gets.

You Incur New Debt

If you fail to pay debts you incur after your plan is confirmed, you can amend your plan so these creditors are paid through your plan. You may have anticipated this by creating a class of postpetition creditors in your plan. If so, your plan should specify that these creditors receive 100% of what they are owed, plus interest. If you didn't create such a class, you'll have to handle postpetition debts as they arise.

No matter what your plan provides, your postpetition creditors will need to file a claim with the trustee in order to get paid through your plan.

If Your Plan Includes a Class of Postpetition Creditors

If your plan includes 100% payment of your postpetition debts, your postpetition creditors are unlikely to object to being paid through the trustee.

If, however, the creditor disagrees with the terms of your plan or you miss a plan payment, the creditor might object. If this happens, you will have to modify your plan to handle the creditor's objection. If the creditor is still not satisfied, the creditor might file a motion with the bankruptcy court asking the court to lift the automatic stay. If the court grants the motion, the creditor would be allowed to go after your postpetition property and income for payment.

EXAMPLE: For the first year and a half of your plan, you will be paying your priority tax debt and your mortgage arrears. Not until Month 19 will the trustee pay your unsecured creditors, including a class of postpetition creditors. Three months into your plan, the court lets you incur a medical debt. The doctor objects to being paid through the plan because the first payment won't come for at least 16 months. You will probably have to amend your plan to add the medical debt to the other debts that will be paid off early in the plan.

If Your Plan Does Not Include a Class of Postpetition Creditors

If your plan does not include a class of postpetition creditors, and you want to pay a new creditor through your plan, you will have to modify your plan. Sometimes, a postpetition creditor files a motion to be included in a modified Chapter 13 plan. The motion is likely to be granted.

If you don't modify your plan to include postpetition creditors to whom you default, the creditor may be able to take collection efforts against property you acquired after filing for bankruptcy.

You Buy Health Insurance

Chapter 13 debtors can reduce what they pay into their repayment plans by the actual amount they spend to buy health insurance for themselves and their families. This is intended to help reduce the number of people who go without health insurance.

To take advantage of this new rule, you have to demonstrate a number of facts, including:

- The insurance is necessary.
- The cost of the insurance is reasonable.
- The cost is not significantly more than the cost of your previous policy or the cost necessary to maintain the lapsed policy (if you were previously insured).
- You have not already claimed the cost as an expense for purposes of determining your disposable income (on Form 22C or Schedule J).
- You actually purchased the policy.

Attempts to Revoke Your Confirmation

If a creditor or the trustee thinks you obtained your confirmation fraudulently—for example, because you used a false name, address, or Social Security number—one of them may file something called an adversary proceeding asking the court to revoke your confirmation. This is extremely rare. An adversary proceeding to revoke a confirmation must be filed within 180 days of the confirmation.

An adversary proceeding is much more formal than a motion. It creates an entirely new lawsuit, separate from your bankruptcy case, and proceeds like any other lawsuit. You will need a lawyer to help you.

The bankruptcy court won't revoke your confirmation because of fraud unless it finds that:

- You made a materially (significant) false statement in your papers, in a deposition, or in court.
- You either knew the statement was false or made the statement with reckless disregard to its truth.
- You intended to induce the court into relying on the statement.
- The court did rely on the statement.

When You Complete Your Plan

It's quite an accomplishment—and something to be proud of—to stick with a Chapter 13 plan to the end. After you have made all of your payments under your plan, filed a certificate showing that you have completed your financial management counseling, and certified that you are current on your domestic support obligations (if any), the court grants a "full payment" discharge. In most courts, the trustee simply files the discharge order on behalf of the court after determining that all payments have been made. In other courts, you must ask the trustee (by phone is fine) to file the discharge order.

 TIP

File Form 23 right away. You must complete a financial management counseling course—and file a certification, Form 23, stating that you have done so—before you make your last plan payment. If you don't file Form 23 on time, the court will close your case without granting you a discharge. To get your discharge, you will have to reopen the case and pay fees. To avoid this fate, file Form 23 as soon as you complete your counseling, even if you haven't yet reached your final plan payment.

Debts Covered by the Discharge

Your Chapter 13 discharge wipes out the balance owed on all of your debts, as long as the debt is included in your plan and does not fall into one of these categories:

- long-term obligations for which the last payment is still due—that is, it will be paid after you've made the final payment on your plan
- nondischargeable debts, as described in Ch. 1, or
- debts you incurred after filing your Chapter 13 case, if the creditor was not paid or was only partially paid through the plan.

The Discharge Hearing

After struggling for years to repay your debts, the long-awaited end of your bankruptcy case may be a little anticlimactic. The court may hold a brief hearing, called a discharge hearing, and require you to attend. At the hearing, the judge explains the effects of discharging your debts in bankruptcy and may lecture you about staying clear of debt.

Few courts, however, schedule a discharge hearing in Chapter 13 cases. Whether or not you must attend a discharge hearing, you'll receive a copy of your discharge order from the court within about four weeks after you complete your payments. If you don't, call the trustee. Make several photocopies of the order and keep them in a safe place. If it's necessary, send copies to creditors who attempt to collect their debt after your case is over or to credit bureaus that continue to report that you owe a discharged debt.

Ending the Income Deduction Order

The trustee will probably remember to stop your income deduction order after you've made your last payment. If the trustee forgets, however, you may need to call and raise the issue.

Debtor Rehabilitation Program

A few Chapter 13 bankruptcy courts have created debtor rehabilitation/credit reestablishment programs. The purpose is to reward people who choose Chapter 13 bankruptcy instead of Chapter 7 bankruptcy and who succeed in completing their Chapter 13 cases.

If you have paid off a high percentage of your unsecured debts (often 75% or more), you may apply for credit from certain creditors.

In the typical program, the court staff includes a "credit liaison." This person will help you:

- acquire, review, and correct your credit file—in particular, to get your credit file to show that you completed a Chapter 13 bankruptcy in which you paid back a high percentage of your debts
- set up a budget
- analyze your ability to repay new debts
- understand the different types of credit
- identify possible sources of credit and credit limits
- fill out credit applications
- obtain information to support your application, such as your Chapter 13 payment history and completed plan
- prepare for any in-person interview with a creditor (for a car loan, for example), and
- understand how creditors make their decisions about extending credit.

Ask the trustee whether your court has a rehabilitation program. If it doesn't, find out from the trustee if a nearby bankruptcy court has one in which you might participate. If there's nothing nearby, you'll have to take your own steps to rebuild your credit. (See Ch. 14.)

If You Cannot Complete Your Plan

Despite your best efforts to keep a handle on your finances and make your regular plan payments, you may be unable to complete your plan. If this happens to you, take solace in the fact that you aren't alone—a significant percentage of Chapter 13 debtors eventually find themselves in this position.

If you can't complete your plan, you have three options: Dismiss your case, convert it to a Chapter 7 bankruptcy, or ask the court to grant you a hardship discharge.

Dismiss Your Case

You have the absolute right to dismiss your Chapter 13 bankruptcy case at any time, as long as:

- The court doesn't believe that you filed your bankruptcy case in bad faith (see Ch. 11).
- You didn't start in another type of bankruptcy (typically, Chapter 7) and then convert to Chapter 13 bankruptcy.

If you converted to Chapter 13 from a different type of bankruptcy, you have to file a noticed motion asking the court for permission to dismiss your case. (See Ch. 11 for information on noticed motions.) The court may deny your request—and order you to convert to Chapter 7 bankruptcy—if it feels that you are abusing the bankruptcy system. Or, it may grant your request, but sanction (fine) you or issue an order barring you from filing for bankruptcy again for a certain period of time.

If your case is dismissed, there are several important consequences:

- All liens that you had removed from your property in your Chapter 13 case are reinstated.
- All money you have paid the trustee that has not yet been disbursed to your creditors will be returned to you, less the trustee's expenses.
- The automatic stay ends, which means that your creditors are free to go after you and your assets for payment.
- Interest (and in some cases penalties) that stopped accruing during your bankruptcy will be added on to your debts.
- You cannot refile for bankruptcy—Chapter 13, Chapter 7, or any other kind—within 180 days if

you dismissed your case because a creditor filed a motion asking the bankruptcy court to lift the automatic stay.

If you change your mind and decide that you want your case to proceed, you can file a motion with the bankruptcy court within ten days of the dismissal asking that your case be reinstated. Unless you have a history of filing and dismissing, or you've had serious problems making the payments under this plan, the court will probably grant your motion.

Convert Your Case to Chapter 7 Bankruptcy

You have an absolute right to convert your Chapter 13 bankruptcy case to a Chapter 7 bankruptcy case at any time, as long as you haven't received a Chapter 7 discharge in a case filed within the previous eight years.

When you convert to Chapter 7, the bankruptcy forms you filed for your Chapter 13 case will usually become a part of your new case. A few bankruptcy courts require you to file an entirely new set of schedules, even if nothing has changed. Within 30 days after you convert, you must file one additional bankruptcy form called the *Statement of Intention*. It tells the court what you plan to do with your secured debts. You will also have to attend a new meeting of creditors.

Because any debts you incurred after filing your Chapter 13 case can be discharged in your Chapter 7 case (if they are otherwise dischargeable), you must amend the appropriate forms to list these new debts.

If, in your Chapter 13 case, the court established a value for certain items of property or determined the amount of a secured claim, those values and amounts will not necessarily apply in the converted case. (11 U.S.C. § 348(f)(1)(B).)

Some courts determine your exemptions as of the date you filed for Chapter 13 bankruptcy, while other courts determine them as of the date you convert to Chapter 7. In the latter situation, if you've acquired nonexempt property after filing your Chapter 13 case, you will be at risk of losing it in your Chapter 7 case. In addition, if the court determines that your conversion to Chapter 7 bankruptcy is in bad faith, the court can order that the new property be included in your Chapter 7 bankruptcy estate. (11 U.S.C. § 348(f)(2).)

If your creditors have filed *Proofs of Claim*, those claims carry over to your Chapter 7 case. However, if you dismiss your Chapter 13 case and refile a Chapter 7 case, your creditors will have to file new claims, assuming you have assets to be distributed.

> ! CAUTION
>
> **You may have to pass the means test when you convert to Chapter 7.** Just because you have a right to convert your Chapter 13 case to Chapter 7 doesn't mean you will necessarily qualify for Chapter 7 relief. In particular, if you cannot pass the means test because of your income, you may run into trouble in some districts. Some bankruptcy courts (and one Bankruptcy Appellate Panel) have ruled that if you convert to Chapter 7 from a Chapter 13 case, you must still pass the means test in order to be eligible for Chapter 7 relief. (See, e.g., *In re Chapman*, 447 B.R. 250 (B.A.P. 8th Cir. 2011); *In re Lassiter*, 2011 WL 2039363 (Bankr. E.D. Va. 2011); *In re Phillips*, 417 B.R. 30 (Bankr. S.D. Ohio 2009).) Other courts, however, have ruled that the means test doesn't apply to Chapter 7 cases that have been converted from Chapter 13. (See, e.g., *In re Guarin*, 2009 WL 4500476 (Bankr. D. Mass. 2009); *In re Willis*, 408 B.R. 803 (Bankr. W.D. Missouri 2009); *In re Dudley*, 405 B.R. 790 (Bankr. W.D. Va. 2009).)

> 📖 RESOURCE
>
> **Resource for Chapter 7 bankruptcy.** *How to File for Chapter 7 Bankruptcy*, by Stephen Elias, Albin Renauer, and Robin Leonard (Nolo), contains detailed information on Chapter 7 bankruptcy. It includes the instructions you will need to file the additional form (the *Statement of Intention*) and to amend the forms you've already filed.

Seek a Hardship Discharge

If you cannot complete your Chapter 13 repayment plan, you can file a motion with the bankruptcy court asking for a hardship discharge. (11 U.S.C. § 1328(b).)

The court will grant your request only if three conditions are met:

- You failed to complete your plan payments due to circumstances "for which you should not justly be held accountable." Your burden is to show the maximum possible misery and the worst of awfuls—that is, more than just a temporary job loss or temporary physical disability. Proving that your condition is permanent is usually key; you may need to bring medical evidence to court.
- Based on what you have already paid into the plan, your unsecured creditors have received at least what they would have received if you had filed for Chapter 7. (This is typically a hard condition to meet unless you have little or no nonexempt property.)
- Modification of your plan is not practical. To meet this requirement, you do not have to file a motion for modification and lose it; you just have to show the bankruptcy court that you wouldn't be able to make payments even under a modified plan.

Debts That Are Not Discharged

If the court grants your motion for a hardship discharge, only unsecured, nonpriority, dischargeable debts are discharged. The following debts typically are not wiped out in a hardship discharge:

- priority debts
- secured debts
- arrears on secured debts
- debts you didn't list in your bankruptcy papers
- student loans
- most federal, state, and local taxes, as well as any amounts you borrowed or charged on a credit card to pay those taxes
- child support, alimony, and debts resulting from a divorce or separation decree
- fines or restitution imposed in a criminal-type proceeding
- debts for death or personal injury resulting from your intoxicated driving
- debts for dues or special assessments you owe to a condominium or cooperative association
- debts you couldn't discharge in a previous bankruptcy that was dismissed due to fraud or misfeasance, and

- debts you owe to a pension, profit-sharing, stock bonus, or other plan established under various sections of the Internal Revenue Code.

Debts That Are Not Discharged If the Creditor Successfully Objects

Some debts will be discharged in a hardship discharge unless the creditor files a successful objection to the discharge in court. These debts include:

- debts incurred through your fraudulent acts, including using a credit card when you knew you would be unable to pay the bill

- debts from willful and malicious injury you caused to another person or property, and
- debts from embezzlement, larceny, or breach of trust (fiduciary duty).

If you have a debt that falls into one of these categories, your best strategy is to do nothing and hope the creditor does the same. If the creditor objects, the court will examine the circumstances in which you incurred the debt to determine whether or not it can be legally eliminated. If you want the debt to be discharged, you should respond to the creditor's objection.

Life After Bankruptcy

Congratulations! After you receive your final discharge and your case is closed, you can get on with your life and enjoy the fresh start that bankruptcy offers. This chapter explains how you can start to rebuild your credit and how to deal with any problems that come up.

Rebuilding Your Credit

A bankruptcy filing can legally remain on your credit record for ten years after you filed your papers, although most credit bureaus remove a Chapter 13 bankruptcy filing after seven years.

What effect a Chapter 13 bankruptcy will have on your credit score depends on several factors, including the status of your credit before filing and how many accounts were included in the bankruptcy. According to Fair Isaac (the largest credit scoring company in the nation), if you have good credit prior to bankruptcy, your score will likely plummet (at least initially) when you file. However, if you have lots of negative marks on your credit report and a low credit score, filing for bankruptcy will probably have only a modest impact on your credit. Fair Isaac also warns that the more accounts included in your bankruptcy, the more the bankruptcy will negatively affect your score.

Many people believe that filing for Chapter 7 bankruptcy is worse for your credit than filing for Chapter 13. Fair Isaac, however, says both types of bankruptcy have an equally negative impact on your score.

Ironically, in many cases, filing for bankruptcy will help you start building good credit sooner than if you don't file. If you are struggling with more debt than you can pay, the late and missed payments will mount up, and you'll max out your available credit (both big negatives for your credit rating).

Postbankruptcy, your strategy for rebuilding credit is simple: Stick to a budget, always pay your bills on time, and gradually take on credit that you can afford to pay off each month.

RESOURCE

Resource for rebuilding credit. For more information on rebuilding your credit—including obtaining a copy of your credit file, requesting that the credit bureau correct mistakes, contacting creditors directly, and getting positive information into your credit file—see *Credit Repair*, by Robin Leonard and Margaret Reiter (Nolo).

Don't Take on Too Much Debt Too Soon

Habitual overspending can be just as hard to overcome as excessive gambling or drinking. If you think you may be a compulsive spender, avoid getting new credit. Instead, get a handle on your spending habits.

Debtors Anonymous, a 12-step support program similar to Alcoholics Anonymous, has programs nationwide. If a Debtors Anonymous group or a therapist recommends that you stay out of the credit system for a while, follow that advice. Even if you don't feel you're a compulsive spender, paying as you spend may still be the way to go.

To find a Debtors Anonymous meeting close by, go to www.debtorsanonymous.org or call 781-453-2743.

Create a Budget

The first step in rebuilding your credit is to create a budget. Making a budget will help you control impulses to overspend and help you start saving money.

Fortunately, the bankruptcy law requires you to participate in budget counseling prior to getting a discharge. You will be able to apply what you learn in your budget counseling class to our suggestions in this chapter.

Before you try to limit how much you spend, take some time to find out exactly how much money you spend now. Tally up all of your regular expenses, like your mortgage or rent, car payments, insurance, health care costs, food, dry cleaning, and the like. It's often helpful to track your spending for a month by writing down everything you spend each day. This helps you figure out how much you spend on things like entertainment and gifts. Don't forget to add in yearly or quarterly expenses, like homeowners' insurance or car insurance.

When you review your expenses and spending log, look for problem areas. Do you buy things on impulse? Are you spending more than you thought in a certain category? Also think about changes you can make so that you can save money at the end of each week, even if it's just a small amount. Then set a weekly or monthly savings goal.

Once you understand your spending habits and identify the changes you need to make, you're ready to make a budget. At the top of a sheet of paper, write down your monthly net income—that is, the amount you bring home after taxes and other mandatory deductions. At the left, list everything you spend money on in a month, any investments you plan to make (including into a savings or money market account), and any nondischargeable or other debts you make payments on. To the right of each item, write down the amount of money you spend, deposit, or pay each month. Finally, total up the amount. If it exceeds your monthly income, make some changes—eliminate or reduce expenditures for nonnecessities—and start over. Once your budget is final, stick to it.

Keep Your Credit Report Accurate

When you apply for credit, the creditor will contact a credit reporting agency and request a copy of your credit report or it will get your credit score from a credit scoring company, such as Fair Isaac. Your credit score is based on information in your report. Creditors use your report and score to decide whether to grant or deny your credit requests. In addition, some insurance companies, landlords, and employers obtain credit reports when evaluating potential insurance policyholders, tenants, or employees.

To make sure that creditors and others who use your credit report see you in the best light, review your report regularly and take steps to remove inaccurate and old information and add current positive information.

Start by obtaining a copy of your report from each of the "big three" reporting agencies (Equifax, Experian, and TransUnion). You are entitled to a free copy of your report from each agency every 12 months. To get your free report, contact the Annual Credit Report Service. Here's how:

- online at www.annualcreditreport.com
- by phone at 877-322-8228, or
- by mail at Annual Credit Report Request Services, P.O. Box 105281, Atlanta, GA 30348-5281.

Avoiding Financial Problems

These nine rules, suggested by people who have been through bankruptcy, will help you stay out of financial hot water.

1. Create a realistic budget and stick to it.
2. Don't buy on impulse. When you see something you hadn't planned to purchase, go home and think it over. It's unlikely you'll return to the store and buy it.
3. Avoid sales unless you are looking for something you absolutely need. Buying a $500 item on sale for $400 isn't a $100 savings if you didn't need the item in the first place—it's spending $400 unnecessarily.
4. Get medical insurance. You can't avoid medical emergencies, but living without medical insurance is an invitation to financial ruin.
5. Charge items only if you can pay for them now. Don't charge based on future income; sometimes that income doesn't materialize.
6. Avoid large house payments. Obligate yourself only for what you can now afford and increase your mortgage payments only as your income increases. Again, don't obligate yourself based on future income that you might not have.
7. Think long and hard before agreeing to cosign or guarantee a loan for someone. Your signature obligates you as if you were the primary borrower. You can't be sure that the other person will pay.
8. If possible, avoid joint obligations with people who have questionable spending habits. If you incur a joint debt, you're probably liable for it all if the other person defaults.
9. Avoid high-risk investments, such as speculative real estate, penny stocks, and junk bonds. Invest conservatively in things such as certificates of deposit, money market funds, and government bonds. And never invest more than you can afford to lose.

If you need your report more than once within 12 months, you can get another free report in certain circumstances, or you can purchase one for a small fee. To learn more, get *Credit Repair*, by Robin Leonard and Margaret Reiter (Nolo).

In addition to your credit history, your credit report will contain the sources of the information and the names of people or businesses who have requested your report within the last year, or within the last two years if those people sought your report for employment reasons.

Most types of negative credit information can remain on your report for seven years. Bankruptcies can remain on your report for up to ten years, although they often drop off after seven years. Some adverse information about student loans can remain on your report even longer.

Review your report for errors, inaccuracies, and incomplete or old information. You have the right to dispute all incomplete, inaccurate or outdated information. You can do this online or by mail. The credit reporting agency has three days to remove the information, or between 30 and 45 days to investigate, and then an additional five days to remove the information or notify you of its decision.

If the credit reporting agency does not remove the information, you can submit a brief statement giving your side of the story which will be included in your report. Be aware, however, that your sample statement will remain on your report for seven years, which may be longer than the negative item you write about. Most creditors don't read sample statements, but it usually doesn't hurt to include one (unless you don't want it in your report for seven years).

You also want to keep new negative information out of your report. To do this, remain current on your bills. What you owe, as well as how long it takes you to pay, will go in your report.

In addition to information about credit accounts, credit reports also contain information from public records, including criminal records. After receiving your bankruptcy discharge, be sure to modify public records to reflect what occurred in the bankruptcy, so wrong information won't appear in your credit report. For example, if a court case was pending against you at the time you filed for bankruptcy, and, as part of the bankruptcy, the potential judgment against you was discharged, be sure the court case is formally dismissed. You may need the help of an attorney. (See Ch. 15 for information on finding one.)

Avoid Credit Repair Agencies

You've probably seen ads for companies that claim they can fix your credit, qualify you for a loan, and get you a credit card. Stay clear of these companies. Their practices are almost always deceptive and sometimes illegal. Some steal the credit reports or Social Security numbers of people who have died or live in places like Guam or the U.S. Virgin Islands and replace your report with these other reports. Others create new identities for debtors by applying to the IRS for taxpayer ID numbers and telling debtors to use them in place of their Social Security numbers (which is illegal).

Even the legitimate companies can't do anything for you that you can't do yourself. If items in your credit report are correct, these companies cannot get them removed. About the only difference between using a legitimate credit repair agency and doing it yourself is the money you save by doing it yourself.

Negotiate With Current Creditors

If you owe any debts that show up as past due on your credit report (perhaps the debt wasn't discharged in your bankruptcy or was incurred after you filed), you can take steps to make them current. Contact the creditor and ask that the item be removed in exchange for full or partial payment. On a revolving account (with a department store, for example), ask the creditor to "re-age" the account so that it is shown as current. For help in negotiating with your creditors, consider contacting a local consumer credit counseling agency.

 CAUTION

Think carefully before re-aging an account. There is a downside to asking a creditor to re-age an account. It resets the clock on the seven-year period that the creditor can report the delinquent account to credit reporting agencies. If you think you might have trouble paying the account down the line, think twice before asking the creditor to re-age it.

TIP

Choosing a credit counseling agency. Unscrupulous debt relief service agencies abound. They take your money and do little or nothing to help you. Your best bet, when looking for a legitimate credit counseling agency, is to choose one affiliated with the Consumer Credit Counseling Service (CCCS). You can find one at www.nfcc.org or call 800-388-2227. Or use an agency approved by the Office of the U.S. Trustee (the same agencies that you must use to get your prebankruptcy credit counseling).

Stabilize Your Income and Employment

Your credit history and score are not the only thing lenders will consider in deciding whether to give you credit. They also look carefully at the stability of your income and employment. Plus, if you start getting new credit before you're back on your feet financially, you'll end up in the same mess that led you to file for bankruptcy in the first place.

Get Credit and Use It Responsibility

Once you've gotten your finances under control, created a budget, and saved some money, it's time to start adding positive information into your credit report. One of the best ways to do this is to pay your bills on time. Payment history is weighted heavily by creditors and credit scoring agencies. But you can also improve your credit by getting and using small amounts of credit responsibly. Here are a few ways to do that.

Use an Existing Credit Card or Get a New Credit Card

If you have a credit card already, you can charge small amounts and pay the entire balance off each month. This will show creditors that you can use credit responsibly. But be honest with yourself, if you aren't going to pay the balance in full each month, don't use the card.

Getting a new credit card may not be as hard as you think. Many people who have filed for bankruptcy report getting credit card offers shortly after receiving a bankruptcy discharge. Keep in mind, though, that these cards will likely have high interest rates, annual fees, and other charges. Again, use the card to make small charges which you pay off every month.

Get a Secured Credit Card

If you can't get a regular credit card, you may be able to get a secured credit card. This option is good for people who need a credit card to book air travel or hotels. You deposit a sum of money into a bank or credit union savings account and are given a credit card with a credit limit that is a percentage of the amount you deposit (often between 50% and 120% of the amount you deposit).

Secured credit cards often come with extremely high interest rates. So use them carefully. Also, many banks and credit unions don't report payments on secured cards to the credit reporting agencies. If this is the case, using one responsibly will do nothing to improve your credit. Before you get a secured card, find out if the issuer will report payments to the credit reporting agencies. Or look for a secured card that will let you convert it to a regular credit card down the line. Finally, never get a secured credit card that is secured by your home.

CAUTION

Avoid look-alike credit cards. Some lesser-known mail-order companies issue cards that look like credit cards, but allow you to make purchases only from their own catalogues. The items in the catalogue tend to be overpriced and of mediocre (if not poor) quality. And your use of the card isn't reported to credit bureaus, so you won't be rebuilding your credit.

Borrow From a Bank

Bank loans provide an excellent way to rebuild credit. A few banks offer something called a passbook savings loan, which is a lot like a secured credit card. You deposit a sum of money into a savings account, and in exchange the bank makes you a loan. You have no access to your savings account while your loan is outstanding. If you don't repay it, the bank will use the money in your savings account. The amount you can borrow depends on how much the bank requires you to deposit.

In most cases, though, you'll have to apply for a standard bank loan. You probably won't qualify unless you bring in a cosigner, offer some property as collateral, or agree to a very high rate of interest.

Banks that offer passbook loans typically give you one to three years to repay the loan. But don't pay the loan back too soon—give it about six to nine months to appear on your credit report. Standard bank loans are paid back on a monthly schedule, usually for a year or two.

Before you take out any loan, be sure you understand the terms:

- **Interest rate.** The interest rate on the loan is usually between two and six percentage points more than what the bank charges its customers with the best credit.
- **Prepayment penalties.** Usually, you can pay the loan back as soon as you want without incurring any prepayment penalties—fees that banks sometimes charge if you pay back a loan early and the bank doesn't collect as much interest from you as it had expected. The penalty is usually a small percentage of the loan amount.
- **Whether the bank reports the loan to a credit bureau.** This is key; the whole reason you take out the loan is to rebuild your credit. You may have to make several calls to find a bank that reports the loan.

Work With a Local Merchant

Another step to consider in rebuilding your credit is to approach a local merchant, such as a jewelry or furniture store, about purchasing an item on credit. Many local stores will work with you in setting up a payment schedule, but be prepared to put down a deposit of up to 30%, pay a high rate of interest, or find someone to cosign the loan. This isn't an ideal way to rebuild your credit, but if all other lenders turn you down, it may be your only option. Again, ask if the merchant will report your payments to the credit reporting agencies.

Using a Debit Card Instead of a Credit Card

If you can't get a regular credit card, and you need one to book things like rental cars and hotels or to buy things over the Internet, you can probably get a debit card from your bank that doubles as a Visa or MasterCard.

Like secured credit cards, however, debit cards are not an ideal solution. You must use them very carefully to avoid trouble. Some of the downsides:

- No grace period is offered (the money is taken directly from your account).
- Unlike credit cards there's no protection for defective purchases.
- There's less protection than regular credit cards if your card is lost or stolen or someone makes an unauthorized transfer.
- Debit cards are not subject to fee limits and banks may change terms with little or no notice.
- Debit cards are more susceptible to theft than are credit cards.
- Overdraft fees can be extremely expensive. It's easy to incur overdraft fees if you don't keep careful track of your purchases. Fees can be as high as $35 per charge (which means you can incur hundreds of dollars on one day if you make several small charges that are in excess of your account limit). Do not opt into the bank's overdraft protection plan. If you have a debit card, call your bank and make sure you don't have overdraft protection. It's better to have the card declined than to incur overdraft fees.
- Using a debit card provides no benefit to your credit history.

Attempts to Collect Clearly Discharged Debts

If a debt was discharged in bankruptcy, the law prohibits creditors from filing a lawsuit, sending you collection letters, calling you, withholding credit, or threatening to file or actually filing a criminal complaint against you. (11 U.S.C. § 524.) If a creditor tries to collect a debt that clearly was discharged in your bankruptcy, you should respond at once with a letter like the one shown below.

Letter to Creditor

1905 Fifth Road
N. Miami Beach, FL 35466

March 18, 20xx

Bank of Miami
2700 Finances Highway
Miami, FL 36678

To Whom It May Concern:

I've been contacted once by letter and once by phone by Rodney Moore of your bank. Mr. Moore claims that I owe $4,812 on Visa account Number 1234 567 890 123.

As you're well aware, this debt was discharged in bankruptcy (Case number 111-999 in the Western District of Tennessee) on February 1, 20xx. Thus, your collection efforts violate federal law, 11 U.S.C. § 524. If they continue, I won't hesitate to pursue my legal rights, including bringing a lawsuit against you for harassment.

Sincerely,

Dawn Schaffer
Dawn Schaffer

The court doesn't give you a list of debts that were discharged. But you can assume a debt was discharged if you listed it in your bankruptcy papers, the creditor didn't successfully object to its discharge, and it isn't in one of the nondischargeable categories listed in Ch. 1. Also, if you live in a community property state and your spouse filed alone, you can assume that your share of the community debts was also discharged.

If the collection efforts don't immediately stop, you may want to hire a lawyer to write the creditor again—sometimes, a lawyer's letterhead gets results. If that doesn't work, you can sue the creditor for harassment. You can bring a lawsuit in state court or in the bankruptcy court. The bankruptcy court should be more familiar with the prohibitions against collection and more sympathetic to you.

If the creditor sues you over the debt, you'll want to raise the discharge as a defense and sue the creditor yourself to stop the illegal collection efforts. The court has the power to hold the creditor in contempt of court. The court may also fine the creditor for the humiliation, inconvenience, and anguish caused you and order the creditor to pay your attorneys' fees. For example, a bankruptcy court in North Carolina fined a creditor $900 for attempting to collect a discharged debt. (*In re Barbour*, 77 B.R. 530 (E.D. N.C. 1987).)

If the creditor sues you (almost certainly in state court), you or your attorney can file papers requesting that the case be transferred ("removed") to the bankruptcy court.

Anticipating Postbankruptcy Debt Collections

Sometimes you can anticipate that a particular creditor will consider a debt to be nondischargeable and go after you for it after your bankruptcy case is closed. In that event, your attorney can file an action in the bankruptcy court while your case is still open to obtain a determination of whether the debt is dischargeable. If the court rules in your favor, the creditor will be prevented from pursuing the debt in state court.

Postbankruptcy Discrimination

Although filing for bankruptcy has serious consequences, it might not be as bad as you think. There are laws that will protect you from postbankruptcy discrimination by the government and by private employers.

Governmental Discrimination

All federal, state, and local governmental units are prohibited from discriminating against you solely because you filed for bankruptcy. (11 U.S.C. § 525(a).) This includes denying, revoking, suspending, or refusing to renew a license, permit, charter, franchise, or other similar grant. This part of the Bankruptcy Code provides important protections, but it does not insulate debtors from all adverse consequences of filing for bankruptcy. Lenders, for example, can consider a debtor's bankruptcy filing when reviewing an application for a government loan or an extension of credit. (See, for example, *Watts v. Pennsylvania Housing Finance Co.*, 876 F.2d 1090 (3d Cir. 1989) and *Toth v. Michigan State Housing Development Authority,* 136 F.3d 477 (6th Cir. 1998).) Still, under this provision of the Bankruptcy Code, the government cannot:

- deny you a job or fire you
- deny you or terminate your public benefits
- evict you from public housing (although if you have a Section 8 voucher, you may not be protected)
- deny you or refuse to renew your state liquor license
- withhold your college transcript
- deny you a driver's license, or
- deny you a contract, such as one for a construction project.

In addition, lenders can't exclude you from participating in a government-guaranteed student loan program. (11 U.S.C. § 525(c).)

In general, once any government-related debt has been discharged, all acts against you that arise out of that debt also must end. If, for example, you lost your driver's license because you didn't pay a court judgment that resulted from a car accident, once the debt is discharged, you must be granted a license. If, however, the judgment wasn't discharged, you can still be denied your license until you pay up.

Keep in mind that only denials based solely on your bankruptcy are prohibited. You may be denied a loan, a job, or an apartment for reasons unrelated to the bankruptcy or for reasons related to your future creditworthiness—for example, because the government concludes you won't be able to repay a Small Business Administration loan.

Nongovernmental Discrimination

Private employers may not fire you or otherwise discriminate against you solely because you filed for bankruptcy. (11 U.S.C. § 525(b).) While the Bankruptcy Code expressly prohibits employers from firing you, most courts have found that it does not prohibit employers from refusing to hire someone because of a prior bankruptcy.

Other forms of discrimination in the private sector aren't illegal. If you seek to rent an apartment and the landlord does a credit check, sees your bankruptcy, and refuses to rent to you, there's not much you can do other than try to show that you'll pay your rent and be a responsible tenant. Paying several months' rent in advance can work wonders in these situations.

If you suffer illegal discrimination because of your bankruptcy, you can sue in state court or in the bankruptcy court. You'll probably need the assistance of an attorney.

Attempts to Revoke Your Discharge

In extremely rare instances, the trustee or a creditor can ask the bankruptcy court to revoke your discharge. The trustee or creditor must file a complaint within one year of your discharge.

Your discharge can be revoked only if the creditor or trustee proves that you obtained the discharge through fraud, which was discovered after your discharge. If your discharge is revoked, you'll owe your creditors as if you had not filed for bankruptcy. Any payment your creditors received from the trustee, however, will be credited against what you owe.

> **SEE AN EXPERT**
> **Help from a lawyer.** If someone asks the bankruptcy court to revoke your discharge, consult a bankruptcy attorney right away.

Help Beyond the Book

Hiring and Working With a Lawyer

As we've mentioned several times throughout this book, it's very difficult to represent yourself in a Chapter 13 bankruptcy case. The vast majority of filers will benefit from hiring a bankruptcy lawyer. But just because you're going to hire a lawyer doesn't mean you can hide your head in the sand. In order to get the best representation possible, you must hire the right lawyer and then maintain a good working relationship with him or her.

Our advice: Stay informed and actively participate in your case. Finding a lawyer who will let you do this is the first step, and then working with your lawyer effectively is the second step.

Unbundled Legal Services and Chapter 13 Bankruptcy

Since the 1990s, lawyers have been increasingly willing to offer their services on a piecemeal basis, such as reviewing paperwork for a self-represented client or handling a hearing on the dischargeability of a debt. When lawyers do specific jobs at a client's request but don't contract for full-service representation in the underlying case, they are said to be providing unbundled services. They often do so for an hourly fee.

Unfortunately, because filing a Chapter 13 bankruptcy got more complicated with the 2005 bankruptcy law changes, few people can represent themselves effectively in Chapter 13, and even fewer attorneys are willing to handle just a piece of the case. Essentially, unbundled services are not an option for the vast majority of Chapter 13 filers.

If you decide to file for Chapter 7 bankruptcy, however, unbundled services may be a possibility. If you are representing yourself in a Chapter 7 case, you may be able to find an attorney who, for example, is willing to handle a court hearing for an hourly fee, review your paperwork before you file, or give you legal advice before and during your bankruptcy.

What Does Legal Representation Mean?

By agreeing to represent you, your lawyer becomes responsible for making sure that all of your paperwork is filed on time, the information in your paperwork is accurate, and you propose a repayment plan the judge will confirm. These duties require the lawyer to review various documents—for instance, your credit report, tax returns, and home value appraisal—both to ensure the accuracy of your paperwork and that you are filing for bankruptcy under the appropriate chapter.

Your lawyer will also be responsible for appearing with you at the 341 hearing and on your behalf at the plan confirmation hearing. Your lawyer will also represent your interests if a creditor objects to your plan or opposes the discharge of a debt, or if you need to eliminate liens that the bankruptcy laws allow to be stripped from your property.

How to Find a Bankruptcy Lawyer

Bankruptcy lawyers are regular lawyers who specialize in handling bankruptcy cases. When seeking legal representation in a Chapter 13 bankruptcy, look for an experienced bankruptcy lawyer, not a general practitioner.

There are several ways to find the best bankruptcy lawyer for your job:

- **Personal referrals.** This is your best approach. If you know someone who was pleased with the services of a bankruptcy lawyer, call that lawyer first.
- **Referrals from other lawyers.** If you, a family member, or a friend used a lawyer in a nonbankruptcy matter, ask that lawyer if they know of any good bankruptcy attorneys.
- **Group legal plans.** If you're a member of a plan that provides free or low-cost legal assistance and the plan covers bankruptcies, make that your first stop in looking for a lawyer.
- **Lawyer-referral panels.** Most county bar associations will give you the names of bankruptcy attorneys who practice in your area. Keep in mind that most bar associations do not screen the lawyers. It's up to you to check out the credentials and experience of the person to whom you're referred.
- **Internet directories.** Both bar associations and private companies provide lists of bankruptcy lawyers on the Internet. A good directory will

provide lots of information about the lawyer, such as the types of cases they handle, their philosophy on representing clients, and typical fees. One good place to start is Nolo's lawyer directory, at www.nolo.com/lawyers. Also, check out www.nacba.org, a site that provides contact information for members of the National Association of Consumer Bankruptcy Attorneys. Or visit www.legalconsumer.com, a site that provides a variety of free services and information, including bankruptcy lawyer listings by zip code.

- **Legal Aid.** Legal Aid offices are partially funded by the federal Legal Services Corporation and offer legal assistance in many areas. A few offices may do bankruptcies, although most do not. To qualify for Legal Aid, you must have a very low income, so few Chapter 13 bankruptcy filers will qualify.
- **Legal clinics.** Many law schools sponsor legal clinics and provide free legal advice to consumers. Some legal clinics have the same income requirements as Legal Aid; others offer free services to low- and moderate-income people.

Bankruptcy Petition Preparers

Bankruptcy petition preparers (BPPs) are nonlawyers who assist people with filling out and filing bankruptcy forms. BPPs are not allowed to provide legal advice—their services are restricted to entering data on forms, printing the forms, and organizing the forms for filing. If you are filing for Chapter 7 bankruptcy without a lawyer and want someone to input your information onto the forms, you might consider using a BPP. For purposes of Chapter 13 bankruptcy, however, BPPs are really not an option. They cannot help you draft a repayment plan, nor can they provide legal advice. As we've said already, most Chapter 13 filers do best by getting a lawyer.

What to Look for in a Lawyer

A big part of finding the right lawyer to represent you is knowing what to look for. Get some basic information before you make an appointment. Then schedule an initial consultation so you can find out more about the lawyer before you decide who to hire.

Before You Make an Appointment

Whether you are browsing Internet directories, calling lawyers referred to you by friends, or getting names from a bar association referral service, here are some things to look for in a lawyer:

Experience. Look for an experienced bankruptcy attorney. Years of practice are not always the best indication of this. Ask how many bankruptcy cases the attorney has handled and what types. If a lawyer has handled tons of Chapter 7 cases, but not many Chapter 13s, he or she might not be for you. On the other hand, if the lawyer only handles Chapter 13 bankruptcies, that might be a red flag. You don't want to be represented by someone who pushes clients in the direction of Chapter 13 when a Chapter 7 might be better. (Lawyers often make a better profit from Chapter 13 bankruptcies.)

Competence. This is a tricky one to figure out. A lawyer may have practiced bankruptcy law for 20 years, but done a bad job of it. On the flip side, if a lawyer who recently graduated from law school is smart, hard-working, and mentored by an experienced bankruptcy attorney, he or she might be a good choice. Ask for referrals from former clients, and, if possible, speak directly to those clients.

Reasonable fees. Before you make an appointment, find out what the lawyer typically charges for a Chapter 13 case. Cheaper isn't always better—you don't want someone cutting corners nor do you necessarily want your case handled by a "bankruptcy mill" that cranks out bankruptcy paperwork without giving clients individual attention. On the other hand, high fees don't always correlate to the best representation. Shop around to find out what most bankruptcy lawyers charge in your area.

What to Look for in the First Meeting

Many lawyers will provide an initial consultation for free. But even if a lawyer charges for a consultation, it might be worth the money to pay for a few consults to find the right lawyer. Here are some things to assess in the first meeting:

How available is the lawyer? When making an appointment, ask to talk directly to the lawyer. If you can't, this may give you a hint as to how accessible he or she is. Of course, if you're told that a paralegal will be handling the routine aspects of your case under the supervision of a lawyer, you may be satisfied with that arrangement. Ask how long it will take for your phone calls to get returned or how hard it is to schedule appointments.

How does the lawyer communicate? Ask specific questions. Do you get clear, concise answers?

Does the lawyer listen to you? Often people want to "tell their story" to the bankruptcy attorney and get miffed if the attorney isn't interested. Customer service considerations usually dictate that the attorney will let you talk for fifteen minutes or so just to get things off your chest. However, the fact is that most of what Chapter 13 clients are concerned about have little or nothing to do with what must be included in your bankruptcy petition or how your bankruptcy will proceed. As a general rule, most Chapter 13 bankruptcies are routine and after a brief introductory conversation the attorney will probably have you complete an online questionnaire that asks about your debts, assets, and financial affairs over the past couple of years. The attorney (or a member of the attorney's staff) will review the questionnaire and ask a few questions (often by email) about the information you provide or leave out. When the lawyer (or assistant) has everything needed for your bankruptcy, the attorney will contact you about what will happen next. Of course there are exceptions and if you feel you need a full interview with the lawyer, by all means go for it, as long as you realize that bankruptcy lawyers tend to be task-oriented and generally make poor confidants.

How does your lawyer feel about your legal knowledge? If you've read this book, you're already better informed than most clients (and many lawyers). How does the lawyer respond to this? Some lawyers are threatened by clients who have done their homework. Others welcome clients that are well-informed and willing to participate fully in their case.

Does the lawyer carry malpractice insurance? If the answer is no, consider finding a lawyer who does. But keep in mind that malpractice insurance is far more protective of the lawyer than the client, and the fact that a lawyer is insured may make it more, rather than less, difficult to recover damages from the lawyer if he or she is professionally negligent.

Do the lawyer's recommendations seem sound? One of your goals at the initial conference is to find out what the lawyer recommends in your particular case. Go home and think about the lawyer's suggestions. If they don't make sense or you have other reservations, call someone else.

What are the lawyer's fees? Now that you've given the lawyer a brief overview of your situation, and the lawyer has made a preliminary recommendation, find out what the lawyer's services will cost.

Personality. No matter how experienced or competent the lawyer is, if you don't feel comfortable with him or her during the first meeting, you may want to keep looking.

Paying Your Lawyer

Because lawyer duties for even a simple Chapter 13 bankruptcy case have drastically increased under the 2005 bankruptcy law, typical lawyer fees have gone way up.

For a routine Chapter 13 bankruptcy, a lawyer will likely charge you somewhere between $2,500 and $4,000 (plus the $281 filing fee and the fees you'll have to pay for credit counseling and personal debt management counseling, about $50 each).

Attorney fees in bankruptcy cases are somewhat unusual in that they must be disclosed to and approved by the court. The reasoning behind this rule is twofold. First, since every penny you pay to a bankruptcy lawyer is a penny not available to your creditors (at least in theory), the trustee and court have an interest in making sure the fees are reasonable. Second, because many bankruptcy clients are financially vulnerable and even desperate when they seek legal assistance, they are susceptible to fee gouging. Prior to the fee disclosure rule, the bankruptcy bar was known for overcharging clients. (Of course, many bankruptcy lawyers did not engage in this abuse.) Court oversight of attorneys fees was instituted in an attempt to curb this problem.

However, even though the court oversees attorneys' fees, the trustee rarely challenges the rates charged in a particular case. (The U.S. Trustee and the court itself may also challenge fees.) This is because attorneys know the range of fees generally allowed by local bankruptcy judges and set their fees accordingly. Even if challenged, attorneys are given the opportunity to justify a fee that seems unusually large.

Bankruptcy Lawyer Fees Are Not Fixed

Some people think that bankruptcy lawyer fees are fixed. This is not the case. Although some courts do establish presumptive fee maximums, these are not set in stone. An attorney can overcome the maximum by providing reasons why a higher fee is reasonable. Essentially, individual lawyers are free to decide what to charge, based on what services you want and how complicated your case is likely to be.

Standard Fees and Extra Fees

The scope and range of services that the attorney promises you in return for your initial fee will be listed in what's called a Rule 2016 Attorney Fee Disclosure Form. This form is filed as part of your bankruptcy papers. In the typical Chapter 13 case, the attorney's fee will include the routine tasks associated with a bankruptcy filing: counseling, preparing bankruptcy forms, drafting your repayment plan, and attending the creditors' meeting and confirmation hearing. Any task not included in the Rule 2016 disclosure form is subject to a separate fee.

If your case will likely require more attorney time, you may—and probably will—be charged extra, according to the attorney's hourly fee or other criteria he or she uses. A typical bankruptcy attorney charges between $200 and $300 an hour (rural and urban). Many charge a minimum of roughly $400 to $600 for a court appearance.

How those extra fees are covered varies. Some attorneys will add these fees to their standard fee and require you to pay it all in advance. For example, say the attorney's standard fee is $3,000, but the attorney believes she will have to perform work in addition to the usual aspects of representation. The attorney may charge $4,000 or $4,500 up front, in anticipation of the additional hours.

Other attorneys will charge you their standard fee up front and wait until after you file to charge you for the extra work. Because these fees are earned after your bankruptcy filing, they won't be discharged in your bankruptcy and the attorney need not collect them up front; they will be added to your plan payments. Whatever method the attorney uses to charge you, you have some protection against fee gouging. An attorney must file a supplemental Rule 2016 form to obtain the court's permission for any postfiling fees.

How and When Fees Are Paid

Some (but not many) lawyers allow you to pay their full fee through your repayment plan, without paying anything up front. Most lawyers require an initial payment—for example, $2,000—and let you pay the rest through your plan. Sometimes a lawyer's choice as to timing of payment depends on how likely it is that your plan will be confirmed, and whether the lawyer thinks you'll complete it. For example, if you have plenty of income to cover your mandatory debts and you are filing for Chapter 13 to save your home, the lawyer might charge only a minimal initial fee, because you are likely to complete your plan and finish paying the fee that way. On the other hand, if you barely have enough income to propose a confirmable plan and you don't own a home, the lawyer might be skeptical of your ability to complete the plan—and might demand the entire fee up front.

Fee Agreements

When you decide on a lawyer, it's important to get an agreement for services and payment in writing. Your contract should include:

- A description of the services your attorney will provide.
- Fees. Include the type and amount of fees, how they will be paid, and whether extra work is included in the fee or will be charged separately.
- Costs. The agreement should outline likely costs and how they will be paid. These would include, at a minimum, filing fees and fees for debt counseling, but might also include costs for property appraisals and expert witnesses.

- Your obligations. Sometimes fee agreements include your duties as a client. For example it might state that you agree to be truthful with your lawyer and to provide information when requested.

Working With Your Lawyer

A good working relationship between you and your lawyer will help the case go more smoothly, reduce your frustration, and ensure the best results possible. Here are some tips:

- **Stay informed.** Insist that your lawyer update you on what's going on with your case.
- **Provide your lawyer with documents and information.** Provide your lawyer with all information that might pertain to your case. More information is better than less. If your lawyer asks for documents, provide them as quickly as possible.
- **If you don't understand something, ask.** You can't make informed decisions about your case if you don't fully understand what's going on.

Legal Research

While your bankruptcy lawyer will be a good resource for finding out what the law is, especially in your district, there are times when you might want to do some sleuthing yourself. In particular, if you are still in the initial stages of considering bankruptcy, you may want to learn more about a particular issue before you plunk down the money to see a lawyer.

Even if you plan to get a lawyer or already have one, knowing how to find the law if you need it is still valuable. Being informed about the law will allow you to ask the right questions of your lawyer and better equip you to make decisions about your case. Reading the book is an excellent way to get informed, and in most cases will more than suffice. But in the event you are facing an issue that isn't covered in this book (because, for example, it only affects a tiny percentage of filers) or you want to know how a cutting edge issue is being treated in your district, you can also do some legal research on your own.

Legal research can vary from the very simple to the hopelessly complex. In this chapter, we stay on the simple side. If you would like to learn more about legal research or if you find that our suggestions come up a bit short in your particular case, we recommend that you obtain a copy of *Legal Research: How to Find & Understand the Law*, by Stephen Elias and the Editors of Nolo (Nolo), which provides a plain-English tutorial on legal research in the law library and on the Internet.

Sources of Bankruptcy Law

Bankruptcy law comes from a variety of sources:
- federal bankruptcy statutes passed by Congress
- federal rules about bankruptcy procedure issued by a federal judicial agency
- local rules issued by individual bankruptcy courts
- federal and bankruptcy court cases applying bankruptcy laws to specific disputes
- laws (statutes) passed by state legislatures that define the property you can keep in bankruptcy, and
- state court cases interpreting state exemption statutes.

Not so long ago, you would have had to visit a law library to find these resources. Now you can find most

of them on the Internet. However, if you are able to visit a decent-sized law library, your research will be the better for it. Using actual books allows you to more easily find and read relevant court interpretations of the underlying statutes and rules—which are crucial to getting a clear picture of what the laws and rules really mean.

How to Use Law Libraries

Law libraries that are open to the public are most often found in and around courthouses. Law schools also frequently admit the public at least some of the time (typically not during exam time, over the summer, or during other breaks in the academic year).

Almost without exception, law libraries come with law librarians. The law librarians will be helpful as long as you ask them the right questions. For example, the law librarians will help you find specific library resources (for instance, where you can find the federal bankruptcy statutes or rules), but they normally won't teach you the ins and outs of legal research. Nor will they give an opinion about what a law means, how you should deal with the court, or how your particular question should be answered. For instance, if you want to find a state case interpreting a particular exemption, the law librarian will show you where your state code is located on the shelves and may even point out the volumes that contain the exemptions. The librarian won't, however, help you interpret the exemption, apply the exemption to your specific facts, or tell you how to raise the exemption in your bankruptcy case. Nor is the librarian likely to tell you what additional research steps you can or should take. When it comes to legal research in the law library, self help is the order of the day.

There is another important reason to visit the law library. Many have computer terminals that offer access to one or both of the major online legal research libraries: Westlaw and LexisNexis. With proper training, you can find just about anything in these online libraries that you could find in the law library itself. In fact, some libraries have started replacing hardcopy books with online materials, to save money and space. When visiting your local library, ask the librarian whether it has access to Westlaw or Lexis and, if so, for some tips on using the bankruptcy materials the online library carries. For example, Westlaw offers a set of materials under a tab called "Bankruptcy Practitioner," with forms, cases, articles, and treatises, all searchable by key words. Learning how to use these materials will be an enormous timesaver in your research.

Below, we show you how to get to the resources you'll most likely be using, whether you are doing your research on the Internet or in the law library.

Bankruptcy Background Materials: Overviews, Encyclopedias, and Treatises

Before digging into the primary law sources (statutes, rules, cases, and so on) that we discuss below, you may want to do some background reading to get a firm grasp of your issue or question.

The Internet

A number of Internet sites contain large collections of articles written by experts about various aspects of bankruptcy. Good starting places are Nolo's website, at www.nolo.com, and www.legalconsumer.com, which offer lots of information and resources.

If you are using Westlaw at your local library, head for the information under the tab "Bankruptcy Practitioner."

Another approach to searching for bankruptcy-related materials is Google. Both the basic Google search and Google Scholar (http://scholar.google.com) are amazingly responsive to plain-language queries. For example, if you want to know more about discharging student loans, you would use Google Scholar, click the "Articles" radio button and enter "discharging student loans in bankruptcy" in the search box and pull up a bevy of links to related articles. Similarly, if you want to read court opinions about discharging student loans in bankruptcy you would do the same search but use the "Legal Opinions and Journals" button.

The Law Library

Providing you with a good treatise or encyclopedia discussion of bankruptcy is where the law library

shines. You can find these materials in hardcopy or on the Westlaw or Lexis online research libraries.

Collier on Bankruptcy

It's a good idea to get an overview of your subject before trying to find a precise answer to a precise question. The best way to do this is to find a general commentary on your subject by a bankruptcy expert. For example, if you want to find out whether a particular debt is nondischargeable, you should start by reading a general discussion about the type of debt you're dealing with. Or, if you don't know whether you're entitled to claim certain property as exempt, a good overview of your state's exemptions would get you started on the right track.

The most complete source of this type of background information is a set of books known as *Collier on Bankruptcy*, by Lawrence P. King, et al. (Matthew Bender). It's available in virtually all law libraries. *Collier* is both incredibly thorough and meticulously up to date; semiannual supplements, with all the latest developments, are in the front of each volume. In addition to comments on every aspect of bankruptcy law, *Collier* contains the bankruptcy statutes, rules, and exemption lists for every state.

Collier is organized according to the bankruptcy statutes. This means that the quickest way to find information in it is to know what statute you're looking for. (See the Bankruptcy Code sections set out below.) If you still can't figure out the governing statute, start with the *Collier* subject matter index. Be warned, however, that the index can be difficult to use because it contains a lot of bankruptcy jargon you may be unfamiliar with. A legal dictionary will be available in the library.

Bankruptcy (National Edition) Published by The Rutter Group

This is a four-volume set of looseleaf binders that covers every aspect of bankruptcy. Although these books are written for lawyers, they aren't too difficult to understand and use. You'll find information on exemptions, Chapter 13 plans, lien stripping, filing and opposing motions, and much more.

Bankruptcy Code Sections (11 U.S.C.)	
§ 101	Definitions
§ 109	Who May File for Which Type of Bankruptcy; Credit Counseling Requirements
§ 110	Rules for Bankruptcy Petition Preparers
§ 111	Budget and Credit Counseling Agencies
§ 302	Who Can File Joint Cases
§ 326	How Trustees Are Compensated
§ 332	Consumer Privacy Ombudsmen
§ 341	Meeting of Creditors
§ 342	Notice of Creditors' Meeting; Informational Notice to Debtors; Requirements for Notice by Debtors
§ 343	Examination of Debtor at Creditors' Meeting
§ 348	Converting From One Type of Bankruptcy to Another
§ 349	Dismissing a Case
§ 350	Closing and Reopening a Case
§ 362	The Automatic Stay
§ 365	How Leases and Executory Contracts Are Treated in Bankruptcy
§ 366	Continuing or Reconnecting Utility Service
§ 501	Filing of Creditors' Claims
§ 506	Allowed Secured Claims and Lien Avoidance
§ 507	Priority Claims
§ 521	Paperwork Requirements and Deadlines
§ 522	Exemptions; Residency Requirements for Homestead Exemption; Stripping Liens From Property
§ 523	Nondischargeable Debts
§ 524	Effect of Discharge and Reaffirmation of Debts
§ 525	Prohibited Postbankruptcy Discrimination
§ 526	Restrictions on Debt Relief Agencies
§ 527	Required Disclosures by Debt Relief Agencies
§ 528	Requirements for Debt Relief Agencies
§ 541	What Property Is Part of the Bankruptcy Estate
§ 547	Preferences
§ 548	Fraudulent Transfers
§ 554	Trustee's Abandonment of Property in the Bankruptcy Estate
§ 707	The Means Test
§ 1301	Stay of Action Against Codebtor
§ 1305	Proof of Claims

Other Background Resources

For general discussions of bankruptcy issues, there are several other good places to start. An excellent all-around resource is called *Consumer Bankruptcy Law and Practice*. This volume, published by the National Consumer Law Center, is updated every year. It contains a complete discussion of Chapter 13 bankruptcy procedures, the official bankruptcy forms, and a marvelous bibliography.

Another good treatise is a legal encyclopedia called *American Jurisprudence*, 2nd Series. Almost all law libraries carry it. The article on bankruptcy has an extensive table of contents, and the entire encyclopedia has an index. Between these two tools, you should be able to zero in on helpful material. Finally, some large and well-stocked law libraries carry a looseleaf publication known as the Commerce Clearing House (CCH) *Bankruptcy Law Reporter* (BLR). In this publication, you can find all three primary source materials relating to bankruptcy: statutes, rules, and cases.

Finding Federal Bankruptcy Statutes

Title 11 of the United States Code contains all the statutes that govern your bankruptcy.

The Internet

If you are using the Internet, go to the Legal Information Institute of Cornell University Law School site (www.law.cornell.edu), which lets you browse laws by subject matter and also offers a keyword search. To find the Bankruptcy Code, go to www.law.cornell.edu, select "U.S. Code" from the menu available under the "Constitutions and Codes" tab, then select Title 11. Use the table below to find the code sections you need.

The Bankruptcy Code is also available at the website of the American Bankruptcy Institute, www.abiworld. org. Find the link to view the code online from ABI's home page or go straight to the wiki: www.abiworld. org/wiki/index.html.

The Law Library

Virtually every law library has at least one complete set of the annotated United States Code ("annotated" means that each statute is followed by citations and summaries of cases interpreting that provision). If you already have a citation to the statute you are seeking, you can use the citation to find the statute. However, if you have no citation—which is frequently the case—you can use either the index to Title 11 (the part of the Code that applies to bankruptcy) or the table we set out above, which matches various issues that are likely to interest you with specific sections of Title 11.

Once you have found and read the statute, you can browse the one-paragraph summaries of written opinions issued by courts that have interpreted that particular statute. You will be looking to see whether a court has addressed your particular issue. If so, you can find and read the entire case in the law library. Reading what a judge has had to say about the statute regarding facts similar to yours is an invaluable guide to understanding how a judge is likely to handle the issue in your case, although when and where the case was decided may be important.

Finding the Federal Rules of Bankruptcy Procedure (FRBP)

The Federal Rules of Bankruptcy Procedure govern what happens if an issue is contested in the bankruptcy court. They also apply to certain routine bankruptcy procedures, such as deadlines for filing paperwork. Any law library will have these rules. Your bankruptcy court's website will have a link to the rules, as does www.law.cornell.edu.

Finding Local Court Rules

Every bankruptcy court operates under a set of local rules that govern how it does business and what is expected of the parties who use it. Each court also has its own forms that debtors must use, and these forms vary from court to court.

Your bankruptcy court clerk's office will have the local rules available for you. Most courts also post their local rules and forms on their own websites. To find the website for your court, take these steps:

Step 1: Go to www.uscourts.gov/links.html.

Step 2: Click the number on the map that is closest to where you live.

Step 3: Browse the list until you find your court and click on it.

Step 4: Click on the local rules and forms link.

These court websites usually contain other helpful information as well, including case information, official bankruptcy forms, court guidelines (in addition to the local rules), information for lawyers, information about the court and its judges, and the court calendar.

At the law library, the *Collier Bankruptcy Practice Manual* has the local rules for most (if not all) of the nation's bankruptcy courts.

Finding Federal Court Bankruptcy Cases

Court opinions are vital to understanding how a particular law might apply to your individual case. The following levels of federal courts issue bankruptcy-related opinions:

- the U.S. Supreme Court
- the U.S. Courts of Appeals
- the Bankruptcy Appellate Panels
- the U.S. District Courts, and
- the bankruptcy courts.

Most bankruptcy-related opinions are, not surprisingly, issued by the bankruptcy courts. By comparison, very few bankruptcy opinions come out of the U.S. Supreme Court. The other courts are somewhere in the middle.

The Internet

Depending on the date the case was decided, U.S. Supreme Court decisions and U.S. Court of Appeals decisions are available for free on the Internet. For $13.95 a month you can also subscribe to VersusLaw (at www.versuslaw.com), which provides U.S. Court of Appeals cases for an earlier period than you can get for free—often back to 1950. VersusLaw doesn't require you to sign a long-term contract. So, one payment of $13.95 gets you a month's worth of research. Not too shabby. VersusLaw also publishes many U.S. District Court cases on its website. Westlaw and Lexis are generally too costly to use from home, unless you do a lot of research. However, you will be able to find either or both of these online megaresources at your local law library.

U.S. Supreme Court. To find a Supreme Court case, go to http://supreme.nolo.com. Use one of the search options to locate a particular case. If you don't know the case name and you don't have a citation, enter some relevant words relating to your issue and see what you pull up. You can search cases all the way back to 1893.

U.S. Court of Appeals. You can find a U.S Circuit Court of Appeals case back to roughly 1996. Follow these steps:

Step 1: Go to www.law.cornell.edu.

Step 2: Click "Federal Law," then "Federal Courts of Appeals Decisions."

Step 3: Click on "Search All Circuit Court Opinions on the Internet."

Again, if you are looking for a case decided prior to 1996, your best bet is to sign up for VersusLaw, described just above.

U.S. District Court and Bankruptcy Court. Cases reported by the bankruptcy courts are generally not available online unless you use Westlaw or Lexis. However, if you know the name of a particular case, a Google search might lead you to a court's website, where some judges post their decisions. You will probably have to take a trip to a law library if you want to know what the judges are doing in these courts— where the legal rubber meets the judicial road.

The Law Library

U.S. Supreme Court cases are published in three different book series:

- *Supreme Court Reports*
- *Supreme Court Reporter*, and
- *Supreme Court Lawyer's Edition*.

Some law libraries carry all three of these publications; others have only one. The cases are the same, but each series has different editorial enhancements.

U.S. Court of Appeals cases are published in the Federal Reporter (abbreviated simply as "F."). Most law libraries, large and small, carry this series.

Many U.S. District Court cases are published in the Federal Supplement (F.Supp.), a series available in most law libraries.

Written opinions of bankruptcy judges, and related appeals, are published in the *Bankruptcy Reporter* (B.R.), available in most mid- to large-sized libraries. To accurately understand how your bankruptcy court is likely to interpret the laws in your particular case, sooner or later you will need access to the *Bankruptcy Reporter*.

State Statutes

The secret to understanding what property you can keep frequently lies in the exemptions that your state allows you to claim. These exemptions are found in your state's statutes.

The Internet

Every state has its statutes online, including its exemption statutes. This means that you can read your state's exemption statutes for yourself. Follow these steps:

Step 1: Go to Appendix A. At the top of your state's exemption table, you'll see a general reference to the collection of state laws for your state that contain the exemption statutes.

Step 2: Go to www.nolo.com/legal-research/state-law.html. Click on "State Law Resources."

Step 3: Click on your state. This will bring you to your state's website.

Step 4: Look for the link to the state's official code. Click on the link and then look for the collection of statutes mentioned in Appendix A.

Step 5: Use the citation on the far right of your state's exemption table in Appendix A to find exactly what you need.

The Law Library

Your law library will have your state's statutes in book form, usually referred to as your state's code, annotated statutes, or compiled laws. Use Appendix A in this book to find a reference to the exemption statute you want to read, then use that reference to locate the exemption statute in the code. Once you find and read the statute, you can browse the summaries of court opinions interpreting the statute and, if you wish, read the cases in their entirety.

Alternatively, if your library has a copy of *Collier on Bankruptcy* (see above), you can find the exemptions for your state, accompanied by annotations summarizing state court interpretations.

State Court Cases

State courts are sometimes called on to interpret exemption statutes. If a court has interpreted the statute in which you are interested, you'll definitely want to chase down the relevant case and read it for yourself.

The Internet

All states make their more recent cases available free on the Internet—usually back to about 1996. To find these cases for your state:

Step 1: Go to www.law.cornell.edu/opinions. html#state.

Step 2: Click on your state.

Step 3: Locate the link to the court opinions for your state. This may be one link, or there may be separate links for your state's supreme court and your state's courts of appeal (the lower trial courts seldom publish their opinions, so you probably won't be able to find them).

If you want to go back to an earlier case, consider subscribing to VersusLaw at www.versuslaw.com. As mentioned earlier, you don't have to sign a long-term contract.

The Law Library

Your law library will have a collection of books that contain opinions issued by your state's courts. If you have a citation, you can go right to the case. If you don't have a citation, you'll need to use a digest to find relevant bankruptcy cases. Finding cases by subject matter is a little too advanced for this brief summary. See *Legal Research: How to Find & Understand the Law*, by Stephen Elias and the Editors of Nolo (Nolo), for more help.

Other Helpful Resources

Probably the most helpful bankruptcy website is maintained by the Office of the United States Trustee, at www.justice.gov/ust. This site provides lists of approved credit and financial management counseling agencies, median income figures for every state and the IRS national, regional, and local expenses you will need to complete the means test.

You can download official bankruptcy forms from the U.S. Courts website at www.uscourts.gov/bkforms/ index.html. However, this site doesn't include required local forms; for those, you'll have to visit your court or its website.

As part of the bankruptcy process, you are required to give the replacement (retail) value for all of the property you list in Schedule A (real property) and Schedule B (personal property). These figures are also the key to figuring out which of your property is exempt. Here are some tips on finding these values:

- **Cars:** Use the *Kelley Blue Book*, at www.kbb. com, or the website of the National Auto Dealers Association, www.nada.com.
- **Other personal property:** Check prices on eBay, www.ebay.com.
- **Homes:** To value your property, compare it to similar real estate parcels in your neighborhood that have recently sold (comparables). For a modest fee, you can get details on comparables— including neighborhood information, sales history, address, number of bedrooms and baths, square footage, and property tax information—from SmartHomeBuy at www.smarthomebuy.com. Less detailed information (purchase price, sales date, and address) is available free from sites such as www.homevalues.com, www.zillow.com, www. domania.com, www.homeradar.com, and http:// list.realestate.yahoo.com/re/homevalues.

Our Websites

Nolo's website, www.nolo.com, offers lots of free information on bankruptcy, credit repair, student loans, and much more. You can also view information on the Nolo products mentioned in this book, including links to legal updates highlighting important developments that occurred after this book went to press.

Nolo author Albin Renauer also maintains a website that provides a free means test calculator, helpful information about Chapter 7 and Chapter 13 bankruptcies, and a means test law browser that provides summaries and references to developing case law, at www.legalconsumer.com.

Glossary

341 hearing. See "meeting of creditors."

341 notice. A notice sent to the debtor and the debtor's creditors announcing the date, time, and place for the first meeting of creditors. The 341 notice is sent along with the notice of bankruptcy filing and information about important deadlines by which creditors have to take certain actions, such as filing objections.

342 notice. A notice that the court clerk is required to give to debtors pursuant to Section 342 of the Bankruptcy Code, to inform them of their obligations as bankruptcy debtors and the consequences of not being completely honest in their bankruptcy cases.

707(b) action. An action taken by the U.S. Trustee, the regular trustee, or any creditor, under authority of Section 707(b) of the Bankruptcy Code, to dismiss a debtor's Chapter 7 filing on the ground of abuse.

Abuse. Misuse of the Chapter 7 bankruptcy remedy. This term is typically applied to a Chapter 7 bankruptcy filing that should have been filed under Chapter 13 because the debtor appears to have enough disposable income to fund a Chapter 13 repayment plan.

Accounts receivable. Money or other property that one person or business owes to another for goods or services. Accounts receivable most often refer to the debts owed to a business by its customers.

Administrative expenses. The trustee's fee, the debtor's attorneys' fee, and other costs of bringing a bankruptcy case that a debtor must pay in full in a Chapter 13 repayment plan. Administrative costs are typically 10% of the debtor's total payments under the plan.

Administrative Office of the United States Courts. The federal government agency that issues court rules and forms to be used by the federal courts, including bankruptcy courts.

Adversary action. Any lawsuit that begins with the filing of a formal complaint and formal service of process on the parties being sued. In a bankruptcy case, adversary actions are often brought to determine the dischargeability of a debt or to recover property transferred by the debtor shortly before filing for bankruptcy.

Affidavit. A written statement of facts, signed under oath in front of a notary public.

Allowed secured claim. A debt that is secured by collateral or a lien against the debtor's property, for which the creditor has filed a *Proof of Claim* with the bankruptcy court. The claim is secured only to the extent of the value of the property—for example, if a debtor owes $5,000 on a note for a car that is worth only $3,000, the remaining $2,000 is an unsecured claim.

Amendment. A document filed by the debtor that changes one or more documents previously filed with the court. A debtor often files an amendment because the trustee requires changes to the debtor's paperwork based on the testimony at the meeting of creditors.

Animals. An exemption category in many states. Some states specifically exempt pets or livestock and poultry. If your state simply allows you to exempt "animals," you may include livestock, poultry, or pets. Some states exempt only domestic animals, which are usually considered to be all animals except pets.

Annuity. A type of insurance policy that pays out during the life of the insured, unlike life insurance, which pays out at the insured's death. Once the insured reaches the age specified in the policy, he or she receives monthly payments until death.

Appliance. A household apparatus or machine, usually operated by electricity, gas, or propane. Examples include refrigerators, stoves, washing machines, dishwashers, vacuum cleaners, air conditioners, and toasters.

Arms and accoutrements. Arms are weapons (such as pistols, rifles, and swords); accoutrements are the furnishings of a soldier's outfit, such as a belt or pack, but not clothes or weapons.

Arms-length creditor. A creditor with whom the debtor deals in the normal course of business, as opposed to an insider (a friend, relative, or business partner).

Articles of adornment. See "jewelry."

Assessment benefits. See "stipulated insurance."

Assisted person. Any person contemplating or filing for bankruptcy who receives bankruptcy assistance, whose debts are primarily consumer debts, and whose nonexempt property is valued at less than $150,000. A person or an entity that offers help to an assisted person is called a "debt relief agency."

Automatic stay. An injunction automatically issued by the bankruptcy court when a debtor files for bankruptcy. The automatic stay prohibits most creditor collection activities, such as filing or continuing lawsuits, making written requests for payment, or notifying credit reporting bureaus of an unpaid debt.

Avails. Any amount available to the owner of an insurance policy other than the actual proceeds of the policy. Avails include dividend payments, interest, cash or surrender value (the money you'd get if you sold your policy back to the insurance company), and loan value (the amount of cash you can borrow against the policy).

Bankruptcy Abuse Prevention and Reform Act of 2005. The formal name of the bankruptcy law that took effect on October 17, 2005.

Bankruptcy administrator. The official responsible for supervising the administration of bankruptcy cases, estates, and trustees in Alabama and North Carolina, where there is no U.S. Trustee.

Bankruptcy Appellate Panel. A specialized court that hears appeals of bankruptcy court decisions (available only in some regions).

Bankruptcy assistance. Goods or services provided to an "assisted person" for the purpose of providing information, advice, counsel, document preparation or filing, or attendance at a creditors' meeting; appearing in a case or proceeding on behalf of another person; or providing legal representation.

Bankruptcy Code. The federal law that governs the creation and operation of the bankruptcy courts and establishes bankruptcy procedures. (You can find the Bankruptcy Code in Title 11 of the United States Code.)

Bankruptcy estate. All of the property you own when you file for bankruptcy, except for most pensions and educational trusts. The trustee technically takes control of your bankruptcy estate for the duration of your case.

Bankruptcy lawyer. A lawyer who specializes in bankruptcy and is licensed to practice law in the federal courts.

Bankruptcy petition preparer. Any nonlawyer who helps someone with his or her bankruptcy. Bankruptcy petition preparers (BPPs) are a special type of debt relief agency, regulated by the U.S. Trustee. Because they are not lawyers, BPPs can't represent anyone in bankruptcy court or provide legal advice.

Benefit or benevolent society benefits. See "fraternal benefit society benefits."

Building materials. Items, such as lumber, brick, stone, iron, paint, and varnish, that are used to build or improve a structure.

Burial plot. A cemetery plot.

Business bankruptcy. A bankruptcy in which the debts arise primarily from the operation of a business, including bankruptcies filed by corporations, limited liability companies, and partnerships.

Certification. The act of signing a document under penalty of perjury. (The document that is signed is also called a certification.)

Chapter 7 bankruptcy. A liquidation bankruptcy, in which the trustee sells the debtor's nonexempt property and distributes the proceeds to the debtor's creditors. At the end of the case, the debtor receives a discharge of all remaining debts, except those that cannot legally be discharged.

Chapter 9 bankruptcy. A type of bankruptcy restricted to governmental units.

Chapter 11 bankruptcy. A type of bankruptcy intended to help businesses reorganize their debt load in order to remain in business. A Chapter 11 bankruptcy is typically much more expensive than a Chapter 7 or 13 bankruptcy because all of the lawyers must be paid out of the bankruptcy estate.

Chapter 12 bankruptcy. A type of bankruptcy designed to help small farmers reorganize their debts.

Chapter 13 bankruptcy. A type of consumer bankruptcy designed to help individuals reorganize their debts and pay all or a portion of them over three to five years.

Chapter 13 plan. A document filed in a Chapter 13 bankruptcy in which the debtor shows how all of his or her projected disposable income will be used over a three- to five-year period to pay all mandatory debts—for example, back child support, taxes, and mortgage arrearages—as well as some or all unsecured, nonpriority debts, such as medical and credit card bills.

Claim. A creditor's assertion that the bankruptcy filer owes it a debt or obligation.

Clothing. As an exemption category, the everyday clothes you and your family need for work, school, household use, and protection from the elements. In many states, luxury items and furs are not included in the clothing exemption category.

Codebtor. A person who assumes an equal responsibility, along with the debtor, to repay a debt or loan.

Collateral. Property pledged by a borrower as security for a loan.

Common law property states. States that don't use a community property system to classify marital property.

Community property. Certain property owned by married couples in Arizona, California, Idaho, Louisiana, New Mexico, Nevada, Texas, Washington, Wisconsin, and, if both spouses agree, Alaska. Very generally, all property acquired during the marriage is considered community property, belonging equally to both spouses, except for gifts and inheritances by one spouse. Similarly, all debts incurred during the marriage are considered community debts, owed equally by both spouses, with limited exceptions.

Complaint. A formal document that initiates a lawsuit.

Complaint to determine dischargeablity. A complaint initiating an adversary action in bankruptcy court that asks the court to decide whether a particular debt should be discharged at the end of the debtor's bankruptcy case.

Condominium. A building or complex in which separate units, such as townhouses or apartments, are owned by individuals, and the common areas (lobby, hallways, stairways, and so on) are jointly owned by the unit owners.

Confirmation. The bankruptcy judge's ruling approving a Chapter 13 plan.

Confirmation hearing. A court hearing conducted by a bankruptcy judge in which the judge decides whether a debtor's proposed Chapter 13 plan appears to be feasible and meets all applicable legal requirements.

Consumer bankruptcy. A bankruptcy in which most of the debt was incurred for personal, family, or household purposes.

Consumer debt. A debt incurred by an individual for personal, family, or household purposes.

Contingent debts. Debts that may be owed if certain events happen or conditions are satisfied.

Contingent interests in the estate of a decedent. The right to inherit property if one or more conditions to the inheritance are satisfied. For example, a debtor who will inherit property only if he survives his brother has a contingent interest.

Conversion. When a debtor who has filed one type of bankruptcy switches to another type—as when a Chapter 7 debtor converts to a Chapter 13 bankruptcy, or vice versa.

Cooperative housing. A building or another residential structure that is owned by a corporation formed by the residents. In exchange for purchasing stock in the corporation, the residents have the right to live in particular units.

Cooperative insurance. Compulsory employment benefits provided by a state or federal government, such as old age, survivors', disability, and health insurance, to assure a minimum standard of living for lower- and middle-income people. Also called social insurance.

Court clerk. The court employee who is responsible for accepting filings and other documents and generally maintaining an accurate and efficient flow of paper and information in the court.

Cramdown. In a Chapter 13 bankruptcy, the act of reducing a secured debt to the replacement value of the collateral securing the debt.

Credit and debt counseling. Counseling that explores the possibility of repaying debts outside of bankruptcy and educates the debtor about credit, budgeting, and financial management. Under the new bankruptcy law, a debtor must undergo credit counseling with an approved provider before filing for bankruptcy.

Credit insurance. An insurance policy that covers a borrower for an outstanding loan. If the borrower dies or becomes disabled before paying off the loan, the policy will pay off the balance due.

Creditor. A person or an institution to whom money is owed.

Creditor committee. In a Chapter 11 bankruptcy, a committee that represents the unsecured debtors in reorganization proceedings.

Creditor matrix. A specially formatted list of creditors that a debtor must file with the bankruptcy petition. The matrix helps the court notify creditors of the bankruptcy filing and the date and time set for the first meeting of creditors.

Creditors' meeting. See "meeting of creditors."

Crops. Products of the soil or earth that are grown and raised annually and gathered in a single season. Thus, oranges (on the tree or harvested) are crops; an orange tree isn't.

Current market value. What property could be sold for. Prior to 2005, this is how a debtor's property was valued for purposes of determining whether the property is protected by an applicable exemption. Now property must be valued at its "replacement cost."

Current monthly income. As defined by bankruptcy law, a bankruptcy filer's total gross income (whether taxable or not), averaged over the six-month period immediately preceding the month in which the bankruptcy is filed. The current monthly income is used to determine whether the debtor can file for Chapter 7 bankruptcy, among other things.

Debt. An obligation of any type, including a loan, credit, or promise to perform a contract or lease.

Debt relief agency. An umbrella term for any person or agency—including lawyers and bankruptcy petition preparers, but excluding banks, nonprofit and government agencies, and employees of debt relief agencies—that provides "bankruptcy assistance" to an "assisted person."

Debtor. Someone who owes money to another person or business. Also, the generic term used to refer to anyone who files for bankruptcy.

Declaration. A written statement that is made under oath but not witnessed by a notary public.

Declaration and Signature of Non-Attorney Bankruptcy Petition Preparer. A written notice that bankruptcy petition preparers must provide to debtors who use their services. The notice explains that bankruptcy petition preparers aren't attorneys and that they are permitted to perform only certain acts, such as entering information in the bankruptcy petition and schedules under the direction of their clients.

Declaration of homestead. A form filed with the county recorder's office to put on record your right to a homestead exemption. In most states, the homestead exemption is automatic—that is, you are not required to record a homestead declaration in order to claim the homestead exemption. A few states do require such a recording, however.

Deed in lieu of foreclosure. The document created when a homeowner dissolves his or her responsibility for a mortgage by deeding the property over to the mortgage owner. The homeowner's credit report will be negatively affected just as if the home were lost through foreclosure.

Disability benefits. Payments made under a disability insurance or retirement plan when the insured is unable to work (or retires early) because of disability, accident, or sickness.

Discharge. A court order, issued at the conclusion of a Chapter 7 or Chapter 13 bankruptcy case, which legally relieves the debtor of personal liability for debts that can be discharged in that type of bankruptcy.

Discharge exceptions. Debts that are not discharged in a bankruptcy case. The debtor continues to owe these debts even after the bankruptcy is concluded.

Discharge hearing. A hearing conducted by a bankruptcy court to explain the discharge, urge the debtor to stay out of debt, and review reaffirmation agreements to make sure they are feasible and fair.

Dischargeability action. An adversary action brought by a party who asks the court to determine whether a particular debt qualifies for discharge.

Dischargeable debt. A debt that is wiped out at the conclusion of a bankruptcy case, unless the judge decides that it should not be.

Disclosure of Compensation of Bankruptcy Petition Preparer. An official form bankruptcy petition preparers must file with the bankruptcy court to disclose their fees.

Dismissal. When the court orders a case to be closed without providing the relief available under the bankruptcy laws. For example, a Chapter 13 case might be dismissed because the debtor fails to propose a feasible plan; a Chapter 7 case might be dismissed for abuse.

Disposable income. The difference between a debtor's "current monthly income" and allowable expenses.

This is the amount that the bankruptcy law deems available to pay into a Chapter 13 plan.

Domestic animals. See "animals."

Domestic support obligation. An obligation to pay alimony or child support to a spouse, child, or government entity pursuant to an order by a court or other governmental unit.

Doubling. The ability of married couples to double the amount of certain property exemptions when filing for bankruptcy together. The federal bankruptcy exemptions allow doubling. State laws vary—some permit doubling and some do not.

Education individual retirement account. A type of account to which a person can contribute a certain amount of tax-deferred funds every year for the educational benefit of the debtor or certain relatives. Such an account is not part of the debtor's bankruptcy estate.

Emergency bankruptcy filing. An initial bankruptcy filing that includes only the petition and the creditor matrix, filed right away because the debtor needs the protection of the automatic stay to prevent a creditor from taking certain action, such as a foreclosure. An emergency filing case will be dismissed if the other required documents and forms are not filed in a timely manner.

Endowment insurance. An insurance policy that gives an insured who lives for a specified time (the endowment period) the right to receive the face value of the policy (the amount paid at death). If the insured dies sooner, the beneficiary named in the policy receives the proceeds.

Equity. The amount you get to keep if you sell property—typically the property's market value, less the costs of sale and the value of any liens on the property.

ERISA-qualified benefits. Pensions that meet the requirements of the Employee Retirement Income Security Act (ERISA), a federal law that sets minimum standards for such plans and requires beneficiaries to receive certain notices.

Executory contract. A contract in which one or both parties still have a duty to carry out one or more of the contract's terms.

Exempt property. Property described by state and federal laws (exemptions) that a debtor is entitled to keep in a Chapter 7 bankruptcy. Exempt property cannot be taken and sold by the trustee for the benefit of the debtor's unsecured creditors.

Exemptions. State and federal laws specifying the types of property creditors are not entitled to take to satisfy a debt, and the bankruptcy trustee is not entitled to take and sell for the benefit of the debtor's unsecured creditors.

Farm tools. Tools used by a person whose primary occupation is farming. Some states limit farm tools of the trade to items that can be held in the hand, such as hoes, axes, pitchforks, shovels, scythes, and the like. In other states, farm tools also include plows, harnesses, mowers, reapers, and so on.

Federal exemptions. A list of exemptions contained in the federal Bankruptcy Code. Some states give debtors the option of using the federal exemptions rather than state exemptions.

Federal Rules of Bankruptcy Procedure. A set of rules issued by the Administrative Office of the United States Courts, that govern bankruptcy court procedures.

Filing date. The date a bankruptcy petition in a particular case is filed. With few exceptions, debts incurred after the filing date are not discharged. Similarly, property owned before the filing date is part of the bankruptcy estate, while property acquired after the filing date is not.

Fines, penalties, and restitution. Debts owed to a court or a victim as a result of a sentence in a criminal matter. These debts are generally not dischargeable in bankruptcy.

Foreclosure. The process by which a creditor with a lien on real estate forces a sale of the property in order to collect on the lien. Foreclosure typically occurs when a homeowner defaults on a mortgage.

Fraternal benefit society benefits. Benefits, often group life insurance, paid for by fraternal societies, such as the Elks, Masons, Knights of Columbus, or the Knights of Maccabees, for their members. Also called benefit society, benevolent society, or mutual aid association benefits.

Fraud. Generally, an act that is intended to mislead another for the purpose of financial gain. In a bankruptcy case, fraud is any writing or representation intended to mislead creditors for the purpose of obtaining a loan or credit, or any act intended to mislead the bankruptcy court or the trustee.

Fraudulent transfer. In a bankruptcy case, a transfer of property to another for less than the property's value for the purpose of hiding the property from the bankruptcy trustee—for instance, when a debtor signs a car over to a relative to keep it out of the bankruptcy estate. Fraudulently transferred property can be recovered and sold by the trustee for the benefit of the creditors.

Fraudulently concealed assets. Property that a bankruptcy debtor deliberately fails to disclose as required by the bankruptcy rules.

Furnishings. An exemption category recognized in many states, which includes furniture, fixtures in your home (such as a heating unit, furnace, or built-in lighting), and other items with which a home is furnished, such as carpets and drapes.

Good faith. In a Chapter 13 case, when a debtor files for bankruptcy with the sincere purpose of paying off debts over the period of time required by law rather than for manipulative purposes—such as to prevent a foreclosure that by all rights should be allowed to proceed.

Goods and chattels. See "personal property."

Group life or group health insurance. A single insurance policy covering individuals in a group (for example, employees) and their dependents.

Head of household. A person who supports and maintains, in one household, one or more people who are closely related to the person by blood, marriage, or adoption. Also referred to as "head of family."

Health aids. Items needed to maintain their owner's health, such as a wheelchair, crutches, prosthesis, or a hearing aid. Many states require that health aids be prescribed by a physician.

Health benefits. Benefits paid under health insurance plans, such as Blue Cross or Blue Shield, to cover the costs of health care.

Heirloom. An item with special monetary or sentimental value, which is passed down from generation to generation.

Home equity loan. A loan made to a homeowner on the basis of the equity in the home—and secured by the home in the same manner as a mortgage.

Homestead. A state or federal exemption applicable to property where the debtor lives when he or she files bankruptcy—usually including boats and mobile homes.

Homestead declaration. See "declaration of homestead."

Household good. As an exemption category, an item of permanent nature (as opposed to items consumed, like food or cosmetics) used in or about the house. This includes linens, dinnerware, utensils, pots and pans, and small electronic equipment like radios. Many state laws specifically list the types of household goods that fall within this exemption, as do the federal bankruptcy laws.

Householder. A person who supports and maintains a household, with or without other people. Also called a "housekeeper."

Impairs an exemption. When a lien, in combination with any other liens on the property and the amount the debtor is entitled to claim as exempt, exceeds the value of the property the debtor could claim in the absence of any liens. For example, if property is worth $15,000, there are $5,000 worth of liens on the property, and the debtor is entitled to a $5,000 exemption in the property, another lien that exceeded $5,000 would impair the debtor's exemption. Certain types of liens that impair an exemption may be removed (avoided) by the debtor if the court so orders.

Implement. As an exemption category, an instrument, tool, or utensil used by a person to accomplish his or her job.

In lieu of homestead (or burial) exemption. Designates an exemption that is available only if you don't claim the homestead (or burial) exemption.

Individual Debtor's Statement of Intention. An official bankruptcy form that debtors with secured debts must file to indicate what they want to do with the property that secures the debt. For instance, a debtor with a car note must indicate whether he or she wants to keep the car and continue the debt (reaffirmation), pay off the car note at a reduced price (redemption), or give the car back to the creditor and cancel the debt.

Injunction. A court order prohibiting a person or an entity from taking specified actions—for example, the automatic stay (in reality an automatic injunction), which prevents most creditors from trying to collect their debts.

Insider creditor. A creditor with whom the debtor has a personal relationship, such as a relative, friend, or business partner.

Intangible property. Property that cannot be physically touched, such as an ownership share in a corporation or a copyright. Documents—such as a stock certificate—may provide evidence of intangible property.

Involuntary dismissal. When a bankruptcy judge dismisses a case because the debtor fails to carry out his or her duties—such as filing papers in a timely manner and cooperating with the trustee—or because the debtor files the bankruptcy in bad faith or engages in abuse by wrongfully filing for Chapter 7 when he or she should have filed for Chapter 13.

Involuntary lien. A lien that is placed on the debtor's property without the debtor's consent—for instance, when the IRS places a lien on property for back taxes.

IRS expenses. A table of national and regional expense estimates published by the IRS. Debtors whose "current monthly income" is more than their state's "median family income" must use the IRS expenses to calculate their average net income in a Chapter 7 case or their disposable income in a Chapter 13 case.

Jewelry. Items created for personal adornment; usually includes watches. Also called "articles of adornment."

Joint debtors. Married people who file for bankruptcy together and pay a single filing fee.

Judgment proof. A description of a person whose income and property are such that a creditor can't (or won't) seize them to enforce a money judgment—for example, a dwelling protected by a homestead exemption or a bank account containing only a few dollars.

Judicial foreclosure. A foreclosure that occurs through a court proceeding, usually when the party seeking the foreclosure files a complaint in court seeking a court order authorizing it.

Judicial lien. A lien created by the recording of a court money judgment against the debtor's property, usually real estate.

Lease. A contract that governs the relationship between an owner of property (such as a car or real estate) and a person who wishes to use the property for a specific period of time.

Lien. A legal claim against property that must be paid before title to the property can be transferred. Liens can also often be collected through repossession (personal property) or foreclosure (real estate), depending on the type of lien.

Lien avoidance. A bankruptcy procedure in which certain types of liens can be removed from certain types of property. Liens that are not avoided survive the bankruptcy even though the underlying debt may be cancelled. For instance, a lien remains on a car even if the debt evidenced by the car note is discharged in the bankruptcy.

Life estate. The right to live in, but not own, a specific home until your death.

Life insurance. A policy that provides for the payment of money to an individual (called the beneficiary) in the event of the death of another (called the insured). The policy matures (becomes payable) only when the insured dies.

Lifting the stay. When a bankruptcy court allows a creditor to continue with debt collection or other activities that are otherwise banned by the automatic stay. For instance, the court might allow a landlord to proceed with an eviction or a lender to repossess a car because the debtor has defaulted on the note.

Liquid assets. Cash or items that are easily convertible into cash, such as a money market account, stock, U.S. Treasury bill, or bank deposit.

Liquidated debt. An existing debt for a specified amount arising out of a contract or court judgment. In contrast, an unliquidated debt is a claim for an as-yet uncertain amount, such as for injuries suffered in a car accident before the case goes to court.

Lost future earnings. The portion of a lawsuit judgment intended to compensate an injured person for the money he or she won't be able to earn in the future because of the injury. Also called lost earnings payments or recoveries.

Luxuries. In bankruptcy, goods or services purchased by the debtor that a court decides were not appropriate in light of the debtor's insolvency. This might include vacations, jewelry, costly cars, or frequent meals at expensive restaurants.

Mailing matrix. See "creditor matrix."

Marital debts. Debts owed jointly by a married couple.

Marital property. Property owned jointly by a married couple.

Marital settlement agreement. An agreement between a divorcing couple that sets out who gets what percentage (or what specific items) of the marital property, who pays what marital debts, and who gets custody and pays child support if there are children of the marriage.

Materialmen's and mechanics' liens. Liens imposed by statute on real estate when suppliers of materials, labor, and contracting services used to improve the real estate are not properly compensated.

Matured life insurance benefits. Insurance benefits that are currently payable because the insured person has died.

Means test. A formula that uses predefined income and expense categories to determine whether a debtor whose income is more than the median family income for his or her state should be allowed to file a Chapter 7 bankruptcy.

Median family income. An annual income figure for which there are as many families with incomes below that level as there are above that level. The U.S. Census Bureau publishes median family income figures for each state and for different family sizes. In bankruptcy, the median family income is used as a basis for determining whether a debtor must pass the means test to file Chapter 7 bankruptcy, and whether a debtor filing a Chapter 13 bankruptcy must commit all his or her projected disposable income to a five-year repayment plan.

Meeting of creditors. A meeting that the debtor is required to attend in a bankruptcy case, at which the trustee and creditors may ask the debtor questions about his or her property, information in the documents and forms he or she filed, and his or her debts.

Mortgage. A contract in which a loan to purchase real estate is secured by the real estate as collateral. If the borrower defaults on loan payments, the lender can foreclose on the property.

Motion. A formal legal procedure in which the bankruptcy judge is asked to rule on a dispute in the bankruptcy case. To bring a motion, a party must file a document explaining what relief is requested, the facts of the dispute, and the legal reasons why the court should grant the relief. The party bringing the motion must mail these documents to all affected parties and let them know when the court will hear argument on the motion.

Motion to avoid judicial lien on real estate. A motion brought by a bankruptcy debtor that asks the bankruptcy court to remove a judicial lien on

real estate because the lien impairs the debtor's homestead exemption.

Motion to lift stay. A motion in which a creditor asks the court for permission to continue a court action or collection activities in spite of the automatic stay.

Motor vehicle. A self-propelled vehicle suitable for use on a street or road. This includes a car, truck, motorcycle, van, and moped. See also "tools of the trade."

Musical instrument. An instrument having the capacity, when properly operated, to produce a musical sound. Pianos, guitars, drums, drum machines, synthesizers, and harmonicas are all musical instruments.

Mutual aid association benefits. See "fraternal benefit society benefits."

Mutual assessment or mutual life. See "stipulated insurance."

Necessities. Articles needed to sustain life, such as food, clothing, medical care, and shelter.

Newly discovered creditors. Creditors who the debtor discovers after the bankruptcy is filed. If the case is still open, the debtor can amend the list to include the creditor; if the case is closed, it usually can be reopened to accommodate the amendment.

Nonbankruptcy federal exemptions. Federal laws that allow a debtor who has not filed for bankruptcy to keep creditors away from certain property. The debtor can also use these exemptions in bankruptcy if the debtor is using a state exemption system.

Nondischargeable debt. Debt that survives bankruptcy, such as back child support and most student loans.

Nonexempt property. Property in the bankruptcy estate that is unprotected by the exemption system available to the debtor (this is typically—but not always—the exemption system in the state where the debtor files bankruptcy). In a Chapter 7 bankruptcy, the trustee may sell it for the benefit of the debtor's unsecured creditors. In a Chapter 13 bankruptcy, debtors must propose a plan that pays their unsecured creditors at least the value of their unsecured property.

Nonjudicial foreclosure. A foreclosure that occurs outside of court, usually when a trustee of a deed of trust first records a notice of default and then a notice of sale in an auction, typically held on the courthouse steps.

Nonpossessory, nonpurchase-money lien. A lien placed on property that is already owned by the debtor and is used as collateral for the loan without being possessed by the lender. In contrast, a nonpurchase-money, possessory lien exists on collateral that is held by a pawnshop.

Nonpriority debt. A type of debt that is not entitled to be paid first in bankruptcy, as priority debts are. Nonpriority debts do not have to be paid in full in a Chapter 13 case.

Nonpriority, unsecured claim. A claim that is not for a priority debt (such as child support) and is not secured by collateral or other property. Typical examples include credit card debt, medical bills, and student loans. In a Chapter 13 repayment plan, nonpriority, unsecured claims are paid only after all other debts are paid.

Notice of appeal. A form that must be filed with a court when a party wishes to appeal a judgment or an order issued by the court. Often, the notice of appeal must be filed within ten days of the date the order or judgment is entered in the court's records.

Objection. A document one party files to oppose a proposed action by another party—for instance, when a creditor or trustee files an objection to a bankruptcy debtor's claim of exemption.

Order for relief. The court's automatic injunction against certain collection and other activities that might negatively affect the bankruptcy estate. Another name for the "automatic stay."

Oversecured debt. A debt that is secured by collateral that is worth more than the amount of the debt.

PACER. An online, fee-based database containing bankruptcy court dockets (records of proceedings in bankruptcy cases) and federal court documents, such as court rules and recent appellate court decisions.

Pain and suffering damages. The portion of a court judgment intended to compensate for past, present, and future mental and physical pain, suffering, impairment of ability to work, and mental distress caused by an injury.

Partially secured debt. A debt secured by collateral that is worth less than the debt itself—for instance, when a person owes $15,000 on a car that is worth only $10,000.

Party in interest. Any person or entity that has a financial interest in the outcome of a bankruptcy case, including the trustee, the debtor, and all creditors.

Pension. A fund into which payments are made to provide an employee income after retirement. Typically, the beneficiary can't access the account without incurring a significant penalty, usually a tax. There are many types of pensions, including defined benefit pensions provided by many large corporations and individual pensions (such as 401(k) and IRA accounts). In bankruptcy, most pensions are not considered part of the bankruptcy estate and are therefore not affected by a bankruptcy filing.

Personal financial management counseling. Under the new bankruptcy law, a two-hour class intended to teach budget skills. Every consumer bankruptcy filer must attend such a class in order to obtain a discharge in Chapter 7, Chapter 12, or Chapter 13 bankruptcy.

Personal injury cause of action. The right to seek compensation for physical and mental suffering, including injury to body, reputation, or both. For example, someone who is hit and injured by a car might have a personal injury cause of action against the driver.

Personal injury recovery. The portion of a lawsuit judgment or insurance settlement that is intended to compensate someone for physical and mental suffering, including physical injury, injury to reputation, or both. Bankruptcy exemptions usually do not apply to compensation for pain or suffering or punitive damages—in other words, that part of the recovery can be taken by the trustee in a Chapter 7 case.

Personal property. All property not classified as real property, including tangible items, such as cars and jewelry, and intangible property, such as stocks and pensions.

Petition. The document a debtor files to officially begin a bankruptcy case and ask for relief. Other documents and schedules must be filed to support the petition at the time it is filed, or shortly afterwards.

Pets. See "animals."

Preference. A payment made by a debtor to a creditor within a defined period prior to filing for bankruptcy—within three months for arms-length creditors (regular commercial creditors) and one year for insider creditors (friends, family, business associates). Because a preference gives that debtor an edge over other debtors in the bankruptcy case, the trustee can recover the preference and distribute it among all of the creditors.

Prepetition. Any time prior to the moment the bankruptcy petition is filed.

Prepetition counseling. Debt or credit counseling that occurs before the bankruptcy petition is filed—as opposed to personal financial management counseling, which occurs after the petition is filed.

Presumed abuse. In a Chapter 7 bankruptcy, when the debtor has a current monthly income in excess of the family median income for the state where the debtor lives, and has sufficient income to propose a Chapter 13 plan under the "means test." If abuse is presumed, the debtor has to prove that his or her Chapter 7 filing is not abusive in order to proceed further.

Primarily business debts. When the majority of debt owed by a bankruptcy debtor—in dollar terms—arises from debts incurred to operate a business.

Primarily consumer debts. When the majority of debt owed by a bankruptcy debtor—in dollar terms—arises from debts incurred for personal or family purposes.

Priority claim. See "priority debt."

Priority creditor. A creditor who has filed a *"Proof of Claim"* showing that the debtor owes it a priority debt.

Priority debt. A type of debt that is paid first if there are distributions to be made from the bankruptcy estate. Priority debts include alimony and child support, fees owed to the trustee and attorneys in the case, and wages owed to employees. With one exception (back child support obligations assigned to government entities), priority claims must be paid in full in a Chapter 13 bankruptcy.

Proceeds for damaged exempt property. Money received through insurance coverage, arbitration, mediation, settlement, or a lawsuit to pay for exempt property that has been damaged or destroyed. For example, if a debtor had the right to use a $30,000 homestead exemption, but his or her home was destroyed by fire, the debtor can instead exempt $30,000 of the insurance proceeds.

Projected disposable income. The amount of income a debtor will have left over each month, after deducting allowable expenses, payments on

mandatory debts, and administrative expenses from his or her current monthly income. This is the amount the debtor must pay toward his or her unsecured nonpriority debts in a Chapter 13 plan.

Proof of Claim. A formal document filed by bankruptcy creditors in a bankruptcy case to assert their right to payments from the bankruptcy estate, if any payments are made.

Proof of Service. A document signed under penalty of perjury by the person serving a document showing how the service was made, who made it, and when.

Property of the estate. See "bankruptcy estate."

Purchase-money loans. Loans that are made to purchase specific property items and that use the property as collateral to assure repayment, such as car loans and mortgages.

Purchase-money security interest. A claim on property owned by the holder of a loan that was used to purchase the property and that is secured by the property (as collateral).

Reaffirmation. An agreement entered into after a bankruptcy filing (postpetition) between the debtor and a creditor in which the debtor agrees to repay all or part of a prepetition debt after the bankruptcy is over. For instance, a debtor makes an agreement with the holder of a car note that the debtor can keep the car and must continue to pay the debt after bankruptcy.

Real property. Real estate (land and buildings on the land, usually including mobile homes attached to a foundation).

Reasonable investigation. Bankruptcy attorneys' obligation, under bankruptcy law, to look into the information provided to them by their clients.

Redemption. In a Chapter 7 bankruptcy, when the debtor obtains legal title to collateral for a secured debt by paying the secured creditor the replacement value of the collateral in a lump sum. For example, a debtor may redeem a car note by paying the lender the replacement value of the car (what a retail vendor would charge for the car, considering its age and condition).

Reopen a case. To open a closed bankruptcy case, usually for the purpose of adding an overlooked creditor or filing a motion to avoid an overlooked lien. A debtor must request that the court reopen the case.

Repayment plan. An informal plan to repay creditors most or all of what they are owed outside of bankruptcy. Also refers to the plan proposed by a debtor in a Chapter 13 case.

Replacement cost. What it would cost to replace a particular item by buying it from a retail vendor, considering its age and condition—for instance, when buying a car from a used car dealer, furniture from a used furniture shop, or electronic equipment on eBay.

Repossession. When a secured creditor takes property used as collateral because the debtor has defaulted on the loan secured by the collateral.

Request to lift the stay. A written request filed in bankruptcy court by a creditor, which seeks permission to engage in debt collection activity otherwise prohibited by the automatic stay.

Schedule A. The official bankruptcy form a debtor must file to describe all of his or her real property.

Schedule B. The official bankruptcy form a debtor must file to describe all personal property owned by the debtor, including tangible property, such as jewelry and vehicles, and intangible property, such as investments and accounts receivable.

Schedule C. The official bankruptcy form a debtor must file to describe the property the debtor is claiming as exempt and the legal basis for the claims of exemption.

Schedule D. The official bankruptcy form a debtor must file to describe all secured debts owed by the debtor, such as car notes and mortgages.

Schedule E. The official bankruptcy form a debtor must file to describe all priority debts owed by the debtor, such as back child support and taxes.

Schedule F. The official bankruptcy form a debtor must file to describe all nonpriority, unsecured debts owed by the debtor, such as most credit card and medical bills.

Schedule G. The official bankruptcy form a debtor must file to describe any leases and executory contracts (contracts under which one or both parties still have obligations) to which the debtor is a party.

Schedule H. The official bankruptcy form a debtor must file to describe all codebtors that might be affected by the bankruptcy.

Schedule I. The official bankruptcy form a debtor must file to describe the debtor's income.

Schedule J. The official bankruptcy form a debtor must file to describe the debtor's actual monthly expenses.

Schedules. Official bankruptcy forms a debtor must file, detailing the debtor's property, debts, income, and expenses.

Second deed of trust. A loan against real estate made after the original mortgage (or first deed of trust). Most home equity loans are second deeds of trust.

Secured claim. A debt secured by collateral under a written agreement (for instance, a mortgage or car note) or by operation of law—such as a tax lien.

Secured creditor. The owner of a secured claim.

Secured debt. A debt secured by collateral.

Secured interest. A claim to property used as collateral. For instance, a lender on a car note retains legal title to the car until the loan is paid off.

Secured property. Property that is collateral for a secured debt.

Serial bankruptcy filing. A practice used by some debtors to file and dismiss one bankruptcy after another to obtain the protection of the automatic stay, even though the bankruptcies themselves offer no debt relief—for instance, when a debtor files successive Chapter 13 cases to prevent foreclosure of his or her home even though there are no debts to repay.

Short sale. When a homeowner sells his or her home for less than is owed on the mortgage and turns the proceeds over to the mortgage owner. The homeowner's credit report will be negatively affected just as if the home were lost through foreclosure.

Sickness benefits. See "disability benefits."

State exemptions. State laws that specify the types of property creditors are not entitled to take to satisfy a debt, and the bankruptcy trustee is not entitled to take and sell for the benefit of the debtor's unsecured creditors.

Statement of Financial Affairs. The official bankruptcy form a debtor must file to describe the debtor's legal, economic, and business transactions for the several years prior to filing, including gifts, preferences, income, closing of deposit accounts, lawsuits, and other information that the trustee needs to assess the legitimacy of the bankruptcy and the true extent of the bankruptcy estate.

Statement of Current Monthly Income and Calculation of Commitment Period and Disposable Income. The official bankruptcy form a debtor must file in a Chapter 13 case, setting out the debtor's current monthly income and calculating the debtor's projected disposable income that will determine how much will be paid to the debtor's unsecured creditors.

Statement of Current Monthly Income and Means-Test Calculation. The official bankruptcy form a debtor must file in a Chapter 7 filing that shows the debtor's current monthly income, calculates whether the debtor's income is higher than the state's median family income, and, if so, uses the means test to determine whether a Chapter 7 bankruptcy would constitute abuse.

Statement of Intention. The official bankruptcy form a debtor must file in a Chapter 7 case to tell the court and secured creditors how the debtor plans to treat his or her secured debts—that is, reaffirm the debt, redeem the debt, or surrender the property and discharge the debt.

Statement of Social Security Number. The official bankruptcy form a debtor must file to disclose the debtor's complete Social Security number.

Statutory lien. A lien imposed on property by law, such as tax liens and mechanics' liens, as opposed to voluntary liens (such as mortgages) and liens arising from court judgments (judicial liens).

Stay. See "automatic stay."

Stipulated insurance. An insurance policy that allows the insurance company to assess an amount on the insured, above the standard premium payments, if the company experiences losses worse than had been calculated into the standard premium. Also called assessment, mutual assessment, or mutual life insurance.

Stock options. A contract between a corporation and an employee that gives the employee the right to purchase corporate stock at a specific price mentioned in the contract (the strike price).

Strip down of lien. In a Chapter 13 bankruptcy, when the amount of a lien on collateral is reduced to the collateral's replacement value. See "cramdown."

Student loan. A type of loan made for educational purposes by nonprofit or commercial lenders with repayment and interest terms dictated by federal law. Student loans are not dischargeable in bankruptcy unless the debtor can show that repaying the loan would impose an "undue hardship."

Substantial abuse. Under pre-2005 bankruptcy law, filing a Chapter 7 bankruptcy when a Chapter 13 bankruptcy was feasible.

Suits, executions, garnishments, and attachments. Activities engaged in by creditors to enforce money judgments, typically involving the seizure of wages and bank accounts.

Summary of Schedules. The official bankruptcy form a debtor must file to summarize the property and debt information contained in a debtor's schedules

Surrender value. See "avails."

Surrendering collateral. In Chapter 7 bankruptcy, the act of returning collateral to a secured lender in order to discharge the underlying debt—for example, returning a car to discharge the car note.

Tangible personal property. See "tangible property" and "personal property."

Tangible property. Property that may be physically touched. Examples include money, furniture, cars, jewelry, artwork, and houses. Compare "intangible property."

Tax lien. A statutory lien imposed on property to secure payment of back taxes—typically income and property taxes.

Tenancy by the entirety. A way that married couples can hold title to property in about half of the states. When one spouse dies, the surviving spouse automatically owns 100% of the property. In most cases, this type of property is not part of the bankruptcy estate if only one spouse files.

To ____ acres. A limitation on the size of a homestead that may be exempted.

Tools of the trade. Items needed to perform a line of work that you are currently doing and relying on for support. For a mechanic, plumber, or carpenter, for example, tools of trade are the implements used to repair, build, and install. Traditionally, tools of the trade were limited to items that could be held in the hand. Most states, however, now embrace a broader definition, and a debtor may be able to fit many items under a tools of trade exemption.

Transcript of tax return. A summary of a debtor's tax return provided by the IRS upon the debtor's request, usually acceptable as a substitute for the return in the instances when a return must be filed under bankruptcy law.

Trustee. An official appointed by the bankruptcy court to carry out the administrative tasks associated with a bankruptcy and to seize and sell nonexempt property in the bankruptcy estate for the benefit of the debtor's unsecured creditors.

U.S. Trustee. An official employed by Office of the U.S. Trustee (a division of the U.S. Department of Justice) who is responsible for overseeing the bankruptcy trustees, regulating credit and personal financial management counselors, regulating bankruptcy petition preparers, auditing bankruptcy cases, ferreting out fraud, and generally making sure that the bankruptcy laws are obeyed.

Undersecured debt. A debt secured by collateral that is worth less than the debt.

Undue hardship. The conditions under which a debtor may discharge a student loan—for example, when the debtor has no income and little chance of earning enough to repay the loan in the future.

Unexpired lease. A lease that is still in effect.

Unmatured life insurance. A policy that is not yet payable because the insured is still alive.

Unscheduled debt. A debt that is not included in the schedules accompanying a bankruptcy filing, perhaps because it was overlooked or intentionally left out.

Unsecured creditor. A creditor whose debt is not secured by collateral, and who therefore has no right to seize a particular item of the debtor's property if the debtor defaults on the debt.

Unsecured priority claims. Priority claims that aren't secured by collateral, such as back child support or taxes for which no lien has been placed on the debtor's property.

Valuation of property. The act of determining the replacement value of property for the purpose of describing it in the bankruptcy schedules, determining whether it is protected by an applicable exemption, redeeming secured property, or cramming down a lien in Chapter 13 bankruptcy.

Voluntary dismissal. When a bankruptcy debtor dismisses his or her Chapter 7 or Chapter 13 case on his or her own, without coercion by the court.

Voluntary lien. A lien agreed to by the debtor, as when the debtor signs a mortgage, car note, or second deed of trust.

Weekly net earnings. The earnings a debtor has left after mandatory deductions, such as income tax, mandatory union dues, and Social Security contributions, have been subtracted from his or her gross income.

Wildcard exemption. A dollar value that the debtor can apply to any type of property to make it—or more of it—exempt. In some states, filers may use the unused portion of a homestead exemption as a wildcard exemption.

Willful and malicious act. An act done with the intent to cause harm. In a Chapter 7 bankruptcy, a debt arising from the debtor's willful and malicious act is not discharged if the victim proves to the bankruptcy court's satisfaction that the act occurred.

Willful or malicious act resulting in a civil judgment. A bad act that was careless or reckless, but was not necessarily intended to cause harm. In a Chapter 13 case, a debt arising from the debtor's act that was either willful or malicious is not discharged if it is part of a civil judgment.

Wrongful death cause of action. The right to seek compensation for having to live without a deceased person. Usually only the spouse and children of the deceased have a wrongful death cause of action.

Wrongful death recoveries. The portion of a lawsuit judgment intended to compensate a plaintiff for having to live without a deceased person. The compensation is intended to cover the earnings and the emotional comfort and support the deceased would have provided.

State and Federal Exemption Charts

The charts in this appendix summarize the laws that determine how much property people can keep when they file for Chapter 7 bankruptcy. When you file for Chapter 13 bankruptcy, your repayment plan must pay at least what your unsecured, nonpriority creditors would have received from the sale of your nonexempt property—the property that you would not get to keep if you had filed under Chapter 7. (See Chs. 3, 4, and 5 for more on this requirement.)

As you will see, the charts are divided into categories of property, such as insurance, personal property, and wages. Following each exemption, we provide the numerical citation to the state statute that includes the exemption.

The states are listed alphabetically, followed by the federal exemptions. We also note which states allow you to choose between the federal and state bankruptcy exemptions.

> **RELATED TOPIC**
>
> **Need help understanding a term?** Many of the categories, types of property, and other terms used in these charts are defined in the Glossary, which you'll find right before this appendix.

Doubling

When a married couple files for bankruptcy jointly, federal law and the laws of some states allow them each to claim the full amount of an exemption. (11 U.S.C. § 522.) Because a couple gets to claim twice the amount available to those who file alone, this practice is informally known as "doubling."

Not all states allow doubling, however. And some states allow married filers to double only certain exemptions (for example, they can double personal property exemptions but not the homestead exemption). In the charts that follow, we indicate exemptions that cannot be doubled (and states that don't allow doubling at all). Unless you see a note stating that you cannot double, assume that you can.

> **CAUTION**
>
> **These charts provide general information only.** There are exceptions to state exemption laws that are much too detailed to include here. Consider doing further legal research or consulting an attorney about the exemptions you plan to claim, particularly if you anticipate—or are facing—a challenge to your exemption claims.

Retirement Accounts

Virtually all types of tax-exempt retirement accounts are exempt in bankruptcy, whether you use the state or federal exemptions. You can exempt 401(k)s, 403(b)s, profit-sharing and money purchase plans, IRAs (including Roth, SEP, and SIMPLE IRAs), and defined-benefit plans.

These exemptions are unlimited—that is, the entire account is exempt, regardless of how much money is in it—except in the case of traditional and Roth IRAs. For these types of IRAs only, the exemption is limited to a total value of $1,171,650 per person (this figure will be adjusted every three years for inflation). If you have more than one traditional or Roth IRA, you don't get to exempt $1,171,650 per account: Your total exemption, no matter how many accounts you have, is $1,171,650.

If you are using the federal bankruptcy exemptions, you can find this new retirement account provision at 11 U.S.C. § 522(d)(12). If you are using state exemptions, cite 11 U.S.C. § 522(b)(3)(C) as the applicable exemption when you complete your bankruptcy papers.

Special Considerations in States With "Bankruptcy-specific" Exemptions

Eight states have exemption schemes that apply only in bankruptcy (which means debtors cannot use these exemptions against judgment creditors). These states are: California, Colorado, Georgia, Michigan, Montana, New York, Ohio, and West Virginia. While most of these schemes have been deemed constitutional—including West Virginia's scheme, in 2010, by the Fourth Circuit Court of Appeals (*Sheehan v. Peveich*, 574 F.3d 248 (4th Cir. 2009))—a few lower courts over the years have determined that such "bankruptcy-specific" exemption schemes are unconstitutional, most recently, in 2011, when Michigan's scheme was found to be unconstitutional by a Sixth Circuit Bankruptcy Appellate Panel. (*In re Schafer,* 2011 WL 650545 (6th Cir. BAP (Mich.)) (See "Attention Michigan Residents," below.)

And while Michigan's scheme has been declared invalid, another lower court has ruled that Georgia's bankruptcy-specific exemptions are not only allowed, but *required*—that is, if you're filing bankruptcy, you *must* use the bankruptcy-specific exemption instead of a broader, more general one, at least where it is narrower in scope than a corresponding general exemption. (*In re Allen,* 2010 WL 3958171 (Bankr. M.D. Ga. 2010).)

Although the majority of bankruptcy courts in states with bankruptcy-specific exemption schemes allow debtors to use these exemptions, you may wish to consult with an attorney if you live in one of these states to determine what exemptions are permitted in your local bankruptcy court.

Attention Michigan Residents

In 2011, the Bankruptcy Appellate Panel of the Sixth Circuit ruled that Michigan's bankruptcy-only exemption scheme (at Michigan Compiled Laws 600.5451) is unconstitutional. (*In re: Schafer,* 2011 WL 650545 (6th Cir. BAP (Mich.)). This case is currently being appealed to the Sixth Circuit Court of Appeals. It is unclear what courts are bound by this decision—all bankruptcy courts in Michigan, or just those in the Western District. For now, it's wise to check with a local bankruptcy attorney regarding which exemptions to use.

In this appendix, we provide two sets of exemptions — those available if you can use the Michigan bankruptcy-only exemptions, and those available if you cannot use the Michigan bankruptcy-only exemptions (these are called the "general exemptions"). Michigan also allows debtors to use the federal exemptions instead of the state exemptions.

 CAUTION

Some states have other exemptions that apply to judgment creditors. Some states (including but not limited to Arkansas, Georgia, Maryland, and West Virginia) have other exemption amounts that apply to judgment creditors only. Most often, these other amounts apply to the homestead exemption only, but some apply to other property as well. The state exemptions listed in this appendix do not include these judgment-creditor-only exemptions. If you want to use an exemption against a judgment creditor, check to see if an amount different from the bankruptcy exemption amount listed in this appendix, applies. You can find all of your state's exemptions (both bankruptcy and nonbankruptcy) in the National Consumer Law Center's *Bankruptcy Law & Practice* manual or *Fair Debt Collection* manual (many law libraries have these books, as do some public libraries). Or contact a local consumer attorney.

Confirm the Information in the Exemption Charts Before Relying on It

The exemptions in the following charts were current when this book went to press, but your state may have changed the law since then. In addition, states often carve out exceptions to the exemptions, which are far too detailed to list here. For instance, even if an item is listed as exempt in one of these charts, you might have to give it up to pay child support or a tax debt.

Before relying on any particular exemption, consider:

- reading the exemption statute yourself, using the research information in Ch. 16, and
- cross-checking the chart's information against the exemptions for your state listed on www.legalconsumer.com.

Last, but certainly not least, consult with a bankruptcy lawyer.

Alabama

Federal bankruptcy exemptions not available. All law references are to Alabama Code unless otherwise noted.

ASSET	EXEMPTION	LAW
homestead	Real property or mobile home to $5,000; property cannot exceed 160 acres	6-10-2
	Must record homestead declaration before attempted sale of home	6-10-20
insurance	Annuity proceeds or avails to $250 per month	27-14-32
	Disability proceeds or avails to an average of $250 per month	27-14-31
	Fraternal benefit society benefits	27-34-27
	Life insurance proceeds or avails	6-10-8; 27-14-29
	Life insurance proceeds or avails if clause prohibits proceeds from being used to pay beneficiary's creditors	27-15-26
	Mutual aid association benefits	27-30-25
pensions	Tax-exempt retirement accounts, including 401(k)s, 403(b)s, profit-sharing and money purchase plans, SEP and SIMPLE IRAs, and defined-benefit plans	11 U.S.C. § 522(b)(3)(C)
	Traditional and Roth IRAs to $1,171,650 per person	11 U.S.C. § 522(b)(3)(C); (n)
	IRAs & other retirement accounts	19-3B-508
	Judges (only payments being received)	12-18-10(a),(b)
	Law enforcement officers	36-21-77
	Spendthrift trusts (with exceptions)	19-3B-501 to 503
	State employees	36-27-28
	Teachers	16-25-23
personal property	Books of debtor & family	6-10-6
	Burial place for self & family	6-10-5
	Church pew for self & family	6-10-5
	Clothing of debtor & family	6-10-6
	Family portraits or pictures	6-10-6
public benefits	Aid to blind, aged, disabled & other public assistance	38-4-8
	Crime victims' compensation	15-23-15(e)
	Southeast Asian War POWs' benefits	31-7-2
	Unemployment compensation	25-4-140
	Workers' compensation	25-5-86(b)
tools of trade	Arms, uniforms, equipment that state military personnel are required to keep	31-2-78
wages	With respect to consumer loans, consumer credit sales & consumer leases, 75% of weekly net earnings or 30 times the federal minimum hourly wage; all other cases, 75% of earned but unpaid wages; bankruptcy judge may authorize more for low-income debtors	5-19-15; 6-10-7
wildcard	$3,000 of any personal property, except wages	6-10-6

Alaska

Alaska law states that only the items found in Alaska Statutes §§ 9.38.010, 9.38.015(a), 9.38.017, 9.38.020, 9.38.025, and 9.38.030 may be exempted in bankruptcy. In *In re McNutt*, 87 B.R. 84 (9th Cir. 1988), however, an Alaskan debtor used the federal bankruptcy exemptions. All law references are to Alaska Statutes unless otherwise noted.

Alaska exemption amounts are adjusted regularly by administrative order. Current amounts are found at 8 Alaska Admin. Code tit. 8, § 95.030.

ASSET	EXEMPTION	LAW
homestead	$70,200 (joint owners may each claim a portion, but total can't exceed $70,200)	09.38.010(a)
insurance	Disability benefits	09.38.015(b); 09.38.030(e)(1),(5)
	Fraternal benefit society benefits	21.84.240
	Life insurance or annuity contracts, total avails to $500,000	09.38.025
	Medical, surgical, or hospital benefits	09.38.015(a)(3)
miscellaneous	Alimony, to extent wages exempt	09.38.030(e)(2)
	Child support payments made by collection agency	09.38.015(b)
	Liquor licenses	09.38.015(a)(7)
	Property of business partnership	09.38.100(b)
pensions	Tax-exempt retirement accounts, including 401(k)s, 403(b)s, profit-sharing and money purchase plans, SEP and SIMPLE IRAs, and defined-benefit plans	11 U.S.C. § 522(b)(3)(C)
	Traditional and Roth IRAs to $1,171,650 per person	11 U.S.C. § 522(b)(3)(C); (n)
	Elected public officers (only benefits building up)	09.38.015(b)
	ERISA-qualified benefits deposited more than 120 days before filing bankruptcy	09.38.017
	Judicial employees (only benefits building up)	09.38.015(b)
	Public employees (only benefits building up)	09.38.015(b); 39.35.505
	Roth & traditional IRAs, medical savings accounts	09.38.017(e)(3)
	Teachers (only benefits building up)	09.38.015(b)
	Other pensions, to extent wages exempt (only payments being received)	09.38.030(e)(5)
personal property	Books, musical instruments, clothing, family portraits, household goods & heirlooms to $3,900 total	09.38.020(a)
	Building materials	34.35.105
	Burial plot	09.38.015(a)(1)
	Cash or other liquid assets to $1,820; for sole wage earner in household, $2,860 (restrictions apply—see *wages*)	09.38.030(b)
	Deposit in apartment or condo owners' association	09.38.010(e)
	Health aids needed	09.38.015(a)(2)
	Jewelry to $1,300	09.38.020(b)
	Money held in mortgage escrow accounts after July 1, 2008	09.38.015(e)
	Motor vehicle to $3,900; vehicle's market value can't exceed $26,000	09.38.020(e)
	Personal injury recoveries, to extent wages exempt	09.38.030(e)(3)
	Pets to $1,300	09.38.020(d)
	Proceeds for lost, damaged, or destroyed exempt property	09.38.060
	Tuition credits under an advance college tuition payment contract	09.38.015(a)(8)
	Wrongful death recoveries, to extent wages exempt	09.38.030(e)(3)

public benefits	Adult assistance to elderly, blind, disabled	47.25.550
	Alaska benefits for low-income seniors	09.38.015(a)(11)
	Alaska longevity bonus	09.38.015(a)(5)
	Crime victims' compensation	09.38.015(a)(4)
	Federally exempt public benefits paid or due	09.38.015(a)(6)
	General relief assistance	47.25.210
	Senior care (prescription drug) benefits	09.38.015(a)(10)
	20% of permanent fund dividends	43.23.065
	Unemployment compensation	09.38.015(b); 23.20.405
	Workers' compensation	23.30.160
tools of trade	Implements, books & tools of trade to $3,640	09.38.020(c)
wages	Weekly net earnings to $456; for sole wage earner in a household, $716; if you don't receive weekly or semimonthly pay, you can claim $1,820 in cash or liquid assets paid any month; for sole wage earner in household, $2,860	9.38.030(a),(b); 9.38.050(b)
wildcard	None	

Arizona

Federal bankruptcy exemptions not available. All law references are to Arizona Revised Statutes unless otherwise noted.

ASSET	EXEMPTION	LAW
homestead	Real property, an apartment, or mobile home you occupy to $150,000; sale proceeds exempt 18 months after sale or until new home purchased, whichever occurs first (spouses may not double)	33-1101(A)
	May record homestead declaration to clarify which one of multiple eligible parcels is being claimed as homestead	33-1102
insurance	Fraternal benefit society benefits	20-877
	Group life insurance policy or proceeds	20-1132
	Health, accident, or disability benefits	33-1126(A)(4)
	Life insurance cash value or proceeds, or annuity contract if owned at least two years and beneficiary is dependent family member	33-1126(A)(6); 20-1131(D)
	Life insurance proceeds to $20,000 if beneficiary is spouse or child	33-1126(A)(1)
miscellaneous	Alimony, child support needed for support	33-1126(A)(3)
	Minor child's earnings, unless debt is for child	33-1126(A)(2)
pensions *see also wages*	Tax-exempt retirement accounts, including 401(k)s, 403(b)s, profit-sharing and money purchase plans, SEP and SIMPLE IRAs, and defined-benefit plans	11 U.S.C. § 522(b)(3)(C)
	Traditional and Roth IRAs to $1,171,650 per person	11 U.S.C. § 522(b)(3)(C); (n)
	Board of regents members, faculty & administrative officers under board's jurisdiction	15-1628(I)
	District employees	48-227
	ERISA-qualified benefits deposited over 120 days before filing	33-1126(B)
	IRAs & Roth IRAs	33-1126(B); *In re Herrscher*, 121 B.R. 29 (D. Ariz. 1989)
	Firefighters	9-968
	Police officers	9-931
	Public Safety Personnel Retirement System	38-850(c)
	Rangers	41-955
	State employees' retirement & disability	38-792; 38-797.11

personal property *spouses may double all personal property*	2 beds & bedding; 1 living room chair per person; 1 dresser, table, lamp; kitchen table; dining room table & 4 chairs (1 more per person); living room carpet or rug; couch; 3 lamps; 3 coffee or end tables; pictures, paintings, personal drawings, family portraits; refrigerator, stove, washer, dryer, vacuum cleaner; TV, radio, stereo, alarm clock to $4,000 total	33-1123
	Bank deposit to $150 in one account	33-1126(A)(9)
	Bible; bicycle; sewing machine; typewriter; burial plot; rifle, pistol, or shotgun to $500 total	33-1125
	Books to $250; clothing to $500; wedding & engagement rings to $1,000; watch to $100; pets, horses, milk cows & poultry to $500; musical instruments to $250	33-1125
	Food & fuel to last 6 months	33-1124
	Funeral deposits to $5,000	32-1391.05(4)
	Health aids	33-1125(9)
	Motor vehicle to $5,000 ($10,000, if debtor is physically disabled)	33-1125(8)
	Prepaid rent or security deposit to $1,000 or 1½ times your rent, whichever is less, in lieu of homestead	33-1126(C)
	Proceeds for sold or damaged exempt property	33-1126(A)(5),(8)
	Wrongful death awards	12-592
public benefits	Unemployment compensation	23-783(A)
	Welfare benefits	46-208
	Workers' compensation	23-1068(B)
tools of trade *husband & wife may double*	Arms, uniforms & accoutrements of profession or office required by law	33-1130(3)
	Farm machinery, utensils, seed, instruments of husbandry, feed, grain & animals to $2,500 total	33-1130(2)
	Library & teaching aids of teacher	33-1127
	Tools, equipment, instruments & books to $2,500	33-1130(1)
wages	75% of earned but unpaid weekly net earnings or 30 times the federal minimum hourly wage; 50% of wages for support orders; bankruptcy judge may authorize more for low-income debtors	33-1131
wildcard	None	

Arkansas

Federal bankruptcy exemptions available. All law references are to Arkansas Code Annotated unless otherwise noted.

Note: *In re Holt*, 894 F.2d 1005 (8th Cir. 1990) held that Arkansas residents are limited to exemptions in the Arkansas Constitution. Statutory exemptions can still be used within Arkansas for nonbankruptcy purposes, but they cannot be claimed in bankruptcy.

ASSET	EXEMPTION	LAW
homestead *choose Option 1 or 2*	1. For married person or head of family: unlimited exemption on real or personal property used as residence to ¼ acre in city, town, or village, or 80 acres elsewhere; if property is between ¼ and 1 acre in city, town, or village, or 80 to 160 acres elsewhere, additional limit is $2,500; homestead may not exceed 1 acre in city, town, or village, or 160 acres elsewhere (spouses may not double)	Constitution 9-3; 9-4, 9-5; 16-66-210; 16-66-218(b)(3), (4); *In re Stevens*, 829 F.2d 693 (8th Cir. 1987)
	2. Real or personal property used as residence to $800 if single; $1,250 if married	16-66-218(a)(1)

insurance	Annuity contract	23-79-134
	Disability benefits	23-79-133
	Fraternal benefit society benefits	23-74-403
	Group life insurance	23-79-132
	Life, health, accident, or disability cash value or proceeds paid or due to $500	16-66-209; Constitution 9-1, 9-2; *In re Holt*, 894 F.2d 1005 (8th Cir. 1990)
	Life insurance proceeds if clause prohibits proceeds from being used to pay beneficiary's creditors	23-79-131
	Life insurance proceeds or avails if beneficiary isn't the insured	23-79-131
	Mutual assessment life or disability benefits to $1,000	23-72-114
	Stipulated insurance premiums	23-71-112
pensions	Tax-exempt retirement accounts, including 401(k)s, 403(b)s, profit-sharing and money purchase plans, SEP and SIMPLE IRAs, and defined-benefit plans	11 U.S.C. § 522(b)(3)(C)
	Traditional and Roth IRAs to $1,171,650 per person	11 U.S.C. § 522(b)(3)(C); (n)
	Disabled firefighters	24-11-814
	Disabled police officers	24-11-417
	Firefighters	24-10-616
	IRA deposits to $20,000 if deposited over 1 year before filing for bankruptcy	16-66-218(b)(16)
	Police officers	24-10-616
	School employees	24-7-715
	State police officers	24-6-205; 24-6-223
personal property	Burial plot to 5 acres, if choosing federal homestead exemption (Option 2)	16-66-207; 16-66-218(a)(1)
	Clothing	Constitution 9-1, 9-2
	Motor vehicle to $1,200	16-66-218(a)(2)
	Prepaid funeral trusts	23-40-117
	Wedding rings	16-66-219
public benefits	Crime victims' compensation	16-90-716(e)
	Unemployment compensation	11-10-109
	Workers' compensation	11-9-110
tools of trade	Implements, books & tools of trade to $750	16-66-218(a)(4)
wages	Earned but unpaid wages due for 60 days; in no event less than $25 per week	16-66-208; 16-66-218(b)(6)
wildcard	$500 of any personal property if married or head of family; $200 if not married	Constitution 9-1, 9-2; 16-66-218(b)(1),(2)

California—System 1

Federal bankruptcy exemptions not available. California has two systems; you must select one or the other. All law references are to California Code of Civil Procedure unless otherwise noted. Many exemptions do not apply to claims for child support.

Note: California's exemption amounts are no longer updated in the statutes themselves. California Code of Civil Procedure Section 740.150 deputized the California Judicial Council to update the exemption amounts every three years. (The next revision will be in 2013.) As a result, the amounts listed in this chart will not match the amounts that appear in the cited statutes. The current exemption amounts can be found on the California Judicial Council website, www.courts.ca.gov/forms.htm.

ASSET	EXEMPTION	LAW
homestead	Real or personal property you occupy including mobile home, boat, stock cooperative, community apartment, planned development, or condo to $75,000 if single & not disabled; $100,000 for families if no other member has a homestead (if only one spouse files, may exempt one-half of amount if home held as community property & all of amount if home held as tenants in common); $175,000 if 65 or older, or physically or mentally disabled; $175,000 if 55 or older, single & earn gross annual income under $15,000 or married & earn gross annual income under $20,000 & creditors seek to force the sale of your home; forced sale proceeds received exempt for 6 months after (spouses may not double); separated married debtor may claim homestead in community property homestead occupied by other spouse	704.710; 704.720; 704.730; *In re McFall*, 112 B.R. 336 (9th Cir. BAP 1990)
	May file homestead declaration to protect exemption amount from attachment of judicial liens and to protect proceeds of voluntary sale for 6 months	704.920
insurance	Disability or health benefits	704.130
	Fidelity bonds	Labor 404
	Fraternal benefit society benefits	704.170
	Fraternal unemployment benefits	704.120
	Homeowners' insurance proceeds for 6 months after received, to homestead exemption amount	704.720(b)
	Life insurance proceeds if clause prohibits proceeds from being used to pay beneficiary's creditors	Ins. 10132; Ins. 10170; Ins. 10171
	Matured life insurance benefits needed for support	704.100(c)
	Unmatured life insurance policy cash surrender value completely exempt; loan value exempt to $11,475	704.100(b)
miscellaneous	Business or professional licenses	695.060
	Inmates' trust funds to $1,425 (spouses may not double)	704.090
	Property of business partnership	Corp. 16501-04
pensions	Tax-exempt retirement accounts, including 401(k)s, 403(b)s, profit-sharing and money purchase plans, SEP and SIMPLE IRAs, and defined-benefit plans	11 U.S.C. § 522(b)(3)(C)
	Traditional and Roth IRAs to $1,171,650 per person	11 U.S.C. § 522(b)(3)(C); (n)
	County employees	Gov't 31452
	County firefighters	Gov't 32210
	County peace officers	Gov't 31913
	Private retirement benefits, including IRAs & Keoghs	704.115
	Public employees	Gov't 21255
	Public retirement benefits	704.110

personal property	Appliances, furnishings, clothing & food	704.020
	Bank deposits from Social Security Administration to $2,875 ($4,300 for husband & wife); unlimited if SS funds are not commingled with other funds	704.080
	Bank deposits of other public benefits to $1,425 ($2,150 for husband & wife)	
	Building materials to repair or improve home to $2,875 (spouses may not double)	704.030
	Burial plot	704.200
	Funds held in escrow	Fin. 17410
	Health aids	704.050
	Jewelry, heirlooms & art to $7,175 total (spouses may not double)	704.040
	Motor vehicles to $2,725, or $2,725 in auto insurance for loss or damages (spouses may not double)	704.010
	Personal injury & wrongful death causes of action	704.140(a); 704.150(a)
	Personal injury & wrongful death recoveries needed for support; if receiving installments, at least 75%	704.140(b),(c),(d); 704.150(b),(c)
public benefits	Aid to blind, aged, disabled; public assistance	704.170
	Financial aid to students	704.190
	Relocation benefits	704.180
	Unemployment benefits	704.120
	Union benefits due to labor dispute	704.120(b)(5)
	Workers' compensation	704.160
tools of trade	Tools, implements, materials, instruments, uniforms, one commercial vehicle, books, furnishings & equipment to $7,175 total ($14,350 total if used by both spouses in same occupation)	704.060
	Commercial vehicle (Vehicle Code § 260) to $4,850 ($9,700 total if used by both spouses in same occupation) (this counts toward total tools of trade exemption)	704.060
wages	Minimum 75% of wages paid within 30 days prior to filing	704.070
	Public employees' vacation credits; if receiving installments, at least 75%	704.113
wildcard	None	

California—System 2

Refer to the notes for California—System 1, above.

Note: Married couples may not double any exemptions. (*In re Talmadge*, 832 F.2d 1120 (9th Cir. 1987); *In re Baldwin*, 70 B.R. 612 (9th Cir. BAP 1987).)

One court has argued that System 2 exemptions are not available to debtors in bankruptcy. To date, the vast majority of (if not all) California bankruptcy courts accept System 2 exemptions. However, you may wish to check with a bankruptcy attorney to find out which exemptions are acceptable in your local court. See, "Special Considerations in States With 'Bankruptcy-Specific' Exemptions," at the beginning of this appendix for more information.

ASSET	EXEMPTION	LAW
homestead	Real or personal property, including co-op, used as residence to $22,075; unused portion of homestead may be applied to any property	703.140(b)(1)

insurance	Disability benefits	703.140(b)(10)(C)
	Life insurance proceeds needed for support of family	703.140(b)(11)(C)
	Unmatured life insurance contract accrued avails to $11,800	703.140(b)(8)
	Unmatured life insurance policy other than credit	703.140(b)(7)
miscellaneous	Alimony, child support needed for support	703.140(b)(10)(D)
pensions	Tax-exempt retirement accounts, including 401(k)s, 403(b)s, profit-sharing and money purchase plans, SEP and SIMPLE IRAs, and defined-benefit plans	11 U.S.C. § 522(b)(3)(C)
	Traditional and Roth IRAs to $1,171,650 per person	11 U.S.C. § 522(b)(3)(C); (n)
	ERISA-qualified benefits needed for support	703.140(b)(10)(E)
personal property	Animals, crops, appliances, furnishings, household goods, books, musical instruments & clothing to $550 per item	703.140(b)(3)
	Burial plot to $22,075, in lieu of homestead	703.140(b)(1)
	Health aids	703.140(b)(9)
	Jewelry to $1,425	703.140(b)(4)
	Motor vehicle to $3,525	703.140(b)(2)
	Personal injury recoveries to $22,075 (not to include pain & suffering; pecuniary loss)	703.140(b)(11)(D),(E)
	Wrongful death recoveries needed for support	703.140(b)(11)(B)
public benefits	Crime victims' compensation	703.140(b)(11)(A)
	Public assistance	703.140(b)(10)(A)
	Social Security	703.140(b)(10)(A)
	Unemployment compensation	703.140(b)(10)(A)
	Veterans' benefits	703.140(b)(10)(B)
tools of trade	Implements, books & tools of trade to $2,200	703.140(b)(6)
wages	None (use federal nonbankruptcy wage exemption)	
wildcard	$1,175 of any property	703.140(b)(5)
	Unused portion of homestead or burial exemption of any property	703.140(b)(5)

Colorado

Federal bankruptcy exemptions not available. All law references are to Colorado Revised Statutes unless otherwise noted.

Some of the exemptions in this table may not be available to you in some bankruptcy courts. Before filing bankruptcy, check with a bankruptcy attorney to find out which exemptions are acceptable in your court. See, "Special Considerations in States With 'Bankruptcy-Specific' Exemptions," at the beginning of this appendix for more information.

ASSET	EXEMPTION	LAW
homestead	Real property, mobile home, manufactured home, or house trailer you occupy to $60,000; $90,000 if owner, spouse, or dependent is disabled or at least 60 years old; sale proceeds exempt 2 years after received	38-41-201; 38-41-201.6; 38-41-203; 38-41-207; *In re Pastrana*, 216 B.R. 948 (D. Colo., 1998)
	Spouse or child of deceased owner may claim homestead exemption	38-41-204

insurance	Disability benefits to $200 per month; if lump sum, entire amount exempt	10-16-212
	Fraternal benefit society benefits	10-14-403
	Group life insurance policy or proceeds	10-7-205
	Homeowners' insurance proceeds for 1 year after received, to homestead exemption amount	38-41-209
	Life insurance cash surrender value to $100,000, except contributions to policy within past 48 months	13-54-102(1)(l)
	Life insurance proceeds if clause prohibits proceeds from being used to pay beneficiary's creditors	10-7-106
miscellaneous	Child support or domestic support obligation	13-54-102(u) 13-54-102.5
	Property of business partnership	7-60-125
pensions *see also wages*	Tax-exempt retirement accounts, including 401(k)s, 403(b)s, profit-sharing and money purchase plans, SEP and SIMPLE IRAs, and defined-benefit plans	11 U.S.C. § 522(b)(3)(C)
	Traditional and Roth IRAs to $1,171,650 per person	11 U.S.C. § 522(b)(3)(C); (n)
	ERISA-qualified benefits, including IRAs & Roth IRAs	13-54-102(1)(s)
	Firefighters & police officers	31-30.5-208; 31-31-203
	Public employees' pensions, deferred compensation & defined contribution plans	24-51-212
	Veteran's pension for veteran, spouse, or dependents if veteran served in war or armed conflict	13-54-102(1)(h); 13-54-104
personal property	1 burial plot per family member	13-54-102(1)(d)
	Clothing to $1,500	13-54-102(1)(a)
	Food & fuel to $600	13-54-102(1)(f)
	Health aids	13-54-102(1)(p)
	Household goods to $3,000	13-54-102(1)(e)
	Jewelry & articles of adornment to $2,000	13-54-102(1)(b)
	Motor vehicles or bicycles used for work to $5,000; $10,000 if used by a debtor or by a dependent who is disabled or 60 or over	13-54-102(j)(I), (II)
	Personal injury recoveries	13-54-102(1)(n)
	Family pictures & books to $1,500	13-54-102(1)(c)
	Proceeds for damaged exempt property	13-54-102(1)(m)
	Security deposits	13-54-102(1)(r)
public benefits	Aid to blind, aged, disabled; public assistance	26-2-131
	Crime victims' compensation	13-54-102(1)(q); 24-4.1-114
	Disability benefits to $3,000	13-54-102(v)
	Earned income tax credit or refund	13-54-102(1)(o)
	Unemployment compensation	8-80-103
	Veteran's benefits for veteran, spouse, or child if veteran served in war or armed conflict	13-54-102(1)(h)
	Workers' compensation	8-42-124
tools of trade	Livestock or other animals, machinery, tools, equipment & seed of person engaged in agriculture, to $50,000 total	13-54-102(1)(g)
	Professional's library to $3,000 (if not claimed under other tools of trade exemption)	13-54-102(1)(k)

tools of trade (continued)	Stock in trade, supplies, fixtures, tools, machines, electronics, equipment, books & other business materials, to $20,000 total	13-54-102(1)(i)
	Military equipment personally owned by members of the National Guard	13-54-102(1)(h.5)
wages	Minimum 75% of weekly net earnings or 30 times the federal or state minimum wage, whichever is greater, including pension & insurance payments	13-54-104
wildcard	None	

Connecticut

Federal bankruptcy exemptions available. All law references are to Connecticut General Statutes Annotated unless otherwise noted.

ASSET	EXEMPTION	LAW
homestead	Owner-occupied real property, including co-op or mobile manufactured home, to $75,000; applies only to claims arising after 1993, but to $125,000 in the case of a money judgment arising out of services provided at a hospital	52-352a(e); 52-352b(t)
insurance	Disability benefits paid by association for its members	52-352b(p)
	Fraternal benefit society benefits	38a-637
	Health or disability benefits	52-352b(e)
	Life insurance proceeds if clause prohibits proceeds from being used to pay beneficiary's creditors	38a-454
	Life insurance proceeds or avails	38a-453
	Unmatured life insurance policy avails to $4,000 if beneficiary is dependent	52-352b(s)
miscellaneous	Alimony, to extent wages exempt	52-352b(n)
	Child support	52-352b(h)
	Farm partnership animals & livestock feed reasonably required to run farm where at least 50% of partners are members of same family	52-352d
pensions	Tax-exempt retirement accounts, including 401(k)s, 403(b)s, profit-sharing and money purchase plans, SEP and SIMPLE IRAs, and defined-benefit plans	11 U.S.C. § 522(b)(3)(C)
	Traditional and Roth IRAs to $1,171,650 per person	11 U.S.C. § 522(b)(3)(C); (n)
	ERISA-qualified benefits, including IRAs, Roth IRAs & Keoghs, to extent wages exempt	52-321a; 52-352b(m)
	Medical savings account	52-321a
	Municipal employees	7-446
	State employees	5-171; 5-192w
	Teachers	10-183q
personal property	Appliances, food, clothing, furniture, bedding	52-352b(a)
	Burial plot	52-352b(c)
	Health aids needed	52-352b(f)
	Motor vehicle to $1,500	52-352b(j)
	Proceeds for damaged exempt property	52-352b(q)
	Residential utility & security deposits for 1 residence	52-3252b(l)
	Spendthrift trust funds required for support of debtor & family	52-321(d)
	Transfers to a licensed debt adjuster	52-352b(u)
	Tuition savings accounts	52-321a(E)
	Wedding & engagement rings	52-352b(k)

public benefits	Crime victims' compensation	52-352b(o); 54-213
	Public assistance	52-352b(d)
	Social Security	52-352b(g)
	Unemployment compensation	31-272(c); 52-352b(g)
	Veterans' benefits	52-352b(g)
	Workers' compensation	52-352b(g)
tools of trade	Arms, military equipment, uniforms, musical instruments of military personnel	52-352b(i)
	Tools, books, instruments & farm animals needed	52-352b(b)
wages	Minimum 75% of earned but unpaid weekly disposable earnings, or 40 times the state or federal hourly minimum wage, whichever is greater	52-361a(f)
wildcard	$1,000 of any property	52-352b(r)

Delaware

Federal bankruptcy exemptions not available. All law references are to Delaware Code Annotated (in the form "title number-section number") unless otherwise noted.

Note: A single person may exempt no more than $25,000 total in all exemptions (not including retirement plans and principal residence); a husband & wife may exempt no more than $50,000 total (10-4914).

ASSET	EXEMPTION	LAW
homestead	Real property or manufactured home used as principal residence to $75,000 in 2010, $100,000 in 2011, and $125,000 in 2012; $125,000 for working or married persons where one spouse is 65 or older (spouses may not double)	10-4914(c)
	Property held as tenancy by the entirety may be exempt against debts owed by only one spouse	*In re Kelley*, 289 B.R. 38 (Bankr. D. Del. 2003)
insurance	Annuity contract proceeds to $350 per month	18-2728
	Fraternal benefit society benefits	18-6218
	Group life insurance policy or proceeds	18-2727
	Health or disability benefits	18-2726
	Life insurance proceeds if clause prohibits proceeds from being used to pay beneficiary's creditors	18-2729
	Life insurance proceeds or avails	18-2725
pensions	Tax-exempt retirement accounts, including 401(k)s, 403(b)s, profit-sharing and money purchase plans, SEP and SIMPLE IRAs, and defined-benefit plans	11 U.S.C. § 522(b)(3)(C)
	Traditional and Roth IRAs to $1,171,650 per person	11 U.S.C. § 522(b)(3)(C); (n)
	IRAs, Roth IRAs & any other retirement plans	10-4915
	Kent County employees	9-4316
	Police officers	11-8803
	State employees	29-5503
	Volunteer firefighters	16-6653
personal property	Bible, books & family pictures	10-4902(a)
	Burial plot	10-4902(a)
	Church pew or any seat in public place of worship	10-4902(a)

personal property (continued)	Clothing, includes jewelry	10-4902(a)
	College investment plan account (limit for year before filing is $5,000 or average of past two years' contribution, whichever is more)	10-4916
	Principal and income from spendthrift trusts	12-3536
	Pianos & leased organs	10-4902(d)
	Sewing machines	10-4902(c)
public benefits	Aid to blind	31-2309
	Aid to aged, disabled; general assistance	31-513
	Crime victims' compensation	11-9011
	Unemployment compensation	19-3374
	Workers' compensation	19-2355
tools of trade	Tools of trade and/or vehicle necessary for employment to $15,000 each	10-4914(c)
	Tools, implements & fixtures to $75 in New Castle & Sussex Counties; to $50 in Kent County	10-4902(b)
wages	85% of earned but unpaid wages	10-4913
wildcard	$500 of any personal property, except tools of trade, if head of family	10-4903

District of Columbia

Federal bankruptcy exemptions available. All law references are to District of Columbia Code unless otherwise noted.

ASSET	EXEMPTION	LAW
homestead	Any property used as a residence or co-op that debtor or debtor's dependent uses as a residence	15-501(a)(14)
	Property held as tenancy by the entirety may be exempt against debts owed by only one spouse	*Estate of Wall*, 440 F.2d 215 (D.C. Cir. 1971)
insurance	Disability benefits	15-501(a)(7); 31-4716.01
	Fraternal benefit society benefits	31-5315
	Group life insurance policy or proceeds	31-4717
	Life insurance payments	15-501(a)(11)
	Life insurance proceeds if clause prohibits proceeds from being used to pay beneficiary's creditors	31-4719
	Life insurance proceeds or avails	31-4716
	Other insurance proceeds to $200 per month, maximum 2 months, for head of family; else $60 per month	15-503
	Unmatured life insurance contract other than credit life insurance	15-501(a)(5)
miscellaneous	Alimony or child support	15-501(a)(7)
pensions *see also wages*	Tax-exempt retirement accounts, including 401(k)s, 403(b)s, profit-sharing and money purchase plans, SEP and SIMPLE IRAs, and defined-benefit plans	11 U.S.C. § 522(b)(3)(C)
	Traditional and Roth IRAs to $1,171,650 per person	11 U.S.C. § 522(b)(3)(C); (n)
	ERISA-qualified benefits, IRAs, Keoghs, etc. to maximum deductible contribution	15-501(b)(9)
	Any stock bonus, annuity, pension, or profit-sharing plan	15-501(a)(7)
	Judges	11-1570(f)
	Public school teachers	38-2001.17; 38-2021.17

ASSET	EXEMPTION	LAW
personal property	Appliances, books, clothing, household furnishings, goods, musical instruments, pets to $425 per item or $8,625 total	15-501(a)(2)
	Cemetery & burial funds	43-111
	Cooperative association holdings to $50	29-928
	Food for 3 months	15-501(a)(12)
	Health aids	15-501(a)(6)
	Higher education tuition savings account	47-4510
	Residential condominium deposit	42-1904.09
	All family pictures; all the family library to $400	15-501(a)(8)
	Motor vehicle to $2,575	15-501(a)(1)
	Payment, including pain & suffering, for loss of debtor or person depended on	15-501(a)(11)
	Uninsured motorist benefits	31-2408.01(h)
	Wrongful death damages	15-501(a)(11); 16-2703
public benefits	Aid to blind, aged, disabled; general assistance	4-215.01
	Crime victims' compensation	4-507(e); 15-501(a)(11)
	Social Security	15-501(a)(7)
	Unemployment compensation	51-118
	Veterans' benefits	15-501(a)(7)
	Workers' compensation	32-1517
tools of trade	Library, furniture, tools of professional or artist to $300	15-501(a)(13)
	Tools of trade or business to $1,625	15-501(a)(5)
	Mechanic's tools to $200	15-503(b)
	Seal & documents of notary public	1-1206
wages	Minimum 75% of earned but unpaid wages, pension payments; bankruptcy judge may authorize more for low-income debtors	16-572
	Nonwage (including pension & retirement) earnings to $200 per month for head of family; else $60 per month for a maximum of two months	15-503
	Payment for loss of future earnings	15-501(e)(11)
wildcard	Up to $850 in any property, plus up to $8,075 of unused homestead exemption	15-501(a)(3)

Florida

Federal bankruptcy exemptions not available. All law references are to Florida Statutes Annotated unless otherwise noted.

ASSET	EXEMPTION	LAW
homestead	Real or personal property including mobile or modular home to unlimited value; cannot exceed half acre in municipality or 160 acres elsewhere; spouse or child of deceased owner may claim homestead exemption	222.01; 222.02; 222.03; 222.05; Constitution 10-4 *In re Colwell*, 196 F.3d 1225 (11th Cir. 1999)
	May file homestead declaration	222.01
	Property held as tenancy by the entirety may be exempt against debts owed by only one spouse	*Havoco of America, Ltd. v. Hill*, 197 F.3d 1135 (11th Cir. 1999)
insurance	Annuity contract proceeds; does not include lottery winnings	222.14; *In re Pizzi*, 153 B.R. 357 (S.D. Fla. 1993)
	Death benefits payable to a specific beneficiary, not the deceased's estate	222.13
	Disability or illness benefits	222.18
	Fraternal benefit society benefits	632.619
	Life insurance cash surrender value	222.14
miscellaneous	Alimony, child support needed for support	222.201
	Damages to employees for injuries in hazardous occupations	769.05
pensions *see also wages*	Tax-exempt retirement accounts, including 401(k)s, 403(b)s, profit-sharing and money purchase plans, SEP and SIMPLE IRAs, and defined-benefit plans	11 U.S.C. § 522(b)(3)(C)
	Traditional and Roth IRAs to $1,171,650 per person	11 U.S.C. § 522(b)(3)(C); (n)
	County officers, employees	122.15
	ERISA-qualified benefits, including IRAs & Roth IRAs	222.21(2)
	Firefighters	175.241
	Police officers	185.25
	State officers, employees	121.131
	Teachers	238.15
personal property	Any personal property to $1,000 (husband & wife may double); to $4,000 if no homestead claimed	Constitution 10-4; *In re Hawkins*, 51 B.R. 348 (S.D. Fla. 1985)
	Federal income tax refund or credit	222.25
	Health aids	222.25
	Motor vehicle to $1,000	222.25
	Preneed funeral contract deposits	497.56(8)
	Prepaid college education trust deposits	222.22(1)
	Prepaid hurricane savings accounts	222.22(4)
	Prepaid medical savings account deposits	222.22(2)
public benefits	Crime victims' compensation, unless seeking to discharge debt for treatment of injury incurred during the crime	960.14
	Public assistance	222.201
	Social Security	222.201
	Unemployment compensation	222.201; 443.051(2),(3)
	Veterans' benefits	222.201; 744.626
	Workers' compensation	440.22
tools of trade	None	
wages	100% of wages for heads of family up to $750 per week either unpaid or paid & deposited into bank account for up to 6 months	222.11
	Federal government employees' pension payments needed for support & received 3 months prior	222.21
wildcard	See personal property	

Georgia

Federal bankruptcy exemptions not available. All law references are to the Official Code of Georgia Annotated unless otherwise noted.

Some of the exemptions in this table may not be available to you in some bankruptcy courts. Before filing bankruptcy, check with a bankruptcy attorney to find out which exemptions are acceptable in your court. See, "Special Considerations in States With 'Bankruptcy-Specific' Exemptions," at the beginning of this appendix for more information.

ASSET	EXEMPTION	LAW
homestead	Real or personal property, including co-op, used as residence to $10,000 (to $20,000 if married and debtor spouse is sole owner); up to $5,000 of unused portion of homestead may be applied to any property	44-13-100(a)(1); 44-13-100(a)(6); *In re Burnett*, 303 B.R. 684 (M.D. Ga. 2003)
insurance	Annuity & endowment contract benefits	33-28-7
	Disability or health benefits to $250 per month	33-29-15
	Fraternal benefit society benefits	33-15-62
	Group insurance	33-30-10
	Proceeds & avails of life insurance	33-26-5; 33-25-11
	Life insurance proceeds if policy owned by someone you depended on, needed for support	44-13-100(a)(11)(C)
	Unmatured life insurance contract	44-13-100(a)(8)
	Unmatured life insurance dividends, interest, loan value, or cash value to $2,000 if beneficiary is you or someone you depend on	44-13-100(a)(9)
miscellaneous	Alimony, child support needed for support	44-13-100(a)(2)(D)
pensions	Tax-exempt retirement accounts, including 401(k)s, 403(b)s, profit-sharing and money purchase plans, SEP and SIMPLE IRAs, and defined-benefit plans	11 U.S.C. § 522(b)(3)(C)
	Traditional and Roth IRAs to $1,171,650 per person	11 U.S.C. § 522(b)(3)(C); (n)
	Employees of nonprofit corporations	44-13-100(a)(2.1)(B)
	ERISA-qualified benefits & IRAs	18-4-22
	Public employees	44-13-100(a)(2.1)(A); 47-2-332
	Payments from IRA necessary for support	44-13-100(a)(2)(F)
	Other pensions needed for support	18-4-22; 44-13-100(a)(2)(E); 44-13-100(a)(2.1)(C)
personal property	Animals, crops, clothing, appliances, books, furnishings, household goods, musical instruments to $300 per item, $5,000 total	44-13-100(a)(4)
	Burial plot, in lieu of homestead	44-13-100(a)(1)
	Compensation for lost future earnings needed for support to $7,500	44-13-100(a)(11)(E)
	Health aids	44-13-100(a)(10)
	Jewelry to $500	44-13-100(a)(5)
	Motor vehicles to $3,500	44-13-100(a)(3)
	Personal injury recoveries to $10,000	44-13-100(a)(11)(D)
	Wrongful death recoveries needed for support	44-13-100(a)(11)(B)
public benefits	Aid to blind	49-4-58
	Aid to disabled	49-4-84
	Crime victims' compensation	44-13-100(a)(11)(A)
public benefits (continued)	Local public assistance	44-13-100(a)(2)(A)
	Old age assistance	49-4-35
	Social Security	44-13-100(a)(2)(A)
	Unemployment compensation	44-13-100(a)(2)(A)
	Veterans' benefits	44-13-100(a)(2)(B)
	Workers' compensation	34-9-84
tools of trade	Implements, books & tools of trade to $1,500	44-13-100(a)(7)
wages	Minimum 75% of earned but unpaid weekly disposable earnings, or 30 times the state or federal hourly minimum wage, whichever is greater, for private & federal workers; bankruptcy judge may authorize more for low-income debtors	18-4-20; 18-4-21
wildcard	$600 of any property	44-13-100(a)(6)
	Unused portion of homestead exemption to $5,000	44-13-100(a)(6)

Hawaii

Federal bankruptcy exemptions available. All law references are to Hawaii Revised Statutes unless otherwise noted.

ASSET	EXEMPTION	LAW
homestead	Head of family or over 65 to $30,000; all others to $20,000; property cannot exceed 1 acre; sale proceeds exempt for 6 months after sale (spouses may not double)	651-91; 651-92; 651-96
	Property held as tenancy by the entirety may be exempt against debts owed by only one spouse	*Security Pacific Bank v. Chang*, 818 F.Supp. 1343 (D. Haw. 1993)
insurance	Annuity contract or endowment policy proceeds if beneficiary is insured's spouse, child, or parent	431:10-232(b)
	Accident, health, or sickness benefits	431:10-231
	Fraternal benefit society benefits	432:2-403
	Group life insurance policy or proceeds	431:10-233
	Life insurance proceeds if clause prohibits proceeds from being used to pay beneficiary's creditors	431:10D-112
	Life or health insurance policy for spouse or child	431:10-234
miscellaneous	Property of business partnership	425-125
pensions	Tax-exempt retirement accounts, including 401(k)s, 403(b)s, profit-sharing and money purchase plans, SEP and SIMPLE IRAs, and defined-benefit plans	11 U.S.C. § 522(b)(3)(C)
	Traditional and Roth IRAs to $1,171,650 per person	11 U.S.C. § 522(b)(3)(C); (n)
	IRAs, Roth IRAs, and ERISA-qualified benefits deposited over 3 years before filing bankruptcy	651-124
	Firefighters	88-169
	Police officers	88-169
	Public officers & employees	88-91; 653-3
personal property	Appliances & furnishings	651-121(1)
	Books	651-121(1)
	Burial plot to 250 sq. ft. plus tombstones, monuments & fencing	651-121(4)
	Clothing	651-121(1)

personal property (continued)	Jewelry, watches & articles of adornment to $1,000	651-121(1)
	Motor vehicle to wholesale value of $2,575	651-121(2)
	Proceeds for sold or damaged exempt property; sale proceeds exempt for 6 months after sale	651-121(5)
public benefits	Crime victims' compensation & special accounts created to limit commercial exploitation of crimes	351-66; 351-86
	Public assistance paid by Department of Health Services for work done in home or workshop	346-33
	Temporary disability benefits	392-29
	Unemployment compensation	383-163
	Unemployment work relief funds to $60 per month	653-4
	Workers' compensation	386-57
tools of trade	Tools, implements, books, instruments, uniforms, furnishings, fishing boat, nets, motor vehicle & other property needed for livelihood	651-121(3)
wages	Prisoner's wages held by Department of Public Safety (except for restitution, child support & other claims)	353-22.5
	Unpaid wages due for services of past 31 days	651-121(6)
wildcard	None	

Idaho

Federal bankruptcy exemptions not available. All law references are to Idaho Code unless otherwise noted.

ASSET	EXEMPTION	LAW
homestead	Real property or mobile home to $100,000; sale proceeds exempt for 6 months (spouses may not double)	55-1003; 55-1113
	Must record homestead exemption for property that is not yet occupied	55-1004
insurance	Annuity contract proceeds to $1,250 per month	41-1836
	Death or disability benefits	11-604(1)(a); 41-1834
	Fraternal benefit society benefits	41-3218
	Group life insurance benefits	41-1835
	Homeowners' insurance proceeds to amount of homestead exemption	55-1008
	Life insurance proceeds if clause prohibits proceeds from being used to pay beneficiary's creditors	41-1930
	Life insurance proceeds or avails for beneficiary other than the insured	11-604(d); 41-1833
	Medical, surgical, or hospital care benefits & amount in medical savings account	11-603(5)
	Unmatured life insurance contract, other than credit life insurance, owned by debtor	11-605(9)
	Unmatured life insurance contract interest or dividends to $5,000 owned by debtor or person debtor depends on	11-605(10)
miscellaneous	Alimony, child support	11-604(1)(b)
	Liquor licenses	23-514

pension *see also wages*	Tax-exempt retirement accounts, including 401(k)s, 403(b)s, profit-sharing and money purchase plans, SEP and SIMPLE IRAs, and defined-benefit plans	11 U.S.C. § 522(b)(3)(C)
	Traditional and Roth IRAs to $1,171,650 per person	11 U.S.C. § 522(b)(3)(C); (n)
	ERISA-qualified benefits	55-1011
	Firefighters	72-1422
	Government & private pensions, retirement plans, IRAs, Roth IRAs, Keoghs, etc.	11-604A
	Police officers	50-1517
	Public employees	59-1317
personal property	Appliances, furnishings, books, clothing, pets, musical instruments, family portraits & sentimental heirlooms to $750 per item, $7,500 total	11-605(1)
	Building materials	45-514
	Burial plot	11-603(1)
	College savings program account	11-604A(4)(b)
	Crops cultivated on maximum of 50 acres, to $1,000; water rights to 160 inches	11-605(6) and (7)
	Firearm (1) to $750	11-605(8)
	Health aids	11-603(2)
	Jewelry to $1,000	11-605(2)
	Motor vehicle to $7,000	11-605(3)
	Personal injury recoveries	11-604(1)(c)
	Proceeds for damaged exempt property for 3 months after proceeds received	11-606
	Provisions (food, water, and storage equipment) sufficient for up to 12 months	11-605(4)
	Wrongful death recoveries	11-604(1)(c)
public benefits	Aid to blind, aged, disabled	56-223
	Federal, state & local public assistance	11-603(4)
	General assistance	56-223
	Social Security	11-603(3)
	Unemployment compensation	11-603(6)
	Veterans' benefits	11-603(3)
	Workers' compensation	72-802
tools of trade	Arms, uniforms & accoutrements that peace officer, National Guard, or military personnel is required to keep	11-605(6)
	Implements, books & tools of trade to $2,500	11-605(3)
wages	Minimum 75% of earned but unpaid weekly disposable earnings, or 30 times the federal hourly minimum wage, whichever is greater but not more than $1,500 in a calendar year; pension payments; bankruptcy judge may authorize more for low-income debtors	11-207; 11-605-12; 11-206
wildcard	$800 in any tangible personal property	11-605(11)

Illinois

Federal bankruptcy exemptions not available. All law references are to Illinois Compiled Statutes Annotated unless otherwise noted.

ASSET	EXEMPTION	LAW
homestead	Real or personal property including a farm, lot & buildings, condo, co-op, or mobile home to $15,000; sale proceeds exempt for 1 year	735-5/12-901; 735-5/12-906

homestead (continued)	Spouse or child of deceased owner may claim homestead exemption	735-5/12-902
	Illinois recognizes tenancy by the entirety, with limitations	750-65/22; 765-1005/1c; *In re Gillissie*, 215 B.R. 370 (Bankr. N.D. Ill. 1998); *Great Southern Co. v. Allard*, 202 B.R. 938 (N.D. Ill. 1996)
insurance	Fraternal benefit society benefits	215-5/299.1a
	Health or disability benefits	735-5/12-1001(g)(3)
	Homeowners' proceeds if home destroyed, to $15,000	735-5/12-907
	Life insurance, annuity proceeds, or cash value if beneficiary is insured's child, parent, spouse, or other dependent	215-5/238; 735-5/12-1001(f)
	Life insurance proceeds to a spouse or dependent of debtor to extent needed for support	735-5/12-1001(f),(g)(3)
miscellaneous	Alimony, child support	735-5/12-1001(g)(4)
	Property of business partnership	805-205/25
pensions	Tax-exempt retirement accounts, including 401(k)s, 403(b)s, profit-sharing and money purchase plans, SEP and SIMPLE IRAs, and defined-benefit plans	11 U.S.C. § 522(b)(3)(C)
	Traditional and Roth IRAs to $1,171,650 per person	11 U.S.C. § 522(b)(3)(C); (n)
	Civil service employees	40-5/11-223
	County employees	40-5/9-228
	Disabled firefighters; widows & children of firefighters	40-5/22-230
	IRAs and ERISA-qualified benefits	735-5/12-1006
	Firefighters	40-5/4-135; 40-5/6-213
	General Assembly members	40-5/2-154
	House of correction employees	40-5/19-117
	Judges	40-5/18-161
	Municipal employees	40-5/7-217(a); 40-5/8-244
	Park employees	40-5/12-190
	Police officers	40-5/3-144.1; 40-5/5-218
	Public employees	735-5/12-1006
	Public library employees	40-5/19-218
	Sanitation district employees	40-5/13-805
	State employees	40-5/14-147
	State university employees	40-5/15-185
	Teachers	40-5/16-190; 40-5/17-151
personal property	Bible, family pictures, schoolbooks & clothing	735-5/12-1001(a)
	Health aids	735-5/12-1001(e)
	Illinois College Savings Pool accounts invested more than 1 year before filing if below federal gift tax limit, or 2 years before filing if above	735-5/12-1001(j)
	Motor vehicle to $2,400	735-5/12-1001(c)
	Personal injury recoveries to $15,000	735-5/12-1001(h)(4)
	Preneed cemetery sales funds, care funds & trust funds	235-5/6-1; 760-100/4; 815-390/16

personal property (continued)	Prepaid tuition trust fund	110-979/45(g)
	Proceeds of sold exempt property	735-5/12-1001
	Wrongful death recoveries	735-5/12-1001(h)(2)
public benefits	Aid to aged, blind, disabled; public assistance	305-5/11-3
	Crime victims' compensation	735-5/12-1001(h)(1)
	Restitution payments on account of WWII relocation of Aleuts & Japanese Americans	735-5/12-1001(12)(h)(5)
	Social Security	735-5/12-1001(g)(1)
	Unemployment compensation	735-5/12-1001(g)(1),(3)
	Veterans' benefits	735-5/12-1001(g)(2)
	Workers' compensation	820-305/21
	Workers' occupational disease compensation	820-310/21
tools of trade	Implements, books & tools of trade to $1,500	735-5/12-1001(d)
wages	Minimum 85% of earned but unpaid weekly wages or 45 times the federal minimum hourly wage (or state minimum hourly wage, if higher); bankruptcy judge may authorize more for low-income debtors (some judges may not allow this exemption)	735-5/12-803
wildcard	$4,000 of any personal property (does not include wages)	735-5/12-1001(b)

Indiana

Federal bankruptcy exemptions not available. All law references are to Indiana Statutes Annotated unless otherwise noted.

ASSET	EXEMPTION	LAW
homestead *see also* wildcard	Real or personal property used as residence to $17,600	34-55-10-2(c)(1)
	Property held as tenancy by the entirety may be exempt against debts incurred by only one spouse	34-55-10-2(c)(5); 32-17-3-1
insurance	Employer's life insurance policy on employee	27-1-12-17.1
	Fraternal benefit society benefits	27-11-6-3
	Group life insurance policy	27-1-12-29
	Life insurance policy, proceeds, cash value, or avails if beneficiary is insured's spouse or dependent	27-1-12-14
	Life insurance proceeds if clause prohibits proceeds to be used to pay beneficiary's creditors	27-2-5-1
	Mutual life or accident proceeds needed for support	27-8-3-23; *In re Stinnet*, 321 B.R. 477 (S.D. Ind. 2005)
miscellaneous	Property of business partnership	23-4-1-25
pensions	Tax-exempt retirement accounts, including 401(k)s, 403(b)s, profit-sharing and money purchase plans, SEP and SIMPLE IRAs, and defined-benefit plans	11 U.S.C. § 522(b)(3)(C)
	Traditional and Roth IRAs to $1,171,650 per person	11 U.S.C. § 522(b)(3)(C); (n)
	Firefighters	36-8-7-22 36-8-8-17
	Police officers	36-8-8-17; 10-12-2-10

pensions (continued)	Public employees	5-10.3-8-9
	Public or private retirement benefits & contributions	34-55-10-2(c)(6)
	Sheriffs	36-8-10-19
	State teachers	5-10.4-5-14
personal property	Earned income tax credit	34-55-10-2(c)(11)
	Education savings account (529 and Coverdell) contributions made more than 2 years prior to filing; contributions made more than 1 but less than 2 years prior to filing to $5,000; no exemption for contributions made less than 1 year prior to filing	34-55-10-2(c) (9), (10)
	Health aids	34-55-10-2(c)(4)
	Money in medical care savings account or health savings account	34-55-10-2(c) (7), (8)
	Spendthrift trusts	30-4-3-2
	$350 of any intangible personal property, except money owed to you	34-55-10-2(c)(3)
public benefits	Crime victims' compensation, unless seeking to discharge the debts for which the victim was compensated	5-2-6.1-38
	Unemployment compensation	22-4-33-3
	Veterans' disability benefits	34-55-10-2(c)(12)
	Workers' compensation	22-3-2-17
tools of trade	National Guard uniforms, arms & equipment	10-16-10-3
wages	Minimum 75% of earned but unpaid weekly disposable earnings, or 30 times the federal hourly minimum wage; bankruptcy judge may authorize more for low-income debtors	24-4.5-5-105
wildcard	$9,350 of any real estate or tangible personal property	34-55-10-2(c)(2)

Iowa

Federal bankruptcy exemptions not available. All law references are to Iowa Code Annotated unless otherwise noted.

ASSET	EXEMPTION	LAW
homestead	May record homestead declaration	561.4
	Real property or an apartment to an unlimited value; property cannot exceed ½ acre in town or city, 40 acres elsewhere (spouses may not double)	499A.18; 561.2; 561.16
insurance	Accident, disability, health, illness, or life proceeds or avails	627.6(6)
	Disability or illness benefit	627.6(8)(c)
	Employee group insurance policy or proceeds	509.12
	Fraternal benefit society benefits	512B.18
	Life insurance proceeds if clause prohibits proceeds from being used to pay beneficiary's creditors	508.32
	Life insurance proceeds paid to spouse, child, or other dependent (limited to $10,000 if acquired within 2 years of filing for bankruptcy)	627.6(6)
	Upon death of insured, up to $15,000 total proceeds from all matured life, accident, health, or disability policies exempt from beneficiary's debts contracted before insured's death	627.6(6)
miscellaneous	Alimony, child support needed for support	627.6(8)(d)
	Liquor licenses	123.38

pensions *see also wages*	Tax-exempt retirement accounts, including 401(k)s, 403(b)s, profit-sharing and money purchase plans, SEP and SIMPLE IRAs, and defined-benefit plans	11 U.S.C. § 522(b)(3)(C)
	Traditional and Roth IRAs to $1,171,650 per person	11 U.S.C. § 522(b)(3) (C); (n)
	Disabled firefighters, police officers (only payments being received)	410.11
	Federal government pension	627.8
	Firefighters	411.13
	Other pensions, annuities & contracts fully exempt; however, contributions made within 1 year prior to filing for bankruptcy not exempt to the extent they exceed normal & customary amounts	627.6(8)(e)
	Peace officers	97A.12
	Police officers	411.13
	Public employees	97B.39
	Retirement plans, Keoghs, IRAs, Roth IRAs, ERISA-qualified benefits	627.6(8)(f)
personal property	Bibles, books, portraits, pictures & paintings to $1,000 total	627.6(3)
	Burial plot to 1 acre	627.6(4)
	Clothing & its storage containers, household furnishings, appliances, musical instruments, and other personal property to $7,000	627.6(5)
	Health aids	627.6(7)
	Jewelry to $2,000	627.6(1)(6)
	Residential security or utility deposit, or advance rent, to $500	627.6(14)
	Rifle or musket; shotgun	627.6(2)
	One motor vehicle to $7,000	627.6(9)
	Wedding or engagement rings, limited to $7,000 if purchased after marriage and within last two years	627.6(1)(a)
	Wrongful death proceeds and awards needed for support of debtor and dependents	627.6(15)
public benefits	Adopted child assistance	627.19
	Aid to dependent children	239B.6
	Any public assistance benefit	627.6(8)(a)
	Social Security	627.6(8)(a)
	Unemployment compensation	627.6(8)(a)
	Veterans' benefits	627.6(8)(b)
	Workers' compensation	627.13
tools of trade	Farming equipment; includes livestock, feed to $10,000	627.6(11)
	National Guard articles of equipment	29A.41
	Nonfarming equipment to $10,000	627.6(10)

wages	Expected annual earnings	Amount NOT exempt per year	642.21
	$0 to $11,999	$250	
	$12,000 to $15,999	$400	
	$16,000 to $23,999	$800	
	$24,000 to $34,999	$1,000	
	$35,000 to $49,999	$2,000	
	More than $50,000	10%	
	Not exempt from spousal or child support		
	Wages or salary of a prisoner		356.29
wildcard	$1,000 of any personal property, including cash		627.6(14)

Kansas

Federal bankruptcy exemptions not available. All law references are to Kansas Statutes Annotated unless otherwise noted.

ASSET	EXEMPTION	LAW
homestead	Real property or mobile home you occupy or intend to occupy to unlimited value; property cannot exceed 1 acre in town or city, 160 acres on farm	60-2301; Constitution 15-9
insurance	Cash value of life insurance; not exempt if obtained within 1 year prior to bankruptcy with fraudulent intent	60-2313(a)(7); 40-414(b)
	Disability & illness benefits	60-2313(a)(1)
	Fraternal life insurance benefits	60-2313(a)(8)
	Life insurance proceeds	40-414(a)
miscellaneous	Alimony, maintenance & support	60-2312(b)
	Liquor licenses	60-2313(a)(6); 41-326
pensions	Tax-exempt retirement accounts, including 401(k)s, 403(b)s, profit-sharing and money purchase plans, SEP and SIMPLE IRAs, and defined-benefit plans	11 U.S.C. § 522(b)(3)(C)
	Traditional and Roth IRAs to $1,171,650 per person	11 U.S.C. § 522(b) (3)(C); (n)
	Elected & appointed officials in cities with populations between 120,000 & 200,000	13-14a10
	ERISA-qualified benefits	60-2308(b)
	Federal government pension needed for support & paid within 3 months of filing for bankruptcy (only payments being received)	60-2308(a)
	Firefighters	12-5005(e); 14-10a10
	Judges	20-2618
	Police officers	12-5005(e); 13-14a10
	Public employees	74-4923; 74-49,105
	State highway patrol officers	74-4978g
	State school employees	72-5526
	Payment under a stock bonus, pension, profit-sharing, annuity, or similar plan or contract on account of illness, disability, death, age, or length of service, to the extent reasonably necessary for support	60-2312(b)
personal property	Burial plot or crypt	60-2304(d)
	Clothing to last 1 year	60-2304(a)
	Food & fuel to last 1 year	60-2304(a)
	Funeral plan prepayments	60-2313(a)(10); 16-310(d)
	Furnishings & household equipment	60-2304(a)
	Jewelry & articles of adornment to $1,000	60-2304(b)
	Motor vehicle to $20,000; if designed or equipped for disabled person, no limit	60-2304(c)
public benefits	Crime victims' compensation	60-2313(a)(7); 74-7313(d)
	General assistance	39-717(c)
	Social Security	60-2312(b)
	Unemployment compensation	60-2313(a)(4); 44-718(c)

ASSET	EXEMPTION	LAW
public benefits (continued)	Veterans' benefits	60-2312(b)
	Workers' compensation	60-2313(a)(3); 44-514
tools of trade	Books, documents, furniture, instruments, equipment, breeding stock, seed, grain & stock to $7,500 total	60-2304(e)
	National Guard uniforms, arms & equipment	48-245
wages	Minimum 75% of disposable weekly wages or 30 times the federal minimum hourly wage per week, whichever is greater; bankruptcy judge may authorize more for low-income debtors	60-2310
wildcard	None	

Kentucky

Federal bankruptcy exemptions available. All law references are to Kentucky Revised Statutes unless otherwise noted.

ASSET	EXEMPTION	LAW
homestead	Real or personal property used as residence to $5,000; sale proceeds exempt	427.060; 427.090
insurance	Annuity contract proceeds to $350 per month	304.14-330
	Cooperative life or casualty insurance benefits	427.110(1)
	Fraternal benefit society benefits	427.110(2)
	Group life insurance proceeds	304.14-320
	Health or disability benefits	304.14-310
	Life insurance policy if beneficiary is a married woman	304.14-340
	Life insurance proceeds if clause prohibits proceeds from being used to pay beneficiary's creditors	304.14-350
	Life insurance proceeds or cash value if beneficiary is someone other than insured	304.14-300
miscellaneous	Alimony, child support needed for support	427.150(1)
pensions	Tax-exempt retirement accounts, including 401(k)s, 403(b)s, profit-sharing and money purchase plans, SEP and SIMPLE IRAs, and defined-benefit plans	11 U.S.C. § 522(b)(3)(C)
	Traditional and Roth IRAs to $1,171,650 per person	11 U.S.C. § 522(b)(3) (C); (n)
	ERISA-qualified benefits, including IRAs, SEPs & Keoghs deposited more than 120 days before filing	427.150
	Firefighters	67A.620; 95.878
	Police officers	427.120; 427.125
	State employees	61.690
	Teachers	161.700
	Urban county government employees	67A.350
personal property	Burial plot to $5,000, in lieu of homestead	427.060
	Clothing, jewelry, articles of adornment & furnishings to $3,000 total	427.010(1)
	Health aids	427.010(1)
	Lost earnings payments needed for support	427.150(2)(d)
	Medical expenses paid & reparation benefits received under motor vehicle reparation law	304.39-260
	Motor vehicle to $2,500	427.010(1)

personal property (continued)	Personal injury recoveries to $7,500 (not to include pain & suffering or pecuniary loss)	427.150(2)(c)
	Prepaid tuition payment fund account	164A.707(3)
	Wrongful death recoveries for person you depended on, needed for support	427.150(2)(b)
public benefits	Aid to blind, aged, disabled; public assistance	205.220(c)
	Crime victims' compensation	427.150(2)(a)
	Unemployment compensation	341.470(4)
	Workers' compensation	342.180
tools of trade	Library, office equipment, instruments & furnishings of minister, attorney, physician, surgeon, chiropractor, veterinarian, or dentist to $1,000	427.040
	Motor vehicle of auto mechanic, mechanical, or electrical equipment servicer, minister, attorney, physician, surgeon, chiropractor, veterinarian, or dentist to $2,500	427.030
	Tools, equipment, livestock & poultry of farmer to $3,000	427.010(1)
	Tools of nonfarmer to $300	427.030
wages	Minimum 75% of disposable weekly earnings or 30 times the federal minimum hourly wage per week, whichever is greater; bankruptcy judge may authorize more for low-income debtors	427.010(2),(3)
wildcard	$1,000 of any property	427.160

Louisiana

Federal bankruptcy exemptions not available. All law references are to Louisiana Revised Statutes Annotated unless otherwise noted.

ASSET	EXEMPTION	LAW
homestead	Property you occupy to $25,000 (if debt is result of catastrophic or terminal illness or injury, limit is full value of property as of 1 year before filing); cannot exceed 5 acres in city or town, 200 acres elsewhere (spouses may not double)	20:1(A)(1),(2),(3)
	Spouse or child of deceased owner may claim homestead exemption; spouse given home in divorce gets homestead	20:1(B)
insurance	Annuity contract proceeds & avails	22:912
	Fraternal benefit society benefits	22:298
	Group insurance policies or proceeds	22:944
	Health, accident, or disability proceeds or avails	22:1015
	Life insurance proceeds or avails; if policy issued within 9 months of filing, exempt only to $35,000	22:912
miscellaneous	Property of minor child	13:3881(A)(3); Civil Code Art. 223
pensions	Tax-exempt retirement accounts, including 401(k)s, 403(b)s, profit-sharing and money purchase plans, SEP and SIMPLE IRAs, and defined-benefit plans	11 U.S.C. § 522(b)(3)(C)
	Traditional and Roth IRAs to $1,171,650 per person	11 U.S.C. § 522(b)(3)(C); (n)
	Assessors	11:1403
	Court clerks	11:1526
	District attorneys	11:1583

pensions (continued)	ERISA-qualified benefits, including IRAs, Roth IRAs & Keoghs, if contributions made over 1 year before filing for bankruptcy	13:3881; 20:33(1)
	Firefighters	11:2263
	Gift or bonus payments from employer to employee or heirs whenever paid	20:33(2)
	Judges	11:1378
	Louisiana University employees	11:952.3
	Municipal employees	11:1735
	Parochial employees	11:1905
	Police officers	11:3513
	School employees	11:1003
	Sheriffs	11:2182
	State employees	11:405
	Teachers	11:704
	Voting registrars	11:2033
personal property	Arms, military accoutrements; bedding; dishes, glassware, utensils, silverware (nonsterling); clothing, family portraits, musical instruments; bedroom, living room & dining room furniture; poultry, 1 cow, household pets; heating & cooling equipment, refrigerator, freezer, stove, washer & dryer, iron, sewing machine	13:3881(A)(4)
	Cemetery plot, monuments	8:313
	Disaster relief insurance proceeds	13:3881(A)(7)
	Engagement & wedding rings to $5,000	13:3881(A)(5)
	Motor vehicle to $7,500	13:3881(A)(7)
	Motor vehicle modified for disability to $7,500	13:3881(A)(8)
	Spendthrift trusts	9:2004
public benefits	Aid to blind, aged, disabled; public assistance	46:111
	Crime victims' compensation	46:1811
	Earned income tax credit	13:3881 (A)(6)
	Unemployment compensation	23:1693
	Workers' compensation	23:1205
tools of trade	Tools, instruments, books, $7,500 of equity in a motor vehicle, one firearm to $500, needed to work	13:3881(A)(2)
wages	Minimum 75% of disposable weekly earnings or 30 times the federal minimum hourly wage per week, whichever is greater; bankruptcy judge may authorize more for low-income debtors	13:3881(A)(1)
wildcard	None	

Maine

Federal bankruptcy exemptions not available. All law references are to Maine Revised Statutes Annotated, in the form "title number-section number," unless otherwise noted.

ASSET	EXEMPTION	LAW
homestead	Real or personal property (including cooperative) used as residence to $47,500; if debtor has minor dependents in residence, to $95,000; if debtor over age 60 or physically or mentally disabled, $95,000; proceeds of sale exempt for six months	14-4422(1)

insurance	Annuity proceeds to $450 per month	24-A-2431
	Death benefit for police, fire, or emergency medical personnel who die in the line of duty	25-1612
	Disability or health proceeds, benefits, or avails	14-4422(13)(A),(C); 24-A-2429
	Fraternal benefit society benefits	24-A-4118
	Group health or life policy or proceeds	24-A-2430
	Life, endowment, annuity, or accident policy, proceeds or avails	14-4422(14)(C); 24-A-2428
	Life insurance policy, interest, loan value, or accrued dividends for policy from person you depended on, to $4,000	14-4422(11)
	Unmatured life insurance policy, except credit insurance policy	14-4422(10)
miscellaneous	Alimony & child support needed for support	14-4422(13)(D)
pensions	Tax-exempt retirement accounts, including 401(k)s, 403(b)s, profit-sharing and money purchase plans, SEP and SIMPLE IRAs, and defined-benefit plans	11 U.S.C. § 522(b)(3)(C)
	Traditional and Roth IRAs to $1,171,650 per person	11 U.S.C. § 522(b)(3)(C); (n)
	ERISA-qualified benefits	14-4422(13)(E)
	Judges	4-1203
	Legislators	3-703
	State employees	5-17054
personal property	Animals, crops, musical instruments, books, clothing, furnishings, household goods, appliances to $200 per item	14-4422(3)
	Balance due on repossessed goods; total amount financed can't exceed $2,000	9-A-5-103
	Burial plot in lieu of homestead exemption	14-4422(1)
	Cooking stove; furnaces & stoves for heat	14-4422(6)(A),(B)
	Food to last 6 months	14-4422(7)(A)
	Fuel not to exceed 10 cords of wood, 5 tons of coal, or 1,000 gal. of heating oil	14-4422(6)(C)
	Health aids	14-4422(12)
	Jewelry to $750; no limit for one wedding & one engagement ring	14-4422(4)
	Lost earnings payments needed for support	14-4422(14)(E)
	Military clothes, arms & equipment	37-B-262
	Motor vehicle to $5,000	14-4422(2)
	Personal injury recoveries to $12,500	14-4422(14)(D)
	Seeds, fertilizers & feed to raise & harvest food for 1 season	14-4422(7)(B)
	Tools & equipment to raise & harvest food	14-4422(7)(C)
	Wrongful death recoveries needed for support	14-4422(14)(B)
public benefits	Maintenance under the Rehabilitation Act	26-1411-H
	Crime victims' compensation	14-4422(14)(A)
	Federal, state, or local public assistance benefits; earned income and child tax credits	14-4422(13)(A); 22-3180, 22-3766
	Social Security	14-4422(13)(A)
	Unemployment compensation	14-4422(13)(A),(C)
	Veterans' benefits	14-4422(13)(B)
	Workers' compensation	39-A-106

tools of trade	Books, materials & stock to $5,000	14-4422(5)
	Commercial fishing boat, 5-ton limit	14-4422(9)
	One of each farm implement (& its maintenance equipment needed to harvest & raise crops)	14-4422(8)
wages	None (use federal nonbankruptcy wage exemption)	
wildcard	Unused portion of exemption in homestead to $6,000; or unused exemption in animals, crops, musical instruments, books, clothing, furnishings, household goods, appliances, tools of the trade & personal injury recoveries	14-4422(16)
	$400 of any property	14-4422(15)

Maryland

Federal bankruptcy exemptions not available. All law references are to Maryland Code of Courts & Judicial Proceedings unless otherwise noted. New Maryland homestead exemption is indexed for inflation by matching the federal homestead amount.

ASSET	EXEMPTION	LAW
homestead	Owner-occupied residential property to $21,625 (spouses may double). Property held as tenancy by the entirety is exempt against debts owed by only one spouse	11-504(f); In re Birney, 200 F.3d 225 (4th Cir. 1999)
insurance	Disability or health benefits, including court awards, arbitrations & settlements	11-504(b)(2)
	Fraternal benefit society benefits	Ins. 8-431; Estates & Trusts 8-115
	Life insurance or annuity contract proceeds or avails if beneficiary is insured's dependent, child, or spouse	Ins. 16-111(a); Estates & Trusts 8-115
	Medical insurance benefits deducted from wages plus medical insurance payments to $145 per week or 75% of disposable wages	Commercial Law 15-601.1(3)
miscellaneous	Child support	11-504(b)(6)
	Alimony to same extent wages are exempt	11-504(b)(7)
pensions	Tax-exempt retirement accounts, including 401(k)s, 403(b)s, profit-sharing and money purchase plans, SEP and SIMPLE IRAs, and defined-benefit plans	11 U.S.C. § 522(b)(3)(C)
	Traditional and Roth IRAs to $1,171,650 per person	11 U.S.C. § 522(b)(3)(C); (n)
	ERISA-qualified benefits, including IRAs, Roth IRAs & Keoghs	11-504(h)(1), (4)
	State employees	State Pers. & Pen. 21-502
personal property	Appliances, furnishings, household goods, books, pets & clothing to $1,000 total	11-504(b)(4)
	Burial plot	Bus. Reg. 5-503
	Health aids	11-504(b)(3)
	Perpetual care trust funds	Bus. Reg. 5-603
	Prepaid college trust funds	Educ. 18-1913
	Lost future earnings recoveries	11-504(b)(2)

public benefits	Baltimore Police death benefits	Code of 1957 art. 24, 16-103
	Crime victims' compensation	Crim. Proc. 11-816(b)
	Unemployment compensation	Labor & Employment 8-106
	Workers' compensation	Labor & Employment 9-732
tools of trade	Clothing, books, tools, instruments & appliances to $5,000	11-504(b)(1)
wages	Earned but unpaid wages, the greater of 75% or $145 per week; in Kent, Caroline, Queen Anne's & Worcester Counties, the greater of 75% or 30 times federal minimum hourly wage	Commercial Law 15-601.1
wildcard	$6,000 in cash or any property, if claimed within 30 days of attachment or levy	11-504(b)(5)
	An additional $5,000 in real or personal property	11-504(f)

Massachusetts

Federal bankruptcy exemptions available. All law references are to Massachusetts General Laws Annotated, in the form "title number-section number," unless otherwise noted.

ASSET	EXEMPTION	LAW
homestead	Property held as tenancy by the entirety may be exempt against debt for nonnecessity owed by only one spouse	209-1
	Automatic homestead for principal residence (including mobile home) to $125,000; to $500,000 if homestead declaration is recorded and complies with MA law; spouses may not double; trust beneficiaries are eligible for exemption; owners with a disability or 62 or older may each exempt up to $500,000, but aggregate cannot be more than $1,000,000.	188-1, 2, 5
	Spouse or children of deceased owner may claim homestead exemption	188-2
insurance	Disability benefits to $400 per week	175-110A
	Fraternal benefit society benefits	176-22
	Group annuity policy or proceeds	175-132C
	Group life insurance policy	175-135
	Life insurance or annuity contract proceeds if clause prohibits proceeds from being used to pay beneficiary's creditors	175-119A
	Life insurance policy if beneficiary is a married woman	175-126
	Life or endowment policy, proceeds, or cash value	175-125
	Medical malpractice self-insurance	175F-15
miscellaneous	Property of business partnership	108A-25
pensions *see also wages*	Tax-exempt retirement accounts, including 401(k)s, 403(b)s, profit-sharing and money purchase plans, SEP and SIMPLE IRAs, and defined-benefit plans	11 U.S.C. § 522(b)(3)(C)
	Traditional and Roth IRAs to $1,171,650 per person	11 U.S.C. § 522(b)(3)(C); (n)
	Credit union employees	171-84
	ERISA-qualified benefits, including IRAs & Keoghs to specified limits	235-34A; 246-28

pensions (continued)	Private retirement benefits	32-41
	Public employees	32-19
	Savings bank employees	168-41; 168-44
personal property	2 cows, 12 sheep, 2 swine, 4 tons of hay	235-34(4)
	Bank deposits to $2,500	235-34(15), 235-28A
	Beds & bedding; heating unit, stove, refrigerator, freezer & hot water heater; clothing	235-34(1)
	Bibles & books to $500 total	235-34(3)
	Burial plots, tombs & church pew	235-34(11),(8)
	Cash for fuel, heat, water, or light to $500 per month	235-34(1)
	Cash to $2,500/month for rent, in lieu of homestead	235-34(14)
	Cooperative association shares to $100	235-34(13)
	Food or cash for food to $600	235-34(7)
	Household furnishings to $15,000	235-34(2)
	Jewelry to $1,225	235-34(18)
	Motor vehicle to $7,500; to $15,000 if used by elderly or disabled debtor	235-34(16)
	Moving expenses for eminent domain	79-6A
	Sewing machine, computer, TV to $300	235-34(12)
	Trust company, bank, or credit union deposits to $2,500	235-34(15)
public benefits	Aid to Families with Dependent Children	118-10
	Public assistance	235-34(15)
	Unemployment compensation	151A-36
	Veterans' benefits	115-5
	Workers' compensation	152-47
tools of trade	Arms, accoutrements & uniforms required	235-34(10)
	Fishing boats, tackle & nets to $1,500	235-34(9)
	Materials you designed & procured to $5,000	235-34(6)
	Tools, implements & fixtures to $5,000 total	235-34(5)
wages	Earned but unpaid wages to 85% or 50x minimum wage per week	246-28
wildcard	$1,000 plus up to $5,000 of unused automobile, tools of the trade, and household furniture exemptions	235-34(17)

Michigan ("Bankruptcy-Specific" Exemptions)**

Federal bankruptcy exemptions available. All law references are to Michigan Compiled Laws Annotated unless otherwise noted.

Under Michigan law, bankruptcy exemption amounts are adjusted for inflation every three years (starting in 2005) by the Michigan Department of Treasury. These amounts have already been adjusted, so the amounts listed in the statutes are not current. You can find the current amounts at www.michigan.gov/documents/BankruptcyExemptions2005_141050_7.pdf or by searching Google for "Property Debtor in Bankruptcy May Exempt, Inflation Adjusted Amounts."

**The extent to which Michigan "bankruptcy-specific" exemptions (found in Section 600.5451) are available to debtors is unclear. See "Attention Michigan Residents," at the beginning of this appendix for more information. The exemptions that come from sections other than 600.5451 are not bankruptcy-specific and can be used even if your judge does not allow the bankruptcy-specific exemptions. See, "Michigan (General Exemptions)," below for a complete list of non-bankruptcy-specific exemptions.

ASSET	EXEMPTION	LAW
homestead	Property held as tenancy by the entirety may be exempt against debts owed by only one spouse	600.5451(1)(o)
	Real property including condo to $35,300 ($52,925 if over 65 or disabled); property cannot exceed 1 lot in town, village, city, or 40 acres elsewhere; spouse or children of deceased owner may claim homestead exemption; spouses or unmarried co-owners may not double	600.5451(1)(n); *Vinson v. Dakmak*, 347 B.R. 620 (E.D. Mich. 2006)
insurance	Disability, mutual life, or health benefits	600.5451(1)(j)
	Employer-sponsored life insurance policy or trust fund	500.2210
	Fraternal benefit society benefits	500.8181
	Life, endowment, or annuity proceeds if clause prohibits proceeds from being used to pay beneficiary's creditors	500.4054
	Life insurance	500.2207
miscellaneous	Property of business partnership	449.25
pensions	Tax-exempt retirement accounts, including 401(k)s, 403(b)s, profit-sharing and money purchase plans, SEP and SIMPLE IRAs, and defined-benefit plans	11 U.S.C. § 522(b)(3)(C)
	Traditional and Roth IRAs to $1,171,650 per person	11 U.S.C. § 522(b)(3)(C); (n)
	ERISA-qualified benefits, except contributions within last 120 days	600.5451(1)(m)
	Firefighters, police officers	38.559(6); 38.1683
	IRAs & Roth IRAs, except contributions within last 120 days	600.5451(1)(l)
	Judges and probate judges	38.2308; 38.1683
	Legislators	38.1057; 38.1683
	Public school employees	38.1346; 38.1683
	State employees	38.40; 38.1683
personal property	Appliances, utensils, books, furniture & household goods to $550 each, $3,525 total	600.5451(1)(c)
	Building & loan association shares to $1,175 par value, in lieu of homestead	600.5451(1)(k)
	Burial plots, cemeteries	600.5451(1)(a)(vii)
	Church pew, slip, seat for entire family to $600	600.5451(1)(d)
	Clothing; family pictures	600.5451(1)(a)
	Food & fuel to last family for 6 months	600.5451(1)(b)
	Crops, animals, and feed to $2,350	600.5451(1)(e)
	1 motor vehicle to $3,250	600.5451(1)(g)
	Computer & accessories to $600	600.5451(1)(h)
	Household pets to $600	600.5451(1)(f)
	Professionally prescribed health aids	600.5451(a)
public benefits	Crime victims' compensation	18.362
	Social welfare benefits	400.63
	Unemployment compensation	421.30
	Veterans' benefits for Korean War veterans	35.977
	Veterans' benefits for Vietnam veterans	35.1027
	Veterans' benefits for WWII veterans	35.926
	Workers' compensation	418.821
tools of trade	Arms & accoutrements required	600.6023(1)(a)
	Tools, implements, materials, stock, apparatus, or other things needed to carry on occupation to $2,350 total	600.5451(1)(i)

wages	Head of household may keep 60% of earned but unpaid wages (no less than $15/week), plus $2/week per nonspouse dependent; if not head of household may keep 40% (no less than $10/week)	600.5311
wildcard	None	

Michigan (General Exemptions)

The extent to which the Michigan "bankruptcy-specific" exemptions are available to debtors is unclear. See "Attention Michigan Residents," at the beginning of this appendix for more information. (We list the Michigan "bankruptcy-specific" right before these exemptions.) If the bankruptcy-specific exemptions are not available, debtors can choose between the general exemptions (listed below) and the federal exemptions.

ASSET	EXEMPTION	LAW
homestead	Real property to $3,500	600.6023(1) (h)
insurance	Disability and life insurance	600.6023(1)(f)
	Employer-sponsored life insurance policy or trust fund	500.2210
	Fraternal benefit society benefits	500.8181
	Life, endowment, or annuity proceeds if clause prohibits proceeds from being used to pay beneficiary's creditors	500.4054
	Life insurance	500.2207
miscellaneous	Property of business partnership	449.25
pensions	Tax-exempt retirement accounts, including 401(k)s, 403(b)s, profit-sharing and money purchase plans, SEP and SIMPLE IRAs, and defined-benefit plans	11 U.S.C. § 522(b)(3)(C)
	Traditional and Roth IRAs to $1,171,650 per person	11 U.S.C. § 522(b)(3)(C); (n)
	Firefighters, police officers	38.559(6); 38.1683
	Judges and probate judges	38.2308; 38.1683
	Legislators	38.1057; 38.1683
	Public school employees	38.1346; 38.1683
	State employees	38.40; 38.1683
personal property	Appliances, utensils, books, furniture & household goods to $1,000	600.6023(1)(b)
	Building & loan association shares to $1,000	600.6023 (1)(g)
	Burial plots, church pew, slip, seat for entire family	600.6023 (1)(c)
	Clothing & family pictures	600.6023 (1)(a)
	Food & fuel to last family for 6 months	600.6023 (1)(a)
	2 cows, 100 hens, 5 roosters, 10 sheep, 5 swine & feed to last 6 months	600.6023 (1)(d)
public benefits	Crime victim's compensation	18.362
	Social welfare benefits	400.63
	Unemployment compensation	421.30
	Veteran's benefits for Korean War, Vietnam, WW II veterans	35.977; 35.1027; 35.926
	Workers' compensation	418.821
tools of trade	Arms and accoutrements required	600.6023 (1)(a)
	Tools and stock needed to carry out occupation to $1,000 total	600.6023 (1)(e)
wages	Head of household may keep 60% of earned but unpaid wages (no less than $15/week), plus $2/week per nonspouse dependent; if not head of household may keep 40% (no less than $10/week)	600.5311
wildcard	None	

Minnesota

Federal bankruptcy exemptions available. All law references are to Minnesota Statutes Annotated, unless otherwise noted.

Note: Section 550.37(4)(a) requires certain exemptions to be adjusted for inflation on July 1 of even-numbered years; this table includes all changes made through July 1, 2010. Exemptions are published on or before the May 1 issue of the Minnesota State Register, www.comm.media.state.mn.us/bookstore/stateregister.asp, or call the Minnesota Dept. of Commerce at 651-296-7977.

ASSET	EXEMPTION	LAW
homestead	Home & land on which it is situated to $360,000; if homestead is used for agricultural purposes, $900,000; cannot exceed ½ acre in city, 160 acres elsewhere (spouses may not double)	510.01; 510.02
	Manufactured home to an unlimited value	550.37 subd. 12
insurance	Accident or disability proceeds	550.39
	Fraternal benefit society benefits	64B.18
	Life insurance proceeds to $44,000 if beneficiary is spouse or child of insured, plus $11,000 per dependent	550.37 subd. 10
	Police, fire, or beneficiary association benefits	550.37 subd. 11
	Unmatured life insurance contract dividends, interest, or loan value to $8,800 if insured is debtor or person debtor depends on	550.37 subd. 23
miscellaneous	Earnings of minor child	550.37 subd. 15
pensions	Tax-exempt retirement accounts, including 401(k)s, 403(b)s, profit-sharing and money purchase plans, SEP and SIMPLE IRAs, and defined-benefit plans	11 U.S.C. § 522(b)(3)(C)
	Traditional and Roth IRAs to $1,171,650 per person	11 U.S.C. § 522(b)(3)(C); (n)
	ERISA-qualified benefits if needed for support, up to $66,000 in present value	550.37 subd. 24
	IRAs or Roth IRAs needed for support, up to $66,000 in present value	550.37 subd. 24
	Public employees	353.15; 356.401
	State employees	352.965 subd. 8; 356.401
	State troopers	352B.071; 356.401
personal property	Appliances, furniture, jewelry, radio, phonographs & TV to $9,900 total	550.37 subd. 4(b)
	Bible & books	550.37 subd. 2
	Burial plot; church pew or seat	550.37 subd. 3
	Clothing, one watch, food & utensils for family	550.37 subd. 4(a)
	Motor vehicle to $4,400 (up to $44,000 if vehicle has been modified for disability)	550.37 subd. 12(a)
	Personal injury recoveries	550.37 subd. 22
	Proceeds for damaged exempt property	550.37 subds. 9, 16
	Wedding rings to $2,695	550.37 subd. 4(c)
	Wrongful death recoveries	550.37 subd. 22
public benefits	Crime victims' compensation	611A.60
	Public benefits	550.37 subd. 14
	Unemployment compensation	268.192 subd. 2
	Veterans' benefits	550.38
	Workers' compensation	176.175
tools of trade total (except teaching materials) can't exceed $13,000	Farm machines, implements, livestock, produce & crops	550.37 subd. 5
	Teaching materials of college, university, public school, or public institution teacher	550.37 subd. 8
	Tools, machines, instruments, stock in trade, furniture & library to $11,000 total	550.37 subd. 6
wages	Minimum 75% of weekly disposable earnings or 40 times federal minimum hourly wage, whichever is greater	571.922
	Wages deposited into bank accounts for 20 days after depositing	550.37 subd. 13
	Wages paid within 6 months of returning to work after receiving welfare or after incarceration; includes earnings deposited in a financial institution in the last 60 days	550.37 subd. 14
wildcard	None	

Note: In cases of suspected fraud, the Minnesota constitution permits courts to cap exemptions that would otherwise be unlimited. (*In re Tveten*, 402 N.W.2d 551 (Minn. 1987); *In re Medill*, 119 B.R. 685 (Bankr. D. Minn. 1990); *In re Sholdan*, 217 F.3d 1006 (8th Cir. 2000).)

Mississippi

Federal bankruptcy exemptions not available. All law references are to Mississippi Code unless otherwise noted.

ASSET	EXEMPTION	LAW
homestead	May file homestead declaration	85-3-27; 85-3-31
	Mobile home does not qualify as homestead unless you own land on which it is located (see *personal property*)	*In re Cobbins*, 234 B.R. 882 (S.D. Miss. 1999)
	Property you own & occupy to $75,000; if over 60 & married or widowed may claim a former residence; property cannot exceed 160 acres; sale proceeds exempt	85-3-1(b)(i); 85-3-21; 85-3-23
insurance	Disability benefits	85-3-1(b)(ii)
	Fraternal benefit society benefits	83-29-39
	Homeowners' insurance proceeds to $75,000	85-3-23
	Life insurance proceeds if clause prohibits proceeds from being used to pay beneficiary's creditors	83-7-5; 85-3-11
pensions	Tax-exempt retirement accounts, including 401(k)s, 403(b)s, profit-sharing and money purchase plans, SEP and SIMPLE IRAs, and defined-benefit plans	11 U.S.C. § 522(b)(3)(C)
	Traditional and Roth IRAs to $1,171,650 per person	11 U.S.C. § 522(b)(3)(C); (n)
	ERISA-qualified benefits, IRAs, Keoghs deposited over 1 year before filing bankruptcy	85-3-1(e)
	Firefighters (includes death benefits)	21-29-257; 45-2-1
	Highway patrol officers	25-13-31
	Law enforcement officers' death benefits	45-2-1
	Police officers (includes death benefits)	21-29-257; 45-2-1
	Private retirement benefits to extent tax deferred	71-1-43

pensions (continued)	Public employees retirement & disability benefits	25-11-129
	State employees	25-14-5
	Teachers	25-11-201(1)(d)
	Volunteer firefighters' death benefits	45-2-1
personal property	Mobile home to $30,000	85-3-1(d)
	Personal injury judgments to $10,000	85-3-17
	Sale or insurance proceeds for exempt property	85-3-1(b)(i)
	State health savings accounts	85-3-1(g)
	Tangible personal property to $10,000: any items worth less than $200 each; furniture, dishes, kitchenware, household goods, appliances, 1 radio, 1 TV, 1 firearm, 1 lawn-mower, clothing, wedding rings, motor vehicles, tools of the trade, books, crops, health aids, domestic animals (does not include works of art, antiques, jewelry, or electronic entertainment equipment)	85-3-1(a)
	Tax-qualified § 529 education savings plans, including those under the Mississippi Prepaid Affordable College Tuition Program	85-3-1(f)
public benefits	Assistance to aged	43-9-19
	Assistance to blind	43-3-71
	Assistance to disabled	43-29-15
	Crime victims' compensation	99-41-23(7)
	Federal income tax refund to $5,000; earned income tax credit to $5,000; state tax refunds to $5,000	85-3-1(h); (i); (j); (k)
	Social Security	25-11-129
	Unemployment compensation	71-5-539
	Workers' compensation	71-3-43
tools of trade	See personal property	
wages	Earned but unpaid wages owed for 30 days; after 30 days, minimum 75% of earned but unpaid weekly disposable earnings or 30 times the federal hourly minimum wage, whichever is greater; bankruptcy judge may authorize more for low-income debtors	85-3-4
wildcard	$50,000 of any property, including deposits of money, available to Mississippi resident who is at least 70 years old; also see personal property	85-3-1(h)

Missouri

Federal bankruptcy exemptions not available. All law references are to Annotated Missouri Statutes unless otherwise noted.

ASSET	EXEMPTION	LAW
homestead	Property held as tenancy by the entirety may be exempt against debts owed by only one spouse	In re Eads, 271 B.R. 371 (Bankr. W.D. Mo. 2002)
	Real property to $15,000 or mobile home to $5,000 (joint owners may not double)	513.430(6); 513.475 In re Smith, 254 B.R. 751 (Bankr. W.D. Mo. 2000)
insurance	Assessment plan or life insurance proceeds	377.090
	Disability or illness benefits	513.430(10)(c)
	Fraternal benefit society benefits to $5,000, bought over 6 months before filing	513.430(8)
insurance (continued)	Life insurance dividends, loan value, or interest to $150,000, bought over 6 months before filing	513.430(8)
	Stipulated insurance premiums	377.330
	Unmatured life insurance policy	513.430(7)
miscellaneous	Alimony, child support to $750 per month	513.430(10)(d)
	Property of business partnership	358.250
pensions	Tax-exempt retirement accounts, including 401(k)s, 403(b)s, profit-sharing and money purchase plans, SEP and SIMPLE IRAs, and defined-benefit plans	11 U.S.C. § 522(b)(3)(C)
	Traditional and Roth IRAs to $1,171,650 per person	11 U.S.C. § 522(b)(3)(C); (n)
	Employee benefit spendthrift trust	456.014
	Employees of cities with 100,000 or more people	71.207
	ERISA-qualified benefits, IRAs, Roth IRAs & other retirement accounts needed for support	513.430(10)(e), (f)
	Firefighters	87.090; 87.365; 87.485
	Highway & transportation employees	104.250
	Police department employees	86.190; 86.353; 86.1430
	Public officers & employees	70.695; 70.755
	State employees	104.540
	Teachers	169.090
personal property	Appliances, household goods, furnishings, clothing, books, crops, animals & musical instruments to $3,000 total	513.430(1)
	Burial grounds to 1 acre or $100	214.190
	Health aids	513.430(9)
	Motor vehicle to $3,000	513.430(5)
	Wedding ring to $1,500 & other jewelry to $500	513.430(2)
	Wrongful death recoveries for person you depended on	513.430(11)
public benefits	Crime victim's compensation	595.025
	Public assistance	513.430(10)(a)
	Social Security	513.430(10)(a)
	Unemployment compensation	288.380(10)(l); 513.430(10)(c)
	Veterans' benefits	513.430(10)b)
	Workers' compensation	287.260
tools of trade	Implements, books & tools of trade to $3,000	513.430(4)
wages	Minimum 75% of weekly earnings (90% of weekly earnings for head of family), or 30 times the federal minimum hourly wage, whichever is more; bankruptcy judge may authorize more for low-income debtors	525.030
	Wages of servant or common laborer to $90	513.470
wildcard	$1,250 of any property if head of family, else $600; head of family may claim additional $350 per child	513.430(3); 513.440

Montana

Federal bankruptcy exemptions not available. All law references are to Montana Code Annotated unless otherwise noted.

Some of the exemptions in this table may not be available to you in some bankruptcy courts. Before filing bankruptcy, check with a bankruptcy attorney to find out which exemptions are acceptable in your court. See, "Special Considerations in States With 'Bankruptcy-Specific' Exemptions," at the beginning of this appendix for more information.

ASSET	EXEMPTION	LAW
homestead	Must record homestead declaration before filing for bankruptcy	70-32-105
	Real property or mobile home you occupy to $250,000; sale, condemnation, or insurance proceeds exempt for 18 months	70-32-104; 70-32-201; 70-32-213
insurance	Annuity contract proceeds to $350 per month	33-15-514
	Disability or illness proceeds, avails, or benefits	25-13-608(1)(d); 33-15-513
	Fraternal benefit society benefits	33-7-522
	Group life insurance policy or proceeds	33-15-512
	Hail insurance benefits	80-2-245
	Life insurance proceeds if clause prohibits proceeds from being used to pay beneficiary's creditors	33-20-120
	Medical, surgical, or hospital care benefits	25-13-608(1)(f)
	Unmatured life insurance contracts	25-13-608(1)(k)
miscellaneous	Alimony, child support	25-13-608(1)(g)
pensions	Tax-exempt retirement accounts, including 401(k)s, 403(b)s, profit-sharing and money purchase plans, SEP and SIMPLE IRAs, and defined-benefit plans	11 U.S.C. § 522(b)(3)(C)
	Traditional and Roth IRAs to $1,171,650 per person	11 U.S.C. § 522(b)(3)(C); (n)
	IRAs & ERISA-qualified benefits deposited over 1 year before filing bankruptcy or up to 15% of debtor's gross annual income	31-2-106
	Firefighters	19-18-612(1)
	IRA & Roth IRA contributions & earnings made before judgment filed	25-13-608(1)(e)
	Police officers	19-19-504(1)
	Public employees	19-2-1004; 25-13-608(i)
	Teachers	19-20-706(2); 25-13-608(j)
	University system employees	19-21-212
personal property	Appliances, household furnishings, goods, animals with feed, crops, musical instruments, books, firearms, sporting goods, clothing & jewelry to $600 per item, $4,500 total	25-13-609(1)
	Burial plot	25-13-608(1)(h)
	Cooperative association shares to $500 value	35-15-404
	Health aids	25-13-608(1)(a)
	Motor vehicle to $2,500	25-13-609(2)
	Proceeds from sale or for damage or loss of exempt property for 6 months after received	25-13-610
public benefits	Aid to aged, disabled needy persons	53-2-607
	Crime victims' compensation	53-9-129

ASSET	EXEMPTION	LAW
public benefits (continued)	Local public assistance	25-13-608(1)(b)
	Silicosis benefits	39-73-110
	Social Security	25-13-608(1)(b)
	Subsidized adoption payments to needy persons	53-2-607
	Unemployment compensation	31-2-106(2); 39-51-3105
	Veterans' benefits	25-13-608(1)(c)
	Vocational rehabilitation to blind needy persons	53-2-607
	Workers' compensation	39-71-743
tools of trade	Implements, books & tools of trade to $3,000	25-13-609(3)
	Uniforms, arms & accoutrements needed to carry out government functions	25-13-613(b)
wages	Minimum 75% of earned but unpaid weekly disposable earnings, or 30 times the federal hourly minimum wage, whichever is greater; bankruptcy judge may authorize more for low-income debtors	25-13-614
wildcard	None	

Nebraska

Federal bankruptcy exemptions not available. All law references are to Revised Statutes of Nebraska unless otherwise noted.

ASSET	EXEMPTION	LAW
homestead	$60,000 for head of family or an unmarried person age 65 or older; cannot exceed 2 lots in city or village, 160 acres elsewhere; sale proceeds exempt 6 months after sale (spouses may not double)	40-101; 40-111; 40-113
	May record homestead declaration	40-105
insurance	Fraternal benefit society benefits to $100,000 loan value unless beneficiary convicted of a crime related to benefits	44-1089
	Life insurance proceeds and avails to $100,000	44-371
pensions see also wages	Tax-exempt retirement accounts, including 401(k)s, 403(b)s, profit-sharing and money purchase plans, SEP and SIMPLE IRAs, and defined-benefit plans	11 U.S.C. § 522(b)(3)(C)
	Traditional and Roth IRAs to $1,171,650 per person	11 U.S.C. § 522(b)(3)(C); (n)
	County employees	23-2322
	Deferred compensation of public employees	48-1401
	ERISA-qualified benefits including IRAs & Roth IRAs needed for support	25-1563.01
	Military disability benefits	25-1559
	School employees	79-948
	State employees	84-1324
personal property	Burial plot	12-517
	Clothing	25-1556(2)
	Crypts, lots, tombs, niches, vaults	12-605
	Furniture, household goods & appliances, household electronics, personal computers, books & musical instruments to $1,500	25-1556(3)
	Health aids	25-1556(5)

personal property (continued)	Medical or health savings accounts to $25,000	8-1, 131(2)(b)
	Perpetual care funds	12-511
	Personal injury recoveries	25-1563.02
	Personal possessions	25-1556
public benefits	Aid to disabled, blind, aged; public assistance	68-1013
	General assistance to poor persons	68-148
	Unemployment compensation	48-647
	Workers' compensation	48-149
tools of trade	Equipment or tools including a vehicle used in or for commuting to principal place of business to $2,400 (husband & wife may double)	25-1556(4); *In re Keller*, 50 B.R. 23 (D. Neb. 1985)
wages	Minimum 85% of earned but unpaid weekly disposable earnings or pension payments for head of family; minimum 75% of earned but unpaid weekly disposable earnings or 30 times the federal hourly minimum wage, whichever is greater, for all others; bankruptcy judge may authorize more for low-income debtors	25-1558
wildcard	$2,500 of any personal property except wages, in lieu of homestead	25-1552

Nevada

Federal bankruptcy exemptions not available. All law references are to Nevada Revised Statutes Annotated unless otherwise noted.

ASSET	EXEMPTION	LAW
homestead	Must record homestead declaration before filing for bankruptcy	115.020
	Real property or mobile home to $550,000 Spouses may not double	115.010; 21.090(1)(m)
insurance	Annuity contract proceeds	687B.290
	Fraternal benefit society benefits	695A.220
	Group life or health policy or proceeds	687B.280
	Health proceeds or avails	687B.270
	Life insurance policy or proceeds	21.090(1)(k); *In re Bower*, 234 B.R. 109 (Nev. 1999)
	Life insurance proceeds if you're not the insured	687B.260
miscellaneous	Alimony & child support	21.090(1)(s)
	Property of some business partnerships	87.250
	Security deposits for a rental residence, except landlord may enforce terms of lease or rental agreement	21.090(1)(n)
pensions	Tax-exempt retirement accounts, including 401(k)s, 403(b)s, profit-sharing and money purchase plans, SEP and SIMPLE IRAs, and defined-benefit plans	11 U.S.C. § 522(b)(3)(C)
	Traditional and Roth IRAs to $1,171,650 per person	11 U.S.C. § 522(b)(3)(C); (n)
	ERISA-qualified benefits, deferred compensation, SEP IRA, Roth IRA, or IRA to $500,000	21.090(1)(r)
	Public employees	286.670
personal property	Appliances, household goods, furniture, home & yard equipment to $12,000 total	21.090(1)(b)

personal property (continued)	Books, works of art, musical instruments & jewelry to $5,000	21.090(1)(a)
	Burial plot purchase money held in trust	689.700
	Funeral service contract money held in trust	689.700
	Health aids	21.090(1)(q)
	Interests in qualifying trusts	21.090(1)(cc)
	Keepsakes & pictures	21.090(1)(a)
	Metal-bearing ores, geological specimens, art curiosities, or paleontological remains; must be arranged, classified, cataloged & numbered in reference books	21.100
	Mortgage impound accounts	645B.180
	Motor vehicle to $15,000; no limit on vehicle equipped for disabled person	21.090(1)(f),(o)
	1 gun	21.090(1)(i)
	Personal injury compensation to $16,500	21.090(1)(u)
	Restitution received for criminal act	21.090(1)(x)
	Stock in certain closely held corporations	21.090(1)(bb)
	Tax refunds derived from the earned income credit	21.090(1)(aa)
	Wrongful death awards to survivors	21.090(1)(v)
public benefits	Aid to blind, aged, disabled; public assistance	422.291
	Crime victim's compensation	21.090
	Industrial insurance (workers' compensation)	616C.205
	Public assistance for children	432.036
	Social Security retirement, disability, SSI, survivor benefits	21.090(1)(y)
	Unemployment compensation	612.710
	Vocational rehabilitation benefits	615.270
tools of trade	Arms, uniforms & accoutrements you're required to keep	21.090(1)(j)
	Cabin or dwelling of miner or prospector; mining claim, cars, implements & appliances to $4,500 total (for working claim only)	21.090(1)(e)
	Farm trucks, stock, tools, equipment & seed to $4,500	21.090(1)(c)
	Library, equipment, supplies, tools, inventory & materials to $10,000	21.090(1)(d)
wages	Minimum 75% of disposable weekly earnings or 30 times the federal minimum hourly wage per week, whichever is more; bankruptcy judge may authorize more for low-income debtors	21.090(1)(g)
wildcard	$1,000 of any personal property	21.090(1)(z)

New Hampshire

Federal bankruptcy exemptions available. All law references are to New Hampshire Revised Statutes Annotated unless otherwise noted.

ASSET	EXEMPTION	LAW
homestead	Real property or manufactured housing (& the land it's on if you own it) to $100,000	480:1

insurance	Firefighters' aid insurance	402:69
	Fraternal benefit society benefits	418:17
	Homeowners' insurance proceeds to $5,000	512:21(VIII)
miscellaneous	Jury, witness fees	512:21(VI)
	Property of business partnership	304-A:25
	Wages of minor child	512:21(III)
pensions	Tax-exempt retirement accounts, including 401(k)s, 403(b)s, profit-sharing and money purchase plans, SEP and SIMPLE IRAs, and defined-benefit plans	11 U.S.C. § 522(b)(3)(C)
	Traditional and Roth IRAs to $1,171,650 per person	11 U.S.C. § 522(b)(3)(C); (n)
	ERISA-qualified retirement accounts including IRAs & Roth IRAs	512:2 (XIX)
	Federally created pension (only benefits building up)	512:21(IV)
	Firefighters	102:23
	Police officers	103:18
	Public employees	100-A:26
personal property	Beds, bedding & cooking utensils	511:2(II)
	Bibles & books to $800	511:2(VIII)
	Burial plot, lot	511:2(XIV)
	Church pew	511:2(XV)
	Clothing	511:2(I)
	Cooking & heating stoves, refrigerator	511:2(IV)
	Domestic fowl to $300	511:2(XIII)
	Food & fuel to $400	511:2(VI)
	Furniture to $3,500	511:2(III)
	Jewelry to $500	511:2(XVII)
	Motor vehicle to $4,000	511:2(XVI)
	Proceeds for lost or destroyed exempt property	512:21(VIII)
	Sewing machine	511:2(V)
	1 cow, 6 sheep & their fleece, 4 tons of hay	511:2(XI); (XII)
	1 hog or pig or its meat (if slaughtered)	511:2(X)
public benefits	Aid to blind, aged, disabled; public assistance	167:25
	Unemployment compensation	282-A:159
	Workers' compensation	281-A:52
tools of trade	Tools of your occupation to $5,000	511:2(IX)
	Uniforms, arms & equipment of military member	511:2(VII)
	Yoke of oxen or horse needed for farming or teaming	511:2(XII)
wages	50 times the federal minimum hourly wage per week	512:21(II)
	Deposits in any account designated a payroll account.	512:21(XI)
	Earned but unpaid wages of spouse	512:21(III)
wildcard	$1,000 of any property	511:2(XVIII)
	Unused portion of bibles & books, food & fuel, furniture, jewelry, motor vehicle & tools of trade exemptions to $7,000	511:2(XVIII)

New Jersey

Federal bankruptcy exemptions available. All law references are to New Jersey Statutes Annotated unless otherwise noted.

ASSET	EXEMPTION	LAW
homestead	None, but survivorship interest of a spouse in property held as tenancy by the entirety is exempt from creditors of a single spouse	*Freda v. Commercial Trust Co. of New Jersey*, 570 A.2d 409 (N.J. 1990)
insurance	Annuity contract proceeds to $500 per month	17B:24-7
	Disability benefits	17:18-12
	Disability, death, medical, or hospital benefits for civil defense workers	App. A:9-57.6
	Disability or death benefits for military member	38A:4-8
	Group life or health policy or proceeds	17B:24-9
	Health or disability benefits	17:18-12; 17B:24-8
	Life insurance proceeds if clause prohibits proceeds from being used to pay beneficiary's creditors	17B:24-10
	Life insurance proceeds or avails if you're not the insured	17B:24-6b
pensions	Tax-exempt retirement accounts, including 401(k)s, 403(b)s, profit-sharing and money purchase plans, SEP and SIMPLE IRAs, and defined-benefit plans	11 U.S.C. § 522(b)(3)(C)
	Traditional and Roth IRAs to $1,171,650 per person	11 U.S.C. § 522(b)(3)(C); (n)
	Alcohol beverage control officers	43:8A-20
	City boards of health employees	43:18-12
	Civil defense workers	App. A:9-57.6
	County employees	43:10-57; 43:10-105
	ERISA-qualified benefits for city employees	43:13-9
	Firefighters, police officers, traffic officers	43:16-7; 43:16A-17
	IRAs	*In re Yuhas*, 104 F.3d 612 (3d Cir. 1997)
	Judges	43:6A-41
	Municipal employees	43:13-44
	Prison employees	43:7-13
	Public employees	43:15A-53
	School district employees	18A:66-116
	State police	53:5A-45
	Street & water department employees	43:19-17
	Teachers	18A:66-51
	Trust containing personal property created pursuant to federal tax law, including 401(k) plans, IRAs, Roth IRAs & higher education (529) savings plans	25:2-1; *In re Yuhas*, 104 F.3d 612 (3d Cir. 1997)
personal property	Burial plots	45:27-21
	Clothing	2A:17-19
	Furniture & household goods to $1,000	2A:26-4
	Personal property & possessions of any kind, stock or interest in corporations to $1,000 total	2A:17-19
public benefits	Old age, permanent disability assistance	44:7-35
	Unemployment compensation	43:21-53
	Workers' compensation	34:15-29
tools of trade	None	

wages	90% of earned but unpaid wages if annual income is less than 250% of federal poverty level; 75% if annual income is higher	2A:17-56
	Wages or allowances received by military personnel	38A:4-8
wildcard	None	

New Mexico

Federal bankruptcy exemptions available. All law references are to New Mexico Statutes Annotated unless otherwise noted.

ASSET	EXEMPTION	LAW
homestead	$60,000	42-10-9
insurance	Benevolent association benefits to $5,000	42-10-4
	Fraternal benefit society benefits	59A-44-18
	Life, accident, health, or annuity benefits, withdrawal or cash value, if beneficiary is a New Mexico resident	42-10-3
	Life insurance proceeds	42-10-5
miscellaneous	Ownership interest in unincorporated association	53-10-2
	Property of business partnership	54-1A-501
pensions	Tax-exempt retirement accounts, including 401(k)s, 403(b)s, profit-sharing and money purchase plans, SEP and SIMPLE IRAs, and defined-benefit plans	11 U.S.C. § 522(b)(3)(C)
	Traditional and Roth IRAs to $1,171,650 per person	11 U.S.C. § 522(b)(3)(C); (n)
	Pension or retirement benefits	42-10-1; 42-10-2
	Public school employees	22-11-42A
personal property	Books & furniture	42-10-1; 42-10-2
	Building materials	48-2-15
	Clothing	42-10-1; 42-10-2
	Cooperative association shares, minimum amount needed to be member	53-4-28
	Health aids	42-10-1; 42-10-2
	Jewelry to $2,500	42-10-1; 42-10-2
	Materials, tools & machinery to dig, drill, complete, operate, or repair oil line, gas well, or pipeline	70-4-12
	Motor vehicle to $4,000	42-10-1; 42-10-2
public benefits	Crime victims' compensation	31-22-15
	General assistance	27-2-21
	Occupational disease disablement benefits	52-3-37
	Unemployment compensation	51-1-37
	Workers' compensation	52-1-52
tools of trade	$1,500	42-10-1; 42-10-2
wages	Minimum 75% of disposable earnings or 40 times the federal hourly minimum wage, whichever is more; bankruptcy judge may authorize more for low-income debtors	35-12-7
wildcard	$500 of any personal property	42-10-1
	$5,000 of any real or personal property, in lieu of homestead	42-10-10

New York

Federal bankruptcy exemptions are available. All references are to Consolidated Laws of New York unless otherwise noted; Civil Practice Law & Rules are abbreviated C.P.L.R.

Some of the exemptions in this table may not be available to you in some bankruptcy courts. Before filing bankruptcy, check with a bankruptcy attorney to find out which exemptions are acceptable in your court. See, "Special Considerations in States With 'Bankruptcy-Specific' Exemptions," at the beginning of this appendix for more information.

ASSET	EXEMPTION	LAW
homestead	Real property including co-op, condo, or mobile home, to $75,000, $125,000, or $150,000, depending on the county	C.P.L.R. 5206(a); In re Pearl, 723 F.2d 193 (2nd Cir. 1983)
insurance	Annuity contract benefits due the debtor, if debtor paid for the contract; $5,000 limit if purchased within 6 months prior to filing & not tax deferred	Ins. 3212(d); Debt. & Cred. 283(1)
	Disability or illness benefits to $400 per month	Ins. 3212(c)
	Life insurance proceeds & avails if the beneficiary is not the debtor, or if debtor's spouse has taken out policy	Ins. 3212(b)
	Life insurance proceeds left at death with the insurance company, if clause prohibits proceeds from being used to pay beneficiary's creditors	Est. Powers & Trusts 7-1.5(a)(2)
miscellaneous	Alimony, child support	C.P.L.R. 5205 (d)(3); Debt. & Cred. 282(2)(d)
	Property of business partnership	Partnership 51
pensions	Tax-exempt retirement accounts, including 401(k)s, 403(b)s, profit-sharing and money purchase plans, SEP and SIMPLE IRAs, and defined-benefit plans	11 U.S.C. § 522(b)(3)(C)
	Traditional and Roth IRAs to $1,171,650 per person	11 U.S.C. § 522(b)(3)(C); (n)
	ERISA-qualified benefits, IRAs, Roth IRAs & Keoghs & income needed for support	C.P.L.R. 5205(c); Debt. & Cred. 282(2)(e)
	Public retirement benefits	Ins. 4607
	State employees	Ret. & Soc. Sec. 10
	Teachers	Educ. 524
	Village police officers	Unconsolidated 5711-o
	Volunteer ambulance workers' benefits	Vol. Amb. Wkr. Ben. 23
	Volunteer firefighters' benefits	Vol. Firefighter Ben. 23
personal property	Religious texts, schoolbooks, other books to $500; pictures; clothing; church pew or seat; sewing machine, refrigerator, TV, radio; furniture, cooking utensils & tableware, dishes; food to last 120 days; stoves with fuel to last 120 days; domestic animal with food to last 120 days, to $1,000; wedding ring; watch, jewelry, art to $1,000; exemptions may not exceed $10,000 total (including tools of trade & limited annuity)	C.P.L.R. 5205(a)(1)-(6); Debt. & Cred. 283(1)
	Burial plot without structure to ¼ acre	C.P.L.R. 5206(f)
	Cash (including savings bonds, tax refunds, bank & credit union deposits) to $5,000, or to $10,000 after exemptions for personal property taken, whichever amount is less (for debtors who do not claim homestead)	Debt. & Cred. 283(2)

personal property (continued)	College tuition savings program trust fund	C.P.L.R. 5205(j)
	Electronic deposits of exempt property into bank account in last 45 days	C.P.L.R. 5205(l)(1)
	Health aids, including service animals with food	C.P.L.R. 5205(h)
	Lost future earnings recoveries needed for support	Debt. & Cred. 282(3)(iv)
	Motor vehicle to $4,000; $10,000 if equipped for disabled person (except if municipality is creditor)	Debt. & Cred. 282(1); *In re Miller*, 167 B.R. 782 (S.D. N.Y. 1994)
	Personal injury recoveries up to 1 year after receiving	Debt. & Cred. 282(3)(iii)
	Recovery for injury to exempt property up to 1 year after receiving	C.P.L.R. 5205(b)
	Savings & loan savings to $600	Banking 407
	Security deposit to landlord, utility company	C.P.L.R. 5205(g)
	Spendthrift trust fund principal, 90% of income if not created by debtor	C.P.L.R. 5205(c),(d)
	Wrongful death recoveries for person you depended on	Debt. & Cred. 282(3)(ii)
public benefits	Aid to blind, aged, disabled	Debt. & Cred. 282(2)(c)
	Crime victims' compensation	Debt. & Cred. 282(3)(i)
	Home relief, local public assistance	Debt. & Cred. 282(2)(a)
	Public assistance	Soc. Serv. 137
	Social Security	Debt. & Cred. 282(2)(a)
	Unemployment compensation	Debt. & Cred. 282(2)(a)
	Veterans' benefits	Debt. & Cred. 282(2)(b)
	Workers' compensation	Debt. & Cred. 282(2)(c); Work. Comp. 33, 218
tools of trade	Farm machinery, team & food for 60 days; professional furniture, books & instruments to $3,000 total	C.P.L.R. 5205(a),(b)
	Uniforms, medal, emblem, equipment, horse, arms & sword of member of military	C.P.L.R. 5205(e)
wages	90% of earned but unpaid wages received within 60 days before & anytime after filing	C.P.L.R. 5205(d)
	90% of earnings from dairy farmer's sales to milk dealers	C.P.L.R. 5205(f)
	100% of pay of noncommissioned officer, private, or musician in U.S. or N.Y. state armed forces	C.P.L.R. 5205(e)
wildcard	$1,000 of personal property, bank account, or cash in lieu of homestead	C.P.L.R. 5205(a)(9)

North Carolina

Federal bankruptcy exemptions not available. All law references are to General Statutes of North Carolina unless otherwise noted.

ASSET	EXEMPTION	LAW
homestead	Property held as tenancy by the entirety may be exempt against debts owed by only one spouse	*In re Chandler*, 148 B.R. 13 (E.D. N.C. 1992)

homestead (continued)	Real or personal property, including co-op, used as residence to $35,000; $60,000 if 65 or older, property owned with spouse as tenants by the entirety or joint tenants with right of survivorship, and spouse has died; up to $5,000 of unused portion of homestead may be applied to any property	1C-1601(a)(1),(2)
insurance	Employee group life policy or proceeds	58-58-165
	Fraternal benefit society benefits	58-24-85
	Life insurance on spouse or children	1C-1601(a)(6); Const. Art. X § 5
miscellaneous	Alimony, support, separate maintenance, and child support necessary for support of debtor and dependents	1C-1601(a)(12)
	Property of business partnership	59-55
	Support received by a surviving spouse for 1 year, up to $10,000	30-15
pensions	Tax-exempt retirement accounts, including 401(k)s, 403(b)s, profit-sharing and money purchase plans, SEP and SIMPLE IRAs, and defined-benefit plans	11 U.S.C. § 522(b)(3)(C)
	Traditional and Roth IRAs to $1,171,650 per person	11 U.S.C. § 522(b)(3)(C); (n)
	Firefighters & rescue squad workers	58-86-90
	IRAs & Roth IRAs	1C-1601(a)(9)
	Law enforcement officers	143-166.30(g)
	Legislators	120-4.29
	Municipal, city & county employees	128-31
	Retirement benefits from another state to extent exempt in that state	1C-1601(a)(11)
	Teachers & state employees	135-9; 135-95
personal property	Animals, crops, musical instruments, books, clothing, appliances, household goods & furnishings to $5,000 total; may add $1,000 per dependent, up to $4,000 total additional (all property must have purchased at lease 90 days before filing)	
	Burial plot to $18,500, in lieu of homestead	1C-1601(a)(1)
	College savings account established under 26 U.S.C. § 529 to $25,000, excluding certain contributions within prior year	1C-1601(a)(10)
	Health aids	1C-1601(a)(7)
	Motor vehicle to $3,500	1C-1601(a)(3)
	Personal injury & wrongful death recoveries for person you depended on	1C-1601(a)(8)
public benefits	Aid to blind	111-18
	Crime victims' compensation	15B-17
	Public adult assistance under work first program	108A-36
	Unemployment compensation	96-17
	Workers' compensation	97-21
tools of trade	Implements, books & tools of trade to $2,000	1C-1601(a)(5)
wages	Earned but unpaid wages received 60 days before filing for bankruptcy, needed for support	1-362
wildcard	$5,000 of unused homestead or burial exemption	1C-1601(a)(2)
	$500 of any personal property	Constitution Art. X § 1

North Dakota

Federal bankruptcy exemptions not available. All law references are to North Dakota Century Code unless otherwise noted.

ASSET	EXEMPTION	LAW
homestead	Real property, house trailer, or mobile home to $100,000 (spouses may not double)	28-22-02(10); 47-18-01
insurance	Fraternal benefit society benefits Any unmatured life insurance contract, other than credit life insurance	26.1-15.1-18; 26.1-33-40; 28-22-03.1(4)
	Life insurance proceeds payable to deceased's estate, not to a specific beneficiary	26.1-33-40
	Life insurance surrender value to $8,000 per policy, if beneficiary is insured's dependent & policy was owned over 1 year before filing for bankruptcy; limit does not apply if more needed for support	28-22-03.1(5)
miscellaneous	Child support payments	14-09-09.31; 28-22-03.1(8)(d)
pensions	Tax-exempt retirement accounts, including 401(k)s, 403(b)s, profit-sharing and money purchase plans, SEP and SIMPLE IRAs, and defined-benefit plans	11 U.S.C. § 522(b)(3)(C)
	Traditional and Roth IRAs to $1,171,650 per person	11 U.S.C. § 522(b)(3)(C); (n)
	Disabled veterans' benefits, except military retirement pay	28-22-03.1(4)(d)
	ERISA-qualified benefits, IRAs, Roth IRAs & Keoghs to $100,000 per plan; no limit if more needed for support; total of all accounts cannot exceed $200,000	28-22-03.1(7)
	Public employees deferred compensation	54-52.2-06
	Public employees pensions	28-22-19(1)
personal property	One Bible or other religious text; schoolbooks; other books	28-22-02(4)
	Burial plots, church pew	28-22-02(2),(3)
	Wearing apparel to $5,000 and all clothing & family pictures	28-22-02(1),(5)
	Crops or grain raised by debtor on 160 acres where debtor resides	28-22-02(8)
	Food & fuel to last 1 year	28-22-02(6)
	Health aids	28-22-03.1(6)
	Insurance proceeds for exempt property	28-22-02(9)
	One motor vehicle to $2,950 (or $32,000 for vehicle that has been modified to accommodate owner's disability)	28-22-03.1(2)
	Personal injury recoveries to $15,000	28-22-03.1(4)(b)
	Wrongful death recoveries to $15,000	28-22-03.1(4)(a)
	Head of household not claiming crops or grain may claim $5,000 of any personal property	28-22-03
	Unmarried with no dependents not claiming crops or grain may claim $3,750 of any personal property	28-22-05
public benefits	Crime victims' compensation	28-22-03.1(4); 28-22-19(2)
	Old age & survivor insurance program benefits	52-09-22
	Public assistance	28-22-19(3)
	Social Security	28-22-03.1(8)(a)
public benefits (continued)	Unemployment compensation	52-06-30
	Veteran's disability benefits	28-22-03.1(8)(b)
	Workers' compensation	65-05-29
tools of trade	Books, tools & implements of trade to $1,500	28-22-03.1(3)
wages	Minimum 75% of disposable weekly earnings or 40 times the federal minimum wage, whichever is more; bankruptcy judge may authorize more for low-income debtors	32-09.1-03
wildcard	$7,500 of any property in lieu of homestead	28-22-03.1(1)

Ohio

Federal bankruptcy exemptions not available. All law references are to Ohio Revised Code unless otherwise noted. Amounts are adjusted for inflation by tracking federal exemption amounts.

Some of the exemptions in this table may not be available to you in some bankruptcy courts. Before filing bankruptcy, check with a bankruptcy attorney to find out which exemptions are acceptable in your court. See, "Special Considerations in States With 'Bankruptcy-Specific' Exemptions," at the beginning of this appendix for more information.

ASSET	EXEMPTION	LAW
homestead	Property held as tenancy by the entirety may be exempt against debts owed by only one spouse	*In re Pernus*, 143 B.R. 856 (N.D. Ohio 1992)
	Real or personal property used as residence to $21,625	2329.66(A)(1)(b)
insurance	Benevolent society benefits to $5,000	2329.63; 2329.66(A)(6)(a)
	Disability benefits needed for support	2329.66(A)(6)(e); 3923.19
	Fraternal benefit society benefits	2329.66(A)(6)(d); 3921.18
	Group life insurance policy or proceeds	2329.66(A)(6)(c); 3917.05
	Life, endowment, or annuity contract avails for your spouse, child, or dependent	2329.66(A)(6)(b); 3911.10
	Life insurance proceeds for a spouse	3911.12
	Life insurance proceeds if clause prohibits proceeds from being used to pay beneficiary's creditors	3911.14
miscellaneous	Alimony, child support needed for support	2329.66(A)(11)
	Property of business partnership	1775.24; 2329.66(A)(14)
pensions	Tax-exempt retirement accounts, including 401(k)s, 403(b)s, profit-sharing and money purchase plans, SEP and SIMPLE IRAs, and defined-benefit plans	11 U.S.C. § 522(b)(3)(C)
	Traditional and Roth IRAs to $1,171,650 per person	11 U.S.C. § 522(b)(3)(C); (n)
	ERISA-qualified benefits needed for support	2329.66(A)(10)(b)
	Firefighters, police officers	742.47
	IRAs, Roth IRAs & Keoghs needed for support	2329.66(A)(10)(c), (a)
	Public employees	145.56
	Public safety officers' death benefit	2329.66(A)(10)(a)

pensions (continued)	Public school employees	3309.66
	State highway patrol employees	5505.22
	Volunteer firefighters' dependents	146.13
personal property	Animals, crops, books, musical instruments, appliances, household goods, furnishings, firearms, hunting & fishing equipment to $525 per item; jewelry to $1,450 for 1 or more items; $11,525 total	2329.66(A)(4) (b),(c),(d); In re Szydlowski, 186 B.R. 907 (N.D. Ohio 1995)
	Burial plot	517.09; 2329.66(A)(8)
	Cash, money due within 90 days, tax refund, bank, security & utility deposits to $425 total	2329.66(A)(3); In re Szydlowski, 186 B.R. 907 (N.D. Ohio 1995)
	Compensation for lost future earnings needed for support, received during 12 months before filing	2329.66(A)(12)(d)
	Health aids (professionally prescribed)	2329.66(A)(7)
	Motor vehicle to $3,450	2329.66(A)(2)(b)
	Personal injury recoveries to $21,625, received during 12 months before filing	2329.66(A)(12)(c)
	Tuition credit or payment	2329.66(A)(16)
	Wrongful death recoveries for person debtor depended on, needed for support, received during 12 months before filing	2329.66(A)(12)(b)
public benefits	Crime victim's compensation, received during 12 months before filing	2329.66(A)(12)(a); 2743.66(D)
	Disability assistance payments	2329.66(A)(9)(f); 5115.07
	Public assistance	2329.66(A)(9)(d); (e); 5107.75; 5108.08
	Unemployment compensation	2329.66(A)(9)(c); 4141.32
	Vocational rehabilitation benefits	2329.66(A)(9)(a); 3304.19
	Workers' compensation	2329.66(A)(9)(b); 4123.67
tools of trade	Implements, books & tools of trade to $2,175	2329.66(A)(5)
wages	Minimum 75% of disposable weekly earnings or 30 times the federal hourly minimum wage, whichever is higher; bankruptcy judge may authorize more for low-income debtors	2329.66(A)(13)
wildcard	$1,150 of any property	2329.66(A)(18)

Oklahoma

Federal bankruptcy exemptions not available. All law references are to Oklahoma Statutes Annotated (in the form "title number-section number"), unless otherwise noted.

ASSET	EXEMPTION	LAW
homestead	Real property or manufactured home to unlimited value; property cannot exceed 1 acre in city, town, or village, or 160 acres elsewhere; $5,000 limit if more than 25% of total sq. ft. area used for business purposes; okay to rent homestead as long as no other residence is acquired	31-1(A)(1); 31-1(A)(2); 31-2

insurance	Annuity benefits & cash value	36-3631.1
	Assessment or mutual benefits	36-2410
	Fraternal benefit society benefits	36-2718.1
	Funeral benefits prepaid & placed in trust	36-6125
	Group life policy or proceeds	36-3632
	Life, health, accident & mutual benefit insurance proceeds & cash value, if clause prohibits proceeds from being used to pay beneficiary's creditors	36-3631.1
	Limited stock insurance benefits	36-2510
miscellaneous	Alimony, child support	31-1(A)(19)
	Beneficiary's interest in a statutory support trust	6-3010
	Liquor license	37-532
	Property of business partnership	54-1-504
pensions	Tax-exempt retirement accounts, including 401(k)s, 403(b)s, profit-sharing and money purchase plans, SEP and SIMPLE IRAs, and defined-benefit plans	11 U.S.C. § 522(b) (3)(C)
	Traditional and Roth IRAs to $1,171,650 per person	11 U.S.C. § 522(b) (3)(C); (n)
	County employees	19-959
	Disabled veterans	31-7
	ERISA-qualified benefits, IRAs, Roth IRAs, Education IRAs & Keoghs	31-1(A)(20), (24)
	Firefighters	11-49-126
	Judges	20-1111
	Law enforcement employees	47-2-303.3
	Police officers	11-50-124
	Public employees	74-923
	Tax-exempt benefits	60-328
	Teachers	70-17-109
personal property	Books, portraits & pictures	31-1(A)(6)
	Burial plots	31-1(A)(4); 8-7
	Clothing to $4,000	31-1(A)(7)
	College savings plan interest	31-1A(24)
	Deposits in an IDA (Individual Development Account)	31-1A(22)
	Federal earned income tax credit	31-1(A)(23)
	Food & seed for growing to last 1 year	31-1(A)(17)
	Guns for household use to $2,000	31-1A(14)
	Health aids (professionally prescribed)	31-1(A)(9)
	Household & kitchen furniture; personal computer and related equipment	31-1(A)(3)
	Livestock for personal or family use: 5 dairy cows & calves under 6 months; 100 chickens; 20 sheep; 10 hogs; 2 horses, bridles & saddles; forage & feed to last 1 year	31-1(A)(10),(11), (12),(15),(16),(17)
	Motor vehicle to $7,500	31-1(A)(13)
	Personal injury & wrongful death recoveries to $50,000	31-1(A)(21)
	Prepaid funeral benefits	36-6125(H)
	War bond payroll savings account	51-42
	Wedding and anniversary rings to $3,000	31-1(A)(8)

public benefits	Crime victims' compensation	21-142.13
	Public assistance	56-173
	Social Security	56-173
	Unemployment compensation	40-2-303
	Workers' compensation	85-48
tools of trade	Implements needed to farm homestead; tools, books & apparatus to $10,000 total	31-1(A)(5); 31-1(C)
wages	75% of wages earned in 90 days before filing bankruptcy; bankruptcy judge may allow more if you show hardship	12-1171.1; 31-1(A)(18); 31-1.1
wildcard	None	

Oregon

Federal bankruptcy exemptions not available. All law references are to Oregon Revised Statutes unless otherwise noted.

ASSET	EXEMPTION	LAW
homestead	Prepaid rent & security deposit for renter's dwelling	*In re Casserino*, 379 F.3d 1069 (9th Cir. 2004)
	Real property of a soldier or sailor during time of war	408.440
	Real property you occupy or intend to occupy to $40,000 ($50,000 for joint owners); property cannot exceed 1 block in town or city or 160 acres elsewhere; sale proceeds exempt 1 year from sale if you intend to purchase another home or use sale proceeds for rent	18.395; 18.402; *In re Wynn*, 369 B.R. 605 (D. Or. 2007)
	Tenancy by entirety not exempt, but subject to survivorship rights of nondebtor spouse	*In re Pletz*, 225 B.R. 206 (D. Or. 1997)
insurance	Annuity contract benefits to $500 per month	743.049
	Fraternal benefit society benefits to $7,500	748.207; 18.348
	Group life policy or proceeds not payable to insured	743.047
	Health or disability proceeds or avails	743.050
	Life insurance proceeds or cash value if you are not the insured	743.046; 743.047
miscellaneous	Alimony, child support needed for support	18.345(1)(i)
	Liquor licenses	471.292 (1)
pensions	Tax-exempt retirement accounts, including 401(k)s, 403(b)s, profit-sharing and money purchase plans, SEP and SIMPLE IRAs, and defined-benefit plans	11 U.S.C. § 522(b)(3)(C)
	Traditional and Roth IRAs to $1,171,650 per person	11 U.S.C. § 522(b)(3)(C); (n)
	ERISA-qualified benefits, including IRAs & SEPs & payments to $7,500	18.358; 18.348
	Public officers', employees' pension payments to $7,500	237.980; 238.445; 18.348(2)
personal property	Bank deposits to $7,500; cash for sold exempt property	18.348; 18.345(2)
	Books, pictures & musical instruments to $600 total	18.345(1)(a)
	Building materials for construction of an improvement	87.075
	Burial plot	65.870

personal property (continued)	Clothing, jewelry & other personal items to $1,800 total	18.345(1)(b)
	Compensation for lost earnings payments for debtor or someone debtor depended on, to extent needed	18.345(1)(L),(3)
	Domestic animals, poultry & pets to $1,000 plus food to last 60 days	18.345(1)(e)
	Federal earned income tax credit	18.345(1)(n)
	Food & fuel to last 60 days if debtor is householder	18.345(1)(f)
	Furniture, household items, utensils, radios & TVs to $3,000 total	18.345(1)(f)
	Health aids	18.345(1)(h)
	Higher education savings account to $7,500	348.863; 18.348(1)
	Motor vehicle to $3,000	18.345(1)(d),(3)
	Personal injury recoveries to $10,000	18.345(1)(k),(3)
	Pistol; rifle or shotgun (owned by person over 16) to $1,000	18.362
public benefits	Aid to blind to $7,500	411.706; 411.760; 18.348
	Aid to disabled to $7,500	411.706; 411.760; 18.348
	Civil defense & disaster relief to $7,500	18.348
	Crime victims' compensation	18.345(1)(j)(A),(3); 147.325
	General assistance to $7,500	411.760; 18.348
	Injured inmates' benefits to $7,500	655.530; 18.348
	Medical assistance to $7,500	414.095; 18.348
	Old-age assistance to $7,500	411.706; 411.760; 18.348
	Unemployment compensation to $7,500	657.855; 18.348
	Veterans' benefits & proceeds of Veterans loans	407.125; 407.595; 18.348(m)
	Vocational rehabilitation to $7,500	344.580; 18.348
	Workers' compensation to $7,500	656.234; 18.348
tools of trade	Tools, library, team with food to last 60 days, to $6,000	18.345(1)(c),(3)
wages	75% of disposable wages or $170 per week, whichever is greater; bankruptcy judge may authorize more for low-income debtors	18.385
	Wages withheld in state employee's bond savings accounts	292.070
wildcard	$400 of any personal property not already covered by existing exemption	18.348(1)(o)

Pennsylvania

Federal bankruptcy exemptions available. All law references are to Pennsylvania Consolidated Statutes Annotated unless otherwise noted.

ASSET	EXEMPTION	LAW
homestead	None; however, property held as tenancy by the entirety may be exempt against debts owed by only one spouse	*In re Martin*, 269 B.R. 119 (M.D. Pa. 2001)
insurance	Accident or disability benefits	42-8124(c)(7)
	Fraternal benefit society benefits	42-8124(c)(1),(8)
	Group life policy or proceeds	42-8124(c)(5)

insurance (continued)	Insurance policy or annuity contract payments where insured is the beneficiary, cash value or proceeds to $100 per month	42-8124(c)(3)
	Life insurance & annuity proceeds if clause prohibits proceeds from being used to pay beneficiary's creditors	42-8214(c)(4)
	Life insurance annuity policy cash value or proceeds if beneficiary is insured's dependent, child or spouse	42-8124(c)(6)
	No-fault automobile insurance proceeds	42-8124(c)(9)
miscellaneous	Property of business partnership	15-8342
pensions	Tax-exempt retirement accounts, including 401(k)s, 403(b)s, profit-sharing and money purchase plans, SEP and SIMPLE IRAs, and defined-benefit plans	11 U.S.C. § 522(b)(3)(C)
	Traditional and Roth IRAs to $1,171,650 per person	11 U.S.C. § 522(b)(3)(C); (n)
	City employees	53-13445; 53-23572; 53-39383; 42-8124(b)(1)(iv)
	County employees	16-4716
	Municipal employees	53-881.115; 42-8124(b)(1)(vi)
	Police officers	53-764; 53-776; 53-23666; 42-8124(b)(1)(iii)
	Private retirement benefits to extent tax-deferred, if clause prohibits proceeds from being used to pay beneficiary's creditors; exemption limited to deposits of $15,000 per year made at least 1 year before filing (limit does not apply to rollovers from other exempt funds or accounts)	42-8124(b)(1)(vii), (viii),(ix)
	Public school employees	24-8533; 42-8124(b)(1)(i)
	State employees	71-5953; 42-8124(b)(1)(ii)
personal property	Bibles & schoolbooks	42-8124(a)(2)
	Clothing	42-8124(a)(1)
	Military uniforms & accoutrements	42-8124(a)(4); 51-4103
	Sewing machines	42-8124(a)(3)
public benefits	Crime victims' compensation	18-11.708
	Korean conflict veterans' benefits	51-20098
	Unemployment compensation	42-8124(a)(10); 43-863
	Veterans' benefits	51-20012; 20048; 20098; 20127
	Workers' compensation	42-8124(c)(2)
tools of trade	Seamstress's sewing machine	42-8124(a)(3)
wages	Earned but unpaid wages	42-8127
	Prison inmate's wages	61-3704
	Wages of victims of abuse	42-8127(f)
wildcard	$300 of any property, including cash, real property, securities, or proceeds from sale of exempt property	42-8123

Rhode Island

Federal bankruptcy exemptions available. All law references are to General Laws of Rhode Island unless otherwise noted.

ASSET	EXEMPTION	LAW
homestead	$300,000 in land & buildings you occupy or intend to occupy as a principal residence (spouses may not double)	9-26-4.1
insurance	Accident or sickness proceeds, avails, or benefits	27-18-24
	Fraternal benefit society benefits	27-25-18
insurance (continued)	Life insurance proceeds if clause prohibits proceeds from being used to pay beneficiary's creditors	27-4-12
	Temporary disability insurance	28-41-32
miscellaneous	Earnings of a minor child	9-26-4(9)
	Property of business partnership	7-12-36
pensions	Tax-exempt retirement accounts, including 401(k)s, 403(b)s, profit-sharing and money purchase plans, SEP and SIMPLE IRAs, and defined-benefit plans	11 U.S.C. § 522(b)(3)(C)
	Traditional and Roth IRAs to $1,171,650 per person	11 U.S.C. § 522(b)(3)(C); (n)
	ERISA-qualified benefits	9-26-4(12)
	Firefighters	9-26-5
	IRAs & Roth IRAs	9-26-4(11)
	Police officers	9-26-5
	Private employees	28-17-4
	State & municipal employees	36-10-34
personal property	Beds, bedding, furniture, household goods & supplies, to $9,600 total (spouses may not double)	9-26-4(3); In re Petrozella, 247 B.R. 591 (R.I. 2000)
	Bibles & books to $300	9-26-4(4)
	Burial plot	9-26-4(5)
	Clothing	9-26-4(1)
	Consumer cooperative association holdings to $50	7-8-25
	Debt secured by promissory note or bill of exchange	9-26-4(7)
	Jewelry to $2,000	9-26-4 (14)
	Motor vehicles to $12,000	9-26-4 (13)
	Prepaid tuition program or tuition savings account	9-26-4 (15)
public benefits	Aid to blind, aged, disabled; general assistance	40-6-14
	Crime victims' compensation	12-25.1-3(b)(2)
	State disability benefits	28-41-32
	Unemployment compensation	28-44-58
	Veterans' disability or survivors' death benefits	30-7-9
	Workers' compensation	28-33-27
tools of trade	Library of practicing professional	9-26-4(2)
	Working tools to $1,500	9-26-4(2)

wages	Earned but unpaid wages due military member on active duty	30-7-9
	Earned but unpaid wages due seaman	9-26-4(6)
	Earned but unpaid wages to $50	9-26-4(8)(iii)
	Wages of any person who had been receiving public assistance are exempt for 1 year after going off of relief	9-26-4(8)(ii)
	Wages of spouse & minor children	9-26-4(9)
	Wages paid by charitable organization or fund providing relief to the poor	9-26-4(8)(i)
wildcard	$5,000	9-26-4(16)

South Carolina

Federal bankruptcy exemptions not available. All law references are to Code of Laws of South Carolina unless otherwise noted. (Amounts adjusted for inflation in 2010 (15-41-30(B).)

ASSET	EXEMPTION	LAW
homestead	Real property, including co-op, to $53,375 (single owner); $106,750 (multiple owners)	15-41-30(A)(1)
insurance	Accident & disability benefits	38-63-40(D)
	Benefits accruing under life insurance policy after death of insured, where proceeds left with insurance company pursuant to agreement; benefits not exempt from action to recover necessaries if parties agree	38-63-50
	Disability or illness benefits	15-41-30(A)(10)(C)
	Fraternal benefit society benefits	38-38-330
	Group life insurance proceeds; cash value to $50,000	38-63-40(C); 38-65-90
	Life insurance avails from policy for person you depended on to $4,275	15-41-30(A)(8)
	Life insurance proceeds from policy for person you depended on, needed for support	15-41-30(A)(12)(C)
	Proceeds & cash surrender value of life insurance payable to beneficiary other than insured's estate & for the express benefit of insured's spouse, children, or dependents (must be purchased 2 years before filing)	38-63-40(A)
	Proceeds of life insurance or annuity contract	38-63-40(B)
	Unmatured life insurance contract, except credit insurance policy	15-41-30(A)(8)
miscellaneous	Alimony, child support	15-41-30(A)(10)(D)
	Property of business partnership	33-41-720
pensions	Tax-exempt retirement accounts, including 401(k)s, 403(b)s, profit-sharing and money purchase plans, SEP and SIMPLE IRAs, and defined-benefit plans	11 U.S.C. § 522(b)(3)(C)
	Traditional and Roth IRAs to $1,171,650 per person	11 U.S.C. § 522(b)(3)(C); (n)
	ERISA-qualified benefits; your share of the pension plan fund	15-41-30(10)(E),(13)
	Firefighters	9-13-230
	General assembly members	9-9-180
	IRAs & Roth IRAs needed for support	15-41-30(A)(12)
	Judges, solicitors	9-8-190
	Police officers	9-11-270
	Public employees	9-1-1680

personal property	Animals, crops, appliances, books, clothing, household goods, furnishings, musical instruments to $4,275 total	15-41-30(A)(3)
	Burial plot to $50,000, in lieu of homestead	15-41-30(1)
	Cash & other liquid assets to $5,350, in lieu of burial or homestead exemption	15-41-30(A)(5)
	College investment program trust fund	59-2-140
	Health aids	15-41-30(A)(10)
	Jewelry to $1,075	15-41-30(A)(4)
	Motor vehicle to $5,350	15-41-30(A)(2)
	Personal injury & wrongful death recoveries for person you depended on for support	15-41-30(A)(12)
public benefits	Crime victims' compensation	15-41-30(A)(12); 16-3-1300
	General relief; aid to aged, blind, disabled	43-5-190
	Local public assistance	15-41-30(A)(11)
	Social Security	15-41-30(A)(11)
	Unemployment compensation	15-41-30(A)(11)
	Veterans' benefits	15-41-30(A)(11)
	Workers' compensation	42-9-360
tools of trade	Implements, books & tools of trade to $1,600	15-41-30(A)(6)
wages	None (use federal nonbankruptcy wage exemption)	15-41-30(A)(7)
wildcard	Up to $5,350 for any property from unused exemption amounts	15-41-30(A)(7)

South Dakota

Federal bankruptcy exemptions not available. All law references are to South Dakota Codified Law unless otherwise noted.

ASSET	EXEMPTION	LAW
homestead	Gold or silver mine, mill, or smelter not exempt	43-31-5
	May file homestead declaration	43-31-6
	Real property to unlimited value or mobile home (larger than 240 sq. ft. at its base & registered in state at least 6 months before filing) to unlimited value; property cannot exceed 1 acre in town or 160 acres elsewhere; sale proceeds to $30,000 ($170,000 if over age 70 or widow or widower who hasn't remarried) exempt for 1 year after sale (spouses may not double)	43-31-1; 43-31-2; 43-31-3; 43-31-4; 43-45-3
	Spouse or child of deceased owner may claim homestead exemption	43-31-13
insurance	Annuity contract proceeds to $250 per month	58-12-6; 58-12-8
	Endowment, life insurance, policy proceeds to $20,000; if policy issued by mutual aid or benevolent society, cash value to $20,000	58-12-4
	Fraternal benefit society benefits	58-37A-18
	Health benefits to $20,000	58-12-4
	Life insurance proceeds, if clause prohibits proceeds from being used to pay beneficiary's creditors	58-15-70
	Life insurance proceeds to $10,000, if beneficiary is surviving spouse or child	43-45-6

pensions	Tax-exempt retirement accounts, including 401(k)s, 403(b)s, profit-sharing and money purchase plans, SEP and SIMPLE IRAs, and defined-benefit plans	11 U.S.C. § 522(b)(3)(C)
	Traditional and Roth IRAs to $1,171,650 per person	11 U.S.C. § 522(b)(3)(C); (n)
	City employees	9-16-47
	ERISA-qualified benefits, limited to income & distribution on $1,000,000	43-45-16
	Public employees	3-12-115
personal property	Bible, schoolbooks; other books to $200	43-45-2(4)
	Burial plots, church pew	43-45-2(2),(3)
	Cemetery association property	47-29-25
	Clothing	43-45-2(5)
	Family pictures	43-45-2(1)
	Food & fuel to last 1 year	43-45-2(6)
public benefits	Crime victim's compensation	23A-28B-24
	Public assistance	28-7A-18
	Unemployment compensation	61-6-28
	Workers' compensation	62-4-42
tools of trade	None	
wages	Earned wages owed 60 days before filing bankruptcy, needed for support of family	15-20-12
	Wages of prisoners in work programs	24-8-10
wildcard	Head of family may claim $6,000, or nonhead of family may claim $4,000 of any personal property	43-45-4

Tennessee

Federal bankruptcy exemptions not available. All law references are to Tennessee Code Annotated unless otherwise noted.

ASSET	EXEMPTION	LAW
homestead	$5,000; $7,500 for joint owners; $25,000 if at least one dependent is a minor child (if 62 or older, $12,500 if single; $20,000 if married; $25,000 if spouse is also 62 or older)	26-2-301
	2–15-year lease	26-2-303
	Life estate	26-2-302
	Property held as tenancy by the entirety may be exempt against debts owed by only one spouse, but survivorship right is not exempt	In re Arango, 136 B.R. 740 aff'd, 992 F.2d 611 (6th Cir. 1993); In re Arwood, 289 B.R. 889 (Bankr. E.D. Tenn. 2003)
	Spouse or child of deceased owner may claim homestead exemption	26-2-301
insurance	Accident, health, or disability benefits for resident & citizen of Tennessee	26-2-110
	Disability or illness benefits	26-2-111(1)(C)
	Fraternal benefit society benefits	56-25-1403
	Life insurance or annuity	56-7-203
miscellaneous	Alimony, child support owed for 30 days before filing for bankruptcy	26-2-111(1)(E)
	Educational scholarship trust funds & prepayment plans	49-4-108; 49-7-822

pensions	Tax-exempt retirement accounts, including 401(k)s, 403(b)s, profit-sharing and money purchase plans, SEP and SIMPLE IRAs, and defined-benefit plans	11 U.S.C. § 522(b)(3)(C)
	Traditional and Roth IRAs to $1,171,650 per person	11 U.S.C. § 522(b)(3)(C); (n)
	ERISA-qualified benefits, IRAs & Roth IRAs	26-2-111(1)(D)
	Public employees	8-36-111
	State & local government employees	26-2-105
	Teachers	49-5-909
personal property	Bible, schoolbooks, family pictures & portraits	26-2-104
	Burial plot to 1 acre	26-2-305; 46-2-102
	Clothing & storage containers	26-2-104
	Health aids	26-2-111(5)
	Health savings accounts	26-2-105
	Lost future earnings payments for you or person you depended on	26-2-111(3)
	Personal injury recoveries to $7,500; wrongful death recoveries to $10,000 ($15,000 total for personal injury, wrongful death & crime victims' compensation)	26-2-111(2)(B),(C)
	Wages of debtor deserting family, in hands of family	26-2-109
public benefits	Aid to blind	71-4-117
	Aid to disabled	71-4-1112
	Crime victims' compensation to $5,000 (see personal property)	26-2-111(2)(A); 29-13-111
	Local public assistance	26-2-111(1)(A)
	Old-age assistance	71-2-216
	Relocation assistance payments	13-11-115
	Social Security	26-2-111(1)(A)
	Unemployment compensation	26-2-111(1)(A)
	Veterans' benefits	26-2-111(1)(B)
	Workers' compensation	50-6-223
tools of trade	Implements, books & tools of trade to $1,900	26-2-111(4)
wages	Minimum 75% of disposable weekly earnings or 30 times the federal minimum hourly wage, whichever is more, plus $2.50 per week per child; bankruptcy judge may authorize more for low-income debtors	26-2-106,107
wildcard	$10,000 of any personal property including deposits on account with any bank or financial institution	26-2-103

Texas

Federal bankruptcy exemptions available. All law references are to Texas Revised Civil Statutes Annotated unless otherwise noted.

ASSET	EXEMPTION	LAW
homestead	Unlimited; property cannot exceed 10 acres in town, village, city or 100 acres (200 for families) elsewhere; sale proceeds exempt for 6 months after sale (renting okay if another home not acquired, Prop. 41.003)	Prop. 41.001; 41.002; Const. Art. 16 §§ 50, 51

homestead (continued)	Must file homestead declaration, or court will file it for you & charge you for doing so	Prop. 41.005(f); 41.021 to 41.023
insurance	Fraternal benefit society benefits	Ins. 885.316
	Life, health, accident, or annuity benefits, monies, policy proceeds & cash values due or paid to beneficiary or insured	Ins. 1108.051
	Texas employee uniform group insurance	Ins. 1551.011
	Texas public school employees group insurance	Ins. 1575.006
	Texas state college or university employee benefits	Ins. 1601.008
miscellaneous	Alimony & child support	Prop. 42.001(b)(3)
	Higher education savings plan trust account	Educ. 54.709(e)
	Liquor licenses & permits	Alco. Bev. Code 11.03
	Prepaid tuition plans	Educ. 54.639
pensions	Tax-exempt retirement accounts, including 401(k)s, 403(b)s, profit-sharing and money purchase plans, SEP and SIMPLE IRAs, and defined-benefit plans	11 U.S.C. § 522(b)(3)(C)
	Traditional and Roth IRAs to $1,171,650 per person	11 U.S.C. § 522(b)(3)(C); (n)
	County & district employees	Gov't. 811.006
	ERISA-qualified government or church benefits, including Keoghs & IRAs	Prop. 42.0021
	Firefighters	6243e(5); 6243a-1(8.03); 6243b(15); 6243e(5); 6243e.1(1.04)
	Judges	Gov't. 831.004
	Law enforcement officers, firefighters, emergency medical personnel survivors	Gov't. 615.005
	Municipal employees & elected officials, state employees	6243h(22); Gov't. 811.005
	Police officers	6243d-1(17); 6243j(20); 6243a-1(8.03); 6243b(15); 6243d-1(17)
	Retirement benefits to extent tax-deferred	Prop. 42.0021
	Teachers	Gov't. 821.005
personal property *to $60,000 total for family, $30,000 for single adult (include tools of trade in these aggregate limits)*	Athletic & sporting equipment, including bicycles	Prop. 42.002(a)(8)
	Bible or other book containing sacred writings of a religion (doesn't count toward $30,000 or $60,000 total)	Prop. 42.001(b)(4)
	Burial plots (exempt from total)	Prop. 41.001
	Clothing & food	Prop. 42.002(a)(2),(5)
	Health aids (exempt from total)	Prop. 42.001(b)(2)
	Health savings accounts	Prop. 42.0021
	Home furnishings including family heirlooms	Prop. 42.002(a)(1)
	Jewelry (limited to 25% of total exemption)	Prop. 42.002(a)(6)
	Pets & domestic animals plus their food: 2 horses, mules, or donkeys & tack; 12 head of cattle; 60 head of other livestock; 120 fowl	Prop. 42.002(a)(10),(11)

personal property (continued)	1 two-, three- or four-wheeled motor vehicle per family member or per single adult who holds a driver's license; or, if not licensed, who relies on someone else to operate vehicle	Prop. 42.002(a)(9)
	2 firearms	Prop. 42.002(a)(7)
public benefits	Crime victims' compensation	Crim. Proc. 56.49
	Medical assistance	Hum. Res. 32.036
	Public assistance	Hum. Res. 31.040
	Unemployment compensation	Labor 207.075
	Workers' compensation	Labor 408.201
tools of trade *included in aggregate dollar limits for personal property*	Farming or ranching vehicles & implements	Prop. 42.002(a)(3)
	Tools, equipment (includes boat & motor vehicles used in trade) & books	Prop. 42.002(a)(4)
wages	Earned but unpaid wages	Prop. 42.001(b)(1)
	Unpaid commissions not to exceed 25% of total personal property exemptions	Prop. 42.001(d)
wildcard	None	

Utah

Federal bankruptcy exemptions not available. All law references are to Utah Code unless otherwise noted.

ASSET	EXEMPTION	LAW
homestead	Must file homestead declaration before attempted sale of home	78B-5-504
	Real property, mobile home, or water rights to $20,000 if primary residence; $5,000 if not primary residence	78-23-3(1),(2),(4)
	Sale proceeds exempt for 1 year	78B-5-503(5)(b)
insurance	Disability, illness, medical, or hospital benefits	78B-5-505(1)(a)(iii)
	Fraternal benefit society benefits	31A-9-603
	Life insurance policy cash surrender value, excluding payments made on the contract within the prior year	78B-5-505(i)(a)(xiii)
	Life insurance proceeds if beneficiary is insured's spouse or dependent, as needed for support	78B-5-505(i)(a)(xi)
	Medical, surgical & hospital benefits	78B-5-505(1)(a)(iv)
miscellaneous	Alimony needed for support	78B-5-505(a)(vi),(vii)
	Child support	78B-5-505(1) (f),(k)
pensions	Tax-exempt retirement accounts, including 401(k)s, 403(b)s, profit-sharing and money purchase plans, SEP and SIMPLE IRAs, and defined-benefit plans	11 U.S.C. § 522(b)(3)(C)
	Traditional and Roth IRAs to $1,171,650 per person	11 U.S.C. § 522(b)(3)(C); (n)
	ERISA-qualified benefits, IRAs, Roth IRAs & Keoghs (benefits that have accrued & contributions that have been made at least 1 year prior to filing)	78B-5-505(1)(a)(xiv)
	Other pensions & annuities needed for support	78-23-6(3)
	Public employees	49-11-612

personal property	Animals, books & musical instruments to $500	78B-5-506(1)(c)
	Artwork depicting, or done by, a family member	78B-5-505(1)(a)(ix)
	Bed, bedding, carpets	78B-5-505(1)(a)(viii)
	Burial plot	78B-5-505(1)(a)(i)
	Clothing (cannot claim furs or jewelry)	78B-5-505(1)(a)(viii)
	Dining & kitchen tables & chairs to $500	78B-5-505(1)(b)
	Food to last 12 months	78B-5-505(1)(a)(viii)
	Health aids	78B-5-505(1)(a)(ii)
	Heirlooms to $500	78B-5-505(1)(d)
	Motor vehicle to $2,500	78B-5-506(3)
	Personal injury, wrongful death recoveries for you or person you depended on	78B-5-505(1)(a)(x)
	Proceeds for sold, lost, or damaged exempt property	78B-5-507
	Refrigerator, freezer, microwave, stove, sewing machine, washer & dryer	78B-5-505(1)(a)(viii)
	Sofas, chairs & related furnishings to $500	78B-5-506(1)(a)
public benefits	Crime victims' compensation	63-25a-421(4)
	General assistance	35A-3-112
	Occupational disease disability benefits	34A-3-107
	Unemployment compensation	35A-4-103(4)(b)
	Veterans' benefits	78B-5-505(1)(a)(v)
	Workers' compensation	34A-2-422
tools of trade	Implements, books & tools of trade to $3,500	78B-5-506(2)
	Military property of National Guard member	39-1-47
wages	Minimum 75% of disposable weekly earnings or 30 times the federal hourly minimum wage, whichever is more; bankruptcy judge may authorize more for low-income debtors	70C-7-103
wildcard	None	

Vermont

Federal bankruptcy exemptions available. All law references are to Vermont Statutes Annotated unless otherwise noted.

ASSET	EXEMPTION	LAW
homestead	Property held as tenancy by the entirety may be exempt against debts owed by only one spouse	In re McQueen, 21 B.R. 736 (D. Ver. 1982)
	Real property or mobile home to $75,000; may also claim rents, issues, profits & outbuildings	27-101
	Spouse of deceased owner may claim homestead exemption	27-105
insurance	Annuity contract benefits to $350 per month	8-3709
	Disability benefits that supplement life insurance or annuity contract	8-3707
	Disability or illness benefits needed for support	12-2740(19)(C)
	Fraternal benefit society benefits	8-4478
	Group life or health benefits	8-3708
	Health benefits to $200 per month	8-4086
	Life insurance proceeds for person you depended on	12-2740(19)(H)

insurance (continued)	Life insurance proceeds if clause prohibits proceeds from being used to pay beneficiary's creditors	8-3705
	Life insurance proceeds if beneficiary is not the insure	8-3706
	Unmatured life insurance contract other than credit	12-2740(18)
miscellaneous	Alimony, child support	12-2740(19)(D)
pensions	Tax-exempt retirement accounts, including 401(k)s, 403(b)s, profit-sharing and money purchase plans, SEP and SIMPLE IRAs, and defined-benefit plans	11 U.S.C. § 522(b)(3)(C)
	Traditional and Roth IRAs to $1,171,650 per person	11 U.S.C. § 522(b)(3)(C); (n)
	Municipal employees	24-5066
	Other pensions	12-2740(19)(J)
	Self-directed accounts (IRAs, Roth IRAs, Keoghs); contributions must be made 1 year before filing	12-2740(16)
	State employees	3-476
	Teachers	16-1946
personal property	Appliances, furnishings, goods, clothing, books, crops, animals, musical instruments to $2,500 total	12-2740(5)
	Bank deposits to $700	12-2740(15)
	Cow, 2 goats, 10 sheep, 10 chickens & feed to last 1 winter; 3 swarms of bees plus honey; 5 tons coal or 500 gal. heating oil, 10 cords of firewood; 500 gal. bottled gas; growing crops to $5,000; yoke of oxen or steers, plow & ox yoke; 2 horses with harnesses, halters & chains	12-2740(6), (9)-(14)
	Health aids	12-2740(17)
	Jewelry to $500; wedding ring unlimited	12-2740(3),(4)
	Motor vehicles to $2,500	12-2740(1)
	Personal injury, lost future earnings, wrongful death recoveries for you or person you depended on	12-2740(19)(F), (G),(I)
	Stove, heating unit, refrigerator, freezer, water heater & sewing machines	12-2740(8)
public benefits	Aid to blind, aged, disabled; general assistance	33-124
	Crime victims' compensation needed for support	12-2740(19)(E)
	Social Security needed for support	12-2740(19)(A)
	Unemployment compensation	21-1367
	Veterans' benefits needed for support	12-2740(19)(B)
	Workers' compensation	21-681
tools of trade	Books & tools of trade to $5,000	12-2740(2)
wages	Entire wages, if you received welfare during 2 months before filing	12-3170
	Minimum 75% of weekly disposable earnings or 30 times the federal minimum hourly wage, whichever is greater; bankruptcy judge may authorize more for low-income debtors	12-3170
wildcard	Unused exemptions for motor vehicle, tools of trade, jewelry, household furniture, appliances, clothing & crops to $7,000	12-2740(7)
	$400 of any property	12-2740(7)

Virginia

Federal bankruptcy exemptions not available. All law references are to Code of Virginia unless otherwise noted.

ASSET	EXEMPTION	LAW
homestead	$5,000 plus $500 per dependent; rents & profits; sale proceeds exempt to $5,000 (unused portion of homestead may be applied to any personal property); exemption is $10,000 if over 65	*Cheeseman v. Nachman*, 656 F.2d 60 (4th Cir. 1981); 34-4; 34-18; 34-20
	May include mobile home	*In re Goad*, 161 B.R. 161 (W.D. Va. 1993)
	Must file homestead declaration before filing for bankruptcy	34-6
	Property held as tenancy by the entirety may be exempt against debts owed by only one spouse	*In re Bunker*, 312 F.3d 145 (4th Cir. 2002)
	Surviving spouse may claim $15,000; if no surviving spouse, minor children may claim exemption	64.1-151.3
insurance	Accident or sickness benefits	38.2-3406
	Burial society benefits	38.2-4021
	Cooperative life insurance benefits	38.2-3811
	Fraternal benefit society benefits	38.2-4118
	Group life or accident insurance for government officials	51.1-510
	Group life insurance policy or proceeds	38.2-3339
	Industrial sick benefits	38.2-3549
	Life insurance proceeds	38.2-3122
miscellaneous	Property of business partnership	50-73.108
pensions *see also wages*	Tax-exempt retirement accounts, including 401(k)s, 403(b)s, profit-sharing and money purchase plans, SEP and SIMPLE IRAs, and defined-benefit plans	11 U.S.C. § 522(b)(3)(C)
	Traditional and Roth IRAs to $1,171,650 per person	11 U.S.C. § 522(b)(3)(C); (n)
	City, town & county employees	51.1-802
	ERISA-qualified benefits to same extent permitted by federal bankruptcy law	34-34
	Judges	51.1-300
	State employees	51.1-124.4(A)
	State police officers	51.1-200
personal property	Bible	34-26(1)
	Burial plot	34-26(3)
	Clothing to $1,000	34-26(4)
	Family portraits & heirlooms to $5,000 total	34-26(2)
	Firearm (one) to $3,000	34-26(4b)
	Health aids	34-26(6)
	Household furnishings to $5,000	34-26(4a)
	Motor vehicle to $6,000	34-26(8)
	Personal injury causes of action & recoveries	34-28.1
	Pets	34-26(5)
	Prepaid tuition contracts	23-38.81(E)
	Wedding & engagement rings	34-26(1a)

ASSET	EXEMPTION	LAW
public benefits	Aid to blind, aged, disabled; general relief	63.2-506
	Crime victims' compensation unless seeking to discharge debt for treatment of injury incurred during crime	19.2-368.12
	Payments to tobacco farmers	3.1-1111.1
	Unemployment compensation	60.2-600
	Workers' compensation	65.2-531
tools of trade	For farmer, pair of horses, or mules with gear; one wagon or cart, one tractor to $3,000; 2 plows & wedges; one drag, harvest cradle, pitchfork, rake; fertilizer to $1,000	34-27
	Tools, books & instruments of trade, including motor vehicles, to $10,000, needed in your occupation or education	34-26(7)
	Uniforms, arms, equipment of military member	44-96
wages	Minimum 75% of weekly disposable earnings or 40 times the federal minimum hourly wage, whichever is greater; bankruptcy judge may authorize more for low-income debtors	34-29
wildcard	Unused portion of homestead or personal property exemption	34-13
	$10,000 of any property for disabled veterans	34-4.1

Washington

Federal bankruptcy exemptions available. All law references are to Revised Code of Washington Annotated unless otherwise noted.

ASSET	EXEMPTION	LAW
homestead	Must record homestead declaration before sale of home if property unimproved or home unoccupied	6.15.040
	Real property or manufactured home to $125,000; unimproved property intended for residence to $15,000 (spouses may not double)	6.13.010; 6.13.030
insurance	Annuity contract proceeds to $2,500 per month	48.18.430
	Disability proceeds, avails, or benefits	48.36A.180
	Fraternal benefit society benefits	48.18.400
	Group life insurance policy or proceeds	48.18.420
	Life insurance proceeds or avails if beneficiary is not the insured	48.18.410
miscellaneous	Child support payments	6.15.010(1)(c)(iv)
pensions	Tax-exempt retirement accounts, including 401(k)s, 403(b)s, profit-sharing and money purchase plans, SEP and SIMPLE IRAs, and defined-benefit plans	11 U.S.C. § 522(b)(3)(C)
	Traditional and Roth IRAs to $1,171,650 per person	11 U.S.C. § 522(b)(3)(C); (n)
	City employees	41.28.200; 41.44.240
	ERISA-qualified benefits, IRAs, Roth IRAs & Keoghs	6.15.020
	Judges	2.10.180; 2.12.090
	Law enforcement officials & firefighters	41.26.053
	Police officers	41.20.180
	Public & state employees	41.40.052

pensions (continued)	State patrol officers	43.43.310
	Teachers	41.32.052
	Volunteer firefighters	41.24.240
personal property	Appliances, furniture, household goods, home & yard equipment to $6,500 total for individual ($13,000 for community)	6.15.010(1)(c)(i)
	Books and electronic media to $3,500	6.15.010(1)(b)
	Burial ground	68.24.220
	Burial plots sold by nonprofit cemetery association	68.20.120
	Clothing, no more than $3,500 in furs, jewelry, ornaments	6.15.010(1)(a)
	Fire insurance proceeds for lost, stolen, or destroyed exempt property	6.15.030
	Food & fuel for comfortable maintenance	6.15.010(1)(c)(i)
	Health aids prescribed	6.15.010(1)(c)(v)
	Keepsakes & family pictures	6.15.010(1)(b)
	Motor vehicle to $3,250 total for individual (two vehicles to $6,500 for community)	6.15.010(1)(c)(iii)
	Personal injury recoveries to $20,000	6.15.010(1)(c)(vi)
	Tuition units purchased more than 2 years before	6.15.010(1)(e)
public benefits	Child welfare	74.13.070
	Crime victims' compensation	7.68.070(10)
	General assistance	74.04.280
	Industrial insurance (workers' compensation)	51.32.040
	Old-age assistance	74.08.210
	Unemployment compensation	50.40.020
tools of trade	Farmer's trucks, stock, tools, seed, equipment & supplies to $10,000 total	6.15.010(1)(d)(i)
	Library, office furniture, office equipment & supplies of physician, surgeon, attorney, clergy, or other professional to $10,000 total	6.15.010(1)(d)(ii)
	Tools & materials used in any other trade to $10,000	6.15.010(1)(d)(iii)
wages	Minimum 75% of weekly disposable earnings or 30 times the federal minimum hourly wage, whichever is greater; bankruptcy judge may authorize more for low-income debtors	6.27.150
wildcard	$3,000 of any personal property (no more than $1,500 in cash, bank deposits, bonds, stocks & securities)	6.15.010(1)(c)(ii)

West Virginia

Federal bankruptcy exemptions not available. All law references are to West Virginia Code unless otherwise noted.

Some of the exemptions in this table may not be available to you in some bankruptcy courts. Before filing bankruptcy, check with a bankruptcy attorney to find out which exemptions are acceptable in your court. See, "Special Considerations in States With 'Bankruptcy-Specific' Exemptions," at the beginning of this appendix for more information.

ASSET	EXEMPTION	LAW
homestead	Real or personal property used as residence to $25,000; unused portion of homestead may be applied to any property	38-10-4(a)

insurance	Fraternal benefit society benefits	33-23-21
	Group life insurance policy or proceeds	33-6-28
	Health or disability benefits	38-10-4(j)(3)
	Life insurance payments from policy for person you depended on, needed for support	38-10-4(k)(3)
	Unmatured life insurance contract, except credit insurance policy	38-10-4(g)
	Unmatured life insurance contract's accrued dividend, interest, or loan value to $8,000, if debtor owns contract & insured is either debtor or a person on whom debtor is dependent	38-10-4(h)
miscellaneous	Alimony, child support needed for support	38-10-4(j)(4)
pensions	Tax-exempt retirement accounts, including 401(k)s, 403(b)s, profit-sharing and money purchase plans, SEP and SIMPLE IRAs, and defined-benefit plans	11 U.S.C. § 522(b)(3)(C)
	Traditional and Roth IRAs to $1,171,650 per person	11 U.S.C. § 522(b)(3)(C); (n)
	ERISA-qualified benefits, IRAs needed for support	38-10-4(j)(5)
	Public employees	5-10-46
	Teachers	18-7A-30
personal property	Animals, crops, clothing, appliances, books, household goods, furnishings, musical instruments to $400 per item, $8,000 total	38-10-4(c)
	Burial plot to $25,000, in lieu of homestead	38-10-4(a)
	Health aids	38-10-4(i)
	Jewelry to $1,000	38-10-4(d)
	Lost earnings payments needed for support	38-10-4(k)(5)
	Motor vehicle to $2,400	38-10-4(b)
	Personal injury recoveries to $15,000	38-10-4(k)(4)
	Prepaid higher education tuition trust fund & savings plan payments	38-10-4(k)(6)
	Wrongful death recoveries for person you depended on, needed for support	38-10-4(k)(2)
public benefits	Aid to blind, aged, disabled; general assistance	9-5-1
	Crime victims' compensation	38-10-4(k)(1)
	Social Security	38-10-4(j)(1)
	Unemployment compensation	38-10-4(j)(1)
	Veterans' benefits	38-10-4(j)(2)
	Workers' compensation	23-4-18
tools of trade	Implements, books & tools of trade to $1,500	38-10-4(f)
wages	Minimum 30 times the federal minimum hourly wage per week; bankruptcy judge may authorize more for low-income debtors	38-5A-3
wildcard	$800 plus unused portion of homestead or burial exemption, of any property	38-10-4(e)

Wisconsin

Federal bankruptcy exemptions available. All law references are to Wisconsin Statutes Annotated unless otherwise noted.

ASSET	EXEMPTION	LAW
homestead	Property you occupy or intend to occupy to $75,000; $150,000 for married couples filing jointly; sale proceeds exempt for 2 years if you intend to purchase another home (spouses may not double)	815.20

insurance	Federal disability insurance benefits	815.18(3)(ds)
	Fraternal benefit society benefits	614.96
	Life insurance proceeds for someone debtor depended on, needed for support	815.18(3)(i)(a)
	Life insurance proceeds held in trust by insurer, if clause prohibits proceeds from being used to pay beneficiary's creditors	632.42
	Unmatured life insurance contract (except credit insurance contract) if debtor owns contract & insured is debtor or dependents, or someone debtor is dependent on	815.18(3)(f)
	Unmatured life insurance contract's accrued dividends, interest, or loan value to $4,000 total, if debtor owns contract & insured is debtor or dependents, or someone debtor is dependent on	815.18(3)(f)
miscellaneous	Alimony, child support needed for support	815.18(3)(c)
	Property of business partnership	178.21(3)(c)
pensions	Tax-exempt retirement accounts, including 401(k)s, 403(b)s, profit-sharing and money purchase plans, SEP and SIMPLE IRAs, and defined-benefit plans	11 U.S.C. § 522(b)(3)(C)
	Traditional and Roth IRAs to $1,171,650 per person	11 U.S.C. § 522(b)(3)(C); (n)
	Certain municipal employees	62.63(4)
	Firefighters, police officers who worked in city with population over 100,000	815.18(3)(ef)
	Military pensions	815.18(3)(n)
	Private or public retirement benefits	815.18(3)(j)
	Public employees	40.08(1)
personal property	Burial plot, tombstone, coffin	815.18(3)(a)
	College savings account or tuition trust fund	14.64(7); 14.63(8)
	Deposit accounts to $5,000	815.18(3)(k)
	Fire & casualty proceeds for destroyed exempt property for 2 years from receiving	815.18(3)(e)
	Household goods & furnishings, clothing, keepsakes, jewelry, appliances, books, musical instruments, firearms, sporting goods, animals & other tangible personal property to $12,000 total	815.18(3)(d)
	Lost future earnings recoveries, needed for support	815.18(3)(i)(d)
	Motor vehicles to $4,000; unused portion of $12,000 personal property exemption may be added	815.18(3)(g)
	Personal injury recoveries to $50,000	815.18(3)(i)(c)
	Tenant's lease or stock interest in housing co-op, to homestead amount	182.004(6)
	Wages used to purchase savings bonds	20.921(1)(e)
	Wrongful death recoveries, needed for support	815.18(3)(i)(b)
public benefits	Crime victims' compensation	949.07
	Social services payments	49.96
	Unemployment compensation	108.13
	Veterans' benefits	45.03(8)(b)
	Workers' compensation	102.27
tools of trade	Equipment, inventory, farm products, books & tools of trade to $15,000 total	815.18(3)(b)

wages	75% of weekly net income or 30 times the greater of the federal or state minimum hourly wage; bankruptcy judge may authorize more for low-income debtors	815.18(3)(h)
	Wages of county jail prisoners	303.08(3)
	Wages of county work camp prisoners	303.10(7)
	Wages of inmates under work-release plan	303.065(4)(b)
wildcard	None	

Wyoming

Federal bankruptcy exemptions not available. All law references are to Wyoming Statutes Annotated unless otherwise noted.

ASSET	EXEMPTION	LAW
homestead	Property held as tenancy by the entirety may be exempt against debts owed by only one spouse	*In re Anselmi*, 52 B.R. 479 (D. Wy. 1985)
	Real property you occupy to $10,000 or house trailer you occupy to $6,000	1-20-101; 102; 104
	Spouse or child of deceased owner may claim homestead exemption	1-20-103
insurance	Annuity contract proceeds to $350 per month	26-15-132
	Disability benefits if clause prohibits proceeds from being used to pay beneficiary's creditors	26-15-130
	Fraternal benefit society benefits	26-29-218
	Group life or disability policy or proceeds, cash surrender & loan values, premiums waived & dividends	26-15-131
	Individual life insurance policy proceeds, cash surrender & loan values, premiums waived & dividends	26-15-129
	Life insurance proceeds held by insurer, if clause prohibits proceeds from being used to pay beneficiary's creditors	26-15-133
miscellaneous	Liquor licenses & malt beverage permits	12-4-604
pensions	Tax-exempt retirement accounts, including 401(k)s, 403(b)s, profit-sharing and money purchase plans, SEP and SIMPLE IRAs, and defined-benefit plans	11 U.S.C. § 522(b)(3)(C)
	Traditional and Roth IRAs to $1,171,650 per person	11 U.S.C. § 522(b)(3)(C); (n)
	Criminal investigators, highway officers	9-3-620
	Firefighters' death benefits	15-5-209
	Game & fish wardens	9-3-620
	Police officers	15-5-313(c)
	Private or public retirement funds & accounts	1-20-110
	Public employees	9-3-426
personal property	Bedding, furniture, household articles & food to $2,000 per person in the home	1-20-106(a)(iii)
	Bible, schoolbooks & pictures	1-20-106(a)(i)
	Burial plot	1-20-106(a)(ii)
	Clothing & wedding rings to $1,000	1-20-105
	Medical savings account contributions	1-20-111
	Motor vehicle to $2,400	1-20-106(a)(iv)
	Prepaid funeral contracts	26-32-102
public benefits	Crime victims' compensation	1-40-113
	General assistance	42-2-113(b)
	Unemployment compensation	27-3-319
	Workers' compensation	27-14-702

tools of trade	Library & implements of profession to $2,000 or tools, motor vehicle, implements, team & stock in trade to $2,000	1-20-106(b)
wages	Earnings of National Guard members	19-9-401
	Minimum 75% of disposable weekly earnings or 30 times the federal hourly minimum wage, whichever is more	1-15-511
	Wages of inmates in adult community corrections program	7-18-114
	Wages of inmates in correctional industries program	25-13-107
	Wages of inmates on work release	7-16-308
wildcard	None	

Federal Bankruptcy Exemptions

Spouses filing jointly may double all exemptions. All references are to 11 U.S.C. § 522. These exemptions were last adjusted in 2010. Every three years ending on April 1, these amounts will be adjusted to reflect changes in the Consumer Price Index. Debtors in the following states may select the federal bankruptcy exemptions:

Arkansas	Massachusetts	New Mexico	Texas
Connecticut	Michigan	New York	Vermont
District of Columbia	Minnesota	Pennsylvania	Washington
Hawaii	New Hampshire	Rhode Island	Wisconsin
Kentucky	New Jersey		

ASSET	EXEMPTION	SUBSECTION
homestead	Real property, including co-op or mobile home, or burial plot to $21,625; unused portion of homestead to $10,825 may be applied to any property	(d)(1); (d)(5)
insurance	Disability, illness, or unemployment benefits	(d)(10)(C)
	Life insurance payments from policy for person you depended on, needed for support	(d)(11)(C)
	Life insurance policy with loan value, in accrued dividends or interest, to $11,525	(d)(8)
	Unmatured life insurance contract, except credit insurance policy	(d)(7)
miscellaneous	Alimony, child support needed for support	(d)(10)(D)
pensions	Tax exempt retirement accounts (including 401(k)s, 403(b)s, profit-sharing and money purchase plans, SEP and SIMPLE IRAs, and defined-benefit plans	(b)(3)(C)
	IRAs and Roth IRAs to $1,171,650 per person	(b)(3)(C)(n)
personal property	Animals, crops, clothing, appliances, books, furnishings, household goods, musical instruments to $550 per item, $11,525 total	(d)(3)
	Health aids	(d)(9)
	Jewelry to $1,450	(d)(4)
	Lost earnings payments	(d)(11)(E)
	Motor vehicle to $3,450	(d)(2)
	Personal injury recoveries to $21,625 (not to include pain & suffering or pecuniary loss)	(d)(11)(D)
	Wrongful death recoveries for person you depended on	(d)(11)(B)

public benefits	Crime victims' compensation	(d)(11)(A)
	Public assistance	(d)(10)(A)
	Social Security	(d)(10)(A)
	Unemployment compensation	(d)(10)(A)
	Veterans' benefits	(d)(10)(A)
tools of trade	Implements, books & tools of trade to $2,175	(d)(6)
wages	None	
wildcard	$1,150 of any property	(d)(5)
	Up to $10,825 of unused homestead exemption amount, for any property	(d)(5)

Federal Nonbankruptcy Exemptions

These exemptions are available only if you select your state exemptions. You may use them for any exemptions in addition to those allowed by your state, but they cannot be claimed if you file using federal bankruptcy exemptions. All law references are to the United States Code.

ASSET	EXEMPTION	LAW
death & disability benefits	Government employees	5 § 8130
	Longshoremen & harbor workers	33 § 916
	War risk, hazard, death, or injury compensation	42 § 1717
miscellaneous	Debts of seaman incurred while on a voyage	46 § 11111
	Indian lands or homestead sales or lease proceeds	25 § 410; 412a
	Klamath Indian tribe benefits for Indians residing in Oregon; agricultural or grazing lands to $5,000	25 §§ 543; 545
	Life insurance benefits for serviceman's Group Life Ins. or Veteran's Group Life Ins.	38 § 1970(g)
	Military deposits in savings accounts while on permanent duty outside U.S.	10 § 1035
	Military group life insurance	38 § 1970(g)
	Railroad workers' unemployment insurance	45 § 352(e)
	Seamen's clothing	46 § 11110
	Seamen's wages (except for spousal and child support)	46 § 11109
	Minimum 75% of disposable weekly earnings or 30 times the federal minimum hourly wage, whichever is more; bankruptcy judge may authorize more for low-income debtors	15 § 1673
retirement	CIA employees	50 § 403
	Civil service employees	5 § 8346
	Foreign Service employees	22 § 4060
	Military Medal of Honor roll pensions	38 § 1562(c)
	Military service employees	10 § 1440
	Railroad workers	45 § 231m
	Social Security	42 § 407
	Veterans' benefits	38 § 5301
survivor's benefits	Judges, U.S. court & judicial center directors, administrative assistants to U.S. Supreme Court Chief Justice	28 § 376
	Lighthouse workers	33 § 775
	Military service	10 § 1450

Chart and Tear-Out Forms

Median Family Income Chart

Schedule J—*Current Expenditures of Individual Debtor(s)*

Form 22A—*Chapter 7 Statement of Current Monthly Income and Means-Test Calculation*

Form 22C—*Chapter 13 Statement of Current Monthly Income and Calculation of Commitment Period and Disposable Income*

Median Family Income Chart

State	1 Earner	2 People	3 People	4 People *	State	1 Earner	2 People	3 People	4 People *
Alabama	$38,321	$46,025	$51,182	$61,593	Montana	$38,369	$49,743	$56,308	$68,313
Alaska	$52,611	$70,811	$77,200	$88,003	Nebraska	$39,192	$55,519	$64,700	$71,247
Arizona	$41,385	$53,781	$56,508	$61,267	Nevada	$43,146	$55,573	$60,855	$65,179
Arkansas	$34,203	$44,048	$47,035	$56,275	New Hampshire	$51,550	$61,679	$79,349	$91,750
California	$47,683	$61,539	$66,050	$74,806	New Jersey	$60,322	$67,503	$84,896	$101,957
Colorado	$47,361	$62,431	$69,252	$79,905	New Mexico	$37,246	$49,515	$51,782	$54,640
Connecticut	$56,773	$70,342	$80,263	$99,440	New York	$45,931	$56,113	$66,953	$81,212
Delaware	$48,049	$59,927	$71,259	$79,829	North Carolina	$37,892	$48,710	$54,310	$65,036
DC	$50,552	$78,313	$78,313	$115,995	North Dakota	$42,953	$58,742	$67,244	$79,336
Florida	$40,766	$49,729	$52,840	$62,742	Ohio	$40,471	$50,253	$58,376	$70,599
Georgia	$39,694	$50,712	$55,711	$64,223	Oklahoma	$37,466	$48,313	$53,332	$60,395
Hawaii	$51,099	$62,432	$75,900	$82,726	Oregon	$42,877	$52,316	$57,429	$66,616
Idaho	$39,120	$49,242	$52,077	$61,301	Pennsylvania	$45,092	$53,091	$66,487	$76,682
Illinois	$45,545	$57,964	$66,758	$79,074	Rhode Island	$46,335	$59,624	$66,800	$86,267
Indiana	$39,987	$49,669	$57,696	$67,296	South Carolina	$37,660	$47,853	$50,824	$62,912
Iowa	$40,650	$55,217	$62,251	$72,234	South Dakota	$36,799	$55,026	$61,612	$69,006
Kansas	$41,611	$55,801	$62,850	$72,665	Tennessee	$37,967	$47,234	$51,642	$60,909
Kentucky	$38,356	$44,696	$51,859	$62,583	Texas	$39,673	$53,950	$57,825	$63,859
Louisiana	$37,931	$46,169	$54,638	$65,778	Utah	$48,176	$55,555	$59,626	$64,780
Maine	$40,532	$51,738	$60,195	$74,738	Vermont	$43,544	$55,110	$69,736	$77,296
Maryland	$57,455	$73,947	$84,151	$100,928	Virginia	$50,605	$64,288	$71,644	$87,498
Massachusetts	$53,496	$64,174	$80,337	$99,067	Washington	$51,671	$61,919	$69,195	$80,404
Michigan	$43,677	$50,079	$58,467	$70,237	West Virginia	$40,887	$44,018	$50,987	$61,691
Minnesota	$46,161	$61,170	$71,784	$84,251	Wisconsin	$41,880	$55,671	$64,724	$76,117
Mississippi	$33,126	$41,601	$45,536	$54,765	Wyoming	$48,832	$62,072	$67,059	$73,362
Missouri	$38,895	$50,603	$58,355	$67,255	* Add $7,500 for each individual in excess of 4.				

B6J (Official Form 6J) (12/07)

In re _____ ,   Case No. _____
                    Debtor   **(if known)**

SCHEDULE J - CURRENT EXPENDITURES OF INDIVIDUAL DEBTOR(S)

Complete this schedule by estimating the average or projected monthly expenses of the debtor and the debtor's family at time case filed. Prorate any payments made bi-weekly, quarterly, semi-annually, or annually to show monthly rate. The average monthly expenses calculated on this form may differ from the deductions from income allowed on Form22A or 22C.

☐ Check this box if a joint petition is filed and debtor's spouse maintains a separate household. Complete a separate schedule of expenditures labeled "Spouse."

1. Rent or home mortgage payment (include lot rented for mobile home) $ _____

   a. Are real estate taxes included?   Yes _____   No _____

   b. Is property insurance included?   Yes _____   No _____

2. Utilities: a. Electricity and heating fuel $ _____

         b. Water and sewer $ _____

         c. Telephone $ _____

         d. Other _____ $ _____

3. Home maintenance (repairs and upkeep) $ _____

4. Food $ _____

5. Clothing $ _____

6. Laundry and dry cleaning $ _____

7. Medical and dental expenses $ _____

8. Transportation (not including car payments) $ _____

9. Recreation, clubs and entertainment, newspapers, magazines, etc. $ _____

10.Charitable contributions $ _____

11.Insurance (not deducted from wages or included in home mortgage payments)

       a. Homeowner's or renter's $ _____

       b. Life $ _____

       c. Health $ _____

       d. Auto $ _____

       e. Other _____ $ _____

12. Taxes (not deducted from wages or included in home mortgage payments)
(Specify) _____ $ _____

13. Installment payments: (In chapter 11, 12, and 13 cases, do not list payments to be included in the plan)

       a. Auto $ _____

       b. Other _____ $ _____

       c. Other _____ $ _____

14. Alimony, maintenance, and support paid to others $ _____

15. Payments for support of additional dependents not living at your home $ _____

16. Regular expenses from operation of business, profession, or farm (attach detailed statement) $ _____

17. Other _____ $ _____

18. AVERAGE MONTHLY EXPENSES (Total lines 1-17. Report also on Summary of Schedules and, $ _____
    if applicable, on the Statistical Summary of Certain Liabilities and Related Data.)

19. Describe any increase or decrease in expenditures reasonably anticipated to occur within the year following the filing of this document:

20. STATEMENT OF MONTHLY NET INCOME

    a. Average monthly income from Line 15 of Schedule I $ _____

    b. Average monthly expenses from Line 18 above $ _____

    c. Monthly net income (a. minus b.) $ _____

In re _____
          Debtor(s)

Case Number: _____
               (If known)

According to the information required to be entered on this statement (check one box as directed in Part I, III, or VI of this statement):

☐ **The presumption arises.**
☐ **The presumption does not arise.**
☐ **The presumption is temporarily inapplicable.**

CHAPTER 7 STATEMENT OF CURRENT MONTHLY INCOME AND MEANS-TEST CALCULATION

In addition to Schedules I and J, this statement must be completed by every individual chapter 7 debtor. If none of the exclusions in Part I applies, joint debtors may complete one statement only. If any of the exclusions in Part I applies, joint debtors should complete separate statements if they believe this is required by § 707(b)(2)(C).

Part I. MILITARY AND NON-CONSUMER DEBTORS

1A	**Disabled Veterans.** If you are a disabled veteran described in the Declaration in this Part IA, (1) check the box at the beginning of the Declaration, (2) check the box for "The presumption does not arise" at the top of this statement, and (3) complete the verification in Part VIII. Do not complete any of the remaining parts of this statement. ☐ **Declaration of Disabled Veteran.** By checking this box, I declare under penalty of perjury that I am a disabled veteran (as defined in 38 U.S.C. § 3741(1)) whose indebtedness occurred primarily during a period in which I was on active duty (as defined in 10 U.S.C. § 101(d)(1)) or while I was performing a homeland defense activity (as defined in 32 U.S.C. §901(1)).
1B	**Non-consumer Debtors.** If your debts are not primarily consumer debts, check the box below and complete the verification in Part VIII. Do not complete any of the remaining parts of this statement. ☐ **Declaration of non-consumer debts.** By checking this box, I declare that my debts are not primarily consumer debts.

1C	**Reservists and National Guard Members; active duty or homeland defense activity.** Members of a reserve component of the Armed Forces and members of the National Guard who were called to active duty (as defined in 10 U.S.C. § 101(d)(1)) after September 11, 2001, for a period of at least 90 days, or who have performed homeland defense activity (as defined in 32 U.S.C. § 901(1)) for a period of at least 90 days, are excluded from all forms of means testing during the time of active duty or homeland defense activity and for 540 days thereafter (the "exclusion period"). If you qualify for this temporary exclusion, (1) check the appropriate boxes and complete any required information in the Declaration of Reservists and National Guard Members below, (2) check the box for "The presumption is temporarily inapplicable" at the top of this statement, and (3) complete the verification in Part VIII. **During your exclusion period you are not required to complete the balance of this form, but you must complete the form no later than 14 days after the date on which your exclusion period ends, unless the time for filing a motion raising the means test presumption expires in your case before your exclusion period ends.**
	
	☐ **Declaration of Reservists and National Guard Members.** By checking this box and making the appropriate entries below, I declare that I am eligible for a temporary exclusion from means testing because, as a member of a reserve component of the Armed Forces or the National Guard
	
	a. ☐ I was called to active duty after September 11, 2001, for a period of at least 90 days and
	  ☐ I remain on active duty /or/
	  ☐ I was released from active duty on _____, which is less than 540 days before this bankruptcy case was filed;
	
	 OR
	
	b. ☐ I am performing homeland defense activity for a period of at least 90 days /or/
	  ☐ I performed homeland defense activity for a period of at least 90 days, terminating on _____, which is less than 540 days before this bankruptcy case was filed.

Part II. CALCULATION OF MONTHLY INCOME FOR § 707(b)(7) EXCLUSION

2	**Marital/filing status.** Check the box that applies and complete the balance of this part of this statement as directed. a. ☐ Unmarried. **Complete only Column A ("Debtor's Income") for Lines 3-11.** b. ☐ Married, not filing jointly, with declaration of separate households. By checking this box, debtor declares under penalty of perjury: "My spouse and I are legally separated under applicable non-bankruptcy law or my spouse and I are living apart other than for the purpose of evading the requirements of § 707(b)(2)(A) of the Bankruptcy Code." **Complete only Column A ("Debtor's Income") for Lines 3-11.** c. ☐ Married, not filing jointly, without the declaration of separate households set out in Line 2.b above. **Complete both Column A ("Debtor's Income") and Column B ("Spouse's Income") for Lines 3-11.** d. ☐ Married, filing jointly. **Complete both Column A ("Debtor's Income") and Column B ("Spouse's Income") for Lines 3-11.**		

	All figures must reflect average monthly income received from all sources, derived during the six calendar months prior to filing the bankruptcy case, ending on the last day of the month before the filing. If the amount of monthly income varied during the six months, you must divide the six-month total by six, and enter the result on the appropriate line.	**Column A** Debtor's Income	**Column B** Spouse's Income
3	**Gross wages, salary, tips, bonuses, overtime, commissions.**	$	$
4	**Income from the operation of a business, profession or farm.** Subtract Line b from Line a and enter the difference in the appropriate column(s) of Line 4. If you operate more than one business, profession or farm, enter aggregate numbers and provide details on an attachment. Do not enter a number less than zero. **Do not include any part of the business expenses entered on Line b as a deduction in Part V.** a. Gross receipts $ b. Ordinary and necessary business expenses $ c. Business income Subtract Line b from Line a	$	$
5	**Rent and other real property income.** Subtract Line b from Line a and enter the difference in the appropriate column(s) of Line 5. Do not enter a number less than zero. **Do not include any part of the operating expenses entered on Line b as a deduction in Part V.** a. Gross receipts $ b. Ordinary and necessary operating expenses $ c. Rent and other real property income Subtract Line b from Line a	$	$
6	**Interest, dividends and royalties.**	$	$
7	**Pension and retirement income.**	$	$
8	**Any amounts paid by another person or entity, on a regular basis, for the household expenses of the debtor or the debtor's dependents, including child support paid for that purpose.** Do not include alimony or separate maintenance payments or amounts paid by your spouse if Column B is completed. Each regular payment should be reported in only one column; if a payment is listed in Column A, do not report that payment in Column B.	$	$
9	**Unemployment compensation.** Enter the amount in the appropriate column(s) of Line 9. However, if you contend that unemployment compensation received by you or your spouse was a benefit under the Social Security Act, do not list the amount of such compensation in Column A or B, but instead state the amount in the space below: Unemployment compensation claimed to be a benefit under the Social Security Act Debtor $ _____ Spouse $ _____	$	$

10	**Income from all other sources.** Specify source and amount. If necessary, list additional sources on a separate page. **Do not include alimony or separate maintenance payments paid by your spouse if Column B is completed, but include all other payments of alimony or separate maintenance.** Do not include any benefits received under the Social Security Act or payments received as a victim of a war crime, crime against humanity, or as a victim of international or domestic terrorism.		
	a.	$	
	b.	$	
	Total and enter on Line 10	$	$

11	**Subtotal of Current Monthly Income for § 707(b)(7).** Add Lines 3 thru 10 in Column A, and, if Column B is completed, add Lines 3 through 10 in Column B. Enter the total(s).	$	$

12	**Total Current Monthly Income for § 707(b)(7).** If Column B has been completed, add Line 11, Column A to Line 11, Column B, and enter the total. If Column B has not been completed, enter the amount from Line 11, Column A.	$

Part III. APPLICATION OF § 707(b)(7) EXCLUSION

13	**Annualized Current Monthly Income for § 707(b)(7).** Multiply the amount from Line 12 by the number 12 and enter the result.	$
14	**Applicable median family income.** Enter the median family income for the applicable state and household size. (This information is available by family size at www.usdoj.gov/ust/ or from the clerk of the bankruptcy court.) a. Enter debtor's state of residence: _____ b. Enter debtor's household size: _____	$
15	**Application of Section 707(b)(7).** Check the applicable box and proceed as directed. ☐ **The amount on Line 13 is less than or equal to the amount on Line 14.** Check the box for "The presumption does not arise" at the top of page 1 of this statement, and complete Part VIII; do not complete Parts IV, V, VI or VII. ☐ **The amount on Line 13 is more than the amount on Line 14.** Complete the remaining parts of this statement.	

Complete Parts IV, V, VI, and VII of this statement only if required. (See Line 15.)

	Part IV. CALCULATION OF CURRENT MONTHLY INCOME FOR § 707(b)(2)	
16	**Enter the amount from Line 12.**	$
17	**Marital adjustment.** If you checked the box at Line 2.c, enter on Line 17 the total of any income listed in Line 11, Column B that was NOT paid on a regular basis for the household expenses of the debtor or the debtor's dependents. Specify in the lines below the basis for excluding the Column B income (such as payment of the spouse's tax liability or the spouse's support of persons other than the debtor or the debtor's dependents) and the amount of income devoted to each purpose. If necessary, list additional adjustments on a separate page. If you did not check box at Line 2.c, enter zero.	
	a.	$	
	b.	$	
	c.	$	
	Total and enter on Line 17.	$
18	**Current monthly income for § 707(b)(2).** Subtract Line 17 from Line 16 and enter the result.	$

Part V. CALCULATION OF DEDUCTIONS FROM INCOME

Subpart A: Deductions under Standards of the Internal Revenue Service (IRS)

19A	**National Standards: food, clothing and other items.** Enter in Line 19A the "Total" amount from IRS National Standards for Food, Clothing and Other Items for the applicable number of persons. (This information is available at www.usdoj.gov/ust/ or from the clerk of the bankruptcy court.) The applicable number of persons is the number that would currently be allowed as exemptions on your federal income tax return, plus the number of any additional dependents whom you support.	$

19B	**National Standards: health care.** Enter in Line a1 below the amount from IRS National Standards for Out-of-Pocket Health Care for persons under 65 years of age, and in Line a2 the IRS National Standards for Out-of-Pocket Health Care for persons 65 years of age or older. (This information is available at www.usdoj.gov/ust/ or from the clerk of the bankruptcy court.) Enter in Line b1 the applicable number of persons who are under 65 years of age, and enter in Line b2 the applicable number of persons who are 65 years of age or older. (The applicable number of persons in each age category is the number in that category that would currently be allowed as exemptions on your federal income tax return, plus the number of any additional dependents whom you support.) Multiply Line a1 by Line b1 to obtain a total amount for persons under 65, and enter the result in Line c1. Multiply Line a2 by Line b2 to obtain a total amount for persons 65 and older, and enter the result in Line c2. Add Lines c1 and c2 to obtain a total health care amount, and enter the result in Line 19B.

Persons under 65 years of age			Persons 65 years of age or older			
a1.	Allowance per person		a2.	Allowance per person		
b1.	Number of persons		b2.	Number of persons		
c1.	Subtotal		c2.	Subtotal		$

20A	**Local Standards: housing and utilities; non-mortgage expenses.** Enter the amount of the IRS Housing and Utilities Standards; non-mortgage expenses for the applicable county and family size. (This information is available at www.usdoj.gov/ust/ or from the clerk of the bankruptcy court). The applicable family size consists of the number that would currently be allowed as exemptions on your federal income tax return, plus the number of any additional dependents whom you support.	$

20B	**Local Standards: housing and utilities; mortgage/rent expense.** Enter, in Line a below, the amount of the IRS Housing and Utilities Standards; mortgage/rent expense for your county and family size (this information is available at www.usdoj.gov/ust/ or from the clerk of the bankruptcy court) (the applicable family size consists of the number that would currently be allowed as exemptions on your federal income tax return, plus the number of any additional dependents whom you support); enter on Line b the total of the Average Monthly Payments for any debts secured by your home, as stated in Line 42; subtract Line b from Line a and enter the result in Line 20B. **Do not enter an amount less than zero.**

a.	IRS Housing and Utilities Standards; mortgage/rental expense	$	
b.	Average Monthly Payment for any debts secured by your home, if any, as stated in Line 42	$	
c.	Net mortgage/rental expense	Subtract Line b from Line a.	$

21	**Local Standards: housing and utilities; adjustment.** If you contend that the process set out in Lines 20A and 20B does not accurately compute the allowance to which you are entitled under the IRS Housing and Utilities Standards, enter any additional amount to which you contend you are entitled, and state the basis for your contention in the space below:	$

22A	**Local Standards: transportation; vehicle operation/public transportation expense.** You are entitled to an expense allowance in this category regardless of whether you pay the expenses of operating a vehicle and regardless of whether you use public transportation. Check the number of vehicles for which you pay the operating expenses or for which the operating expenses are included as a contribution to your household expenses in Line 8. ☐ 0 ☐ 1 ☐ 2 or more. If you checked 0, enter on Line 22A the "Public Transportation" amount from IRS Local Standards: Transportation. If you checked 1 or 2 or more, enter on Line 22A the "Operating Costs" amount from IRS Local Standards: Transportation for the applicable number of vehicles in the applicable Metropolitan Statistical Area or Census Region. (These amounts are available at www.usdoj.gov/ust/ or from the clerk of the bankruptcy court.)	$
22B	**Local Standards: transportation; additional public transportation expense.** If you pay the operating expenses for a vehicle and also use public transportation, and you contend that you are entitled to an additional deduction for your public transportation expenses, enter on Line 22B the "Public Transportation" amount from IRS Local Standards: Transportation. (This amount is available at www.usdoj.gov/ust/ or from the clerk of the bankruptcy court.)	$
23	**Local Standards: transportation ownership/lease expense; Vehicle 1.** Check the number of vehicles for which you claim an ownership/lease expense. (You may not claim an ownership/lease expense for more than two vehicles.) ☐ 1 ☐ 2 or more. Enter, in Line a below, the "Ownership Costs" for "One Car" from the IRS Local Standards: Transportation (available at www.usdoj.gov/ust/ or from the clerk of the bankruptcy court); enter in Line b the total of the Average Monthly Payments for any debts secured by Vehicle 1, as stated in Line 42; subtract Line b from Line a and enter the result in Line 23. **Do not enter an amount less than zero.** 	a.	IRS Transportation Standards, Ownership Costs	$
b.	Average Monthly Payment for any debts secured by Vehicle 1, as stated in Line 42	$
c.	Net ownership/lease expense for Vehicle 1	Subtract Line b from Line a.		$
24	**Local Standards: transportation ownership/lease expense; Vehicle 2.** Complete this Line only if you checked the "2 or more" Box in Line 23. Enter, in Line a below, the "Ownership Costs" for "One Car" from the IRS Local Standards: Transportation (available at www.usdoj.gov/ust/ or from the clerk of the bankruptcy court); enter in Line b the total of the Average Monthly Payments for any debts secured by Vehicle 2, as stated in Line 42; subtract Line b from Line a and enter the result in Line 24. **Do not enter an amount less than zero.** 	a.	IRS Transportation Standards, Ownership Costs	$
b.	Average Monthly Payment for any debts secured by Vehicle 2, as stated in Line 42	$
c.	Net ownership/lease expense for Vehicle 2	Subtract Line b from Line a.		$
25	**Other Necessary Expenses: taxes.** Enter the total average monthly expense that you actually incur for all federal, state and local taxes, other than real estate and sales taxes, such as income taxes, self-employment taxes, social-security taxes, and Medicare taxes. **Do not include real estate or sales taxes.**	$
26	**Other Necessary Expenses: involuntary deductions for employment.** Enter the total average monthly payroll deductions that are required for your employment, such as retirement contributions, union dues, and uniform costs. **Do not include discretionary amounts, such as voluntary 401(k) contributions.**	$
27	**Other Necessary Expenses: life insurance.** Enter total average monthly premiums that you actually pay for term life insurance for yourself. **Do not include premiums for insurance on your dependents, for whole life or for any other form of insurance.**	$
28	**Other Necessary Expenses: court-ordered payments.** Enter the total monthly amount that you are required to pay pursuant to the order of a court or administrative agency, such as spousal or child support payments. **Do not include payments on past due obligations included in Line 44.**	$

29	**Other Necessary Expenses: education for employment or for a physically or mentally challenged child.** Enter the total average monthly amount that you actually expend for education that is a condition of employment and for education that is required for a physically or mentally challenged dependent child for whom no public education providing similar services is available.	$
30	**Other Necessary Expenses: childcare.** Enter the total average monthly amount that you actually expend on childcare—such as baby-sitting, day care, nursery and preschool. **Do not include other educational payments.**	$
31	**Other Necessary Expenses: health care.** Enter the total average monthly amount that you actually expend on health care that is required for the health and welfare of yourself or your dependents, that is not reimbursed by insurance or paid by a health savings account, and that is in excess of the amount entered in Line 19B. **Do not include payments for health insurance or health savings accounts listed in Line 34.**	$
32	**Other Necessary Expenses: telecommunication services.** Enter the total average monthly amount that you actually pay for telecommunication services other than your basic home telephone and cell phone service—such as pagers, call waiting, caller id, special long distance, or internet service—to the extent necessary for your health and welfare or that of your dependents. **Do not include any amount previously deducted.**	$
33	**Total Expenses Allowed under IRS Standards.** Enter the total of Lines 19 through 32.	$

Subpart B: Additional Living Expense Deductions
Note: Do not include any expenses that you have listed in Lines 19-32

34	**Health Insurance, Disability Insurance, and Health Savings Account Expenses.** List the monthly expenses in the categories set out in lines a-c below that are reasonably necessary for yourself, your spouse, or your dependents.	
	a. Health Insurance — $ b. Disability Insurance — $ c. Health Savings Account — $ Total and enter on Line 34	$
	If you do not actually expend this total amount, state your actual total average monthly expenditures in the space below: $ _____	
35	**Continued contributions to the care of household or family members.** Enter the total average actual monthly expenses that you will continue to pay for the reasonable and necessary care and support of an elderly, chronically ill, or disabled member of your household or member of your immediate family who is unable to pay for such expenses.	$
36	**Protection against family violence.** Enter the total average reasonably necessary monthly expenses that you actually incurred to maintain the safety of your family under the Family Violence Prevention and Services Act or other applicable federal law. The nature of these expenses is required to be kept confidential by the court.	$
37	**Home energy costs.** Enter the total average monthly amount, in excess of the allowance specified by IRS Local Standards for Housing and Utilities, that you actually expend for home energy costs. **You must provide your case trustee with documentation of your actual expenses, and you must demonstrate that the additional amount claimed is reasonable and necessary.**	$
38	**Education expenses for dependent children less than 18.** Enter the total average monthly expenses that you actually incur, not to exceed $147.92* per child, for attendance at a private or public elementary or secondary school by your dependent children less than 18 years of age. **You must provide your case trustee with documentation of your actual expenses, and you must explain why the amount claimed is reasonable and necessary and not already accounted for in the IRS Standards.**	$

*Amount subject to adjustment on 4/01/13, and every three years thereafter with respect to cases commenced on or after the date of adjustment.

39	**Additional food and clothing expense.** Enter the total average monthly amount by which your food and clothing expenses exceed the combined allowances for food and clothing (apparel and services) in the IRS National Standards, not to exceed 5% of those combined allowances. (This information is available at www.usdoj.gov/ust/ or from the clerk of the bankruptcy court.) **You must demonstrate that the additional amount claimed is reasonable and necessary**.	$
40	**Continued charitable contributions.** Enter the amount that you will continue to contribute in the form of cash or financial instruments to a charitable organization as defined in 26 U.S.C. § 170(c)(1)-(2).	$
41	**Total Additional Expense Deductions under § 707(b).** Enter the total of Lines 34 through 40	$

Subpart C: Deductions for Debt Payment

42	**Future payments on secured claims.** For each of your debts that is secured by an interest in property that you own, list the name of the creditor, identify the property securing the debt, state the Average Monthly Payment, and check whether the payment includes taxes or insurance. The Average Monthly Payment is the total of all amounts scheduled as contractually due to each Secured Creditor in the 60 months following the filing of the bankruptcy case, divided by 60. If necessary, list additional entries on a separate page. Enter the total of the Average Monthly Payments on Line 42.	

	Name of Creditor	Property Securing the Debt	Average Monthly Payment	Does payment include taxes or insurance?	
a.			$	☐ yes ☐ no	
b.			$	☐ yes ☐ no	
c.			$	☐ yes ☐ no	
			Total: Add Lines a, b and c.		$

43	**Other payments on secured claims.** If any of debts listed in Line 42 are secured by your primary residence, a motor vehicle, or other property necessary for your support or the support of your dependents, you may include in your deduction 1/60th of any amount (the "cure amount") that you must pay the creditor in addition to the payments listed in Line 42, in order to maintain possession of the property. The cure amount would include any sums in default that must be paid in order to avoid repossession or foreclosure. List and total any such amounts in the following chart. If necessary, list additional entries on a separate page.	

	Name of Creditor	Property Securing the Debt	1/60th of the Cure Amount	
a.			$	
b.			$	
c.			$	
			Total: Add Lines a, b and c	$

44	**Payments on prepetition priority claims.** Enter the total amount, divided by 60, of all priority claims, such as priority tax, child support and alimony claims, for which you were liable at the time of your bankruptcy filing. **Do not include current obligations, such as those set out in Line 28.**	$

45	**Chapter 13 administrative expenses.** If you are eligible to file a case under chapter 13, complete the following chart, multiply the amount in line a by the amount in line b, and enter the resulting administrative expense.			
	a.	Projected average monthly chapter 13 plan payment.	$	
	b.	Current multiplier for your district as determined under schedules issued by the Executive Office for United States Trustees. (This information is available at www.usdoj.gov/ust/ or from the clerk of the bankruptcy court.)	x	
	c.	Average monthly administrative expense of chapter 13 case	Total: Multiply Lines a and b	$

46	**Total Deductions for Debt Payment.** Enter the total of Lines 42 through 45.	$

Subpart D: Total Deductions from Income

47	**Total of all deductions allowed under § 707(b)(2).** Enter the total of Lines 33, 41, and 46.	$

Part VI. DETERMINATION OF § 707(b)(2) PRESUMPTION

48	**Enter the amount from Line 18 (Current monthly income for § 707(b)(2))**	$
49	**Enter the amount from Line 47 (Total of all deductions allowed under § 707(b)(2))**	$
50	**Monthly disposable income under § 707(b)(2).** Subtract Line 49 from Line 48 and enter the result	$
51	**60-month disposable income under § 707(b)(2).** Multiply the amount in Line 50 by the number 60 and enter the result.	$
52	**Initial presumption determination.** Check the applicable box and proceed as directed. ☐ **The amount on Line 51 is less than $7,025*.** Check the box for "The presumption does not arise" at the top of page 1 of this statement, and complete the verification in Part VIII. Do not complete the remainder of Part VI. ☐ **The amount set forth on Line 51 is more than $11,725*.** Check the box for "The presumption arises" at the top of page 1 of this statement, and complete the verification in Part VIII. You may also complete Part VII. Do not complete the remainder of Part VI. ☐ **The amount on Line 51 is at least $7,025*, but not more than $11,725*.** Complete the remainder of Part VI (Lines 53 through 55).	
53	**Enter the amount of your total non-priority unsecured debt**	$
54	**Threshold debt payment amount.** Multiply the amount in Line 53 by the number 0.25 and enter the result.	$
55	**Secondary presumption determination.** Check the applicable box and proceed as directed. ☐ **The amount on Line 51 is less than the amount on Line 54.** Check the box for "The presumption does not arise" at the top of page 1 of this statement, and complete the verification in Part VIII. ☐ **The amount on Line 51 is equal to or greater than the amount on Line 54.** Check the box for "The presumption arises" at the top of page 1 of this statement, and complete the verification in Part VIII. You may also complete Part VII.	

Part VII: ADDITIONAL EXPENSE CLAIMS

56	**Other Expenses.** List and describe any monthly expenses, not otherwise stated in this form, that are required for the health and welfare of you and your family and that you contend should be an additional deduction from your current monthly income under § 707(b)(2)(A)(ii)(I). If necessary, list additional sources on a separate page. All figures should reflect your average monthly expense for each item. Total the expenses.		
		Expense Description	Monthly Amount
	a.		$
	b.		$
	c.		$
		Total: Add Lines a, b and c	$

*Amounts are subject to adjustment on 4/01/13, and every three years thereafter with respect to cases commenced on or after the date of adjustment.

	Part VIII: VERIFICATION
57	I declare under penalty of perjury that the information provided in this statement is true and correct. *(If this is a joint case, both debtors must sign.)* Date: _____ Signature: _____ *(Debtor)* Date: _____ Signature: _____ *(Joint Debtor, if any)*

In re _____
                    Debtor(s)

Case Number: _____
                    (If known)

<table>
<tr><td colspan="2">According to the calculations required by this statement:</td></tr>
<tr><td>☐</td><td>The applicable commitment period is 3 years.</td></tr>
<tr><td>☐</td><td>The applicable commitment period is 5 years.</td></tr>
<tr><td>☐</td><td>Disposable income is determined under § 1325(b)(3).</td></tr>
<tr><td>☐</td><td>Disposable income is not determined under § 1325(b)(3).</td></tr>
<tr><td colspan="2">(Check the boxes as directed in Lines 17 and 23 of this statement.)</td></tr>
</table>

CHAPTER 13 STATEMENT OF CURRENT MONTHLY INCOME
AND CALCULATION OF COMMITMENT PERIOD AND DISPOSABLE INCOME

In addition to Schedules I and J, this statement must be completed by every individual chapter 13 debtor, whether or not filing jointly. Joint debtors may complete one statement only.

Part I. REPORT OF INCOME		

	Marital/filing status. Check the box that applies and complete the balance of this part of this statement as directed. a. ☐ Unmarried. **Complete only Column A ("Debtor's Income") for Lines 2-10.** b. ☐ Married. **Complete both Column A ("Debtor's Income") and Column B ("Spouse's Income") for Lines 2-10.**		
1			
	All figures must reflect average monthly income received from all sources, derived during the six calendar months prior to filing the bankruptcy case, ending on the last day of the month before the filing. If the amount of monthly income varied during the six months, you must divide the six-month total by six, and enter the result on the appropriate line.	**Column A** Debtor's Income	**Column B** Spouse's Income
2	**Gross wages, salary, tips, bonuses, overtime, commissions.**	$	$
3	**Income from the operation of a business, profession, or farm.** Subtract Line b from Line a and enter the difference in the appropriate column(s) of Line 3. If you operate more than one business, profession or farm, enter aggregate numbers and provide details on an attachment. Do not enter a number less than zero. **Do not include any part of the business expenses entered on Line b as a deduction in Part IV.** <table><tr><td>a.</td><td>Gross receipts</td><td>$</td></tr><tr><td>b.</td><td>Ordinary and necessary business expenses</td><td>$</td></tr><tr><td>c.</td><td>Business income</td><td>Subtract Line b from Line a</td></tr></table>	$	$
4	**Rent and other real property income.** Subtract Line b from Line a and enter the difference in the appropriate column(s) of Line 4. Do not enter a number less than zero. **Do not include any part of the operating expenses entered on Line b as a deduction in Part IV.** <table><tr><td>a.</td><td>Gross receipts</td><td>$</td></tr><tr><td>b.</td><td>Ordinary and necessary operating expenses</td><td>$</td></tr><tr><td>c.</td><td>Rent and other real property income</td><td>Subtract Line b from Line a</td></tr></table>	$	$
5	**Interest, dividends, and royalties.**	$	$
6	**Pension and retirement income.**	$	$
7	**Any amounts paid by another person or entity, on a regular basis, for the household expenses of the debtor or the debtor's dependents, including child support paid for that purpose.** Do not include alimony or separate maintenance payments or amounts paid by the debtor's spouse. Each regular payment should be reported in only one column; if a payment is listed in Column A, do not report that payment in Column B.	$	$

8	**Unemployment compensation.** Enter the amount in the appropriate column(s) of Line 8. However, if you contend that unemployment compensation received by you or your spouse was a benefit under the Social Security Act, do not list the amount of such compensation in Column A or B, but instead state the amount in the space below: Unemployment compensation claimed to be a benefit under the Social Security Act Debtor $ _____ Spouse $ _____	$	$

9	**Income from all other sources.** Specify source and amount. If necessary, list additional sources on a separate page. Total and enter on Line 9. **Do not include alimony or separate maintenance payments paid by your spouse, but include all other payments of alimony or separate maintenance. Do not include** any benefits received under the Social Security Act or payments received as a victim of a war crime, crime against humanity, or as a victim of international or domestic terrorism. a. $ b. $	$	$

10	**Subtotal.** Add Lines 2 thru 9 in Column A, and, if Column B is completed, add Lines 2 through 9 in Column B. Enter the total(s).	$	$

11	**Total.** If Column B has been completed, add Line 10, Column A to Line 10, Column B, and enter the total. If Column B has not been completed, enter the amount from Line 10, Column A.	$

Part II. CALCULATION OF § 1325(b)(4) COMMITMENT PERIOD

12	**Enter the amount from Line 11.**	$

13	**Marital adjustment.** If you are married, but are not filing jointly with your spouse, AND if you contend that calculation of the commitment period under § 1325(b)(4) does not require inclusion of the income of your spouse, enter on Line 13 the amount of the income listed in Line 10, Column B that was NOT paid on a regular basis for the household expenses of you or your dependents and specify, in the lines below, the basis for excluding this income (such as payment of the spouse's tax liability or the spouse's support of persons other than the debtor or the debtor's dependents) and the amount of income devoted to each purpose. If necessary, list additional adjustments on a separate page. If the conditions for entering this adjustment do not apply, enter zero. a. $ b. $ c. $ Total and enter on Line 13.	$

14	**Subtract Line 13 from Line 12 and enter the result.**	$

15	**Annualized current monthly income for § 1325(b)(4).** Multiply the amount from Line 14 by the number 12 and enter the result.	$

16	**Applicable median family income.** Enter the median family income for applicable state and household size. (This information is available by family size at www.usdoj.gov/ust/ or from the clerk of the bankruptcy court.) a. Enter debtor's state of residence: _____ b. Enter debtor's household size: _____	$

17	**Application of § 1325(b)(4).** Check the applicable box and proceed as directed. ☐ **The amount on Line 15 is less than the amount on Line 16.** Check the box for "The applicable commitment period is 3 years" at the top of page 1 of this statement and continue with this statement. ☐ **The amount on Line 15 is not less than the amount on Line 16.** Check the box for "The applicable commitment period is 5 years" at the top of page 1 of this statement and continue with this statement.

Part III. APPLICATION OF § 1325(b)(3) FOR DETERMINING DISPOSABLE INCOME

18	**Enter the amount from Line 11.**	$

19	**Marital adjustment.** If you are married, but are not filing jointly with your spouse, enter on Line 19 the total of any income listed in Line 10, Column B that was NOT paid on a regular basis for the household expenses of the debtor or the debtor's dependents. Specify in the lines below the basis for excluding the Column B income (such as payment of the spouse's tax liability or the spouse's support of persons other than the debtor or the debtor's dependents) and the amount of income devoted to each purpose. If necessary, list additional adjustments on a separate page. If the conditions for entering this adjustment do not apply, enter zero.	
	<table><tr><td>a.</td><td></td><td>$</td></tr><tr><td>b.</td><td></td><td>$</td></tr><tr><td>c.</td><td></td><td>$</td></tr></table>	
	Total and enter on Line 19.	$
20	**Current monthly income for § 1325(b)(3).** Subtract Line 19 from Line 18 and enter the result.	$
21	**Annualized current monthly income for § 1325(b)(3).** Multiply the amount from Line 20 by the number 12 and enter the result.	$
22	**Applicable median family income.** Enter the amount from Line 16.	$
23	**Application of § 1325(b)(3).** Check the applicable box and proceed as directed. ☐ **The amount on Line 21 is more than the amount on Line 22.** Check the box for "Disposable income is determined under § 1325(b)(3)" at the top of page 1 of this statement and complete the remaining parts of this statement. ☐ **The amount on Line 21 is not more than the amount on Line 22.** Check the box for "Disposable income is not determined under § 1325(b)(3)" at the top of page 1 of this statement and complete Part VII of this statement. **Do not complete Parts IV, V, or VI.**	

Part IV. CALCULATION OF DEDUCTIONS FROM INCOME

Subpart A: Deductions under Standards of the Internal Revenue Service (IRS)

24A	**National Standards: food, apparel and services, housekeeping supplies, personal care, and miscellaneous.** Enter in Line 24A the "Total" amount from IRS National Standards for Allowable Living Expenses for the applicable number of persons. (This information is available at www.usdoj.gov/ust/ or from the clerk of the bankruptcy court.) The applicable number of persons is the number that would currently be allowed as exemptions on your federal income tax return, plus the number of any additional dependents whom you support.	$
24B	**National Standards: health care.** Enter in Line a1 below the amount from IRS National Standards for Out-of-Pocket Health Care for persons under 65 years of age, and in Line a2 the IRS National Standards for Out-of-Pocket Health Care for persons 65 years of age or older. (This information is available at www.usdoj.gov/ust/ or from the clerk of the bankruptcy court.) Enter in Line b1 the applicable number of persons who are under 65 years of age, and enter in Line b2 the applicable number of persons who are 65 years of age or older. (The applicable number of persons in each age category is the number in that category that would currently be allowed as exemptions on your federal income tax return, plus the number of any additional dependents whom you support.) Multiply Line a1 by Line b1 to obtain a total amount for persons under 65, and enter the result in Line c1. Multiply Line a2 by Line b2 to obtain a total amount for persons 65 and older, and enter the result in Line c2. Add Lines c1 and c2 to obtain a total health care amount, and enter the result in Line 24B. <table><tr><td colspan="3">Persons under 65 years of age</td><td colspan="3">Persons 65 years of age or older</td></tr><tr><td>a1.</td><td>Allowance per person</td><td></td><td>a2.</td><td>Allowance per person</td><td></td></tr><tr><td>b1.</td><td>Number of persons</td><td></td><td>b2.</td><td>Number of persons</td><td></td></tr><tr><td>c1.</td><td>Subtotal</td><td></td><td>c2.</td><td>Subtotal</td><td></td></tr></table>	$
25A	**Local Standards: housing and utilities; non-mortgage expenses.** Enter the amount of the IRS Housing and Utilities Standards; non-mortgage expenses for the applicable county and family size. (This information is available at www.usdoj.gov/ust/ or from the clerk of the bankruptcy court). The applicable family size consists of the number that would currently be allowed as exemptions on your federal income tax return, plus the number of any additional dependents whom you support.	$

25B	**Local Standards: housing and utilities; mortgage/rent expense.** Enter, in Line a below, the amount of the IRS Housing and Utilities Standards; mortgage/rent expense for your county and family size (this information is available at www.usdoj.gov/ust/ or from the clerk of the bankruptcy court) (the applicable family size consists of the number that would currently be allowed as exemptions on your federal income tax return, plus the number of any additional dependents whom you support); enter on Line b the total of the Average Monthly Payments for any debts secured by your home, as stated in Line 47; subtract Line b from Line a and enter the result in Line 25B. **Do not enter an amount less than zero.**			

a.	IRS Housing and Utilities Standards; mortgage/rent expense	$	
b.	Average Monthly Payment for any debts secured by your home, if any, as stated in Line 47	$	
c.	Net mortgage/rental expense	Subtract Line b from Line a.	$

26	**Local Standards: housing and utilities; adjustment.** If you contend that the process set out in Lines 25A and 25B does not accurately compute the allowance to which you are entitled under the IRS Housing and Utilities Standards, enter any additional amount to which you contend you are entitled, and state the basis for your contention in the space below: _____ _____ _____	$

27A	**Local Standards: transportation; vehicle operation/public transportation expense.** You are entitled to an expense allowance in this category regardless of whether you pay the expenses of operating a vehicle and regardless of whether you use public transportation. Check the number of vehicles for which you pay the operating expenses or for which the operating expenses are included as a contribution to your household expenses in Line 7. ☐ 0 ☐ 1 ☐ 2 or more. If you checked 0, enter on Line 27A the "Public Transportation" amount from IRS Local Standards: Transportation. If you checked 1 or 2 or more, enter on Line 27A the "Operating Costs" amount from IRS Local Standards: Transportation for the applicable number of vehicles in the applicable Metropolitan Statistical Area or Census Region. (These amounts are available at www.usdoj.gov/ust/ or from the clerk of the bankruptcy court.)	$

27B	**Local Standards: transportation; additional public transportation expense.** If you pay the operating expenses for a vehicle and also use public transportation, and you contend that you are entitled to an additional deduction for your public transportation expenses, enter on Line 27B the "Public Transportation" amount from IRS Local Standards: Transportation. (This amount is available at www.usdoj.gov/ust/ or from the clerk of the bankruptcy court.)	$

28	**Local Standards: transportation ownership/lease expense; Vehicle 1.** Check the number of vehicles for which you claim an ownership/lease expense. (You may not claim an ownership/lease expense for more than two vehicles.) ☐ 1 ☐ 2 or more. Enter, in Line a below, the "Ownership Costs" for "One Car" from the IRS Local Standards: Transportation (available at www.usdoj.gov/ust/ or from the clerk of the bankruptcy court); enter in Line b the total of the Average Monthly Payments for any debts secured by Vehicle 1, as stated in Line 47; subtract Line b from Line a and enter the result in Line 28. **Do not enter an amount less than zero.**	

a.	IRS Transportation Standards, Ownership Costs	$	
b.	Average Monthly Payment for any debts secured by Vehicle 1, as stated in Line 47	$	
c.	Net ownership/lease expense for Vehicle 1	Subtract Line b from Line a.	$

29	**Local Standards: transportation ownership/lease expense; Vehicle 2.** Complete this Line only if you checked the "2 or more" Box in Line 28. Enter, in Line a below, the "Ownership Costs" for "One Car" from the IRS Local Standards: Transportation (available at www.usdoj.gov/ust/ or from the clerk of the bankruptcy court); enter in Line b the total of the Average Monthly Payments for any debts secured by Vehicle 2, as stated in Line 47; subtract Line b from Line a and enter the result in Line 29. **Do not enter an amount less than zero.**		

a.	IRS Transportation Standards, Ownership Costs	$	
b.	Average Monthly Payment for any debts secured by Vehicle 2, as stated in Line 47	$	
c.	Net ownership/lease expense for Vehicle 2	Subtract Line b from Line a.	$

30	**Other Necessary Expenses: taxes.** Enter the total average monthly expense that you actually incur for all federal, state, and local taxes, other than real estate and sales taxes, such as income taxes, self-employment taxes, social-security taxes, and Medicare taxes. **Do not include real estate or sales taxes.**	$
31	**Other Necessary Expenses: involuntary deductions for employment.** Enter the total average monthly deductions that are required for your employment, such as mandatory retirement contributions, union dues, and uniform costs. **Do not include discretionary amounts, such as voluntary 401(k) contributions.**	$
32	**Other Necessary Expenses: life insurance.** Enter total average monthly premiums that you actually pay for term life insurance for yourself. **Do not include premiums for insurance on your dependents, for whole life or for any other form of insurance.**	$
33	**Other Necessary Expenses: court-ordered payments.** Enter the total monthly amount that you are required to pay pursuant to the order of a court or administrative agency, such as spousal or child support payments. **Do not include payments on past due obligations included in Line 49.**	$
34	**Other Necessary Expenses: education for employment or for a physically or mentally challenged child.** Enter the total average monthly amount that you actually expend for education that is a condition of employment and for education that is required for a physically or mentally challenged dependent child for whom no public education providing similar services is available.	$
35	**Other Necessary Expenses: childcare.** Enter the total average monthly amount that you actually expend on childcare—such as baby-sitting, day care, nursery and preschool. **Do not include other educational payments.**	$
36	**Other Necessary Expenses: health care.** Enter the total average monthly amount that you actually expend on health care that is required for the health and welfare of yourself or your dependents, that is not reimbursed by insurance or paid by a health savings account, and that is in excess of the amount entered in Line 24B. **Do not include payments for health insurance or health savings accounts listed in Line 39.**	$
37	**Other Necessary Expenses: telecommunication services.** Enter the total average monthly amount that you actually pay for telecommunication services other than your basic home telephone and cell phone service—such as pagers, call waiting, caller id, special long distance, or internet service—to the extent necessary for your health and welfare or that of your dependents. **Do not include any amount previously deducted.**	$
38	**Total Expenses Allowed under IRS Standards.** Enter the total of Lines 24 through 37.	$

Subpart B: Additional Living Expense Deductions
Note: Do not include any expenses that you have listed in Lines 24-37

39	**Health Insurance, Disability Insurance, and Health Savings Account Expenses.** List the monthly expenses in the categories set out in lines a-c below that are reasonably necessary for yourself, your spouse, or your dependents. <table><tr><td>a.</td><td>Health Insurance</td><td>$</td></tr><tr><td>b.</td><td>Disability Insurance</td><td>$</td></tr><tr><td>c.</td><td>Health Savings Account</td><td>$</td></tr></table> Total and enter on Line 39 **If you do not actually expend this total amount**, state your actual total average monthly expenditures in the space below: $ _____		$
40	**Continued contributions to the care of household or family members.** Enter the total average actual monthly expenses that you will continue to pay for the reasonable and necessary care and support of an elderly, chronically ill, or disabled member of your household or member of your immediate family who is unable to pay for such expenses. **Do not include payments listed in Line 34.**		$
41	**Protection against family violence.** Enter the total average reasonably necessary monthly expenses that you actually incur to maintain the safety of your family under the Family Violence Prevention and Services Act or other applicable federal law. The nature of these expenses is required to be kept confidential by the court.		$
42	**Home energy costs.** Enter the total average monthly amount, in excess of the allowance specified by IRS Local Standards for Housing and Utilities that you actually expend for home energy costs. **You must provide your case trustee with documentation of your actual expenses, and you must demonstrate that the additional amount claimed is reasonable and necessary.**		$
43	**Education expenses for dependent children under 18.** Enter the total average monthly expenses that you actually incur, not to exceed $147.92 per child, for attendance at a private or public elementary or secondary school by your dependent children less than 18 years of age. **You must provide your case trustee with documentation of your actual expenses, and you must explain why the amount claimed is reasonable and necessary and not already accounted for in the IRS Standards.**		$
44	**Additional food and clothing expense.** Enter the total average monthly amount by which your food and clothing expenses exceed the combined allowances for food and clothing (apparel and services) in the IRS National Standards, not to exceed 5% of those combined allowances. (This information is available at www.usdoj.gov/ust/ or from the clerk of the bankruptcy court.) **You must demonstrate that the additional amount claimed is reasonable and necessary.**		$
45	**Charitable contributions.** Enter the amount reasonably necessary for you to expend each month on charitable contributions in the form of cash or financial instruments to a charitable organization as defined in 26 U.S.C. § 170(c)(1)-(2). **Do not include any amount in excess of 15% of your gross monthly income.**		$
46	**Total Additional Expense Deductions under § 707(b).** Enter the total of Lines 39 through 45.		$

Subpart C: Deductions for Debt Payment

47	**Future payments on secured claims.** For each of your debts that is secured by an interest in property that you own, list the name of the creditor, identify the property securing the debt, state the Average Monthly Payment, and check whether the payment includes taxes or insurance. The Average Monthly Payment is the total of all amounts scheduled as contractually due to each Secured Creditor in the 60 months following the filing of the bankruptcy case, divided by 60. If necessary, list additional entries on a separate page. Enter the total of the Average Monthly Payments on Line 47.		

	Name of Creditor	Property Securing the Debt	Average Monthly Payment	Does payment include taxes or insurance?	
a.			$	☐ yes ☐ no	
b.			$	☐ yes ☐ no	
c.			$	☐ yes ☐ no	
			Total: Add Lines a, b, and c		$

48	**Other payments on secured claims.** If any of debts listed in Line 47 are secured by your primary residence, a motor vehicle, or other property necessary for your support or the support of your dependents, you may include in your deduction 1/60th of any amount (the "cure amount") that you must pay the creditor in addition to the payments listed in Line 47, in order to maintain possession of the property. The cure amount would include any sums in default that must be paid in order to avoid repossession or foreclosure. List and total any such amounts in the following chart. If necessary, list additional entries on a separate page.	

	Name of Creditor	Property Securing the Debt	1/60th of the Cure Amount
a.			$
b.			$
c.			$
			Total: Add Lines a, b, and c	$

49	**Payments on prepetition priority claims.** Enter the total amount, divided by 60, of all priority claims, such as priority tax, child support and alimony claims, for which you were liable at the time of your bankruptcy filing. **Do not include current obligations, such as those set out in Line 33.**	$

50	**Chapter 13 administrative expenses.** Multiply the amount in Line a by the amount in Line b, and enter the resulting administrative expense.	

a.	Projected average monthly chapter 13 plan payment.	$
b.	Current multiplier for your district as determined under schedules issued by the Executive Office for United States Trustees. (This information is available at www.usdoj.gov/ust/ or from the clerk of the bankruptcy court.)	x
c.	Average monthly administrative expense of chapter 13 case	Total: Multiply Lines a and b	$

51	**Total Deductions for Debt Payment.** Enter the total of Lines 47 through 50.	$

Subpart D: Total Deductions from Income

52	**Total of all deductions from income.** Enter the total of Lines 38, 46, and 51.	$

Part V. DETERMINATION OF DISPOSABLE INCOME UNDER § 1325(b)(2)

53	**Total current monthly income.** Enter the amount from Line 20.	$
54	**Support income.** Enter the monthly average of any child support payments, foster care payments, or disability payments for a dependent child, reported in Part I, that you received in accordance with applicable nonbankruptcy law, to the extent reasonably necessary to be expended for such child.	$
55	**Qualified retirement deductions.** Enter the monthly total of (a) all amounts withheld by your employer from wages as contributions for qualified retirement plans, as specified in § 541(b)(7) and (b) all required repayments of loans from retirement plans, as specified in § 362(b)(19).	$
56	**Total of all deductions allowed under § 707(b)(2).** Enter the amount from Line 52.	$
57	**Deduction for special circumstances.** If there are special circumstances that justify additional expenses for which there is no reasonable alternative, describe the special circumstances and the resulting expenses in lines a-c below. If necessary, list additional entries on a separate page. Total the expenses and enter the total in Line 57. **You must provide your case trustee with documentation of these expenses and you must provide a detailed explanation of the special circumstances that make such expenses necessary and reasonable.**	

	Nature of special circumstances	Amount of expense
a.		$
b.		$
c.		$
		Total: Add Lines a, b, and c	$

58	**Total adjustments to determine disposable income.** Add the amounts on Lines 54, 55, 56, and 57 and enter the result.	$
59	**Monthly Disposable Income Under § 1325(b)(2).** Subtract Line 58 from Line 53 and enter the result.	$

Part VI: ADDITIONAL EXPENSE CLAIMS

| 60 | **Other Expenses.** List and describe any monthly expenses, not otherwise stated in this form, that are required for the health and welfare of you and your family and that you contend should be an additional deduction from your current monthly income under § 707(b)(2)(A)(ii)(I). If necessary, list additional sources on a separate page. All figures should reflect your average monthly expense for each item. Total the expenses. |

	Expense Description	Monthly Amount
a.		$
b.		$
c.		$
	Total: Add Lines a, b, and c	$

Part VII: VERIFICATION

| 61 | I declare under penalty of perjury that the information provided in this statement is true and correct. *(If this is a joint case, both debtors must sign.)*

Date: _____   Signature: _____
(Debtor)

Date: _____   Signature: _____
(Joint Debtor, if any) |

Index

⚖ NOLO   *Keep Up to Date*

 1   Go to Nolo.com/newsletters to sign up for free newsletters and discounts on Nolo products.

- **Nolo's Special Offer.** A monthly newsletter with the biggest Nolo discounts around.

- **Landlord's Quarterly.** Deals and free tips for landlords and property managers.

 2   Don't forget to check for updates. Find this book at **Nolo.com** and click "Legal Updates."

Let Us Hear From You

 3   Register your Nolo product and give us your feedback at Nolo.com/book-registration.

- Once you've registered, you qualify for technical support if you have any trouble with a download (though most folks don't).

- We'll send you a coupon for 15% off your next Nolo.com order!

CHB11

Find an Attorney

Qualified lawyers · In-depth profiles

When you want help with a serious legal problem, you don't want just any lawyer—you want an expert in the field who can give you and your family up-to-the-minute advice. You need a lawyer who has the experience and knowledge to answer your questions about personal injury, wills, family law, child custody, drafting a patent application or any other specialized legal area you are concerned with.

Nolo's Lawyer Directory is unique because it provides an extensive profile of every lawyer. You'll learn about not only each lawyer's education, professional history, legal specialties, credentials and fees, but also about their philosophy of practicing law and how they like to work with clients.

www.nolo.com